Maggie Smith

A View from the Stalls

Maggie Smith

A View from the Stalls

Caroline Fevrier

The Book Guild Ltd

First published in Great Britain in 2018 by
The Book Guild Ltd
9 Priory Business Park
Wistow Road, Kibworth
Leicestershire, LE8 0RX
Freephone: 0800 999 2982
www.bookguild.co.uk
Email: info@bookguild.co.uk
Twitter: @bookguild

Typeset in Garamond

Printed and bound in Great Britain by CPI Group (UK) Ltd, Croydon, CR0 4YY

ISBN 978 1912083 411

British Library Cataloguing in Publication Data.
A catalogue record for this book is available from the British Library.

Illustrations by the author

Cover Image Credit: Photograph by Laura Hynd, Camera Press London

To my master, Jean-Laurent Cochet,
versatile actor and incomparable stage director.

'Players are the only honest hypocrites…
Today kings, tomorrow beggars, it is only when they are themselves that they are nothing.'

William Hazlitt, *On Actors and Acting* (1817)

Acknowledgements

For their help and efficient assistance in the course of my research for this book, I owe thanks to the staff of several libraries: the Archive and Library Study Room at Blythe House (Victoria & Albert's National Theatre and Performance Collections), the BFI Reuben Library at the British Film Institute Southbank, as well as the former BFI National Library on Stephen Street, the British Library (especially the British Library Sound Archive), the National Theatre Archive and, in Paris, the Bibliothèque Gaston Baty and the Bibliothèque du Film (Cinémathèque Française).

I owe an especial thanks to Nick Hern, from Nick Hern Books, Wendy Lesser, editor of *The Threepenny Review*, and Cambridge University Press from permission to quote from copyrighted material. Every effort has been made to trace copyright holders but, should there be any omissions, I apologise and would be grateful to be notified of any corrections that should be incorporated in future editions.

I am greatly indebted to Jeremy Thompson, Jack Wedgbury, Hannah Virk, and all the team at The Book Guild Ltd for their efficiency, their kindness and the interest they showed in my project. A special thanks goes to Lauren Lewis, who submitted my work to my publishers. I am also deeply grateful to Dennis Tredy (University of Paris, Sorbonne Nouvelle), Hélène Valmary (University of Caen), Professor Axel Nissen (University of Oslo) and Professor Christian Viviani (University of Caen) for their kind support.

My heartfelt thanks to Sarah Smithers for her assistance, and Professor Jacqueline Champeaux (University of Paris Sorbonne) for her encouragements and pertinent suggestions.

Contents

Preface

The reader shall not find here an account of Maggie Smith's life, or a chronological survey of her career. When the well-established critic Michael Coveney started writing his biography of the actress,[1] he was acknowledged by her husband, the screenwriter and playwright Beverley Cross, and he even had access to the press cuttings that Nathan Smith, Maggie's father, had carefully and lovingly kept since the very first success of his actress daughter. Published in 1992, this biography was the result of a thorough work – based on testimonies of Smith's colleagues and also on the author's experience as a stage critic – and it remains an exceptional document on the history of British theatre from the mid-1950s to the early 1990s. Although the present study refers to Coveney's book every so often, it adopts quite a different perspective. The idea to research and write it came as early as 2006, and, during this extensive lapse of time, new entries have been added to the initial corpus. Its aim was to analyse – through the prism of typecasting and its exact opposite, characterisation – the roles and types the actress has played from the early 1990s to the present day. Since then, Michael Coveney has updated and completed his work, but it seemed that a study on the typology of characters was not redundant with a biography and thus, that its publication was still pertinent.

To follow the biographical path would have appeared unnecessary and

1 *Maggie Smith. A Bright Particular Star* (London: Victor Gollancz, 1992). The book was updated by its author and published by Weidenfeld & Nicolson under the title *Maggie Smith. A Biography* in September 2015.

inappropriate. One biography is quite enough for such a private person.[2] Even if there is absolutely zero chance that Maggie Smith reads these pages, the purpose of this book is to pay tribute to her talent, not to upset her with an intrusive publication. Her family and her closest friends know the woman she is. Let's be content with watching the actress. However, a monograph was necessary to do justice to an artist of an excessive humility. Discreet and restrained, the marvellous Maggie Smith never shows off. She has absolutely no talent for that. But as regards acting, her abilities are such that they justify all forms of accolade. Besides, as the actress is often given (very) old lady roles, the question of age will necessarily appear, here and there, in the book. Nevertheless, Dame Maggie's date of birth will not be found in these pages. It shall be found anywhere but here. Apart from the fact that it seems rather rude and irrelevant to mention her age in every sentence as journalists tactfully do these days,[3] this would not make sense. Smith has no age. She has the age of the characters she plays and therefore, this is the most inconstant thing about her.

Furthermore, this study will neither aim at exploring the arcane process of acting, nor use psychoanalysis to apprehend her subliminal idea of characterisation. Journalists often ask her to talk about her work and their requests always meet with a flat refusal. In 2010, in a rare interview with *The Times*, she declared that using words to describe the acting process made no sense.[4] Smith does not want to talk about how she acts and, according to

2 See R. Eyre, *Utopia and other places. Memoir of a young director* (London: Bloomsbury, 1993), p. 97. In his memoir, the former director of the National Theatre explains that Smith is one of these restrained, very private performers, who magnificently dazzle when they are under the spotlights, but fiercely defend their privacy when they are not working. As the critic Irving Wardle suggested in a remarkable article, there is a striking contrast between the shy, insecure person the actress is in real life and the dazzling performer who appears on stage; safely keeping away from the maddening world, she nevertheless 'blossoms' when acting; see 'All the angles: Farce or tragedy, stage or screen – no role seems beyond Maggie Smith', *The Independent*, 28 February 1993, p. 50.

3 Back in the 1980s, Smith herself complained about that fact. See J. Bright, 'Delicious pin-head, all eyes and teeth', *The Sunday Times*, 6 January 1985, p. 13; the actress fiercely disapproved of the mention of age in every article that featured famous people.

4 J. Rees, 'The grand dame returns', *The Sunday Times*, 12 September 2010, p. 4. The late Brian Bedford (who played alongside Maggie Smith in *Private Lives*, *The Guardsman* and *Much Ado About Nothing*, during the Stratford years) acknowledged: 'She's rather secretive about her work process. And very very defensive.'; see K. Garebian, 'The Dramatic Art of Brian Bedford. Unravelling the Mystery from the Text', in *A Well-Bred Muse. Selected Theatre Writings* 1978-1988, (Oakville: Mosaic Press, 1991), p. 39.

her, no one, even the greatest performers themselves, can get into it. The actress thinks that absolutely no one can claim to possess a real knowledge of the acting process, the nature of which is necessarily elusive; for her, acting is essentially driven by instinct.[5] Moreover, she often stresses the inanity of such a discussion, especially since a performance is, by its nature, ephemeral and elusive: she considers it a living thing, and cannot understand why some pretend to analyse it.[6] As an artist, Maggie Smith desperately – and quite rightly – wants to preserve that part of mystery which pertains to acting and dramatic illusion, as much as she protects her private life. It was probably the great George Cukor who expressed that reluctance the most aptly, saying that while some people talk about acting all the time, 'Maggie just does it'.[7]

To concur with her, it seems impossible and pointless to think and write about the 'internal mechanism' of the actor. The performer is not an engine, but a human being of flesh and blood. He lends his body and his voice to a character distinct from him, whom he brings alive through the power of thoughts when he has to act and react in a given situation. The process of acting, in its elaboration, is a strange, mysterious and impalpable operation which cannot be comprehended and described in scientific terms. We are only allowed to appreciate its result. The talent of a performer can only be measured in terms of credibility in portraying the character on screen or on stage. John Gielgud himself asserted that 'an actor's work has life and interest only in its execution. It seems to wither away in discussion and become emptily theoretical and insubstantial'.[8] Everything else is technique, hard work and genius, in other words the hidden part of the job that the

5 V. Olliver, 'The Prime of Ms Smith', *The Times*, 7 February 1986, p. 11. Delivering a speech at the Rex Harrison Memorial (New York City, June 1990), Smith asserted: 'As to the wit, that is impossible to analyse, as is timing […]. It is instinctive, and, I always think, destructive to try and define – like reading a review which describes how you got a laugh on a certain line. And then, on the second night, inexplicably the laugh has gone, not to return for many performances'; quoted in R. Harrison, *A Damned Serious Business* (London-New York-Toronto: Bantam, 1990), p. 242-243.

6 J. Watts, 'The Prime of the Marvellous Miss Smith', *The Observer*, 1 December 1985, p. 45.

7 See C. Romano, 'The Prime of Maggie Smith', *The Washington Post*, 14 October 1979, p. 5.

8 Quoted in R. Eyre, 'Directing Hare', in *The Cambridge Companion to David Hare*, ed. by R. Boon (Cambridge: Cambridge University Press, 2007), p. 138. In a recent interview ('Bouquet au cinéma', *Sud Ouest*, 27 December 2011, p. 39), Michel Bouquet, one of the greatest French actors, confessed: 'This is a very lonely job, just like painting. One does it in public, but the essence of it, is secret.'

public must neither see, nor try to discern. Celebrating Edith Evans's 'magic' talent, Michael Redgrave considered that it is not the role of the audience to analyse a performance that results from an actor's work. The audience should only seek entertainment; analysis is not part of it.[9] To observe a great actor in performance is the only way to capture and appreciate his amazing craft. Exceptional acting cannot be explained in scientific terms, it can only be described.

With regard to Maggie Smith, it is impossible to delve into the inner nature of her talent. The actor and screenwriter Bob Balaban – co-producer of *Gosford Park* – summarised this idea metaphorically, comparing the actress to a kind of magician whose mysterious tricks and technique, hidden under a cloak, have not to be seen or revealed.[10] A few years before, the late Sheridan Morley had already referred to 'Maggie's magic', saying that 'she comes of a generation of actors which believes, like conjurors, that the more they talk about their talent to amuse, the more it is likely to vanish like the rabbit in the hat. In the end, it is all about magic and mystery'.[11] This study will not aim at pulling the rabbit out. It will examine the subject – that is, an extraordinarily gifted performer at work – from an exterior point of view. The only one which allows us to consider the way the dramatic artist creates emotion, entertainment and, as the cleverest magician, illusion. That unrestricted point of view is that of the audience.

From the stalls.

9 *The Actor's Ways and Means* (London: Heinemann, 1979), p. 30.

10 'In her prime; actress Maggie Smith', *Sunday Morning* hosted by C. Osgood, CBS News, 20 January 2002.

11 'There's nothing like a dame!', *Theatregoer Magazine*, September 2002, p. 20. According to one of his biographers, Laurence Olivier was reputed to have replied to someone who congratulated him for his performance as Othello, 'I know it was great, dammit, but I don't know *how* I did it.' See A. Holden, *Olivier* (London: Sphere Books, 1988), p. 2-3.

Mrs Smith

Introduction

To dedicate a monograph to Maggie Smith can be considered as ambitious as superfluous. It certainly appears ambitious, insofar as she is one of the best actresses of our time, not to say the greatest ever. As much as it is difficult to embrace a very large subject, it cannot be easy, for the researcher, to write objectively on someone whose craft and talent necessarily impress many of us at the utmost degree. Moreover, it seems superfluous for the reason that the actress's fame is such that spectators from all over the world, if they do not always remember her name, at least recognise her face which has been immortalised in some of the biggest box-office hits (*Sister Act* in 1992, *The Secret Garden* in 1993 and, of course, the *Harry Potter* saga) and in the very popular TV show *Downton Abbey*.

Thanks to Minerva McGonagall, a role nearly tailor-made by J. K. Rowling, Maggie Smith got, at the dawn of the twenty-first century, a whole new generation of admirers – although the youngest of these spectators could probably not imagine her existing without the pointed hat of the Transfiguration Teacher. Officially, the actress reached international star status, as if the film adaptations of Harry Potter's adventures had suddenly brought to the forefront an artist whose career and reputation were already firmly established. Unexpectedly though, just as the series had come to an end with the eighth movie, Smith gained a new, even greater popularity with *Downton Abbey*. As soon as the first episodes aired, her haughty, grumpy dowager would charm millions of viewers around the world, who revelled in listening to Violet Crawley's scathing one-liners.

The present book certainly does not aim at holding forth on these popular successes, but rather at going beyond the preconceived image it provides of the actress. Maggie Smith's body of work has not to be judged in terms of popularity and success, but of skills and greatness. Had she not been involved in the *Harry Potter* franchise or in *Downton Abbey*, her value would have been quite the same. Actually, she played a small role in each of these two huge hits, but being cast in a small role, she gave a special, outstanding performance and managed, as usual, to steal the whole show. Yet, the actress does not owe anything to Minerva McGonagall and Violet Crawley: she is the one who made these characters captivating and forever unforgettable. On account of the fact that Smith is hugely successful, some people come to the conclusion that she must be very talented and worthy of admiration. On the contrary, it is because she is very talented that she deserves this phenomenal success. Success happens, but talent comes first.

The critic Michael Coveney, introducing the first Maggie Smith retrospective at the National Film Theatre in 1992, declared that, having been a queen of the stage and a movie star for over thirty years, with a talent for both comedy and pathos, Smith still was 'an enigma' and remained a very private person considering her huge popularity, even 'cult status'.[12] It was more than twenty years ago, and since the early 1990s, the actress has not stopped learning her craft, developing her skills and expanding her range. Smith now has the status of an international star, even more popular and revered today than she was at that time. However, it is not as such that she will be celebrated here. Nowadays, star-system is about promotion, business and big money. Therefore, to use the word 'star' to describe an artist of this exceptional calibre would seem derogatory. It implies an idea of ostentation and superficiality which is quite unsuited to the actress in question. Maggie Smith belongs to our time, she is a modern and stylish woman, and nevertheless, as the critic Lyn Gardner once wrote, she remains 'an old-fashioned' celebrity. According to L. Garner, unlike those performers who can be called 'modern actors', Smith has a 'camp'

12 See M. Coveney, 'The Prime of Dame Maggie Smith', *National Film Theatre Programme*, September-October 1992, p. 2. The season (1 September-6 October 1992) featured the following titles: *The VIP*, *Young Cassidy*, *The Honey Pot*, *The Prime of Miss Jean Brodie*, *Hot Millions*, *Love and Pain and the Whole Damn Thing*, *Travels with my Aunt*, *Murder by Death*, *California Suite*, *Quartet*, *A Private Function*, *Clash of the Titans* and *The Lonely Passion of Judith Hearne*. The British Film Institute scheduled a second retrospective (featuring Smith's more recent appearances in movies and TV dramas) in December 2014-January 2015 at what is now the BFI Southbank.

touch that only belongs to legends.[13] In an age of utmost vulgarity and over-publicity, Smith stands as an exception, probably because she still has the high standards of the previous generations of actors. She believes in values like hard work, restraint and beautiful manners which are definitely not the most fashionable ones these days. Just like Sybil Thorndike, John Gielgud or Laurence Olivier in their time, she is, above all, a remarkable professional at the height of her art, far beyond mundane considerations such as marketing and stardom. In this respect, she is the exact antithesis of an actress like Sarah Bernhardt (1844-1923). Whereas the eccentric French thespian knew, at the turn of the nineteenth century, how to take advantage of newspapers and publicity – even embarking on a tour in the United States in the 1880s – Maggie Smith lives a quiet life, away from the limelight and the media hype, and she is always utterly puzzled by the fascination that people have for her. In fact, the actress does not seek fame, even if she has already gained it for a long time. She seeks perfection in her work. She aims at offering the most accurate portrayal of the characters she plays. She possesses the elegance and the humility which belong only to the greatest.

It is certain that Smith has played bigger, more significant roles on stage than she has on screen. In a play (apart from *The Breath of Life*, in which she appeared opposite Judi Dench, in 2002), she always gets top billing and the production usually follows her own initiative. With the exception of A, the oldest of the *Three Tall Women*, the characters she has played on stage for the last two decades were quinquagenarians or elegant sexagenarians, much younger at any rate than the characters she has portrayed on screen. Besides, her actual typecasting comes from her onscreen roles rather than her stage performances. Lady Bracknell, the prototype of her usual parts, was only one theatre role among others, and those she has played since then were quite different.

In her career, the actress has played a few leading roles on the big screen – Jean Brodie, of course, Aunt Augusta in Cukor's *Travels with my Aunt*, and Judith Hearne – but she has rarely been the cornerstone of a cinematic project. However, every time she appears in a supporting role, her juicy performance contributes extensively to the success of the whole film. Her name in the credits is enough to attract spectators, as it guarantees a pleasurable moment. Funny or austere, but always touching and convincing,

13 'Smith and moans', *The Guardian*, 17 October 1997, p. 14.

she turns each of her onscreen appearances into a memorable masterpiece. It can be Mother Superior in *Sister Act*, Aunt Betsey in *David Copperfield* or, more recently, Grace, the murderous housekeeper in *Keeping Mum*, whatever film we may consider, its comical side lies, to a great extent, in the character portrayed by Maggie Smith. As for the cameos, these small but remarkable parts she gets in various productions, they often represent the best moment or the only virtue of the film in question. These very short appearances arouse a legitimate frustration when the spectator imagines what the film could have been if the role given to Smith had allowed her to display her talent in its entirety.

On the rare occasions when she gets top billing in a movie, she is – unsurprisingly – dazzling, as in Richard Loncraine's *My House in Umbria* (2003), Dustin Hoffman's *Quartet* (2013) and, of course, Nicholas Hytner's *The Lady in the Van* (2015). This is enough to demonstrate that an actress of such a stature should be given the leading roles she deserves more often, despite the long-settled habit of writing title roles only for actors in their twenties or thirties. Gradually, though, that phenomenon is starting to fade and, following the evolution of society, there are more and more films involving mature or elderly actors as central characters. Nevertheless, this study shall not distinguish title roles from supporting roles. Not because – according to the aphorism Stanislavski used to repeat, 'There are no small parts, only small actors'[14] – but for the reason that, unfortunately for her co-stars, Maggie Smith is the most formidable scene-stealer, whatever the size of the part she plays. She is as brilliant and remarkable in a cameo as she is in a leading part. In that regard, every role is relevant to this survey.

Focusing on the last twenty-five years, the present work will not go back over the actress's debut, and it will omit the main part of her onstage career which has already been scrupulously described in Michael Coveney's book. The critic undertook to write Maggie Smith's biography in 1990, as she was a triumph in Broadway with *Lettice and Lovage*, and he brought it to an end at the moment she finished filming two commercial hits, *Hook* and *Sister Act*, and an excellent TV drama by Jack Clayton, *Memento Mori.* The hardcover edition was published in September 1992 and a paperback edition was issued the following year, including a few extra pages where

14 *My Life in Art* (London: Eyre Methuen, 1980), p. 298.

Coveney commented on Smith's performance in *The Importance of Being Earnest* and her portrayal of Violet Venable in Richard Eyre's *Suddenly Last Summer* for the BBC. It was 1993 and the biographer – temporarily – bade farewell to the actress at the very moment when she was entering one of the most prosperous periods of her career; he would complete his work twenty-two years later, commenting on the successful and challenging roles that the actress had been given from then on.

For the last two decades, Smith has never stopped appearing in movies and she has also given some of her most noticeable stage performances. However, despite the multiplicity of parts she was offered in the 1990s, she also started being strongly typecast. It was a prospect that Coveney had already contemplated in the postscript to his first edition. The critic suggested that the 'very worst thing' that could occur would be for the actress to prematurely tackle these old bag roles which usually belong to the elderly actresses' repertory – Lady Wishfort, Mrs Malaprop and others – and stick with them.[15] Oddly enough, that 'very worst thing' has actually happened. Since 1992, the actress has not played Wishfort, but she has carved out a career portraying many old bags and she is now mostly identified, in people's minds, with snobbish aristocrats, cantankerous harridans or wrinkled nonagenarians. In October 2015, promoting *The Lady in the Van* on television, a resigned but humorous Smith admitted that she was stuck being 'a mean old cow'.[16]

As a matter of fact, this aspect – as much as the variety of parts she has played for twenty-five years – has motivated the present work. Maggie Smith illustrates, more evidently than anyone, the amazing concomitance of typecasting *and* versatility. Being often stuck – just as Coveney feared – with the old bag type, she is perfectly able, if the part requires it, to transform herself in a breathtaking manner. Far from being a one-dimensional performer playing the same character again and again, as those who know very little about her work mindlessly imply, Smith can play almost anything. Mastering her art at the highest degree, she can look back at an outstanding career spanning sixty years and a succession of striking (and always renewed) performances. Maybe the 'worst thing'

15 *Maggie Smith. A Bright Particular Star*, p. 358. These words do not appear in the updated biography.

16 BBC News interview, 10 November 2015.

has happened, but no way has typecasting reduced or limited, for the last two decades, the incredible, immeasurable range of the protean actress she is. On the contrary, her being typecast has challenged and, eventually, spectacularly emphasised her amazing versatility.

As its title suggests, the purpose of this book was to simply take the enviable place of the spectator and to sketch out, through Maggie Smith's example, considerations on consummate acting. Comparing and analysing the various parts she has played for more than twenty years (1991-2015), the present study will try to comprehend to what extent she is, without any doubt, the greatest actress of our time.

1

HANDBAGS AND OLD BAGS

Typecasting a Chameleon

A Jewel of a Crone

To approach Maggie Smith's work, it is necessary to get to grips, straightaway, with a cliché. For the majority of people who know her – in Europe, in the United States and, these days, worldwide – she is an actress specialising in the old bags. Many of the viewers who have recently discovered her through her impersonations of Minerva McGonagall and Violet, the extremely famous Dowager Countess of Grantham, firmly believe that she has never been given anything else. More accurately, the general public considers too often that she does play, and has always played, a unique type that is actually represented by a multiplicity of roles, more or less similar. People seem to ignore a whole part of Smith's career and, of course, mostly the roles she has played against type. Not only do they pass over her ability to transform, but they systematically associate the actress with a type which almost overshadows her.

These reflections lead to the question of type that Maggie Smith illustrates better than anyone. In France, in the seventeenth century, Molière had scrupulously classified the criteria required by each role, contributing to define the notion of *type*. According to the *Dictionnaire de Littré* (1872), the term covers 'the different roles pertaining to the same character'. At the Comédie Française – until the 1960s – each actor was categorised in a type according to his age, means of voice, gesture, and carriage. The performer was simply given the parts which suited him the best. The type's rules mostly applied to the young actors, whose skills and abilities were narrower and thus, these people remained stuck with the same kind of roles. The only advantage of typecasting was that the performer played the same part for years and had time to improve and perfect his rendition of it. Only age and experience could allow the performer to widen his range, tackle more challenging parts and move from one type to another. In fact, the identification between the actor and the character was so radical that some types took the name of the performer who had created them or played them the most successfully.[17] When she came to Paris to perform at the Comédie-Française, in 1945, Sybil Thorndike was bewildered by this French peculiarity.[18] She wrote to her husband, the actor Lewis Casson, that she would find it a bit boring to work there, as these French actors all had their special types and roles, and had to stick to them.[19]

17 In the late nineteenth century, comical duenna roles were called 'thierrets' from the name of Félicia Thierret (1814-1873), a famous actress who had specialised in that type.

18 J. Stokes, *The French Actress and her English Audience* (Cambridge: Cambridge University Press, 2005), p. 4: 'The English have always been aware that in comparison with their own traditions, French acting, both gesture and declamation, appears rigidly codified and ponderously oratorical [...]. Add the fact that the same types (*emplois*) re throughout the classic French repertoire in quite an unEnglish way – *soubrettes, ingénues, grandes coquettes* and so on – and the challenge of difference becomes that much greater.'

19 J. Croall, *Sibyl Thorndike. A Star of Life* (London: Haus Publishing, 2008), p. 352.

Although the definition theoretically applies to the French classical repertory, the notion of type belongs to a more widespread tradition, inherited from the Commedia dell'Arte and its specific characters. In the Italian comedy – in line with the Greco-Roman tradition – actors used masks to transform into whatever character they had to play. In contrast, on the Shakespearean stage and later, when women were allowed to take part, performers specialised in a category of roles which particularly suited them, in accordance with their physical appearance, their voice and their figure. How they looked, spoke and moved was a determining factor to define what type they would be able to play. The academic Shearer West quotes a critic from *The Monthly Mirror*, writing in 1796 about the English actress Priscilla Hopkins Kemble (1756-1845) who specialised in spinsterish roles: 'The shrillness of (her) voice and the squabbishness of her figure are admirable accompaniments to the peevish expression of her features, and thus as far as natural requisites go, she is perfectly suited to old maids and crabbed aunts.'[20] In England, in the eighteenth century, not only did ageing actresses remain cast in the same type, but they kept playing the role they had played during their whole career – the proper expression was 'owning a role' – at the risk of being ridiculous. The Anglo-Irish actress Dorothy Jordan (1761-1816), famously known as Mrs Jordan, still played the young women at a mature age, although her large figure did not really allow her to play an androgynous Rosalind or an enticing Margery Pinchwife – in Wycherley's *The Country Wife* – without being ridiculous.[21] In France, the celebrated thespian Mademoiselle Mars (1779-1847) was mocked for portraying the ingénues and the young women – Suzanne, in Beaumarchais's *The Marriage of Figaro* and Célimène, in Molière's *The Misanthrope* – when she was in

20 *The Image of the Actor. Verbal and visual representation in the age of Garrick and Kemble* (London: Pinter, 1991), p. 140. West (*ibid.*) also notes: 'The personal appearance and demeanour of actors became identified with the character they were portraying, and that character was morally represented in the form of a stereotype.'

21 J. W. Fisher, 'Creating Another Identity: Aging Actresses in the Eighteenth Century', *Journal of Aging and Identity*, 4.2, 1999, p. 61. See also B. Fothergill, *Mrs Jordan. Portrait of an Actress* (London: Faber and Faber, 1965), p. 261; at the end of her career, Mrs Jordan was advised by one stage manager to start tackling more elderly characters; she thought otherwise. Similarly, it must be noticed that Ellen Terry's last stage role was Portia in *The Merchant of Venice*, in 1917; she was seventy by then.

her sixties.[22] This usage had also spread to the United States as soon as the theatre appeared there, in 1752. American theatrical companies cast their actors according to strict lines of business. By 'line of business' (an equivalent of the French word *emploi*), one means the 'systematic distribution of parts within the given repertories of an eighteenth- or nineteenth-century stock company'.[23] The lines of business included, since the Restoration period and the introduction of female performers, the 'leading lady', the 'juvenile lady', the 'chambermaid', the 'first woman' and the 'second old woman'. Of course, beyond that old-fashioned notion of line of business, the word 'type' must be taken in a wider sense, that is the series of roles which exactly correspond to the technical and physical means of an actor.[24]

The notion of type is reductive in itself. When the role exactly corresponds to the means of the actor, it does need a lesser effort in terms of performance and, at the same time, the attempt of the audience is even greater. The actor has no right to make mistakes, as critics and spectators are prone to blame the performers who satisfy themselves with always playing their type; playing his type, the actor seems to acknowledge that he lacks characterisation skills and cautiously sticks to one part.[25] Type is often associated, in a pejorative sense, with the term 'typecasting' which evokes limitation and compartmentalisation, that is 'to pick, for a given part, a man or a woman whose appearance is already close to the surface of the character he must set out to create.'[26] In one of his essays on actors, Stanislavski criticises this constrictive habit that typecasting is and which explains why all these actors are uninteresting and dull, on stage and off stage. According to the theoretician, those who favour being typecast and

22 A. Martin-Fugier, *Comédiennes. De Mademoiselle Mars à Sarah Bernhardt* (Paris: Seuil, 2001), p. 287-288.

23 J. C. Burge, *Lines of Business. Casting Practice and Policy in the American Theatre, 1752-1899*, (New York-Berne-Frankfurt am Main: Peter Lang, 1986), p. 3.

24 See R. Wojcik, 'Typecasting', *Criticism*, Spring 2003, 45.2, p. 227: 'In terms of acting, type refers most broadly to an actor's ability to embody something typical or representative of the human condition.'

25 *Ibid.*, p. 223.

26 E. J. R. Isaacs, 'Type-casting: The eighth deadly sin', *Theatre Arts Monthly*, Vol. XVII, 2, February 1933, p. 132. On typecast actors, see also Wojcik, 'Typecasting', p. 224: 'The assumption seems to be that typecasting is a sign of an actor's limitation, a concession to commercialism, and the antithesis of art and originality.'

choose the easy path are the lazy, 'poorly endowed' performers whose range is strictly limited.[27]

From a large variety of parts at the beginning of her career and even until the 1980s, Maggie Smith has come, as she got older, to a much more restricted line of roles, at least on the surface. It cannot be denied that, for the last two decades, many of the roles she has played correspond to the same type. In 2002, the actress herself admitted that she was forever stuck with cantankerous old bags in wigs[28] and later, in 2010, she declared that she really was typecast, being the one who is systematically offered that kind of role.[29] In trying to define what is Smith's type, it is tempting to identify her with the role which is precisely hers most of the time, the pinched-faced aristocratic lady. Obviously, the actress seems to be stuck with those haughty dowager parts, but that fact pertains to myth rather than reality. Actually, making an inventory of Smith's roles which belong to this type, it appears that they are more notable than numerous. Her portrayal of Lady Bracknell in *The Importance of Being Earnest* (1993), as well as her successive performances – as Constance Trentham in *Gosford Park* (2001), then as Violet Crawley in *Downton Abbey* (2010-2015) – made such a deep impression on the audience that many people imagine from now on that she has never played another kind of character. On one side, they suppose that Maggie Smith is only able to portray the grumpy ladies and forever does her usual turn. On the other side, the type itself has swallowed up the actress, to the point that it seems quite shocking to see her wearing trainers or doing her shopping at the supermarket. Yet, it is the price of success and popularity, as the general public likes to identify the actress with the characters she plays so well.

With the success of *Downton Abbey*, Maggie Smith has been, in a certain way, the victim of prejudice. The most mediocre tabloids propagate now and again false rumours and ridiculous gossip, pretending that the actress is as difficult and haughty as the character she portrays in the show – although some of the greatest directors who have worked with her praise her professionalism, her kindness and her down-to-earth behaviour.

27 'Type of Actors', in *Stanislavski's Legacy. A collection of Comments on a Variety of Aspects of an actor's Art and Life*, ed. by E. R. Hapgood (London: Methuen, 1989), p. 14-16.

28 B. Bardin, 'Idole Chatter: Maggie Smith', *Premiere Magazine*, April 2002, p. 92.

29 Rees, 'The grand dame returns', p. 4.

Maybe it is a rather inelegant way to take revenge for her reluctance to give interviews; in any case, the strategy is effective. *Downton Abbey*'s fans have such a devotion for the dowager countess that they gladly fantasise that Smith resembles her character. Some young actors dread playing opposite her, as shy of working with one of the most talented actresses in the world as frightened by confronting Violet Crawley in the flesh. In his biography of Gladys Cooper,[30] the critic Sheridan Morley says that during the filming of *My Fair Lady* (1964), his grandmother was confused with Mrs Higgins, the character she played in the movie, and she was being considered, when she was on set, a grand dignified dowager on visit rather than one of the performers.[31] At the time of *Gosford Park*, Maggie Smith had already observed that phenomenon of identification which was probably the most objective evidence of a compelling performance; the fact that some spectators got confused, and really thought that she was as detestable as Countess Trentham in real life, was quite rewarding.[32]

Some journalists adopt an equally revealing attitude towards her, as it appeared during the interview that she gave to *60 Minutes* – the famous CBS broadcast – in February 2013. Probably more used to questioning politicians than discreet and shy British actresses, the journalist Steve Kroft did not spare Maggie Smith a few clumsy questions about her private life, but he also interviewed her as if he completely identified Maggie-the-actress with Violet-the-dowager. Dwelling heavily on her age, the journalist seemed to be amazed by the longevity of her career and also by her present success, as if she had not been brought to the public notice until her involvement in the very popular TV show. Thanks to her huge talent, Smith has been a household name for more than fifty years now. To wonder about the longevity of her career does not make sense. Neither does it make sense, after having shown a handful of old pictures, to compliment on her former beauty a mature actress who indisputably still is beautiful.

Besides, as Maggie Smith plays snobs and cantankerous ladies better

---

30 That name does not mean much for the younger generations and, these days, Cooper's filmography (which is mostly concentrated in the 1940-1950 period) does not allow us to fully gauge the popularity of one of the greatest ladies of the London stage. At least, her grandson, the late Sheridan Morley, has done justice to her amazing career in a well-documented and moving biography.

31 *Gladys Cooper. A Biography* (London: Heinemann, 1979), p. 267.

32 Bardin, 'Idole Chatter'.

than anyone, she is systematically offered these roles. Some consummate actors are so good in one kind of part that people would not think of casting them in anything different. That was the case of the great Margaret Rutherford. As one of her biographers, the critic Eric Keown, recalls, Rutherford remained pigeonholed in the farcical old spinster type – from *Blithe Spirit*'s Arcati to Jane Marple – mainly because no other actress would have been able to play these characters as well as she did: 'Noting how often directors have been content to use her [...] as a comic spinster, it is difficult not to be astonished at their lack of enterprise. The trouble is, of course, that she makes a funnier eccentric than any other actress.'[33] In fact, Smith has been locked into the aristocratic type because, most of the time, filmmakers immediately have her in mind. On the other hand, many of them cannot imagine her playing against type, what is an affront to her incredible versatility; therefore, she is deprived of certain parts.

In his biographies of Dames Sybil Thorndike and Gladys Cooper, S. Morley observed that these two distinguished actresses had been pigeonholed, after a certain age, in a type. About Thorndike, the critic admitted that she started being offered a succession of more or less identical parts; characterisation was no longer in order, and she would play, for years, the same old lady roles.[34] In the same way, as she reached her sixties, Gladys Cooper showed, in every new film, a propension to duplicate a bit too mechanically the same type and the same kind of performance,[35] becoming one among many other veteran British actresses, another imperious old dowager like Dame May Whitty.[36] Because of her matronly figure, Margaret Rutherford got typecast as early as her forties and it cut short any hope of proper characterisation. And Rutherford herself confessed that it was as if the performer she really was inside struggled to escape from her own physical body.[37] Unlike these veteran actresses from the past, Maggie Smith remains very malleable and continues playing, in parallel, characters against type. In fact, if her career exemplifies the phenomenon of typecasting, it

33 *Margaret Rutherford. An illustrated study of her work with a list of her appearances on stage and screen* (London: Rockliff, 1956), p. 67. See also, about Dame Edith Evans, S. Richards, *The Rise of the English Actress* (London: MacMillan, 1993), p. 178.

34 *Sybil Thorndike. A Life in the Theatre* (London: Weidenfeld & Nicolson, 1977), p. 132.

35 Morley, *Gladys Cooper*, p. 240.

36 *Ibid.*, p. 211-214.

37 D. L. Simmons, *Margaret Rutherford. A Blithe Spirit* (London: Sphere Books, 1985), p. 30.

is far from being limited to typecasting. At the present time, Smith still looks youthful and, like all that exceptional, prolific generation (Dench, Redgrave, Gambon, Atkins, McKellen, Jacobi…), she has, deep within her, this particular spark which gives the greatest artists an exceptional radiance defying the years. She still has much to give. Only she must be given the roles that her immense talent deserves.

Regarding Maggie Smith's career, that phenomenon of typecasting did not develop until the early 1990s. Between 1970 and 1980, the actress starred in only five movies. Between 1980 and 1990, she is credited in eight features and two TV dramas. From 1991 onwards, while remaining a valued asset of the English stage, she appeared more often on the silver screen. Then, her appearances got more and more frequent: fourteen films between 1990 and 2000, and more than twenty since 2001. It is certain that Smith has, firstly, privileged her theatre career. On screen, she has not been shown off to advantage as much as she deserved, despite the success and the quality of the films she was in. Apart from the extravagant *Murder by Death* (1976), a delightful whodunnit parody where she appears as a sexy vamp,[38] and maybe *Clash of the Titans* (1981) which shows her wearing the mythological attributes of the beautiful goddess Thetis, Maggie Smith plays the old eccentrics (*Travels with my Aunt* in 1972), the deceived wives (*California Suite* in 1978, and J. Ivory's *Quartet* in 1981), the women at a complete loss (*Love and Pain and the Whole Damn Thing* in 1973, and *The Lonely Passion of Judith Hearne* in 1987), the snobs (*A Private Function* in 1984) and, as long ago as the late 1970s, the embittered spinsters (*Death on the Nile* in 1979, and *A Room with a View* in 1985), translating to film her stage acting skills. At the moment when Smith started to frequently appear on screen, she was immediately relegated among the old ladies, despite her relatively young age and a flattering physical appearance. As an American journalist pointed out, directors and filmmakers seem to have picked up all her mannerisms – mistaking her style for her real substance – to create the 'Maggie Smith character', the haughty aristocrat who has been appearing for more than twenty years in period films.[39] Actually, 1991 can be considered a turning point in her career. From then

38 In movies, Smith never appears as a seductress, except through humour and parody – as she does, for instance, in *The Missionary* (R. Loncraine, 1982).

39 J. Clark, 'A Forceful Character', *The Los Angeles Times*, 24 December 2001 <http://articles.latimes.com/2001/dec/24/entertainment/et-clark24/2> [accessed 12 November 2016].

on, she would get much more onscreen work than she did in the previous decades but, at the same time, she would radically specialise – like it or not – in the older parts. Somewhat weary of these stereotypical roles, and mostly resigned, the actress never hesitates to use eloquent appellations to describe the characters she usually plays, such as 'old bags' or 'old boots'. The fact that she is regularly typecast cannot be denied and typecasting seems to be nothing but a shameful waste for such a gifted and versatile actress, but reality is far from being so dark. Since the early 1990s, the actress has had a magnificent career, both on stage and on screen, and although she has often been stuck – as she admits herself – with a certain type, she has been able to create an impressive gallery of characters which each successfully catches the eye of the spectator.

A common archetype in the literature of the nineteenth century, the mature, haughty and pinched aristocrat endowed with a rather unattractive face corresponds to an essential stock character in comedy. It usually fulfils – according to the 'actantial model' established by the narratologist Greimas – the role of the 'opponent' in the story, that is the troublemaker who stands in the way of the hero and obstructs his action. Either crotchety mother-in-law, snobbish cousin or rich aunt, she plays a pivotal role in family issues, obstructing marriages or spoiling Sunday luncheons. These characters are none others than the 'elderly ladies with gigantic tiaras and parrot noses' whom Oscar Wilde mischievously alludes to in *The Picture of Dorian Gray*.[40] Despite being redoubtable, they are always hilarious and comedy always counterbalances what seems frightening in their ageing or imposing bodies.[41] Oddly enough, Maggie Smith's angular features produce the same effects, the actress creating formidable but incredibly funny characters. The dowager type is an omnipresent character in the French boulevard (especially in Georges Feydeau's theatre) and, even if it shows less frequently in the Anglo-American repertory, it is a recurrent figure on screen in the first half of the twentieth century. The academic Axel Nissen has recently published three excellent studies on that character archetype (quite frequent in the movies of the 1930s) and the numerous

40 *The Picture of Dorian Gray* (Oxford: Oxford University Press, 2006), p. 10.

41 S. Harper, 'From Wholesome Girls to Difficult Dowagers. Actresses in 1930's British Cinema', in *British Cinema, Past and Present*, ed. by J. Ashby and A. Higson (London: Routledge, 2000), p. 149.

actresses who had specialised in that category.[42] Page after page, he brings back the memory of these great performers, now almost forgotten: the American thespians Marie Dressler (1868-1934) and Ethel Barrymore (1879-1959), the English actress May Whitty (1865-1948), and many others who all were regularly cast as matriarchs, old crones and dowagers. With her willowy figure and her regal bearing, Maggie Smith seems to be born to play the aristocratic, imperious type. On account of her anteriority, her Lady Bracknell in *The Importance of Being Earnest* could be regarded as a kind of archetype, the initial figure on which Smith's other stage or movie characters are modelled. As such, Lady Bracknell will serve as a starting point for this reflection.

42 *Actresses of A Certain Character* (Jefferson, North Carolina & London: McFarland and Cie, 2006) and its companion pieces, *Mothers, Mammies and Old Maids. Twenty-Five Character Actresses of Golden Age Hollywood*, (Jefferson, North Carolina & London: McFarland and Cie, 2012) and *Accustomed to Her Face: Thirty-five Character Actresses of Golden Age Hollywood* (Jefferson, North Carolina & London: McFarland and Cie, 2016).

The Importance of Being Bracknell

'The natural *grande dame* of the stage with all the true polish and innate dignity of the unmistakable 'lady'. Her walk, her voice, her carriage, her every detail was marvellous [...]. She held a position which has never been filled, to my mind, by any other actress.'[43] All that praise did not go to Maggie Smith, but to Rose Leclercq (1843-1899), the very first actress who played Lady Bracknell, in 1895. According to the author of these lines, the actress Irene

43 I. Vanbrugh, *To Tell my Story* (London: Hutchinson & Co, 1948), p. 33.

Vanbrugh,[44] Miss Leclercq almost merged with her character, conveying the image of a truly high-born lady. 'She was never stagey or exaggerated,' adds Dame Irene, as if Leclercq's performance was the exact antithesis of what Smith would be wrongly accused of, one century later. In actual fact, Miss Leclercq had been cast as Bracknell because she was an obvious choice: the spectators were accustomed to see her in similar parts.[45] One of the most perfect renditions of Lady Bracknell – in accordance with the author's intentions – was probably given by Mabel Terry-Lewis (1872-1957), who, on this occasion, was cast opposite her own nephew, John Gielgud.[46] Being the antithesis of a character actress, Terry-Lewis excelled in that role for the very reason that it corresponded to her real-life personality.[47] She was surprised that the audience laughed, as she did not find her character funny; on the contrary, she thought that Aunt Augusta's behaviour was quite natural.[48] In her time, Mabel Terry-Lewis was already a case of typecasting, being constantly used as patronesses, countesses and 'ladies of the manor' of any kind; her Lady Bracknell was just right, but not overwhelming.[49] For Smith, who played the formidable lady in 1993, the challenge was all the more hazardous since it was a part for which she was tailored. Her portrayal of Aunt Augusta was much awaited by the critics, who unanimously claimed she was born to play the part.[50] Most of them took their hats off to her performance, whereas some others, less numerous, criticised it with a rare fierceness. At least, it left no one indifferent. This production had been

44 Dame Irene Vanbrugh (1872-1949) played the role of Gwendolen Fairfax in that production.

45 See J. Stokes, *Oscar Wilde: myths, miracles and imitations* (Cambridge: Cambridge University Press, 1996), p. 171.

46 *The Importance of Being Earnest* directed by N. Playfair, Lyric, Hammersmith, 1930.

47 J. Gielgud, *Early Stages* (San Francisco: Mercury House, 1987), p. 108.

48 M. Steen, *A Pride of Terrys* (London: Longmans, 1962), p. 287: 'She was not, in the pure sense of the word, an "actress", for all she did was to carry *herself* on to the stage.' See also Stokes, *Oscar Wilde*, p. 172-173.

49 Steen, *A Pride of Terrys*, p. 359: 'Ambitious actors and actresses were already groaning at what had begun to be known as type-casting; Mabel Terry-Lewis was one of its principal victims. Whether or not she was capable of extending herself beyond the narrow boundaries of her particular idiom is unresolved. [...] She went on polishing the small but perfect jewel of her art and, in private life, became more and more like the characters she acted on the stage.'

50 C. Spencer, 'Dame Maggie's night of triumph', *The Daily Telegraph*, 10 March 1993, p. 17; B. Nightingale, 'Mythical monster triumphs', *The Times*, 10 March 1993, p. 31.

initiated by the producer Robert Fox and the whole project was supposed to come to fruition as early as March 1992.[51] However, in the meantime, Richard Eyre directed the actress in *Suddenly Last Summer* for the BBC[52] and *The Importance of Being Earnest* opened only on 9 March 1993 at the Aldwych, Nicholas Hytner eventually replacing Terry Hands as stage director.

The stakes were high, as the main difficulty for Maggie Smith was to stand out from her numerous predecessors, in a play the audience knows by heart. Robert Tanitch, one of the best experts on Oscar Wilde, admits that 'the over-familiarity of the epigrams' is the pitfall inherent in this too well-known play. He recounts that the actress Fay Compton (1894-1978) – playing Bracknell at the Old Vic, in 1959 – was said to have had a lapse of memory during a performance and the audience supposedly prompted her.[53] The role of Lady Bracknell appears as some sort of frightening monster, if only because it is one of the major roles of English comedy. To list all the actresses (and actors) having played the role would be quite lengthy, but Dame Edith Evans undoubtedly left her mark on it for all eternity, remaining, in our collective memory, Bracknell's absolute incarnation.[54] She is the one whom people refer to each time there is a new revival of the play. She is the one who got immortalised in the first screen adaptation of the play.[55] She is, above all, the one who has perpetuated that very particular way of stressing the line 'A handbag?'. In 1947, John Gielgud convinced Margaret Rutherford to don Aunt Augusta's outfit for a revival in the United States and in Canada.[56] At first, Rutherford turned the part down, arguing that Evans's

51 B. Bamigboye, 'Hat's the way back for Maggie', *The Daily Mail*, 26 July 1991, p. 23.

52 In 1992, Smith had also been cast to appear in *The Widow's Peak*, directed by J. Irvin; the shooting was postponed until the spring of 1993 and she was eventually replaced by Joan Plowright.

53 'The Importance of Being Earnest', *Plays and Players*, May 1993, p. 25.

54 J. C. Trewin, *Edith Evans* (London: Rockliff, 1954), p. 82: 'For our generation, Edith Evans is the only conceivable Lady Bracknell. Doubtless the gracious figure of Rose Leclercq has been applauding her from the shades.'

55 *The Importance of Being Earnest* (A. Asquith, 1952), with M. Redgrave and M. Rutherford.

56 Edith Evans felt she was done with the role and thus refused to take part in the US revival (oddly enough, she nevertheless agreed to appear in a TV adaptation of the play in 1960). At the end of her career, she was even upset to be perpetually identified with the character. See E. Johns, *Dames of the Theatre* (London: W. H. Allen, 1974), p. 82; Evans said she did not want to hear Lady Bracknell's name mentioned again.

performance could not be matched. She finally accepted, provided that she would be allowed to exactly model her acting on that of her talented predecessor.[57] On the contrary, in 1993, Smith had not only to make the audience forget the terrifying Gorgon played by Evans, but also to present her own view of the role. And she did. Marvellously.

With one of the major British actresses at the top of the bill, the Aldwych production stood as a most anticipated event. A spectacular set by Bob Crowley – which involved disproportionate props and *trompe-l'oeil* effects – also contributed to make Hytner's sumptuous staging even more special.[58] Nevertheless, in spite of the gigantic size of John Worthing's sofa, Smith was to be the focus of attention and all the reviews concentrated on her performance. When *The Importance of Being Earnest* premiered in 1895, the main character was John Worthing. It is no longer. The peculiarity of Lady Bracknell lies in the fact that, even though she is only a secondary character, she has become the central figure.[59] Therefore, the play is now staged around a leading performer who gets top billing: Judi Dench in 1982, Wendy Hiller in 1987, Barbara Leigh-Hunt and Patricia Routledge in 1995, Penelope Keith in 2008 and, more recently, David Suchet, in 2015. The danger is that the spectators book their seats not to see the play, but to admire the performance of an actress/actor; for that reason, the performer who plays Bracknell has no difficulty outshining the rest of the cast in front of an audience who has come to the theatre just to see her/him. Of course, the phenomenon got amplified with Maggie Smith topping the bill. Described as 'excellent' by the critics of her time, Rose Leclercq knew her place, that of a supporting actress who did not even appear in Act II. As R. Tanitch observes, she was

57 Johns, *Dames of the Theatre*, p. 127.

58 'The set's the surreal thing' was the headline of I. Wardle's notice (*The Independent on Sunday*, 14 March 1993, p. 20). See also J. Kaplan, 'Wilde on the stage', in *The Cambridge Companion to Oscar Wilde*, ed. by P. Raby (Cambridge: Cambridge University Press, 1997), p. 270. Such a boldness led to expect a very original staging and some critics disapproved of Hytner's approach, which was too conventional for their taste and contrasted with the oddity of the set.

59 Stokes, *Oscar Wilde*, p. 172: 'The rise of the dowager to become the foremost character in the play was a gradual process that depended upon the changing attitudes and widening constituency of the theatre audience to the point where she was finally revealed as an extraordinary social product, both culturally remote and eerily familiar.' See also R. Jackson, 'The Importance of Being Earnest', in *The Cambridge Companion to Oscar Wilde*, p. 171.

scarcely mentioned in the first reviews of the play.[60] In fact, this is Edith Evans who, thanks to her impressive performance, has transformed a minor part into a prominent one, setting a very high standard for her successors.[61] Since then, the character has aged and, Judi Dench's young Bracknell being an exception,[62] no one would imagine her as a quadragenarian nowadays. Maggie Smith played the part more than twenty years ago and she could still play it, as convincingly as she did in 1993.[63]

Avoiding all the clichés associated with the character and cleverly skipping a handbag which had become far too cumbersome, Smith managed to give an outstanding and renewed rendition of Bracknell. Even so, as surprising as it may sound, she does not seem to have happy memories of that production. She did not approve of all the choices made by N. Hytner – although it was the beginning of a fruitful collaboration, on stage and on screen[64] – and it caused a few clashes during the rehearsals, to the point that she replied to a journalist who asked her if she would be willing to bring the play to Broadway, that she would not even take it to Woking.[65] To be just one Bracknell among many others was probably not challenging enough for Maggie Smith. A few years ago, she commented on the horror of playing a part that another actress has made unforgettable, blaming *The Importance of Being Earnest* and Evans's famous 'handbag', forever etched in

60 *Oscar Wilde on Stage and Screen* (London: Methuen, 1999), p. 259. Also J. Donohue, 'Reception and Performance History of *The Importance of Being Earnest*', in *Oscar Wilde in Context*, ed. by K. Powell and P. Raby (Cambridge: Cambridge University Press, 2013), p. 310: 'She is by all odds Wilde's single most memorable characterization. [...] It remains a puzzle why the creator of the role did not garner more mention, let alone praise, by first-night reviewers.'

61 See N. Hytner, *Balancing Acts* (London: Jonathan Cape, 2017), p. 178-179.

62 *The Importance of Being Earnest* directed by Hall, National Theatre, 1982, starring Nigel Havers, Zoe Wanamaker and Anna Massey (who would reprise her role as Miss Prism in Oliver Parker's movie, in 2002).

63 Wendy Hiller, who gave a brilliant performance at seventy-six, in 1987, was considered to be a bit too old for the part of Lady Bracknell. But she belonged to another generation and it is not possible to make a decent comparison, three decades later, with actresses like Maggie Smith, Judi Dench or Eileen Atkins. Sian Phillips recently played a superb Lady Bracknell at the Harold Pinter Theatre.

64 Hytner would successfully direct Smith a few years later, in Alan Bennett's *The Lady in the Van* (Queen's Theatre, 1999-2000). His delightful adaptation of Bennett's play for the big screen (2015) corresponded to his third collaboration with the actress.

65 C. Spencer, 'There is nothing like the Dames', *The Daily Telegraph*, 1 October 2002, p. 21.

our memories.[66] As early as 1986, commenting on Ronald Harwood's *The Interpreters*, she declared that the main virtue of this play was the fact that she did not have to follow in the footsteps of other performers, like she did when tackling the classics.[67] In actual fact, few actresses have brought something really new to the character, as it hardly allows any innovation. It is a conventional, stereotyped figure – a caricature of social authority – which requires a conventional, stereotyped interpretation.[68] Having said that, despite her self-deprecating comments, Miss Smith did not prove unworthy. Her Lady Bracknell remains, for those who had the luck to see her at the Aldwych, an unforgettable creation, enough to be mentioned as a reference in the academic studies and papers on Oscar Wilde. In fact, as Peter Mudford points out, her portrayal proved to be the only one able to compare with Evans's Bracknell. According to him, Edith Evans and Maggie Smith remain the two most memorable interpreters of Lady Bracknell, although they gave quite a different rendition of the part: the formidable, haughty aristocrat versus the restless, prickly parvenue.[69]

Smith's physical appearance, as much as her gestures and her extraordinary sharpness, drew new contours for the formidable Lady. Wearing a large hat adorned with an aggressive feather, her angular frame emphasised by the nearly geometric structure of her costume, the actress did not evade the most expressive comparisons and several critics indulged in extending the ornithological metaphor. Her Bracknell took after the hawk, or sometimes the siren – in the ancient meaning of the term, that is the siren bird – or even, when she was at her most redoubtable, the Harpy. The critic Jane Edwardes saw her as a bird of an uncommon species, disdainfully peering at its preys (while Edith Evans's Bracknell had been a still, steady 'tank'),[70] whereas R. Tanitch noted: 'Dressed in all grey, she is

66 T. Teeman, 'Maggie Smith. A bad case of stage fright', *The Times (Times 2)*, 5 October 2009, p. 3. In 2010, she asserted in *The Sunday Times* that, despite the passing of the years, it was impossible to make the audiences forget Evans's Bracknell and her much too notorious line. See Rees, 'The grand dame returns', p. 5.

67 Olliver, 'The Prime of Ms Smith'.

68 St John Hankin, *Fortnightly Review*, 1 May 1908, p. 791-802: 'Though Lady Bracknell is wonderfully drawn, she is not profoundly drawn. [...] Lady Bracknell is brilliantly done but she is a brilliant surface only. She has no depth and no subtlety.'

69 *Making Theatre. From Text to Performance* (London: The Athlone Press, 2000), p. 75.

70 *Time Out*, 17 March 1993 (see *Theatre Record*, 26 February-11 March 1993, p. 262).

like some highly-strung bird, disapproval in every glance.'[71] For his part, Irving Wardle was of the opinion that a grey-feathered vulture stood in for Bracknell,[72] and Benedict Nightingale carried on the metaphor, writing that Smith had created an efficient comical figure, a kind of rapacious, but urbane 'monster', worthy of the predatory creatures who surround Volpone in Ben Johnson's play.[73] As Lady Bracknell, the actress took possession of the stage as a threatening creature, a bird of prey endowed with a sharp beak and piercing eyes, but with an indisputable charm. Jack Tinker mentioned the 'sweep' of the lady's rustling skirt (an implicit comparison with a peacock tail sweeping away everything in its path) and described a fierce plumed bird in full control, dominating all creatures great and small.[74]

Thirty years had passed since *Hay Fever* (National Theatre, 1964), when a young Maggie strived to exasperate – backstage – Dame Edith, the other Bracknell. Thirty years later, Smith had become, in turn, a DBE, but she was, without question, at the height of her beauty. Lady Bracknell had certainly been seen with a younger face, that of Judi Dench; still, she had never appeared with such a regal bearing, looking, with her delicate features, quite remote from the common Bracknell, usually played as an abrupt battle-axe. In the review he wrote for *The Observer*, Coveney highlighted the genuine ambivalence of the Bracknell that Smith had created. Unlike Evans's, hers was no steady old crone frowning her nose at John Worthing's handbag indignities, but stood as an unconventional figure combining imperious elegance and glamorous feminity.[75] The only tangible vestige of this memorable production, the magnificent grey silk two-piece – the costume she wore in Act I – is now gloriously on display in one of the windows of the new Theatre and Performance Museum at the V&A.[76] As they contemplate the innoxious mannequin which is dressed in the spoils of the august Lady, the visitors probably do not imagine the formidable and frenetic creature who formerly sported

71 Tanitch, 'The Importance of Being Earnest'.

72 Wardle, 'The set is the surreal thing'.

73 Nightingale, 'Mythical monster triumphs'.

74 'Masterclass in the serious business of high comedy', *The Daily Mail*, 17 March 1993, p. 3.

75 'Part and parcel of a glittering career', *The Observer*, 14 March 1993, p. 55.

76 For a detailed description of the costume, see the V&A's website, Theatre and Performance Archive <http://collections.vam.ac.uk/item/O100926/importance-of-being-earnest-theatre-costume-crowley-bob/> [accessed 12 November 2016].

this elegant fitted redingote. The 1890s elaborate outfit perfectly suited Smith's slender figure, that was made taller by the extravagant edifice of feathers and ribbons which topped it. Miles away from the female dragon that Edith Evans's Aunt Augusta was,[77] Maggie Smith's looked like a bird of paradise with metallic plumage and prying eyes.

Imposing by her demeanour, impressive by her beauty, the actress nevertheless gave a hilarious performance. Despite her physical appearance – laughter being generally associated with difformity or ugliness (not without humour, C. Spencer described a sexy 'old trout') – she convulsed the audience thanks to a small repetitive gesture, a sideways glance or a scowl which transformed that elegant lady into a comical figure. As J. Edwardes outlined, this effect was produced by quick movements of the chin and the neck, mimicking the particular (and mechanical) way fowl move their heads, and the critic even compared Smith's demeanour to that of a bird 'fluttering' its wings.[78] Without doubt, to mimic an animal is an efficient trick in comedy. A fine bone structure, an angular face with high cheekbones and sharp eyes and, above all, that most recognisable pointy nose which could have inspired Pamela J. Travers when she wrote *Mary Poppins*, all that endows Maggie Smith with an undeniable similarity – in terms of 'animal physiognomy', as defined by the art historian Baltrusaitis[79] – to the winged creatures.[80] 'Birdlike' is a word which recurs frequently when people describe Smith physically and this is an analogy that Coveney often emphasises, not only in his biography of the actress, but also every

77 Trewin, *Evans*, p. 82: 'It would be wrong to say that Edith Evans' Lady Bracknell entered. Suddenly she would fill the skyline, a Himalayan peak of hot ice and wondrous strange snow.'

78 Edwardes, 'The Importance of Being Earnest'. The description sounded a tad less gallant in the (nonetheless) glowing review written by Peter Roberts (*Plays International*, April 1993, p. 15): 'a wizened old boiler in costume and hats'.

79 See J. Baltrusaitis, *Aberrations: An Essay on the Legend of Forms* (Cambridge, Massachusetts: The MIT Press, 1989). Also R. Remshardt, *Staging the Savage God. The Grotesque in Performance* (Carbondale : Southern Illinois University Press, 2004), p. 37: 'The use of the animal metaphor in the depiction of the face is a preferred method of caricature and satire, which draws on an established typology of human traits and similar presumed characteristics in animals.'

80 Nightingale, 'Mythical monster triumphs'; in his review, the critic emphasised this undeniable resemblance, mentioning her pouts, her piercing stares and mostly, these quick (but irresistible) twitches of the head. The critic from *USA Today* (22 July 1993, p. 8) compared Maggie Smith to a majestic flamingo.

time he writes about her.[81] This morphology, despite contributing to increase her comic potential, gets more discreet when she plays a pathetic scene; the actress obliterates anything that is not immediately relevant to the situation. When it is about being funny, though, she cleverly uses her physical skills, making people laugh even if she does not speak. A critic from *The Wall Street Journal* asserted that, in *The Importance of Being Earnest*, the actress stole the show even when she was not delivering dialogue; the audience appreciated as much her faces, her pauses and her silences as her speeches.[82] The comical aspect of the character was reinforced by the details of the costume. Oversized leg-of-mutton sleeves and an ample corolla skirt underlining a waist already tightened by the corset gave a caricatural shape to Lady Bracknell, probably in accordance with Wilde's design in creating a character who epitomised all the faults of the London's upper class.

However, even if they reflected the opinion of very few critics, the negative reviews were particularly harsh. Michael Billington was the one who criticised Maggie Smith's acting the most fiercely, accusing her of hamming it up to seek laughs.[83] The critic blamed her overacting – that he called an 'orgy' of moues and grimaces, in total discordance with the character created by Oscar Wilde – and her persistent attempts to provoke laughs, making use of all her mannerisms. Billington disliked her gesture and demeanour, especially when she 'clutched' her stomach to express her disgust,[84] as if he did not recognise what is probably Smith's most characteristic gesture when she has to express fright or indignation.[85] For him, her Lady Bracknell had nothing of that self-control, that haughty composure which necessarily belongs to a lady of high rank, sure of her privileges and superiority. Billington noted a 'strenuousness' in her

81 M. Coveney, 'I'm very scared of being back on stage', *The Evening Standard*, 2 March 2007, p. 34.

82 P. Levy, 'Theater in the Decadent Decade', *The Wall Street Journal*, 26 March 1993, p. 9.

83 'The Importance of Being Earnest. The Aldwych', *The Guardian*, 11 March 1993, p. 8. For him, she scandalously sought the laughs, instead of letting them come.

84 *Country Life*, 18 March 1993, p. 73.

85 About the very own gestures of the actor, those that regularly appears, here and there, in his cinematic performances, see C. Viviani, *Le Magique et le Vrai* (Aix-en-Provence : Rouge Profond, 2015), p. 36. What Viviani calls the onscreen *gestuelle du théâtral* ('theatrical gesture') is partly based on the particular body language of the actor. Smith, of course, possesses her very own body language that she uses, less or more, in all her performances.

portrayal, which contradicted the quiet Dame-Edith-like self-assurance that is expected from Bracknell.[86] In his words, the actress made the mistake of sacrificing the realism of the character to turn the latter into 'a bundle of fussiness forever fiddling' which contrasted with Dame Edith's remarkable composure.[87] According to Billington, she overplayed the part, warping every line into excess and grotesque. Other critics implied that Smith was a disservice to the role instead of sublimating it. They pretended that, making faces and flailing excessively, the actress transformed the character into a nervous parvenue. Paul Taylor drew a parallel between her Lady Bracknell and another of her roles, the ambitious Joyce Chilvers in *A Private Function* (M. Mowbray, 1984). According to Taylor, Smith did not have the quiet self-assurance of the character, but expressed the compulsive frenzy of an arriviste; considering her imperiousness contrived, he imagined that, once deprived of her sumptuous attire and imposing headgear, the Lady would not look as dignified as she was supposed to.[88] For his part, the critic John Peter thought that Maggie Smith's gestures were much too jerky and her looks too insistent to be those of a proper lady, well experienced in peering at lower-class people through her lorgnette. Much too inquisitive to be a dowager worthy of the title, this Bracknell had the very manners of an arriviste.[89]

As time passed, although Hytner's production was played to full houses, reviews paradoxically got more and more offensive, often unjust and even cruel. In *The Evening Standard*, Neil Norman wrote an aggressive report which sounded more like an indictment than a theatre review. Under the

---

86 *Ibid.*

87 On Edith Evans's performance, see A. Macaulay, 'Laughter beyond Bracknell', *The Times Literary Supplement*, 29 September 2006, p. 18. M. Billington reiterated his criticism two years later, comparing Smith's performance with that of Barbara Leigh-Hunt in the Old Vic production (dir. Terry Hands, 1995), a stiff matriarch only interested in wealth and worldly proprieties. See 'The real divisions between Wilde and Coward', *The Guardian*, 10 July 1995, p. 8.

88 'The Ultimate Status Symbol', *The Independent*, 12 March 1993, p. 21. See also G. Hassell, 'The Importance of Being Earnest', *What's On*, 17 March 1993 (see *Theatre Record*, 26 February-11 March 1993, p. 263). For the critic, Maggie Smith's Bracknell was definitely too mannered to be convincing as a well-bred aristocrat. It led to an unfortunate *mise en abyme*, Smith-the-actress portraying an arriviste who fakes class and imperiousness to pose as a grand lady.

89 'Upper Class Act', *The Sunday Times*, 14 March 1993, p. 19.

deliberately provocative headline 'The importance of being Maggie Smith',[90] the movie critic took a malicious delight in slating, point by point, Smith's work. Suggesting that the actress's main asset was to be 'bankable', he considered that she literally ruined the production. According to Norman, Maggie Smith shamelessly outshone the other actors who were far from being equal to the task. Insinuating that she had attracted the hate of the rest of the cast, he accused her of conspiring with the audience, not only to upstage her co-stars, but also to ridicule the whole production. For him, the 'bird of prey' had turned into a fearsome raptor looking, with some satisfaction, at the havoc that her overpowering performance had wreaked.[91] What took the cake, in Norman's words, was that she even dared to make the audience laugh to such an extent that her co-stars frequently had to pause because of the applause aroused by Bracknell's hilarious one-liners and frenetic gestures. As stated by the critic, she exaggerated and enlarged every effect, disfiguring the play to be funny at any cost. The worst of it was that she did succeed. Brilliantly. With a roll of her eyes, as he admitted, she left the whole audience in stitches. Norman's paper elicited impassioned reactions that were unanimous in defending one of the most talented actresses of the time. Quite predictably, Michael Coveney addressed a vibrant rebuttal to Norman's review[92] and Edward Fox – who had previously co-starred with Maggie Smith in R. Harwood's *The Interpreters* – sent to *The Evening Standard* a long letter which was as much a touching defence of Smith's talent as a glittering tribute to the actress herself. Fox underscored the phenomenal level of the actress's acting skills in playing high comedy. According to him, such a 'colossal' mastery involved, not only sheer talent, but also a considerable expertise in the matter of technique. The actor brilliantly dismissed the critic's abusive allegations which sounded uncalled for, considering her overpowering genius – *Margarita*m *ante porcos*, as would have said the Romans. In conclusion, Fox simply asserted that there was not

90 *The Evening Standard*, 15 June 1993, p. 11. The title was not really original, as it plagiarised S. Morley's review in *The Spectator*.

91 Michael Billington had already written a similar appreciation, considering that Smith's turn overshadowed the whole production, jeopardising its equilibrium (Billington, 'The Importance of Being Earnest. The Aldwych'). Also P. Simon, 'Dead Earnest', *The New York Magazine*, 9 August 1993, p. 83; the critic said that Smith exaggerated the role 'as disgracefully' as she could.

92 See 'Let's all go Wilde on genius of Maggie', *The Evening Standard*, 17 June 1993, p. 53.

one performer in the country who could rival Smith in terms of comedic abilities.[93] Only an actor, and a great one, was able to put so accurately these truths into words. Norman's review was mean and outrageous, but mostly ridiculous, denoting the critic's hopeless inability to perceive the actress's genius. As he admitted himself, the audience burst into applause at the very sight of Maggie Smith; it is hard to imagine that someone could blame her for giving rise to the plaudits of the spectators.[94] He lamented the fact that her co-stars had to stop speaking while the audience roared with laughter, whereas it is exactly the rule in any comical performance – '*laisser passer les rires*', as French actors say – and what must be the goal, when playing comedy, of any actor worthy of the name. Maggie Smith certainly cannot be reproached for making the most, not only of the text that she delivers perfectly, but also of her acting skills. She made Lady Bracknell the central character in the play for the simple reason that, as soon as she walked onto the stage, she outshone the rest of the cast and the play tended to wilt when she was away. The critic Maureen Paton, from *The Daily Express*, entitled her review 'The divine Dame Maggie illustrates the importance of heroic over-acting,' admitting that, thankfully, the part requires from the performer that she overacts.[95] A bad and vain actress willing to overshadow her co-stars would not manage to do so, but in the case of Maggie Smith or Edith Evans, there is an inevitable imbalance; it is very difficult, even for excellent actors, to be equal to performers of that calibre. Smith has committed the unforgivable offence to do her job at the highest level, acting several yards above the stage. All the supposed shortcomings that are weightily underlined by some critics can easily be turned into qualities, reasserting her amazing genius. In actual fact, what precisely he described in pompous, ironic or

93 'Maggie is a shining glory of artistry', *The Evening Standard*, 25 June 1993, p. 45.

94 J. Stokes, the renowned specialist of Oscar Wilde, also underlined that aspect, preferring Evans's Bracknell to Smith's. In a critical article he wrote on Wilde 'on performance', the academic emphasised the innovative character of Maggie Smith's approach to the role, after many other Bracknells. According to him, the actress played Aunt Augusta in a way that she provoked the laughs and 'controlled' the response of the audience. That is probably why some reviewers (like the reputed critic M. Billington) thought that her rendition did not do justice to the complexities of the character, which require more restraint and self-effacement from the performer. To some extent, Stokes himself acknowledged Smith's triumph: that Lady was excessive, overwhelming, but undeniably irresistible. See 'Wilde Interpretations', *Modern Drama*, 37.1, 1994, p. 169.

95 *The Daily Express*, 10 March 1993, p. 3.

reproving terms, could have inspired the panegyric of an exceptional artist. In spite of himself, he sketched out the portrait *in situ* of an extraordinary performer, standing out from the crowd.

Fortunately, most of the critics lauded Smith's performance. Enthusiastic, Kenneth Hurren declared that almost 'everybody in the town' had certainly heard about Smith's magnificent performance.[96] For his part, S. Morley declared that Maggie Smith's 'stupendous' rendition of Bracknell was the first to challenge Dame Edith's after many years, although he remarked, like M. Billington, a substantial difference in the reading of the character, Smith's Bracknell being not an imperious dowager, comfortably sticking to her prerogatives, but a more 'neurotic' parvenue, much less confident in her social status.[97] She was a parvenue, indeed, but a parvenue who perfectly embodied the quintessence of snobbery. Anyway, Smith's interpretation rightfully compared with that of her legendary predecessor and remains the only one which equals it in the collective memory. At any rate, she offered a new tack on the role, as the critic Malcom Rutherford observed, saying that Dame Maggie Smith's renewed approach to Bracknell brilliantly 'teased' the audience.[98] Many hailed her admirable technical mastery, such as C. Spencer, who thought that Smith tackled the part with as much acuteness as gusto, for the greatest joy of the public,[99] or the academic John Stokes, in the article he wrote for *The Times Literary Supplement* as a reputed specialist of Oscar Wilde.[100] J. Tinker evoked 'a miracle of timing and a masterclass in the serious business of high comedy'.[101] According to I. Wardle, Maggie Smith, relying on her prodigious body skills and timing to dominate the stage, gave a masterful performance.[102] Robin Stringer, from *The Evening Standard*, extended the martial metaphor, and compared the glorious warrior's comedic tricks and tools – her voice inflection, witty quips

96 'The Wilde side shines in Maggie', *The Mail on Sunday*, 14 March 1993, p. 38.

97 'The Importance of Being Maggie', *The Spectator*, 20 March 1993, p. 44.

98 'The Importance of Being Earnest', *The Financial Times*, 10 March 1993, p. 19.

99 Spencer, 'Dame Maggie's night of triumph'.

100 'The age demands', *The Times Literary Supplement*, 19 March 1993, p. 18.

101 Tinker, 'Masterclass in the serious business of high comedy'.

102 Wardle, 'The set is the surreal thing'.

and perfect timing – to a redoubtable arsenal in full display.[103] And Clive Hirschhorn concluded in the grand manner: 'Here is a great actress in a great part giving a great performance in a great play.'[104] Rejoicing in the fact that Smith ended a five-year absence from the London stage with a 'magnificent thunderclap', Coveney also described some of the highlights of the play, especially the expected 'handbag trap' that Smith expertly avoided.[105] By contrast with Evans, she delivered the famous sentence quite simply, with a certain indifference, but chose to stress 'The line is immaterial' instead, judiciously picking the most meaningful part of her speech to make an enormous effect.[106] Five years later, the journalist Jason Rees recklessly suggested that, unlike Judi Dench – 'a model of restraint' in the National Theatre production, in 1982 – Smith had exhausted as much as possible all the effects that she could derive from the most celebrated line from the play. According to Rees, the Maggie-Smith-playing-Bracknell 1993 production took the form of a well-anticipated, self-confident star turn, where the actress milked the 'handbag' line as much as it was possible.[107] That was wrong. By the same token, the journalist unintentionally admitted he had neither seen the production, nor read any of the reviews it received. On the other hand, and more generally, it reflects a regrettable tendency to regard Maggie Smith as a ham actress. On the contrary, everything in her performance reflected technical perfection. In *The Independent*, the critic Georgina Brown lauded Maggie Smith's flawless inflection that did masterfully justice to Wilde's script, without ever changing one word. The critic celebrated the actress's perfect delivery and, contradicting those who pretended that Smith had

103 'Cheers as a "genius" returns to the West End', *The Evening Standard*, 10 March 1993, p. 7.

104 'The Importance of Having Maggie Smith', *Theater Week*, 19 April 1993, p. 14.

105 Coveney, 'Part and parcel of a glittering career'.

106 Jackson, 'The Importance of Being Earnest', p. 170: 'the "build" of the sequence is really towards Jack's desperately specific "The Brighton Line" and Lady Bracknell's amazed retort, "the line is immaterial".' See also M. Owen, 'Friday People', *The Evening Standard*, 5 March 1993, p. 27. The journalist explained that, unexpectedly, the great surprise of Hytner's production was Maggie Smith's treatment of the 'handbag' line, which is without any doubt the most crucial line in Oscar Wilde's play. Whereas Dame Edith stressed it as much as her formidable self could ('A haaaaand baaaaaaag?'), Smith deftly overrode it, preferring to emphasise 'the line is immaterial'.

107 'The Big Match: Maggie v. Judi', *The Evening Standard*, 22 July 1998, p. 29.

brought 'embellishments' to the text, stressed the fact that she faithfully rendered Oscar Wilde's famous lines without any alteration. What appealed to G. Brown was that the actress beautifully revealed the weaknesses of Bracknell, suddenly all smiles when she learned about Cecily Cardew's affluent income.[108] With Smith on command, Bracknell's armour fissured, allowing her greed and vulnerability to show.

Maggie Smith definitely has no reason to regret or depreciate her performance as Lady Bracknell. As De Jongh asserted so appropriately in his rave notice, the play allowed Smith to gloriously step into the theatrical legend.[109] Moreover, some critics regretted that she did not reprise the role in Oliver Parker's movie (2002); not only had she just triumphed in the very similar part of Constance Trentham, in R. Altman's *Gosford Park*, but, mostly, what appeared like a role for Dench seemed to be second nature for Smith.[110] Maggie Smith was the only Bracknell to have, if not overshadowed, at least equalled Dame Edith's and, just like her, she remains strongly identified with the character these days.[111] Fifty years after Dame Edith's triumph, Maggie Smith eventually surpassed her illustrious predecessor. Evans was identified with Lady Bracknell. Smith is now identified with the type as a whole.

108 'Things that make you go *oooh! Bah! Ugh!* and *pish!*', *The Independent*, 20 March 1993, p. 32.

109 'Dame Maggie handbags her way into history', *The Evening Standard*, 10 March 1993, p. 7.

110 See S. Holden, 'O.K., but Was It at Least A Designer Handbag?', *The New York Times*, 22 May 2002, p. 5; P. Craven, 'Books – Second look', *The Sunday Age*, 18 August 2002, p. 10.

111 Fisher, 'Creating Another Identity', p. 74: 'The role had become strongly identified with Dame Edith Evans's performance, on stage and then preserved on film. Maggie Smith's own identification with that role is evident in the way that Sheridan Morley juxtaposes her performance with Albee's in his review.' Morley wrote in fact: 'Smith is predictably just wonderful, Lady Bracknell made over as Martha in a bed-jacket' (see his review 'Who's Afraid of Maggie Smith?', *The Spectator*, 26 November 1994, p. 62).

Trentham, Grantham & Gresham.

To the Manor Born

For the general public, in the UK and abroad, Maggie Smith is the ultimate incarnation of the British lady. The type includes an ample gallery of similar – but nevertheless different – characters, representing as many variations on the same theme. Whenever a grumpy aristocrat appears in a play or in a movie, the character systematically gets compared to her. In this respect, the actress has become an archetype; in a recent interview,

Miriam Margolyes explained that she had been given, in a TV drama, 'the Maggie Smith part', as if Smith herself was now a type. Furthermore, when another actress plays a character corresponding to that type, the people wonder why the role has not been offered to her. Recently, some critics were surprised that Smith had not been cast as 'Madame D.' in *The Grand Budapest Hotel* (W. Anderson, 2014), played by the amazing Tilda Swinton.[112] Still, she was approached for the role of Ruth DeWitt Bukater – a model of upper-class haughtiness – in James Cameron's *Titanic* (1997), but the American actress Frances Fisher eventually replaced her. Due to scheduling issues, Maggie Smith also had to turn down another part of redoubtable dowager, Aunt Elizabeth in Stephen Poliakoff's *Glorious 39* (2009). The movie itself is remarkable and allows Romola Garai the opportunity to give an outstanding performance in the titular role. Aunt Elizabeth (portrayed by Julie Christie) is an irritating, snobbish, frivolous aristocrat, who is indifferent to everything that does not pertain to herself, the kind of woman who asks her niece to scrape her muddy shoes after a walk. It is highly probable that Smith's Aunt Elizabeth would have stood as a much more fearsome figure than Christie's, but this minor character cannot sustain comparison with Mary Gilbert, the magnificent role that Poliakoff had offered her three years before. Maggie Smith now represents ideal casting for that sort of role and her name is nearly used as a generic term for every elderly, cantankerous, upper-class bitch wrinkling her nose in front of a plate of crumpets.

Among Smith's roles, Constance Trentham, in *Gosford Park* (R. Altman, 2002), is certainly the character which most resembles Lady Bracknell. In his review, the movie critic Geoffrey Macnab compared Smith to Evans, and thus implicitly to Lady Bracknell, declaring that the Countess Trentham was portrayed with a stiff imperiousness, worthy of Edith Evans, by Maggie Smith.[113] However, could anyone accuse Smith of identically 'replaying' Lady Bracknell through this new character? Surely not. As it will be examined further, she certainly draws on experience from previous roles, building on firm foundations, what explains why there are constants between one part and another. However, the actress does not possess an

112 Swinton was actually replacing Angela Lansbury, who was in Australia, touring with the play *Driving Miss Daisy*.

113 'Gosford Park', *Sight and Sound*, February. 2002, p. 46.

array of standard acting procedures she would rehash at every occasion. She creates, each time, a new character.

Shot just after the first episode of the *Harry Potter* saga, *Gosford Park* allowed Smith the opportunity to fully display her talent in a supporting part. There was nothing discriminatory about it, as none of the other actors had been given a prominent role. Nevertheless, as paradoxical as it may seem in an ensemble cast (which reunited Alan Bates, Michael Gambon, Eileen Atkins, Derek Jacobi and Helen Mirren among others), she impertinently outshines all of her fellow actors. Constance Trentham, the aunt of the housemistress, Lady Sylvia McCordle (K. Scott Thomas), is impressive by her bearing and her haughtiness. However, regarding class and social influence, she does not carry as much weight as Lady Bracknell. The widow of Count Trentham has definitively lost her lustre when the spectators get acquainted with her. Constance is a kind of relic, a vestige of the splendour of the past, who ekes out a living from the pension that Lord McCordle (M. Gambon), her niece's husband, begrudgingly grants her. At Gosford Park, she simply takes advantage of the material comfort that her age and her respectability entitle her to. Through the character and Maggie Smith's sparkling performance, the viewer is offered a satirical depiction of the flaws of the inter-war upper class. Constance Trentham never stops moaning and humiliating those who are unfortunate enough to come her way. In terms of type, she exactly corresponds to the grumpy old relative, that atrabilious parasite whose presence everyone has to endure during family gatherings. This is an essential figure in comedy and it gains, as played by an artist of this calibre, extra depth.

Although Constance Trentham only makes episodic appearances in the film, the actress who plays her magnificently steals the show. Effortlessly, Smith brings to life this formidable woman who clings onto her privileges and what remains of her former glory. She lends her face, her body and her voice to the elderly aristocrat but completely disappears behind the character. Transfigured by the make-up and the 1930s outfits which make her look older than her real age, the actress Maggie Smith does not exist anymore on screen. Despicable, but thoroughly hilarious, Constance Trentham looks as if she had come out from a sepia coloured picture. On the opposite side, with regard to the pictures taken at the 74th Academy Awards ceremony in March 2002, it is hard to believe that the youthful and modern ginger-haired lady who attended the event alongside the actor-producer Bob Balaban was nominated, precisely, for the role of the elderly countess. John Barrett, the famous hairdresser of Fifth Avenue, recounted he had taken great pleasure in transforming Constance Trentham into a resplendent Maggie. Celebrating Smith's beautiful hair for its shine and thickness, J. Barrett underlined the amazing (physical) malleability of the actress, a spry red-haired woman elegantly sporting a black sequined two-piece suit by Armani.[114]

Gosford Park opens with a preamble that has become legendary. In pouring rain, a butler comes out of a big house to check if the car is ready to depart and pompously announces it to his mistress. Wrapped up in a thick fur coat and sheltered from the rain with an umbrella held by her maid, the lady of the manor rushes into her car. At that stage, we know nothing about the character, but it is easy to guess that this woman is someone grand. Aunt Constance makes her first proper appearance a moment later; sitting in the car, she desperately tries to open her Thermos bottle and calls her devoted servant to the rescue. The car stops and the poor maid, already soaked to the skin, has to help her mistress. The bottle eventually gets opened but Her Ladyship, shivering with cold, keeps her scowl and bluntly scorns another guest who had kindly stopped to give her assistance. The film could end here – it would be a real shame, though – as, in less than five minutes, the actress has masterfully established her character.

At Gosford Park, Constance Trentham is unpleasant with almost every person she meets, generously delivering put-downs and sardonic remarks to the guests who belong to an inferior class. She mocks the evening gown of a penniless cousin and chuckles when a footman spills some hot coffee over the trousers of another guest. She doggedly picks on the unfortunate Ivor Novello – alluding to his recent cinematic flop and suggesting that it is probably time for him to 'throw in the towel' – and assures an American producer of whodunnits that absolutely no one among the guests will ever go and see his upcoming feature. Opposed to any form of progress, she disdainfully rejects everything that aims to innovate. Unsurprisingly, her attitude towards the servants is on the same scale as the way she behaves, upstairs, with her peers. Constance is the perfect incarnation of the opposition of classes in the most appalling way possible. She constantly

114 S. Stacey, 'Top of the Crop – or how one magician with scissors has transformed so many beautiful', *The Daily Mail*, 20 April 2002, p. 35.

bullies her young Scottish maid, Mary McIshran, while claiming to go to a lot of trouble to train her. Her imperiousness reaches its peak when she decides to wear the same blouse two days in a row, compelling the poor Mary to do a night-time laundry. As expected, the next morning, the capricious lady has changed her mind. She will not wear the blouse.[115]

Robert Altman and the screenwriter Julian Fellowes have pushed the type beyond caricature. Constance Trentham embodies all the foibles of the aristocracy. She is not only authoritarian, contemptuous and haughty, but also stingy, mean-spirited and gossipy. For bad faith, she has no rival, imperturbably claiming that she hasn't 'a snobbish bone' in her body. In her own way, she is provocative. The accumulation of all these faults in one person makes the character an archetype, endowing it with the greatest comedic efficiency. In January 2002, in an interview for CBS News, Maggie Smith admitted that it is always 'quite fun' to portray these aggressive old bags.[116] We can take her word for it. Nevertheless, as contemptuous as she is, Constance has to swallow her pride and beg in secret to her nephew McCordle to maintain her allowance. Ultimately, it appears that the lady is much less grand and prestigious than it seemed; she is as pitiful as she is hateful. In fact, what is the most striking thing about *Gosford Park*'s grumpy dowager is that the character shows two radically different aspects of her personality. The countess is highly despicable, her excesses make her risible, but she reveals an unexpected side in private. The histrionic Lady Bracknell only has an existence in public and we spectators are allowed to see her only while, being immaculately dressed and groomed, she is picking at a plate of cucumber sandwiches – when there are some left, of course. With Trentham, we enter the privacy of the character.

In her apartments, Countess Trentham unleashes her personality, revealing her little ways which oddly contrast with her demeanour in public. Deprived of a large part of her majesty, the redoubtable lady ridiculously simpers and behaves like a spoiled child. Her austere outfits and the dark velvet gowns that she wears for dinner have been replaced by a cosy dressing gown of a tender pink colour which looks quite incongruous, given the lady's respectable age. What makes the character so enjoyable is that, when

115 On that scene, see J. Pidduck, *Contemporary Costume Film* (London: BFI, 2004), p. 128.

116 Osgood, 'In her Prime: actress Maggie Smith'.

she is having breakfast in her bed, Smith's Trentham does not look like a formidable dowager, but rather like a little mouse which has escaped from a Beatrix Potter album. Being divested of her mundane finery, Constance has substituted her scintillating tiara with an adorable lace nightcap. Under that cute headwear, we can merely discern a pointy nose and a disdainful mouth that will get even more pinched when the lady discovers that she has not been served home-made jam, but 'bought marmalade'. Critics have emphasised the way Constance Trentham delivers her hilarious one-liners, focusing on her distasteful behaviour towards the other guests; still, the most interesting and subtle part of Smith's performance probably lies in these private scenes where the elderly lady takes the utmost care of her own precious self. Sensitive to the cold, Constance keeps herself warm with a hot water bottle and, still very anxious about her appearance, she scrupulously applies slices of cucumber on her eyelids. Behind closed doors, the old battle-axe proves to be a cutie pie. Thanks to the violent opposition between these two aspects, the character gains as much in depth as in comical adeptness. A delightful behind-the-scenes picture – published in *Country Life* magazine – showed an imperious Maggie Smith in evening dress sporting an unsightly hairnet on her smart Marcel wave, what reflected in some way the dual nature of the character.[117] While her Countess Trentham undoubtedly stands as a figure of fun, Smith also makes her sympathetic – although she never plays *for* sympathy. Yet, very few actresses would have managed to convincingly portray the two sides of Constance Trentham. Many veteran performers can play detestable harridans, but only Smith is able to play a cute and vulnerable one.

By comparison, it is probably what is lacking in the character she plays in *Downton Abbey*. In the wake of the considerable success of ITV's show, Violet Crawley has become Maggie Smith's most popular role, just after Professor McGonagall in *Harry Potter*. However, although Minerva sometimes overshadowed the actress who played her – the youngest spectators so strongly identified Smith with the character created by J. K. Rowling that they believed she was able to turn into a cat – the Dowager Countess seems to have invaded the whole public part of Maggie Smith's life. Violet suddenly appeared on the small screen one

117 S. Johnston, 'Assembling Stars below Stairs', *Country Life*, 24 January 2002, p. 57.

evening in September 2010 and the actress who played her got immediate recognition, in both senses of the word. Wherever she goes, Smith is now inevitably recognised by viewers, many of whom feeling perfectly entitled to snap and harass an actress they watch for free on their television. Besides, the professional recognition – through the numerous awards she has won for her supporting role in the show – has unfortunately, and paradoxically, led some people to think that she did not exist before *Downton Abbey*. Not only was she a household name long before the show aired on ITV, but we can hope that she will go on working long after the Crawley family has said its farewell. Maybe the character and the whole show would not have survived without Maggie Smith, but the actress does not need it to pursue her glittering career.

Despite the infatuation of the general public for the character, thanks to Maggie Smith's exceptional comic timing, Violet is mainly a cameo. We know very little about her, at least until Season 5 – when the viewers discover she has had an affair, many years before, with a Russian prince – and she is never involved in the main plots. Nevertheless, the dowager can be seen as a double of Constance Trentham or, more exactly, a caricature of what is already a caricatural type. On a dramatic level, Violet Crawley stands for a stock character. She personifies the figure of the grumpy old aristocrat which traditionally introduces a comic element in the story, just like the numerous wealthy old aunts who fill P. G. Wodehouse's novels. Visually, she reminds us of the formidable battle-axes who appeared in the movies of the 1930s-1950s.[118] She strongly resembles Lady Beldon, the terrifying and unforgettable dowager in *Mrs Miniver* (W. Wyler, 1942). With her cane, her hats and furs, her imposing shape and her imperious chin, Lady Beldon prefigures the Dowager Countess of Grantham. Snob, haughty and rather determined, she is highly resistant to change and social mixing, and immensely aware of her superiority. The great May Whitty played the character as second nature while Maggie Smith does a great job of characterisation, especially in terms of physical appearance. In real life,

118 One could think of several among Marie Dressler's parts, especially Mrs Bouccicault in *Let us be gay* (R. Z. Leonard, 1930). On some pictures, with her waved bun and her perpetual scowl, Dressler looks more imposing and less feminine than Smith's dowager, but the two characters are quite similar; see V. Sturtevant, *A Great Big Girl like Me. The Films of Marie Dressler* (Urbana-Chicago: University of Illinois, 2009), p. 51, fig. 9.

Dame May looked like the character she portrayed, whereas Dame Maggie does not resemble Violet Crawley at all.

Besides, and it is one of the script's weaknesses, the character does not take herself seriously enough to be convincing as the typical dowager. Her wit and sharpness are almost disconcerting. Wittier than Oscar Wilde and Noel Coward reunited, the dowager countess only speaks through one-liners and aphorisms, a fact that cannot seem realistic unless she spends her nights polishing her quips and learning them by heart in advance. But mostly, as the show goes on, Violet seems to have fun with her own witticisms, when a proper cinematic or theatrical dowager should remain imperturbable and narrow-minded. As Estella Tincknell notes, the dowager may be 'invariably permitted the last word', she arouses too much sympathy to sound as reactionary and stubborn as it would be expected from such a figure.[119] The character undoubtedly raises laughs, but she would have been even more efficient, comically speaking, if she had been 'ridiculous' in the bergsonian sense of the word. According to the theory of the philosopher Henri Bergson, a person or a character is 'ridiculous' – derived from the Latin verb *ridere* ('to laugh') – when making the other people laugh *involuntarily*, just like Trentham or Bracknell, two more coherently developed characters who are unconsciously funny. To comply with the type that the character represents, the dowager countess should not be aware of her own bad faith. Lady Beldon, Constance Trentham and Lady Bracknell do not realise how shamelessly or ridiculously they behave. 'What's a weekend?' was an ingenuous question, particularly suited to a disdainful aristocrat, but in the following seasons, Violet pleasantly jokes, prepares her effects and stages her recurring appearances. Instead of being a comical 'opponent', as required by the type it corresponds, the character conspires with the audience. 'Let's have fun!'. She seems to suggest to the viewers, tincturing her voice with precise degrees of irony. With her somehow distanced acting and her mischievous faces, Smith has made Violet a clever, witty and even lovable woman. However, although the role lacks depth to be worth of the

119 'Dowagers, Debs, Nuns and Babies: The Politics of Nostalgia and the Older Woman in the Sunday Night Television Serial', in *Aging Femininities. Troubling Representations*, ed. by J. Dolan and E. Tincknell (Newcastle: Cambridge Scholars, 2012), p. 60.

highly skilled actress who plays it,[120] Maggie Smith manages, once again, to outshine the whole cast and, during six seasons, she has gloriously stood out as the backbone of the show.

Quite accustomed now to period dramas, Smith has nonetheless never portrayed any of Jane Austen's characters, although the novelist remains, with Dickens, a favourite of TV and cinema adaptations. However, the actress has been able to play, indirectly, the role of Lady Catherine De Bourgh, one of the most famous figures in Austen's *Pride and Prejudice*. In 2005, the director Julian Jarrold was commissioned by Ecosse Films to bring to the screen the life of Jane Austen. Shot in Ireland during the spring of 2006, the movie was released in March 2007. The screenplay of *Becoming Jane*, adapted from a recent biography by Jon H. Spence,[121] was based on the assumption that Austen's supposed romance with a certain Tom Lefroy had presumably inspired her writing. In actual fact, the film claimed to be 'a fictional prequel' to the novel and a 'faux remake' of other Austen adaptations.[122] For the audience, the purpose of the game was to try to recognise, through the 'real' characters of the movie, those, probably more famous, of the novels.

Although – to the great disappointment of the spectator – Smith has very little screen time in a film that lasts more than two hours, she gives a remarkable performance as Lady Gresham, another haughty and grumpy elderly aristocrat. Unlike the other characters of the movie, Gresham is

120 When the first series aired on television, in 2010, M. Coveney was more critical about the show than he would be, years later, in his updated biography of the actress. In a short notice he wrote on his *Whatsonstage* blog, M. Coveney admitted that the new ITV period drama involved excellent actors, like Hugh Bonneville and Jim Carter, but he also deplored the fact that, despite her immediate popularity, Maggie Smith's acerbic dowager was not completely worthy of the magnificent actress who played her, suggesting it was not the kind of material which could give Smith 'something to get her teeth into'. See 'Down with *Downton Abbey*', *WhatsOnStage.com Blogs*, 3 November 2010 <http://www.whatsonstage.com/west-end-theatre/news/11-2010/down-with-downton-abbey-_10987.html> [accessed 12 November 2016].

121 Now deceased, the academic Jon Spence was one of the most valued specialists of Austen and thus, he was committed as historical consultant on set. His book, *Becoming Jane Austen: A Life* (London: Hambledon Continuum, 2003), is a thorough study based on the novelist's correspondence with her sister Cassandra.

122 D. F. Sadoff, *Victorian Vogue. British Novels on Screen* (Minneapolis-London: University of Minnesota, 2010), p. 252.

nothing but a fictional figure, completely fabricated to play the role of an 'opponent' in Jane Austen's life. According to the screenplay, Lady Gresham was one of Jane Austen's acquaintances, the one who had inspired her in creating the redoubtable Lady Catherine De Bourgh. Of course, this idea has been developed a posteriori and therefore, ironically, the character takes a lot after the literary figure of which it pretends to be the prototype. It is quite regrettable though, when the spectators consider the delightful (but rare) moments when Smith/Gresham graces the screen, that she has never got to play Lady Catherine in any of the multiple adaptations of *Pride and Prejudice*. As Jarrold himself observed, the role of Lady Gresham was tailor-made for her, precisely because this character is very similar to the mistress of Rosings Park and, in some aspects, very different: 'I had previously worked in the past with Maggie Smith and knew there was no one else who could play the part of Lady Gresham. She has similarities to Lady Catherine De Bourgh in *Pride and Prejudice*, but in this film you get to see her hidden vulnerabilities – the pain of never having had children and her controlling maternal power over Wisley.'[123]

The resemblance with Lady Catherine is clearly stressed from the very beginning. Fully embodying the upper class, Lady Gresham is a wealthy, haughty aristocrat who pretends to rule over the Austen family in the same manner as she rules over her estate. A critic suggested that, as a kind of allegory, Smith's haughty dowager stood for the 'snobbery and social climbing' that are key elements in Austen's novels.[124] In the novel, Lady Catherine's disdainful attitude borders on roughness. Calling at Longbourn – the Bennet family's home – she sharply refuses the refreshments offered by Mrs Bennet. There is a very similar scene in Jarrold's movie. Visiting the Austen's humble manor, a pinched-faced Lady Gresham contemptuously declines the cup of plain black tea that Jane's mother kindly offers her. Quite unfortunately, Her Ladyship only drinks green tea, as smart people do. The beverage she asks for is, at that time, an expensive rarity and, if the svelte and distinguished lady makes a point of drinking it, it is certainly not for the depurative properties it is associated with nowadays, but simply to stand out from the crowd. In a certain way, green tea is to Lady Gresham what cucumber sandwiches

---

123 *Becoming Jane* pressfile, p. 13-14.

124 L. Beardsworth, 'Becoming Jane', *Empire*, April 2007, p. 56.

are to Lady Bracknell. As the critic Irving Wardle rightfully pointed out, looking at Maggie Smith's rich and varied career, undeniable resonances between some of her parts can be observed. He had spotted an intriguing 'crossover' between several of her portrayals, as if each of these characters, similar, but distinct, was the same individual, considered at a different stage of life.[125] She had certainly kept, when playing Lady Bracknell, something of the frenetic gestures of her first Aunt Augusta – Augusta Bertram, in *Travels with my Aunt* (G. Cukor, 1972) – but, conversely, to play Lady Gresham, she has also preserved the prominent features of Bracknell, that is her contempt for the inferior classes as well as her distaste for everything that goes against decorum.

The character also stands for the embodiment of social authority in the turn of the eighteenth century. Lady Gresham watches over the interests of her nephew, Wisley, who has unfortunately set his heart on the young and penniless Jane Austen. Grinning and bearing it, she accepts that he follows his heart and reluctantly opens her arms to Miss Austen, inviting her to a grand ball purposely organised. Like Lady Catherine, Lady Gresham has the power of decision in affairs of the heart and, just like her, she feels scorned as Jane turns down Wisley's advances. The difference between De Bourgh and Gresham lies in the fact that, with regard to the latter, her suffering is greater than her discontent, what makes the character moving. In a short but very touching scene, she reveals that, having had no child of her own, she has raised her nephew as her son and truly wants him to be happy, thus making the viewer realise why Jane's refusal disappoints her so much. Her first motivation is not the social rules, but the motherly love she feels towards Wisley. Jane Austen has ruined the plans she had made for him and, therefore, the young woman will never be forgiven for that. Lady Gresham may seem harsh and merciless until her very last appearance on screen, but despite all that, she remains a very touching, even lovable character that no actress except Maggie Smith could have played with such subtlety.

Dowager or sphinge, Lady Catherine De Bourgh is like a queen having pride of place at court. Jane Austen describes her in detail: 'Lady Catherine was a tall, large woman, with strongly marked features, which might once have been handsome. Her air was not conciliating, nor was

125 Wardle, 'All the angles'.

her manner of receiving them such as to make her visitors forget their inferior rank.'[126] Such a description certainly reminds us of another well-known dowager, but it would not be accurate to evoke the character that Smith plays in *Becoming Jane*. Despite being majestic and imperious, Lady Gresham does not look as healthy and prosperous as Lady Catherine. With her arachnean wig and her diaphanous complexion, she does not resemble a queen mother but rather a desiccated spinster, as angular as the actress who plays her. From that perspective, she is diametrically different from the cheerful and cordial Mrs Austen, played by Julie Walters. As much as the ancestral home of the Gresham family looks lugubrious and decrepit,[127] its mistress looks sad, old-fashioned and austere. The sumptuous costumes created for the actress by Irish costume designer Eimear Ní Mhaoldhomhnaigh aimed at reflecting a gothic aesthetic – where dark colours were dominant – inspired by the fashion of the 1770s.[128] The black evening gown adorned with green ribbons is undoubtedly the most spectacular element in Lady Gresham's wardrobe. Looking imperial, the ageing woman welcomes her guests at the top of the big stairs of her house and, although her livid pallor is even more accentuated by the greenish-black taffeta, what immediately catches the attention is the gracious poise of the mature lady. The eighteenth-century dresses suit Smith particularly well and, thirty-five years apart, her Lady Gresham has the same delicate features and the same elegance as her Mrs Sullen in *The Beaux's Stratagem*.[129] The physical appearance of

126 J. Austen, *Pride and Prejudice*, Vol. II, Chapter VI (Oxford: Oxford University Press, 2004), p. 125.

127 Lady Gresham's house is a mix of two different locations: the exterior belongs to Kilruddery House, County Wicklow, and the interior to Charleville Forrest, County Offaly (see L. Mac Cárthaigh, 'Locating Jane', *Film Ireland*, 111, 2006, p. 24).

128 *Becoming Jane* pressfile, p. 20: 'Everything about her is quite rigid from the skirts to the fabrics. We used quite stiff fabrics to emphasise a woman who was very set in her ways and who was not going to be influenced by anything like fashion. She wears a very large hood called a calash that was very common at the time. No one else in the film is wearing it so it makes her look quite different and even eccentric. Maggie loved it.' Thus her wardrobe was regarded as old-fashioned for Jane Austen's contemporaries. The magnificent burgundy dress that Maggie Smith wears in a luncheon scene was inspired by a historical outfit from the V&A collection. It is now on display at the Jane Austen's Museum, in Chawton.

129 A National Theatre production (1970), directed by W. Gaskill.

Lady Gresham emphasises a vulnerability quite unexpected in that kind of character. Despite her social status and her wealth, she is a miserable woman who lives a sad, lonely life. The scenery, the lightning and the staging, all tended to suggest these aspects.[130] Ultimately, if the intention of the filmmakers was to present Lady Gresham as a hateful, despicable opponent to the leading figure, Jane Austen, it proves to be a total failure. Slightly escaping from her type, Maggie Smith has rarely appeared as vulnerable and lovable on screen while playing her usual aristocratic persona. As paradoxically as it may seem, the character – fragile, delicate and miserable – is incredibly touching. We hate and fear Lady Catherine. We hate Gresham too, but we feel very sorry for her. Although the part is very small, Lady Gresham probably corresponds, within the narrow limits of typecasting, to one of Smith's most subtle performances. A real tour de force.

130 As director of photography Eigil Bryld explained, 'Lady Gresham is about scale and space. We shot and lit her in a way so she seems a little secluded and composed. The colour scheme is also slightly different. I used some cyan (green-blue) for Lady Gresham to create a sense of slight claustrophobia, almost like being in a fish tank. I used more gentle colours for the Austens.' See *Becoming Jane* pressfile, p. 17.

Flower of Evil

Most of the time, when being typecast, Maggie Smith plays distasteful, contrary, snobbish characters, but those cannot be regarded as villains. Lady Gresham stirs our emotions, while Constance Trentham and the dowager countess make us laugh. Mrs Venable, in Tennessee Williams's *Suddenly Last Summer*, is one of the rare obnoxious figures that the actress has portrayed and, considering the greatness of her performance, it would be exciting to see her in such parts more often.

Some movies can be seen as the definitive adaptation of a novel or a play. In the case of *Suddenly Last Summer*, Joseph Mankiewicz's film (1959) had reasonably discouraged any other attempt to adapt the play for the screen. *Suddenly Last Summer* is undoubtedly overshadowed by Tennessee Williams's more celebrated works and their even more famous cinematic adaptations (like *A Streetcar Named Desire* or *A Cat on a Tin Roof*), but Elizabeth Taylor, Katharine Hepburn and Montgomery Clift's unforgettable performances have made Mankiewicz's film a classic. Yet, being certainly less known than the Hollywood version, the TV adaptation directed by Richard Eyre easily rivals it.[131] Broadcast in November 1993, this restrained and meticulously made adaptation is even seen as being superior to Mankiewicz's film, thanks to its righteous faithfulness to Williams's play and the remarkable quality of Natasha Richardson and Maggie Smith's performances.[132] By the strangest coincidence, the TV drama was shot at Shepperton Studios, on the very set used by Joseph Mankiewicz more than three decades ealier.[133] Richard Eyre decided to restore the genuine atmosphere of Tennessee Williams's play, drawing upon excellent performers and sober staging. In the end, this TV drama stands out as a masterful adaptation of the play – adaptation in the sense that it is a transposition to the screen, but an amazingly accurate and faithful transposition. Natasha Richardson received rave notices for her remarkable performance, more nuanced and layered than that of Elizabeth Taylor. As for Maggie Smith, she is true to form. Grandiose.

Suddenly Last Summer's plot is as simple as it is profoundly disturbing. Old and wealthy Violet Venable promises to subsidise Dr Cukrowicz (Rob Lowe) to allow him to pursue his research. In return, the young

131 The DVD is only available in the US version, in the special box-set *Maggie Smith at the BBC* (BBC Worldwide, 2008).

132 Actually, Smith received a nomination for Outstanding Lead Actress at the 1993 Emmy Awards.

133 S. King, '… About "Last Summer"', *The Los Angeles Times*, 3 January 1993, p. 5. The filming was short – it took only nine days, in September 1992 –, but exhausting, as cast and crew had to work in a very hot and moist atmosphere required by the tropical plants which filled out Mrs Venable's garden. See R. Eyre, *National Service. Diary of a decade at the National Theatre* (London: Bloomsbury, 2003), p. 195.

neurosurgeon has accepted to perform a lobotomy on her niece Catharine Holly (Richardson). Catharine has been confined in hospital since the day she witnessed the horrible death of her cousin Sebastian, Mrs Venable's son, on the beach at Cabeza de Lobo; as the young woman never stops telling frightening stories involving human cannibalism, Mrs Venable is prepared to do anything to silence her. At any cost, the elderly lady must prevent Catharine from tarnishing the memory of Sebastian and, to be more exact, from revealing his homosexuality. Although Gore Vidal's screenplay was written just after the play had been created (1958), it took great liberties with Williams's script, adding some new scenes and making explicit Sebastian's sexual inclination – whereas it was only suggested in the play. When the movie was being made, Katharine Hepburn was only fifty-one, thus much younger than the character she played. Her Venable appears as a beautiful, robust woman in full possession of all her faculties, certainly not as an old lady who has become an invalid after a stroke. Violet Venable's tyrannical and evil nature is immediately perceptible behind her tight smile which now and again freezes into a sarcastic grin, but, nevertheless, she remains an attractive, seductive woman. When she confronts the truth, through Catharine's telling of the facts, her only way to escape from reality is to sink into dementia and withdraw into herself forever. The world of dreams where she used to seek refuge, away from the hideous reality, has become her prison for the rest of her life.

Etymologically, literary critics have related Violet's patronym to 'venal', 'venomous' or 'Venus', as an allusion to the Venus flytraps which ornate Sebastian's exotic garden.[134] In actual fact, with her wide brimmed hat and her gossamer silk chiffon dress, Maggie Smith's Violet has the fluttering grace of a translucent seaweed. To extend the botanical metaphor, she looks like a delicate, nearly wilted flower emerging from the scary jungle that her garden is. The actress immaculately portrays the character whom Tennessee Williams describes in the stage directions. Violet's hair has been dyed in a peculiar orange colour and her mauve chiffon gown makes her figure even more evanescent than the lavender

---

134 J. J. Thompson, *Tennessee Williams' Plays. Memory, Myth, and Symbol* (New York: Peter Lang, 2002), p. 110-111. In the oldest Roman religion, Venus was not the goddess of love and seduction, but a deity who reigned over gardens and lush vegetation.

lace outfit described by the playwright would have done. Leaning on her cane or sitting in her wheelchair, Mrs Venable is a disabled elderly lady, one of those magnificent women whom a stroke or an invasive illness has suddenly deprived of their autonomy and reduced to a shadow of their former selves. In 1992, the actress was certainly a bit too young to play the mother of a quadragenarian and maybe she should have been aged for the role. Nevertheless, as usual, and without the help of any specific make-up, she brilliantly manages to make her character convincing. Smith *acts* old and, therefore, it is obvious that Violet Venable *is* old. While Katharine Hepburn was a redoubtable and triumphant Megaera, a formidable tigress full of strength and energy. Maggie Smith's Gorgon looks like a crumbling porcelain doll, a fragile puppet with rusted joints.[135] Diaphanous in her flounces of faded muslin, Violet resembles a beautiful corpse or an ethereal creature. Weakened by the years and, mostly, by her disability, she lives only for and through the memory of Sebastian. The old lady idolises her son to the point that she reinvents and embellishes his story, as if she was trying to protect herself from the doubts and fears which certainly invade her mind. Her obsession – that is to maintain intact the memory of the 'chaste' Sebastian – leads her to the worst. She wants her niece Catharine to undergo a lobotomy, in the hope that the young woman could forget the atrocious events she has witnessed.

In many aspects, Smith's Venable looks like a modern incarnation of Miss Havisham, in Dickens's *Great Expectations*.[136] Just like Miss Havisham, who literally stages her aborted wedding through the display of a decaying banquet, Mrs Venable herself appears as a spectral figure inhabiting an oneiric world. The white sheets covering the furniture in the deserted rooms of her house bring to mind the description of the thick cobwebs which have invaded Havisham's dining room. Just like the latter ridiculously treasures, as a ghastly relic, her desiccated wedding cake where a colony of spiders has taken up residence, Violet Venable harnesses all her energy to preserve a sugar-coated image of her late son,

135 J. Grissom, *Follies of God. Tennessee Williams and the Women of the Fog* (New York: Knopf, 2015), p. 349. Tennessee Williams himself described Violet Venable as 'an authentic gem', a huge diamond of great worth, which was unfortunately 'deeply flawed' and embedded in a diadem of 'dime-store junk'.

136 Even if it has recently been played by younger actresses (from Gillian Anderson to Helena Bonham-Carter), the part would suit Maggie Smith perfectly.

even if it requires that she ignores the sordid, even atrocious, aspects of reality.[137] In the same way as Miss Havisham indirectly takes her revenge on life through young Estella, Violet makes use of her money to exercise her power over Dr Cukrowicz and put Catharine's ranting to an end. Beneath her appearance as a vulnerable elderly woman, Mrs Venable is frighteningly cruel and Machiavellian.

It is on this paradox that Maggie Smith's performance is built. For the actress, the challenge was twofold – she had to play, despite being too young for the part, an old lady who, precisely, does her best to look younger than her age – and, as usual, she is absolutely compelling. With her dyed Marcel wave and meticulous make-up, Violet Venable desperately tries to keep up appearances, in memory of the (more or less) incestuous couple she formed with her son. Like Sebastian, who followed a strict diet, she had simply refused the ageing process until paralysis undermined all her efforts. 'Both of us were young,' she bravely confesses to Dr Cukrowicz. Clearly, Mrs Venable used to see herself as the muse who inspired Sebastian in writing his poems. When she evokes their ostentatious way of life, Violet Venable has the same beautiful nostalgic smile as Emily Delahunty, a character that Smith would play ten years later.[138] Tennessee Williams never phrases the exact nature of the relationship between mother and son, but that fleeting smile emphasises the ambiguities of the odd couple. Nothing is said, though, it is only subtly suggested on the actress's face; it is obvious, at this time, that Violet used to be young. Like Sebastian. With Sebastian.

However, despite her vulnerability, Mrs Venable – 'venerable', as some critics infer from her surname – can be associated with the figure of the cantankerous dowager. In other words, it fully corresponds to Maggie Smith's usual type. Although her Violet is partly wheelchair-bound (while Katharine Hepburn's Violet was able-bodied), she rules like a monarch, not only over her Garden District estate, but also over her relatives and acquaintances. Far from making her look disabled, her wheelchair resembles the throne of a queen or the palanquin of an oriental sovereign.

---

137 J. O'Connor, *Dramatizing Dementia. Madness in the Plays of Tennessee Williams* (Bowling Green: Popular Press, 1997), p. 103: 'Violet Venable, struggling to convince herself of the purity of her son's life, seeks to ensure her own life's usefulness, terrified that Sebastian's sordid death renders her own existence a "trail of debris"!'

138 *My House in Umbria* (R. Loncraine, 2003).

Frail and invalid, Violet Venable turns out to be a domineering, powerful and authoritarian woman holding the cards. That very metaphor could lead to compare Smith's amazing performance with that of Bette Davis in a little-known Italian movie. In *The Scopone Game* (L. Comencini, 1972),[139] the great Davis portrays an elderly American millionairess who enjoys playing endless games of cards with an impoverished Italian couple (Silvana Mangano and Alberto Sordi) when she stays at her luxurious villa in Rome. These people, although they never win, still desperately hope to beat her one day and eventually lose all their possessions in the game. Stuck in a wheelchair after having suffered a stroke, Davis's millionairess strongly resembles Smith's Venable. With her white Marcel wave and her silk chiffon dresses, frail and diaphanous, Bette Davis looks as majestic and authoritarian as an ageing empress, with the difference that her only motivation is her passion for the card game. Violet Venable's motivations are much more complex.

'The revival of Tennessee Williams's outdated *Suddenly Last Summer* was solely a vehicle for Maggie Smith,' the *Encyclopaedia of Television Film Directors* sourly notices.[140] More accurately, it is once again the actress's impressive performance that has transformed the project into a vehicle for her and critics were unanimous to praise her rendition of Mrs Venable. The journalist of *The Seattle Times* underscored the fact that the actress perfectly revealed every nuance of Violet Venable's character – being alternatively a Southern (charming) belle and a terrifying harridan – and gave a mesmerising portrayal.[141] Lynne Truss, in *The Times*, saw her as a perfect incarnation of 'pearl-necklaced control'.[142] Although Smith is often blamed for overacting, this performance is all restraint and sobriety. There is not one moment when the actress makes the spectator laugh or smile. Unlike Judith in *The Lonely Passion of Judith Hearne*, her vulnerability is not pitifully grotesque. Unlike Constance Trentham, her cruelty is not counterbalanced by any comic effect. Violet Venable remains one of

139 The original title was *Lo Scopone Scientifico*.

140 Edited by J. Roberts (London: Scarecrow Press, 2009), p. 159.

141 J. Voorhees, '*Suddenly Last Summer*: The Acting Is Superb', *The Seattle Times*, 3 January 1993 <http:/community.seattletimes.nwsource.com/archive/?date=19930103&slug=1677897> [accessed 12 November 2016].

142 'Feast for sore psyches. Guilt and paranoia in Tennessee Williams's *Suddenly Last Summer*', *The Times*, 8 November 1993, p. 29.

the rare antipathetic characters whom Maggie Smith has played since the early 1990s, the other one being Mabel Pettigrew in Jack Clayton's *Memento Mori*. However, psychologically speaking, Violet is even more terrifying than the sinister Mrs Pettigrew. Whereas Pettigrew is devoured by social ambition and cupidity, Smith's Venable is a tormented mind, on the brink of madness. This is not the old age dementia that finally catches up with Katharine Hepburn's character in the 1959 movie,[143] but an obsessive delusion which urges her to idealise the past and, for this purpose, to remove all the obstacles that come her way, Catharine included. Smith's Venable, weakened and sorrowful, strongly contrasts with the fiery woman portrayed by Hepburn, what the critic of the *New York Magazine* humorously underlined; instead of 'frothing at the mouth' as Violet Venable, Maggie Smith was 'purring her way to screech'.[144] Still, in R. Eyre's film, Violet's frailty and apparent coldness even enhance the violence of the final scene – which could be held superior to that of the Hollywood movie. This grandiose, spectacular moment gives the actress the opportunity to demonstrate, as if it was necessary, her incomparable skills. As the academic Steven Vineberg rightly suggests, Violet is all the more frightening because of her sphinx-like immobility: 'In the climatic scene, sitting in a regal pose in her wheelchair, impeccably suited and coiffed, [...] Smith is as imposing as a statue, and with a statue's mysterious weight – the power to crush, held in magnificent repose.'[145]

As Catharine, encouraged by Dr Cukrowicz, goes further in her narration of Sebastian's last moments, the spectator's attention focuses on Violet's mute reaction. Her delicate features distorted by terror and repulsion, Mrs Venable remains silent but stares at Catharine with hatred and contempt, looking as vulnerable as ferocious. Catharine's discourse seems to tear her entrails and, as the younger woman resurrects the memory of Sebastian, conversely Violet seems to lose her vital energy. The revelation of the truth is gradually crushing her and that is exactly what

143 K. Karbo, *How to Hepburn: Lessons on Living from Kate the Great* (New York: Bloomsbury, 2007), p. 134-135. It was Hepburn's intention to play Violet Venable as a madwoman, but an insane woman would not have been able to hide the sordid truth. Mankiewicz thought she was not mad, just authoritarian and distressed. The director and the actress never stopped arguing about that.

144 J. Leonard, 'Class Menagerie', *The New York Magazine*, 11 January 1993, p. 51.

145 'Post-mortem rites', *The Threepenny Review*, 65, 1996, p. 17.

Maggie Smith expresses on her ravaged face. While Hepburn apparently remains serene just before sinking into dementia, Smith lets us witness the agony of her character until the final crisis, when grief reaches its climax. Like Medea or Hercules in Seneca's plays, Violet is gripped by the *furor*, this destructive insanity that affects the tragic heroes and, instead of quietly losing her mind like Katharine Hepburn in Mankiewicz's movie, she gets possessed by anger. An American critic evoked 'the grandiose histrionics' of Smith, comparing her with 'a hysterical hawk of recrimination'.[146] Violet's rage and violence are inversely proportionate to her physical frailty and the old lady finds the energy to stand up with a surprising vigour. In a desperate outburst, crying and shouting, she pronounces Catharine's final damnation: 'Cut this hideous story out of her brain!' Unlike Katharine Hepburn's Violet, Maggie Smith's, vulnerable and nervous, resembles an older Blanche Dubois.[147]

In what is certainly one of her best portrayals ever, Maggie Smith has definitely the fierceness and, at the same time, the pathetic beauty of a Bette Davis at the top of her game – as Jane Hudson in *What Ever Happened to Baby Jane?* or Charlotte Hollis in *Hush, Hush, Sweet Charlotte.* In his diaries, Eyre praises the actress's powerful performance, beautifully emphasising the incomparable expressivity of her large blue eyes which allows the spectator to dive into Violet Venable's dark soul.[148] This Mrs Venable is, unquestionably, far above the more restricted character initially created by Tennessee Williams. Smith has sublimated it through an exceptional performance. Her Violet is descended from the House of Atreus.

146 M. Roush, 'Gothic and grotesque "Summer" mesmerizes', *USA Today*, 6 January 1993, p. 1. Once again, Maggie Smith called forth the ornithological metaphor.

147 Coincidentally, Maggie Smith's clothes are similar to Vivien Leigh's in the screen adaptation of *A Streetcar Named Desire* (E. Kazan, 1951), with light, translucent muslins and strass. Smith even wears a similar capeline, edged with translucid scallops, which makes her resemble a delicate floating jellyfish.

148 Eyre, *National Service,* p.196. See also Eyre, *Utopia and other places*, p. 97. According to Eyre, she did not even 'act' when playing Venable: the actress literally takes possession of the character's soul, while paradoxically lending Violet her physical appearance. In a disturbing, but fascinating symbiosis, Williams's mad creature inhabits Smith's body.

Those were the Days.
Hester and Myra, Dames of the Past

Among the different variations on the Bracknell type, Lady Hester – the character played by Smith in *Tea with Mussolini* (F. Zeffirelli, 1999) – could easily be Constance Trentham's cousin. In *Sight and Sound*, Andy Medhurst wrote that M. Smith was doing her 'party piece' of stiffness and regal hauteur.[149] However, despite being as much caricatural as *Gosford Park*'s dowager, Lady Hester goes through an evolution which makes her lovable.

149 'Tea with Mussolini', *Sight and Sound*, April 1999, p. 61.

Tea with Mussolini is, above all, a very special movie in Franco Zeffirelli's body of work. Based on his autobiography, but loosely adapted by the screenwriter John Mortimer, the film did not get ecstatic reviews when it got released. The critics blamed not only its complexity in matter of historical references, but mostly its sentimentality.[150] It nevertheless remains a very beautiful movie, tinged with nostalgia and visually striking. Always at ease in Italian settings, Maggie Smith plays for once a major part, Lady Hester Random, the widow of the former ambassador of Great Britain in Italy and also the leader of a team of distinguished Florence-based elderly expats, the *Scorpioni*. Fascinated by Italy and its artists, but still deeply rooted in their native culture, these ladies meet every afternoon at the famous Gran Caffè Doney for their four o'clock tea. Although Lady Hester is a fictional character created by Mortimer, the *Scorpioni* did exist and one of them, Mary O'Neill, raised the young Franco (who was an orphan), instilling in him a taste for Shakespeare.[151] When reading Zeffirelli's autobiography, it is easy to visualise the first appearance of the *Scorpioni*, these old-fashioned ladies who still dressed as if they were living in the nineteenth century. As the director recounts, they invariably drew attention to themselves with their lavish outfits, parasols and outdated hats in pastel colours when they met for tea at Doney's. There was nothing 'gentle' or kind about them, they were exceedingly snooty.[152] Without any surprise, Smith plays the formidable battle-axe who, as Zeffirelli himself relates in his book, ruled with an iron fist over that uncommon bunch of old ladies. Being the leader of the community, she indulged in being snobbish and imperious in every circumstance. Zeffirelli remembered many outrageous things she did. With this material, John Mortimer created the character and Maggie Smith did the rest.[153] Once again, the actress portrays a haughty and contemptuous woman, who is essentially characterised by her pride as the spouse of a

150 See R. W. Matson, 'An Autobiographical Allegory: Franco Zeffirelli's *Tea with Mussolini*', in *Repicturing the Second World War. Representations in Film and Television*, ed. by M. Paris (New York: Palgrave Macmillan, 2007), p. 45-46.

151 In the movie, she is Mary Wallace (played by Joan Plowright). See F. Zeffirelli, *Franco Zeffirelli. The Autobiography* (London: Arena Books, 1987), p. 18.

152 *Ibid.*, p. 17-18.

153 Quoted in D. Lybarger, 'Spreading the Wrong Gospel: An Interview with Franco Zeffirelli', *Pitch Weekly*, 13 March 1999 <http://www.tipjar.com/dan/zeffirelli.htm> [accessed 12 November 2016].

dignitary – whenever she can, she doggedly refers to her 'late husband, the Ambassador', to the point that it becomes a catchphrase – her hate of Americans and her contempt for everything which pertains to modernity. She gets indignant at a respectable *gelato* disfigured, in Yankee mode, by a profligacy of whipped cream and candied cherries. She rubs shoulders with Elsa Morgenthal (played by Cher), a wealthy American Jewish woman she despises, and, although she benefits from her generosity, she sarcastically criticises her. When Elsa publicly announces her imminent departure from Florence and treats all the guests to Champagne, Hester gladly has her glass filled but hastens to whisper, with a poisonous smile: 'I'd bath in the stuff to celebrate her departure!'. For Lady Hester, Elsa Morgenthal exemplifies the nouveau riche mentality, as well as a vulgarity she abhors. Being unpleasant with Elsa and also with Georgie (Lily Tomlin), an American archaeologist, she behaves in quite an authoritarian manner with the *Scorpioni*, over whom she rules with a firm hand. Unlike the other dowagers and grumpy old aristocrats played by Smith, Lady Hester is not presented as an individual, she stands for the British upper class in its entirety.

Of course, Maggie Smith shines in a role which exactly corresponds to her type and, as usual, she lends her distinction and her aristocratic bearing to the character. From *Death On the Nile* to *Gosford Park*, as well as in *Ladies in Lavender*,[154] 1930s outfits suit the actress particularly well and, here, she wears with an incomparable elegance the floral wide-brimmed hats and flounced dresses designed by Jenny Beavan. Paradoxically, Lady Hester is as funny as she is stylish; with her chin out and her sharp nose, the ambassador's widow has a fierce appearance which enhances the comical efficiency of the character. Evoking Hester's long neck and bulging eyes, the American critic Stephen Holden thought that Maggie Smith suggested some rare species of 'shore bird' haughtily peering down its beak at its more common congeners on the beach.[155] Just like Lady Bracknell, Hester Random resembles a bird of prey, redoubtable but still funny and good looking. Certainly much too young to play Lady Random (as behind the scenes pictures testify), Smith nevertheless makes the best

154 Funnily enough, watching *Ladies in Lavender*, the spectator may notice that Janet Widdington wears a sun hat and a cardigan already worn by Lady Hester in the church scene.

155 'Munching Scenery Like Crumpets', *The New York Times,* 14 May 1999, p. 14.

of it, as usual. Too slight, too pretty to become a character who would have been played, fifty years earlier, by a May Whitty or a Marie Lohr,[156] she compensates by her technical skills.

Although Lady Hester is supposed to be an odious curmudgeon whom everyone fears and hates – the spectators get to see that little boys aim their blowpipes at her in the street – she represents an essentially comical figure. The lady is quite unaware of her abusive behaviour; she remains impassible, grand and pompous, and it is precisely because of her composure that she is always laughable. As early as the first scene, in the graveyard, when she pronounces her fustian speech in honour of the poet Elizabeth Barrett Browning, the character is sketched out at once. Lady Hester takes herself very seriously and is well aware of being someone important.[157] This naive self-confidence leads her to think she is involved in a mission. In a moment of hubris, she decides to inform the Duce himself about the activities of the fascist troops – that she confuses with anarchists. 'Perhaps I should take the role of the ex-ambassador himself and go to Rome myself,' she concludes. Hester Random is a woman of duty and she immediately acts out. She eventually manages to meet Benito Mussolini and the ineffable moment when they have tea together – 'Shall I be mother?' she suggests, teapot in hand – is immortalised by a picture taken by the English journalist who accompanies her.[158] That picture, which gets published in the newspapers, is carefully cut and framed by a triumphant Lady Hester who proudly displays it on every occasion. She feels like a heroine, proud to have successfully met the dictator and mostly reassured by this gesture of entente cordiale. From then on, she blindly trusts Mussolini, being convinced that he will preserve the British expats. Her naivety, her obtuse credulity and, above all, her assertiveness become risible.[159] In San Gimignano, where the British ladies have been confined,

156 Marie Lohr (1890-1975) was an Australian-born actress, who, after playing beautiful ingenues, was pigeonholed in dowager roles in the major part of her career.

157 This is the lack of humour that makes the difference between Lady Hester and Constance Trentham. Constance knows how to use irony and sarcasm, Hester does not.

158 That fictional scene is based on a real event, the meeting of the Duce and Violet Trefusis, one of the *Scorpioni* (a woman who had been, like V. Woolf, Vita Sackville-West's lover).

159 Matson, 'An Autobiographical Allegory', p. 44-45.

she even foolishly believes that Il Duce pays for their hotel to spare them from their sordid dormitory. Whatever happens, Hester is obstinately convinced to be right, as the actress herself explained during the shooting: Lady Hester Random was not an insane, dotty woman; she was not funny either but simply wrong in placing Mussolini on a pedestal. For Maggie Smith, Hester is not a risible character *per se*.[160] This authoritarian and obstinate character gave Alessandra Stanley, from *The New York Times*, the opportunity to establish a comparison with Jean Brodie, one of Smith's most emblematic roles; playing another wrongheaded woman, the actress mixed it with the hauteur of Wilde's Lady Bracknell.[161] Like Lady Hester, Miss Brodie is a stubborn, passionate and dangerously naive woman who idealises Mussolini and reigns over her 'girls' just in the same way as Hester Random reigns over the *Scorpioni*. Still, Lady Hester, despite her hauteur and self-confidence, is not as egocentric and mythomaniac as Miss Brodie was and she finally goes through a positive transformation.

With her obstinance, her arrogance and her prejudices, Hester undoubtedly stands as a caricatural figure, as hateful as funny, but it must be admitted that the actress successfully makes the character attractive. More accurately, Lady Hester is despicable, but Maggie-Smith-playing-Lady-Hester is just adorable. Originally, Violet Crawley was the most obnoxious character in *Downton Abbey* and, nonetheless, she has immediately become the viewers' favourite. Once again, despite Joan Plowright's very moving performance in a much lovable role and Cher's flamboyant portrayal, Maggie Smith steals the show. In *Tea with Mussolini*, though, Lady Hester plays an important role in the story and, mostly, she goes through an evolution. Informed by Mary Wallace that it is Elsa Morgenthal who has given the money to pay for the hotel rooms where the *Scorpioni* are staying in San Gimignano, Lady Hester suddenly realises, on one side, that Mussolini has lied to her, and on the other side, that she has completely misjudged Elsa. The haughty aristocrat turns into a woman of action, a real *pasionaria*. She persuades Elsa to run away with the French Resistance in order to escape the fascists and, with the *Scorpioni*, she chains herself to

160 M. Owen, 'The Golden Girls', *The Mail on Sunday*, 9 August 1998, p. 53.

161 'Dotty, Determined and Excessively Fond of Il Duce', *The New York Times*, 23 August 1998, p. 9. See also J. Christopher, 'Travails with my giddy aunts', *The Times*, 1 April 1999, p. 38.

San Gimignano's towers to prevent the Germans from destroying them. Hester does not resemble the lady she used to be. She displays as much energy to confront the soldiers as she previously did when behaving haughtily and spitefully. Of course, the turnaround is quite sudden and the scenes are more enjoyable than realistic. Blaming the film for its 'camp' aspect, A. Medhurst made fun of the moment Lady Hester stops a Nazi soldier from shooting Arabella (Judi Dench) by shouting 'Stop this nonsense at once!'.[162] But Maggie Smith has no difficulty, thanks to her vulnerable appearance, to make the spectator feel empathy with her character. Angela Lansbury had been approached for the role and, in quite a different style, she would have perfectly managed to play the haughty aristocrat and turn the part into a figure of strength and tenderness.[163] But what Lansbury would have brought in sweetness, Smith replaces it with a disarming vulnerability. Her Lady Hester is a heroine, but – conveniently to an old-fashioned movie filled with nostalgic tones – an obsolete one. She is the survivor of a society of which the values are gradually waning.

Like Lady Hester, Myra Naylor in *The Last September* (1999) is also a survivor from a world that is fading away. 'This is the story of the end of a world'; *The Last September* opens with this title superimposed upon the picture of a lovely Irish countryside in the late afternoon. The story takes place at the outset of the Irish republicans' struggle for independence in the early 1920s. After the 1916 Easter Rising, the native Irish engaged in a merciless battle against the British Army (the 'Black and Tans' war) to put an end to British rule in Ireland and establish an independent Irish republic. It would lead to the 1922 Treaty and the partition of Ireland. This domestic and – all the more – bloody war of independence provides a framework for Deborah Warner's movie, based on Elizabeth Bowen's acclaimed novel (1929) and written for the screen by John Banville. Lady Myra is the snobbish spouse of a wealthy, protestant Anglo-Irish landowner, Richard Naylor (Michael Gambon), settled in County Cork, Southern Ireland. Their vast country house, Danielstown,[164] stands as a

162 Medhurst, 'Tea with Mussolini', 61. E. Cochrane also condemned the 'rose-tinted view of the conflict' ('Tea with Mussolini', *Total Film*, 28, May 1999, p. 91).

163 Matson, 'An Autobiographical Allegory', p. 42.

164 In fact Dowth Hall, in Slane, County Meath.

kind of preserved enclave, a cosy bubble isolated from the outer world and refractory to the upheavals which surround it. Lord and Lady Naylor belong to the Protestant 'Ascendancy', that Anglo-Irish gentry which dominated Ireland for several centuries. Just pretending this guerrilla war is of no importance, being caught between their British inheritance and their Irish temperament, the Naylors keep entertaining their guests as they always did, with upper-class leisures and smart garden parties.

Maggie Smith, as Lady Myra, embodies all the prerogatives and the self-assurance of that aristocracy on the decline. Snobbish and old-fashioned, she seems oblivious of the utter change which is going to happen. She lives in denial of the historical events and indulges in an anachronistic way of life. The fact that many exterior scenes are shot within the frame of a window emphasises the opposition between a safe, well-mannered inside world and the outdoor dangers. This is also Lady Myra's point of view; as 'lady of the manor', she sees from the distance and through deep glass the real events that happen outside. When we discover her, at the very beginning of the movie, she seems a charming but rather irritating lady, returning from a walk in the garden. Despite her unaffected clothing and an air of graciousness, the character definitely looks like one of Lady Bracknell's counterparts. She has the same moues, the same upper-class chuckles and, above all, the same imperiousness which characterise Smith's usual type, with the bonus of a pronounced Irish accent. Lady Myra can be considered a caricatural figure, the function of which is to represent the whole aristocratic class, indifferent to the political tensions and unaware of its upcoming downfall. Clinging to the past, she takes refuge in social niceties without being involved in the political and historical tragedy which is going on outside her big estate. Of course, some critics deplored the fact that the actress was playing, once again, her standard type. The movie critic Mark Steyn, in *The Spectator*, innocently wondered if it was a real necessity to have Maggie Smith playing Lady Myra, the lady of the house, in *The Last September*. In fact, he saw no objection to it, except that the public had already seen her 'snobby, snooty' turn many times.[165] It is unclear whether the reviewer intended to cleverly

165 'Imperial sunset', *The Spectator*, 6 May 2000, p. 48. See also A. O. Scott, 'Oblivious to Revolution, The Gentry Loses Ground', *The New York Times*, 21 April 2000, p. 18; similarly, the critic suggests that Maggie Smith's 'fluttering snobbery' refers more to a schematic type, than it defines the individuality of a character.

display his abilities to use alliterations or simply to assert that the actress is now stuck with a kind of caricatural acting mode. This is quite wrong, all the more since Myra is really different from the other old-fashioned aristocratic ladies whom Smith has previously played.

Oddly enough, Maggie Smith's physical appearance in this movie is the exact opposite of what she usually looks like when being typecast. From that point of view, for once, the actress does not look the part. Myra Naylor has nothing of the redoubtable aristocrat whom she portrays most of the time. More modern and less formally dressed than the likes of Lady Hester or Constance Trentham, Lady Myra literally glows in delicate fabrics and faded autumnal colours which, just like the scenery, metaphorically echo the twilight of the Ascendancy. Being as conservative and haughty as the leader of the *Scorpioni* is, Myra does not look like a female dragon, though. Softer, less angular and effortlessly elegant with her casual – 'bucolic', as she says – outfits and her magnificent untidy bun, Smith looks stunningly beautiful and feminine as Lady Myra. It may even be said that she has rarely looked that gorgeous and attractive on screen. *The Last September* was filmed in the autumn of 1998, a few months after Zeffirelli's *Tea with Mussolini*, but Myra seems to be much younger than Hester is. Welcoming her friend Francie (Jane Birkin) in the guestroom, she radiantly beams, as if nothing was threatening her peaceful life. In softened colours and worn, shapeless pieces of clothing, Myra resembles the blooming, nearly fading roses that ornate her house.

Playing Lady Myra, Maggie Smith has actually very little screen time. Being a key element in Bowen's story, in the sense that the character itself embodies all the flaws and weaknesses of the social class she belongs to, Myra nevertheless remains a secondary figure which is part of the background. However, the actress makes the most of the small partition she has to play and, once more, she shines without indulging in excess or overacting. For the major part of the film, the character is an epitome of snobbery and preciosity, unexpectedly transposed in the Irish countryside. She abhors ants, especially when they colonise her doorstep, as much as Constance Trentham dreaded bought marmalade. With her affected tone and her exaggerated smiles, this dignified Anglo-Irish lady reminds us a lot of the ambitious Joyce Chilvers in *A Private Function*. Even in her usual 'haughty-and-grumpy-aristocrat' roles, Smith has rarely sounded that posh. Of course, the gathering scenes give Myra the opportunity to surpass herself as the perfect housemistress, fussing around and caring for the comfort of her guests. Following straight on from celebrated dowagers like Lady Catherine de Bourgh or Lady Bracknell, she also finds enjoyment in interfering in other people's affairs of the heart. Apart from throwing parties, Lady Myra closely watches over the nineteen-year-old niece of her husband, Lois Farquar (Keeley Hawes), to ensure that she does not meet an ineligible suitor – 'He of course is charming, but he seems to have no relations. One cannot trace him' – and, in that way, she is a countryside equivalent of Bracknell. She intends to put a stop to Lois's engagement to Gerald Colthurst (David Tennant), a young British subaltern, ignoring that, at the same time, the girl is hiding another – non-platonic – lover, an IRA rebel, in a remote mill on the Naylor estate. The scene in the conservatory, where Lady Myra tries to discourage Gerald's aspirations by convincing him, with a large smile, that he is not worthy of Lois, inevitably echoes Wilde's *The Importance of Being Earnest.* Pruning shear in hand, Myra displays the same contemptuous hauteur as Lady Bracknell visiting Algernon and her discourse is as sharp as the blade she uses to cut the stems of her roses: 'There is money, for example. I mean you haven't any.' No infamous handbag here, but still, the impossibility to give her blessing to what she considers a misalliance.

However, just like Lady Hester in *Tea with Mussolini*, the character goes through an evolution which takes the form of a heartbreaking change. Proud and confident, the snobbish Lady Myra progressively loses ground.[166] Quite antipathetic and irritating from the start, the character proves to be moving and almost lovable by the end. The unexpected death of Gerald provokes her sudden disarray and her psychological balance is disturbed. Lady Myra appears on the verge of a breakdown, she screams and cries. The delicate porcelain cracks and reveals her inner uncertainty. Fear and anxiety invade her previously composed mind and, unlike Hester Random who becomes a kind of heroine, Myra turns into an utmost vulnerable woman, as fragile as the chandelier's delicate tassels which gloomily rustle by intervals. The movie ends with suspension points; as Warner and Banville wanted to avoid the image of Danielstown reduced

166 J. McBride, 'The Last September: The Rules of the Ascendancy', *Irish America*, 31 July 2000, p. 58.

to ashes, we do not get to watch the last days of the House of Naylor and its inhabitants. But within a few short scenes, Maggie Smith has suggested enough to let the spectators imagine the awareness which takes hold of Lady Myra, now helpless and resigned to her fate. Like the blooming purple bouquet on which the camera was lingering in the opening scene, the mature, vulnerable rose is beginning to lose its petals.

Housekeeper, or Lady of the House?

As a matter of fact, Maggie Smith's typecasting is not confined to the snobbish aristocrats. In terms of type, the actress is usually cast in two distinct categories. Apart from the haughty dowagers, she regularly plays authority figures, such as housekeepers and governesses. The most notorious of these parts is undeniably Mrs Medlock in *The Secret Garden.* Now supplanted by Minerva McGonagall and Violet Crawley, Medlock, the redoubtable head housekeeper at Misselthwaite Manor, was for a long time the actress's most popular role, especially among younger audiences. When the movie was released, more than twenty years ago, Smith already thought she had been given the kind of role she was used to playing, a 'sour-faced' woman 'in corset'.[167] Agnieszka Holland's movie was the latest of the multiple adaptations of Frances Hodgson Burnett's novel and it has eventually outdone the other versions.[168] For the children of the mid-1990s, and also for those who now discover the film on TV or on DVD, Smith stands out as the sole and unique Medlock, unrivalled and unsurpassable.

Mrs Medlock is not, a priori, one of Maggie Smith's major roles – all the more that the housekeeper is only a secondary character in the famous children's novel – but the actress does not content herself with playing it to perfection. Giving the character some more depth, she makes the sharp housekeeper a thin-skinned and moving woman. Filmed for the most part at Pinewood studios[169] and, for some exterior scenes, among the impressive ruins of Fountains Abbey (Yorkshire), Holland's *The Secret Garden* is certainly the most lavish onscreen adaptation of the novel. Apart from an American silent movie,[170] the first major adaptation was directed by Fred M. Wilcox for MGM in 1949, with Margaret O'Brien as Mary Lennox. In this very theatrical version, entirely shot in studio. Mr Craven's manor looks as gloomy as the scenery for a horror movie and a dour and chilling Mrs Medlock (Gladys Cooper) strangely reminds us of Mrs Danvers greeting the second Mrs de Winter at Manderley. Draped in black veils which emphasise her aquiline profile and make her resemble a sinister bird of prey, Dame Gladys at sixty-one portrays a character

167 R. Wallace, 'Sour-faced dame', *The Daily Mirror*, 4 October 1993, p. 17.

168 In 2012, Universal Pictures had announced a new adaptation, transposed into the American South of 1900. The project does not seem to have gone any further since then.

169 Where the garden was recreated, as it was impossible to shoot on location. The sets were designed by Stuart Craig (stage designer on the Harry Potter franchise). See M. Wolf, '"The Secret Garden" and How It Grew', *The New York Times*, 8 August 1993, p. 11.

170 G. Von Seyffertitz, 1919. In the script, by Marion Fairfax, 'Mrs Medlock is a punishing crone who forces Mary to hem towels as a penalty for having helped Colin remove a brace prescribed by the sadistic Dr Craven.' See S. S. Stokes, 'Painting the Garden: Noel Streatfeild, the Garden as Restorative, and Pre-1950 Dramatizations of *The Secret Garden*', in *In the Garden. Essays in Honor of Frances Hodgson Burnett*, ed. by A. S. Carpenter (Lanham: Scarecrow Press, 2006), p. 174.

who is miles away from the angelic icon of beauty that Miss Cooper once had been. Yet, despite looking like the Statue of the Commander, Cooper's Medlock is only a minor character in this film and, above all, a housekeeper whose task is to carry Mary's luggage when she welcomes her at the station. On television, Hodgson Burnett's novel was adapted no less than four times – in 1952, 1960, 1975 and 1987[171] – but the 1975 series (directed by D. Brooking for the BBC) remains, until now, the most faithful adaptation of the novel. Mrs Medlock is a brusque and unmannerly woman who perfectly corresponds to the character depicted by F. H. Burnett. Therefore, Maggie Smith's Medlock was coming after several others whom she would, inevitably, outshine. According to an American critic, Smith turns a one-dimensional repressive character – what he called 'a Dame-Judith-Anderson-type role' – into a richer and more sympathetic figure.[172]

In fact, the actress had not been cast by chance. When the Polish director Agnieszka Holland was commissioned by American Zoetrope (Francis Ford Coppola's production company) for Warner Bros, she considered it a great opportunity to work with an actress she particularly admired: 'I saw Maggie on the stage in London doing *Lettice and Lovage* and I thought she was the best living actress. As soon as this film came along, I knew I had a part for her.'[173] Directing Smith, Holland realised a longstanding dream and it clearly shows on screen. Caroline Thompson's script had already been completed when she agreed to direct the movie; in consultation with Holland, Thompson (writer of *Edward Scissorhands*, *The Addams Family* and *The Nightmare Before Christmas*) rewrote her screenplay – which was strongly tinged with Gothic elements – to make it more

171 It is impossible to have access to the two series produced by the BBC in 1952 and 1960, but the 1975 and 1987 TV adaptations are available on DVD. The Anglo-American series of 1987 (directed by A. Grint, Hallmark Productions) can be considered a good one, even if Mrs Medlock radically differs from the original character: blonde-haired and sweet, she does seem to be truly concerned by Mary Lennox's welfare – the little girl describes her as 'loving and compassionate' – and she has nothing of Gladys Cooper's fearsome aura.

172 M. Baumgarten, review of 'The Secret Garden', *The Austin Chronicle*, 20 August 1993 http://www.austinchronicle.com/calendar/film/1993-08-20/the-secret-garden/ [accessed 12 November 2016].

173 *The Secret Garden* Press File, Warner Bros Productions, p. 4. Also 'Out of the Ruins: Lonely People', interview with A. Taubin and M. Burman, *Sight and Sound*, October 1993, p. 29.

faithful to the novel.[174] As Agnieszka Holland admitted herself, most of the changes pertained to the character Maggie Smith was going to play. The role was developed to fit an actress of her calibre: 'I wanted her to be a complicated character who has her own reasons for behaving as she does. I didn't want a clichéd wicked housekeeper. Maggie is such a complex actress and full of unexpected resources.'[175] Eventually, Smith's Medlock appears as a hybrid figure, taking after both the housekeeper and the matriarch.

For those who know Burnett's novel well, it could seem surprising to have cast Maggie Smith as Mrs Medlock. According to the description that the novelist gives of the housekeeper, the actress appears to be the worst choice ever: 'She was a stout woman, with very red cheeks and sharp black eyes. She wore a very purple dress, a black silk mantle with jet fringe on it and a black bonnet with purple velvet flowers.'[176] Mrs Medlock, with 'her common, highly colored face' is 'the most disagreeable person' whom Mary Lennox has ever seen, to the point that the little girl is ashamed of having to walk beside her. Such an account does not sound the most appropriate to outline the distinguished lady who, in the 1993 movie, reluctantly comes to pick up young Mary at Liverpool docks. On the contrary, Holland has literally staged a spectacular entrance for Medlock, in a scene reminiscent of Gothic. On the large, deserted dock, an elegant figure suddenly emerges from the fog. It is a woman, wearing a large cloak which makes her look like a bat at rest. Tall and patrician, she is dressed in Parisian fashion, with an immense ribbonned hat on her head. That Medlock has absolutely nothing in common with the Yorkshire woman described by Burnett. With her chin up, her regal bearing and a corset particularly tight-fitted, Maggie Smith wears as effortlessly as usual the magnificent Edwardian costumes designed by Marit Allen, making the housekeeper look like a high-born lady. As one critic rightly underscored, Smith plays Mrs Medlock with a nearly oxymoronic combination of 'imperiousness and servility'.[177]

Smith has often portrayed characters belonging to the servant class,

174 D. Gritten, 'Tending her dark "Garden"', *The Los Angeles Times*, 1 November 1992, p. 5.

175 *The Secret Garden* Press File, p. 4.

176 F. H. Burnett, *The Secret Garden*, Chapter 2 (Oxford: Oxford University Press, 2011), p. 12.

177 L. Nicholls, 'Magical lustre: "The Secret Garden" will unlock your heart', *The Kitchener-Waterloo Record*, 16 August 1993, p. 8.

but most of the time, those are fallen women who were born into the upper class and have eventually lost their status. A parallel can be drawn between Mrs Medlock and another character magnificently portrayed by the actress, Mabel Pettigrew in Jack Clayton's *Memento Mori* (1992). Mrs Pettigrew, a spry and elegant septuagenarian working as a housekeeper, is much too sophisticated for the position she occupies; circumstances have reduced her to becoming a housekeeper and this situation is far from pleasing her. According to Noel Sinyard, Mabel's unforgiving attitude might be motivated by her sense of having always been 'unjustly undervalued'.[178] She feels humiliated and out of place, just like Smith's Miss Bowers was a reluctant lady's companion in *Death on the Nile* (J. Guillermin, 1979). Bowers never stops moaning and crying over the downfall of her family, which has led her to earn a living; thus, she attends very unwillingly to her difficult boss. These two characters, Miss Bowers and Mabel Pettigrew, are quite similar, except that Mrs Pettigrew's employer, the harmless Charmian Colston (Renée Asherson), has not much in common with the formidable Mrs Van Schuyler (Bette Davis) in *Death on the Nile*. In an excellent article focusing on Maggie Smith's career, S. Vineberg highlights the recurrence of that kind of role in her filmography. She specialises and excels at playing characters who belong to a kind of 'disenfranchised' aristocracy; she marvellously brings out that stoic, but bitter frustration which characterises those mighty who may have fallen, but try to maintain 'some vestige of style'.[179] Only Grace Hawkins, the efficient and well-intentioned housekeeper in *Keeping Mum* (N. Johnson, 2005) may be regarded as an exception. Despite her murderous instincts, Grace is above all a caring mother and grandmother, and the actress portrays that incredible character in such a way that she has nothing of a grand dame fallen on hard times.

Actually, Smith's Medlock is significantly different from the character created by F. H. Burnett. She looks like an aristocrat, a lady of the manor. In one of Thompson's first drafts, Mrs Medlock was seen going to the village with a basket in her hands to buy some food. Such a scene would

178 *Jack Clayton* (Manchester: Manchester University Press, 2000), p. 197.

179 'Maggie Smith', *Salon.com*, 6 June 2000 <http://www.salon.com/2000/06/06/smith_12/> [accessed 12 November 2016]. This aspect may also be found in the parts of helpless spinsters and 'poor relatives' that the actress has regularly played.

be unthinkable in the movie. The housekeeper does not help Mary carry her luggage at the dock, and the ancillary tasks have been given to young Martha, her own servant. It is Martha, and not Mrs Medlock, who dresses the little girl and, unlike the character of the novel, the housekeeper does not handle her education. Played by Smith, Medlock has been upgraded to the rank of a proper lady. Still, C. Thompson has reinserted in her final draft a scene (omitted in the 1991 version of the script) which happens to be one of the funniest moments in the film, precisely because it emphasises the originality and the ambiguity of the character. When leaving the docks, Mrs Medlock and Mary Lennox get into a carriage which takes them to Misselthwaite Manor. While the little girl stays immobile, worrying about what to expect, the housekeeper is enjoying a copious picnic. Although the scene did not appear in the 1949, 1975 and 1987 adaptations, it existed in the novel: 'Mrs Medlock cheered up very much over her tea and chicken and beef. She ate a great deal and afterwards fell asleep herself, and Mary sat and stared at her and watched her fine bonnet slip on one side.'[180] Burnett describes Medlock as a lower-class woman, with a ferocious appetite and boorish manners. Of course, that Dickensian creature seems quite remote from Smith's Medlock who nibbles chicken thighs and peels a hard-boiled egg like the most well-bred lady. In any case, this short sequence suffices to sketch out the character and demonstrates, once more, the genius of the actress. Indeed, who, apart from Maggie Smith, would be able to bite chicken drumsticks while staring at her young fellow traveller with the same contemptuous air as an offended sovereign?

Furthermore, unlike Mabel Pettigrew or Miss Bowers – who struggle in vain against their misfortune – Medlock has an indisputable power and, in Lord Craven's absence, rules over Misselthwaite Manor. However, her use of authority is as excessive as inefficient; she maintains Colin in his physical debility, overprotecting him and compelling him to a ridiculous medical regime. Being both the keyholder – she holds on her belt as many keys as a prison warder – and an amateur physician,[181] the well-named 'Med-Lock' submits poor Colin to a shock-treatment, using the most recent technologies, from electrical discharge to hydrotherapy. She certainly

180 *The Secret Garden*, Chapter 3, p. 17.

181 Dr Medlock does not appear in Holland's film, probably because Medlock has replaced him.

appears much stiffer and more narrow-minded than she was in the novel. In the original story, the housekeeper, a kind and practical woman having common sense, realises quickly that the health of her young protégé is improving thanks to Mary. In Agnieszka Holland's film, on the contrary, she seems to be upset by that. Mrs Medlock is stubborn, obsessed with her sense of duty, just like Daphné du Maurier's most famous villain, Mrs Danvers, remains pathologically loyal to the memory of Rebecca. This ladylike Cerberus guards Colin's room as if it was a fortress and, having become a kind of dehumanised figure, she behaves somewhat mechanically. With respect to that, Mary Lennox comes as the grain of sand in the gear, causing trouble in a perfectly settled routine.[182]

It cannot be denied that Smith's Medlock has become a much darker character than she was in the novel. She resembles the wicked stepmother in fairy tales and it certainly accentuates the magical atmosphere of the film.[183] At the docks, the housekeeper was stern and unpleasant, but at Misselthwaite Manor, she turns out to be very brusque, not to say brutal. An American critic asserted that the actress was marvellous, playing 'the sourpuss' part as if she trained on 'a steady diet of persimmons',[184] while another praised Maggie Smith in her 'Victorian-shrew mode'.[185] Rarely has the actress been as agitated and frenetic on screen, rushing, fussing around, and yelling. When Lord Craven suddenly comes home, the kitchen maids are scarcely able to untie the apron of an overexcited Medlock, fidgeting and screaming 'Get me OUT of it !' Still, her authority is exclusively repressive.

182 J. Maslin, 'Blossom Time for a Lonely Girl', *The New York Times*, 13 August 1993, p. 3. See also M. Hearn, 'Heidi Goes to America', in *Johanna Spyri und ihr Werk*, ed. by V. Rutschmann, (Zurich: Chronos Verlag, 2003), p. 179. As pointed out by Michael Hearn, a specialist of children's literature, 'Although Burnett never admitted it, her critically acclaimed and best novel *The Secret Garden* (1911) is almost character for character an imitation of *Heidi*. [...] Craven's ten-year-old son Colin is bedridden like Clara Seseman, and a new English garden replaces the Alps to restore the child to health. Mary Lennox is a new Heidi but morose and contrary.' The famous novel by Johanna Spyri was published in 1880, more than three decades before *The Secret Garden* (1911). Hearn does not mention Medlock, but it is quite obvious here that she reminds us, in many aspects, of Fraülein Rottenmeyer, the redoubtable housekeeper who rules over the house of Herr Seseman, Heidi's tutor.

183 J. Gillispie, 'American Film Adaptations of "The Secret Garden": Reflections of Sociological and Historical Changes', *The Lion and the Unicorn*, June 1996, 20.1, p. 144-145.

184 S. Means, '*Secret Garden* blossoms as a magical film', *The Salt Lake Tribune*, 13 August 1993, p. 3.

185 B. D. Johnson, 'Child's Play', *Maclean's*, 16 August 1993, p. 48.

She only knows how to forbid and punish. If the positive evolution that the two young leading characters have to go through can be considered the main plot of the story, Mrs Medlock stands for the main opponent to that process. As S. Marchalonis suggests, Smith's Medlock becomes a powerful and fearsome enemy: 'Mrs Medlock, in her expanded role, becomes a tyrant whom the children fear [...] Colin, a tyrant in other versions, is afraid of her and the brutal "treatments" she supervises. She treats Mary as no housekeeper would treat an upperclass child.'[186] As imperious and impressive as a lady of high rank would be, the housekeeper has superbly escaped the social class which was hers. Nevertheless, the character proves to be as vulnerable as she is rigid and stubborn. When facing difficulties, she falls apart; she loses all her confidence when Colin opposes her authority. The inflexible Medlock collapses on the stairs and cries out, helpless and desperate, while Martha kindly gives her a comforting embrace, in a gesture of filial devotion. Maggie Smith eventually makes the spectator feel compassion, or even affection, for a rather unpleasant character. In a few seconds, the actress has transformed the austere housekeeper into a lovable character, Medlock revealing at last her vulnerability. That scene, some sort of in-extremis redemption is undoubtedly one of the most moving moments in the movie. Thanks to it, Mrs Medlock has touched the heart of many viewers, all generations considered.

In the film, Smith portrays a more complex figure than the rustic and off-putting housekeeper of the novel. She rightly keeps Mrs Medlock from being a one-dimensional monster by letting show the frustration and the sense of duty within the domestic tyrant.[187] Yet, although the actress makes the most of the material that has been given to her, it would have been impossible to develop the character further without betraying Burnett's original work. Agnieszka Holland's first intention was also to make Mrs Medlock a comical figure and, for that purpose, the script included a new scene written for Smith. When Mary, awakened by Colin's crying, wandered around the corridors to discover where the noise came from, she was supposed to pass Mrs Medlock's apartment. There, she witnessed quite an astonishing scene. The stern housekeeper, dressed only

186 '*Filming the Nineteenth Century*: "The Secret Garden" and "Little Women"', *American Transcendentalist Quarterly*, 10, 4, 1996, p. 282.

187 R. Alleva, 'A Garden to Remember', *Commonweal,* 120, 8 October 1993, p. 17.

in her undergarments and wearing her big hat ornated with red peonies, was standing before her mirror, admiring her reflection.[188] If Medlock's impressive hat still features in the movie, the scene did not make the final cut. It is regrettable, as Maggie Smith would have been – necessarily – hilarious, but it was certainly out of line with the tone of the novel and the character initially created by F. H. Burnett. Indisputably, a scene showing Medlock in corset and drawers would have become the highlight of the movie, disfiguring what was intended to be a faithful adaptation.[189] Instead of that, a quick, furtive shot allows the spectators to get a glimpse of Mrs Medlock climbing up the big stairs of Misselthwaite Manor in the middle of the night, wearing a – surprisingly – vermilion dressing-gown, her huge keyring clinging to her waist. But Smith's pale face is sorrowful enough to make us forget the eccentricity of her nightwear. Mrs Medlock is only a supporting character and the actress, a remarkable scene stealer, has successfully turned her into an unforgettable figure, making her performance an outstanding achievement.

Mrs Medlock could be seen as an antithetic double of Mary Poppins, the nanny archetype – 'double' rather than 'opposite', as the two characters share many similarities. Considering, not the Walt Disney movie, but P. J. Travers's novels, Mary Poppins stands as a prim and intransigent nanny, a woman of much sterner appearance than the pretty red-cheeked young lady of the 1964 film. When reading the description that Travers gives of her heroine – and without undermining Julie Andrews's marvellous performance – we can assume that Maggie Smith would have been, at forty or forty-five, ideal casting for the part. Physically, the two actresses are radically different; Smith has a pointy nose and angular features, whereas Andrews has a pert nose and plump cheekbones. Whereas Andrews played the sweet and radiant Maria in *The Sound of Music*, Smith portrayed the possessive, narcissistic and unsettling Jean Brodie.[190] As Valerie Lawson

188 *The Secret Garden*'s shooting script by C. Thompson, sc. 64 (Alexander Street Press, 2003, via *American Film Scripts Online*). During the shooting, this scene was to appear in the movie, as reported by E. Freud, 'Elephants in the Garden', *Premiere*, September 1993, p. 76.

189 Holland would take her revenge a few years later, with *Washington Square* and the delightful scene when a concupiscent Lavinia – also in her undergarments – encloses a lock of Morris's hair in her medallion.

190 Ironically, Julie Andrews had turned down the role of Miss Brodie that had been offered to her first.

underlines in her biography of P. J. Travers's, Mary Poppins was more complex than the 'saccharine' figure which appears in Walt Disney's film. What makes Mary Poppins so special is the fact that she is as peculiar and stiff as she is sweet and comforting.[191] Stern and pinched, Travers's Mary Poppins was a character just tailor-made for Smith. According to Lawson, a musical had been considered as early as 1982 and, at that time, Maggie Smith and Vanessa Redgrave were the only actresses that P. J. Travers wanted to be given the titular role.[192] Unfortunately, Smith never played in the musical, but at least, she got the opportunity to lend her inimitable voice to the most famous English nanny and to have it kept for posterity. No less than five audiobooks were released by Caedmon editions in the late 1960s and early 1970s – *Mary Poppins* (1968), *Mary Poppins Comes Back* (1969), *Mary Poppins and the Banks Family* (1970), *Mary Poppins Opens the Door* (1970) and *Balloons Balloons* (1971) – allowing Maggie Smith to become a larger than life Mary Poppins. Quick, clever and witty, Mary has an answer for everything and behaves extremely harshly with the children, 'Spit spot into bed' being her favourite motto. Such a profile fitted Smith and her nasal inflections particularly well. The actress also had (and still has) in her a bit of magic and a little touch of eccentricity which make her the ideal actress to play the white witch. Her extravagance is always tempered by dignified restraint, just like Mary Poppins who remains prim and imperturbable even in the most incredible situations. Yet, Mrs Medlock has neither that practical mind nor this whimsical touch which both characterise Mary Poppins. She does not have the same quick mind and, on the contrary, she displays an obtuse zele which leads her to failure. She makes use of brutal and inefficient treatments, while Poppins rules with one simple 'spoonful of sugar'. From that point of view, Mrs Medlock is not a heroine, but an anti-heroine. Anyhow, for Maggie Smith, that character was the first on a long list of authoritarian, but big-hearted figures of whom Jean Brodie had probably been the reverse side. Oddly enough, the positive aspects of Travers's heroine can nevertheless be found in another character portrayed, years later, by the actress. In fact, Smith would get to play the Mary Poppins type. She would play it indirectly, through Minerva McGonagall.

---

191 *Mary Poppins, She Wrote* (New York: Simon & Schuster, 2013), p. 2. The book has subsequently been adapted for the big screen, as *Saving Mr Banks* (J. L. Hancock, 2014).

192 *Ibid.*, p. 348.

Taking the Habit

Halfway between Mrs Medlock and Minerva McGonagall, Maggie Smith gives a memorable portrayal of what was, originally, a supporting figure aimed at acting as a foil to the character played by Whoopi Goldberg. Mother Superior in *Sister Act* (E. Ardolino, 1992) unexpectedly happened to be one of her most significant performances. To tell the truth, Smith was not particularly thrilled at the prospect of being involved in that light, unpretentious US comedy – which had been conceived as a vehicle for Goldberg, recently oscarised for her remarkable performance in *Ghost*

(1990) – and she was unsure about its success. Nevertheless, the actress agreed to take part and, in the autumn of 1991, she flew to Reno, Nevada, where that uncommon movie was to be filmed. Being by nature quite shy and restrained, Maggie Smith got along very well with her exuberant co-star and both seem to have fond memories of their collaboration. Whoopi Goldberg, as an iconoclast and hilarious mistress of ceremony at the 2002 Academy Awards, reduced Maggie Smith to tears of laughter by announcing that 'the Smith family' had been conveniently reunited in the theatre (the actress was indeed sitting next to Will and Jada Smith) and, more than twenty years after their collaboration, the two actresses remain good friends. In the end, thanks to the vibrancy of its actors – not only Goldberg and Smith, but also excellent supporting performers like Kathy Najimy, Joseph Maher (who had worked with Maggie Smith in Stoppard's *Night and Day*, in 1979) or Mary Wickes (the formidable Sister Mary Lazarus) – and a fantastic original score by Marc Shaiman, the film proved to be not only a success, but a huge hit at the box-office.

The role of Mother Superior gained Smith a wider international fame which would even increase, a few years later, with the *Harry Potter* saga. Setting aside *Harry Potter* and *Downton Abbey*, Mother Superior remains, with Mrs Medlock in *The Secret Garden*, one of her most famous roles on screen. These two incursions into Hollywood cinema not only allowed her the opportunity to deliver outstanding performances, but also led her, from that time onwards, to be ineluctably identified with stern and imperious figures. In a certain way, Mother Superior foreshadowed Professor McGonagall and it is probably because we all have also the stiff and pinched-faced nun in mind when watching one episode of the *Harry Potter* series, that we find the role of the transfiguration teacher so well suited for Maggie Smith. All the aspects which characterise Minerva McGonagall were already present, to a greater or lesser extent, in the austere nun.

However, to see Mother Superior as a kind of prototype for the Head of Gryffindor House would sound in some way depreciatory. On the contrary, and even if Minerva McGonagall has become much more famous thanks to the success of the *Harry Potter* franchise, Mother Superior is a fully elaborated character and represents a more substantial role for the actress who plays her. Functionally speaking, the character had been developed as the major 'opponent' to the leading figure, Deloris Van Cartier, the sparkling cabaret singer played by Whoopi Goldberg. Deloris, having witnessed a cold-blooded murder committed by her ex-lover (a shabby casino manager whose activities include crime and drug dealing), runs away and reports the murder to the local police. To ensure the woman's safety, the police inspector decides to hide her in a San Francisco convent until they put the criminals under lock and key. Although the false nun immediately wins the sympathy of her fellow sisters, her *faux-pas* and her nonconformism come up against Mother Superior's stiffness. As a punishment, the latter entrusts her with the choir rehearsals but, unexpectedly, Sister Mary Clarence does marvels, turning the convent's wheezy singers into a group of swinging nuns.

The first time she meets Deloris, Mother Superior remains speechless, but Maggie Smith lets her highly malleable face express the terror and consternation that she feels when considering the provocative creature she is supposed to shelter in her convent. As odd as it may sound, the actress does not seem to *play* a nun. Emphasised by the habit, her pale, bony face and her slender figure radiate asceticism and monastic rigour to such a point that the spectator is prone to believe that this woman is a real nun, hired by the casting director who probably thought she would look more convincing in the part than any Hollywood experienced actress. When Mother Superior has to transform Deloris into Sister Mary Clarence, making her literally take the habit, we feel almost uncomfortable when seeing that chaste, dignified woman handling with distaste the enticing spoils of the cabaret singer. Maybe we forget, then, that Smith herself has played an exquisite music hall singer in *Oh, What a Lovely War!* (R. Attenborough, 1969) and a nymphomaniac aristocrat in *The Missionary* (R. Loncraine, 1982). Mother Superior incarnates the rule of God and acts as a pillar of the institution. Every time Sister Mary Clarence makes a misstep, Maggie Smith intervenes to sanction the unruly nun and to restore order in the convent. However, unlike Mrs Medlock who is terrifying, Mother Superior makes us laugh. Her witty one-liners always hit the mark and her murderous glares crucify – if we may say so – the troublemaker that Mary Clarence is. The critics were not indifferent to the quality of Maggie Smith's performance and they saw it as one of the major assets of the film. The critic Alexander Walker compared the actress's piercing gaze to an 'X-ray' scanner, underscoring the fact that, once again, Smith's incredible bodily tools were efficiently put into action to build a formidable nun, daunting enough to scare Goldberg herself.[193]

One of the juiciest scenes of the movie shows Deloris, already bored by her new (pious) life, luring her fellow sisters into a night stroll. At a late hour, the apprentice nun escapes from the convent to have a drink at the local disco bar, and her new friends Sister Mary Patrick and Sister Mary Robert recklessly join her. Of course, the nuns arouse the interest of drunken lads, and before things go wrong, the three women hastily return to the convent. Unfortunately, Mother Superior was wide awake and frostily welcomes them back. No burst of anger here, but a frightening expression of disapproval that only Maggie Smith is capable of. By contrast with Whoopi/Deloris's cheerful character, Mother Superior appears as the very embodiment of stiffness and sadness. Never, even in the most pathetic scenes of *The Lonely Passion of Judith Hearne*, has the actress looked that pale and sorrowful. Against the Deloris joyous storm, Mother Superior stands as a first-rate killjoy and each scene which brings together the two women involves colourful exchanges. The comical effects result, for a large part, from the strong contrast between the personalities and physical appearances of Deloris and Mother Superior, just like, at the circus, the whiteface clown contrasts with the August.[194]

The whiteface often draws tears and, in *Sister Act* as well, the laughs suddenly fade. At some moments, Smith's face is so full of disarray, so moving that the audience cannot help but empathise with her, especially when she reprimands Whoopi/Deloris for having misled the nuns about the dangers of the outside world from which, as a caring mother, she has always wanted to protect them. In *Sight and Sound*, the critic Kim Newman declared that Maggie Smith's Mother Superior undoubtedly was the most interesting character in the movie.[195] When she realises that Sister Mary Clarence, thanks to her good mood and her dynamism, has outdone her at the convent, Mother Superior feels disavowed and decides to resign. As usual, the actress brings a heartbreaking insecurity to the character. Maggie

193 'Sisters of the superior sort', *The Evening Standard*, 19 November 1992, p. 32.

194 Thus it may seem quite inopportune to have cast – for a few performances – Whoopi Goldberg herself as Mother Superior. She succeeded Sheila Hancock in the London production of the musical (London Palladium, 2010).

195 'Sister Act', *Sight and Sound*, December 1992, p. 49.

Smith could have played Mother Superior as a redoubtable female dragon making life tough for Sister Mary Clarence, but a one-sided character, a cantankerous and strong-minded nun would have make the spectators laugh at her own expense. Here, her human weaknesses make her incredibly touching. Moreover, Sister Mary Clarence's kidnapping turns this mournful, vulnerable nun into a heroine. She quickly handles the situation, uses a clever stratagem to borrow a helicopter and brings the sisters with her to rescue Deloris in Reno. 'Try to blend in!' she famously enjoins them when they enter, in full habit, the casino. The rigid and narrow-minded nun proves to be a woman of action, brave and generous, who is prepared to risk her own life for the woman she first hated. In the last part of the movie, the spectators get to see a complete metamorphosis of the character. Being an 'opponent' at the beginning of the story, Mother Superior becomes the most efficient 'helper',[196] concretising, in quite an edifying manner, her religious vow of assistance to people in need. Thanks to Mother Superior, Deloris escapes death and the two antagonist women reconcile for ever. The last ordeal has revealed the courage and generosity of a woman who, at first, seemed quite unsympathetic. Still, this evolution, quite satisfying in the screenplay, spoils the character's journey in the second opus and pulls down its impact. In the sequel, *Sister Act II* (B. Duke, 1993), Smith's Mother Superior is necessarily – in accordance with the ending of the first movie – a kind woman, trusting and generous beneath her stern exterior. Therefore, the character does not make us laugh anymore. The audience is happy to see the return of Mother Superior, but she does not play the pivotal role she had in the first movie. Still, with the huge commercial success of *Sister Act*, the role of Mother Superior, just like Mrs Medlock, contributed to building the image the general public now has of Maggie Smith. From then on, when not playing grumpy snobs, the actress would specialise in that kind of character – the imperious, prim but big-hearted women – of which Minerva McGonagall is certainly the most famous incarnation.

196 As opposed to an 'opponent', according to Greimas's actantial model.

Bewitched

No one could deny that Minerva McGonagall has been, for more than ten decades, Maggie Smith's most popular part and the *Harry Potter* saga has constituted a cultural phenomenon in itself. Thanks to this role, she has gained millions of new fans around the world, even if many of them know better McGonagall than the actress who plays her. It may be said that Smith was very fortunate to take part in the Potter adventure, but it is certain that the movies have benefited even more from the presence of her name in the credits. For the younger generation, the actress is identified (not to say assimilated to, or confused) with the transfiguration teacher, just like the rest of the public identifies her with the wider type of the haughty aristocrat. Surprisingly, these two figures – or 'types', to be precise – are completely distinct, both at a functional and at a physical level. One major difference is that the character of the grumpy snob provokes laughs because of her provocative haughtiness, while Minerva McGonagall is a positive figure, deeply loved by the audience. Smith excels in portraying these two antithetic types and, oddly enough, the public does not marvel or wonder about the feat it represents, in terms of acting; the two types – McGonagall and the dowager countess – are thoroughly incompatible, but the journalists never point it out.

It must be admitted that, on the scale of the whole franchise, the role of Professor McGonagall is only a supporting one. Even if the die-hard fans of the novels have bemoaned, for such or such instalment, the fact that the screenwriters had omitted several scenes where McGonagall was involved, conversely, it is obvious that Maggie Smith's exceptional performance has given a new depth to the character created by J. K. Rowling. In other words, the actress appears rarely and briefly on screen, but each time, she steals the whole show. Once again. Of course, the heroes of the story are Harry, Hermione and Ron, and the fantasy tone of the film represents a major element of interest for the young spectators, but precisely, if all the special effects were removed, Smith's performance would remain intact, and mostly far above those of the leading actors. Of course, it would be excessive to see Minerva as one of Maggie Smith's most elaborate and compelling parts, although it fits her to perfection. Her participation, in term of screen time, remains quite limited and the role cannot be considered challenging for an actress of that stature. 'I'm Pottering,' she often said. Like the other actors in the series, Maggie Smith has been a victim of *Harry Potter*'s success; being discreet and restrained, she has been chased by autograph hunters for years. Minerva McGonagall has also engulfed the actress to the point that it has overshadowed her other roles. Nonetheless, if – as she recognises herself – taking part in this unique adventure was extraordinary, Smith has been the most extraordinary wizard on screen.

Minerva McGonagall, transfiguration teacher and Deputy Headmistress of Hogwarts School, needs no introduction. Present in the first episode, she welcomes Harry and his classmates on their arrival. Like Mrs Medlock in *The Secret Garden* and Mother Superior in *Sister Act*, Professor McGonagall is the embodiment of authority and stiffness. But unlike *Sister Act*'s austere nun, the character does not go through an evolution. At the outset, the spectators can guess that beneath a stern appearance and an impressive witch hat, Minerva will be, not an 'opponent', but a 'helper' in Harry Potter's initiatory journey. From the start, it is an established fact that she is a fair and magnanimous woman. Of course, as long as Harry, Hermione and Ron are depicted as boisterous kids, Minerva McGonagall behaves like a rigid and harsh schoolmistress who does not hesitate to punish the pupils if needed. She sternly scolds them when they arrive late for her transfiguration class, as well as she waits for their return, hands on her hips and eyebrows drawn in a frown, when they embark on a night-time stroll. But the teacher is as benevolent and well-balanced as Jean Brodie – the other role which McGonagall is often compared with – was narcissistic and dangerously temperamental. From that point of view, Minerva McGonagall can be seen as a variation on the Mary Poppins type. She embodies the same characteristics as Cherry Tree Lane's famous nanny does, positive authority and strictness, combined with moral values and a heart of gold. As an incarnation of cleverness (just like the mythological deity whose name she has inherited), Minerva is as much a model as a tutelary figure for the children. The part seems to have been cut for Maggie Smith. Everyone knows that J. K. Rowling herself expressed the wish that the actress was cast as Professor McGonagall but, at the same time, Smith has totally appropriated the character, lending Minerva her unique distinction and imperiousness. Christopher Columbus once said that her very first scene – filmed on location, in the majestic staircase of Christ Church College at Oxford – had been quite easy to shoot. The young actors were even more impressed than the pupils whom they were supposed to play when seeing the commanding actress who was standing in front of them. With regard to that, one of the most spectacular moments in the first movie is probably McGonagall's entrance in the Great Hall of Hogwarts. As hieratic as a queen with her large green cloak, Smith majestically steps forward into the hall, the first-year students meekly following her.

However, in the first two movies – which are quite faithful to the books – the character remains somewhat schematic and, apart from her ability to turn into a cat, Minerva McGonagall is essentially defined by her function. She represents the school as an institution, she welcomes the students and places the sorting hat on their heads, she awards the house points as well as she dispenses the punishments. In the course of the series, the physical appearance of Minerva McGonagall significantly evolves. In the first instalment, *Harry Potter and the Philosopher's Stone* (2001), Smith's Minerva reflects quite accurately the figure described by J. K. Rowling in her novel. With a tight bun perched on the top of her head and a reproving stare behind her round-rimmed spectacles, the transfiguration teacher looks as if she had come right out of the book. The Scottish touch, with the McGonagall's tartan, gets pride of place. Born to a Glaswegian mother, Maggie Smith herself had contributed to creating her costume, as designer Julianna Makovski recounts. The actress had a clear idea of the kind of costume she could wear as McGonagall; Smith wanted something 'that was Scottish' and she eventually wore a traditional Scottish 'tam' which just happened to be a witch hat.[197] Actually, Minerva McGonagall incarnates a perfect compromise between the wizard and the schoolmistress, combining the witch hat with scholar glasses. With the intention of making the adult characters age on screen (for the reason that the teen actors were going to change a lot over the years), Minerva's hair goes greyish in the second instalment, *Harry Potter and the Chamber of Secrets* (2002), whereas it was red in the first movie. Looking worried, her hair tightly pulled back, Professor McGonagall looks at least ten years older than she did in the first movie.

In the course of the series, as the young heroes grow up and the story becomes more intricate, Minerva gets away from her stern-but-fair-schoolteacher look to take part in the action. In the third movie, *Harry Potter and the Prisoner of Azkaban* (2004), Alfonso Cuarón considerably enlarges Hogwarts scenery and the story takes a much darker tone. Minerva's appearances are quite brief in this film, but the transfiguration teacher nevertheless plays a determinant role, being the one who provides a time turner to Hermione. It is also revealed that the Head of Gryffindor is not only a conscientious teacher at Hogwarts School, but also a member of the Order of the Phoenix, involved in the war against Voldemort and

197 B. McCabe, *Harry Potter: Page to Screen* (New York: Harper, 2011), p. 260.

the Death Eaters. In the fourth movie, *Harry Potter and the Goblet of Fire* (2005), Minerva McGonagall takes part in the Yule Ball – her hilarious dance lesson is probably one of the highlights of the *Harry Potter* saga – and also protects Harry from Snape's evil machinations. In the fifth movie, *Harry Potter and the Order of the Phoenix* (2007), she fights Professor Umbridge's iniquity and stands out as a positive figure, an ally of Harry and his friends. If her appearances are really scarce in the sixth movie, *Harry Potter and the Half-Blood Prince* (2009), it is in the second chapter of the seventh episode, *Harry Potter and the Deathly Hallows* (2011), that McGonagall masterfully dazzles, fighting Snape in single combat and defending Hogwarts against Lord Voldemort's army in spectacular sequences. The schoolteacher has turned into a heroine. At an aesthetical level, it must be noticed that, since the third movie, her outfit and her hairstyle have gone through a perceptible change. The Scottish green has disappeared, giving way to black and grey tones, more suitable for the heroic fantasy. Minerva now looks like a mature, but very attractive woman, who is as gorgeous as she is majestic. She does not wear spectacles anymore, and a very elegant, more elaborated high chignon has replaced the austere bun of the first instalments. Smith has now lent her beauty and her feminine grace to Minerva who wears more structured outfits, ample medieval-style sleeves and fitted robes that give the character a Gothic appearance. Tall, slender and diaphanously pale in her black witch cloak, Minerva looks like a character from an Ann Radcliffe novel. She keeps an original touch with the cute Scottish hat and matching mittens she wears when attending the Quidditch matches, but the costume designer spares her with the unflattering red outfit she was supposed to sport at the Yule Ball. Instead of that, she glows in a magnificent green robe, inspired by the style of medieval illuminations. From then on, McGonagall resembles a fairy more than a wizard.

This physical transformation also corresponds to the change of tonality in the films, which, just like the books, become darker and darker. Yet, from an aesthetical point of view, Minerva McGonagall – a benevolent and positive character – looks more like a maleficent creature than a 'helper'. In other words, if equivalents had to be found in animated films, since *Harry Potter and the Prisoner of Azkaban*, Minerva astonishingly resembles the most frightening – and also the most beautiful – of all the 'baddies' created by Walt Disney, Maleficent in *Sleeping Beauty*.[198] Technically speaking, Disney's Maleficent is in fact a composite figure resulting from the pictorial combination of the queen from *Snow White and the Seven Dwarfs* and the wicked stepmother in *Cinderella*.[199] The recent spin-off *Maleficent* (R. Stromberg, 2014) was an action-fantasy movie involving a young Maleficent played by Angelina Jolie. However, beyond doubt, Maggie Smith would have been just as beautiful and even more imposing if she had had to play the role of an older Maleficent; actually, when Minerva is at her most angular, the resemblance between the Hogwarts teacher and Disney's famous cartoon character is breathtaking. In this respect, Oscar Wilde is to be believed, 'Life imitates Art far more than Art imitates Life'.[200] In *Harry Potter*, McGonagall's general appearance also owes a lot, aesthetically, to that of the American actress Margaret Hamilton (1902-1985), best known for her role in *The Wizard of Oz* (V. Fleming, 1939).[201] It looks as if the beautiful and magnanimous Minerva had borrowed the whole outfit of the memorable Wicked Witch of the West, minus the green foundation and the striped socks. Paradoxically, Minerva McGonagall belongs, by her aesthetics and the structure of her costume, to the category of the wicked creatures, although she is nothing but a positive figure. Likewise, if her schedule had allowed her to play in (the mediocre) *Bewitched* (N. Ephron, 2005), Maggie Smith would have certainly been a delightful Endora, as sharp and funny as Agnes Moorehead in the 1960s TV show.

Anyway, while she is a 'helper', McGonagall is far from being a good fairy from the World of Noddy. As time goes by, her character is confronted with some dangerous situations and she displays qualities of bravery and self-control which reveal the warrior she truly is. Heroic fantasy is close to epic and J. K. Rowling's Minerva resembles a Homeric goddess, who is powerful and redoubtable, but remains a dispenser of blessings. In the last episode, in the wake of her namesake the warrior Athena, she even confronts Voldemort's army. A close-up on Minerva's face, when she raises her huge aquamarine eyes to heaven just before the ultimate battle, allows

198 See A. M. Davis, *Good Girls and Wicked Witches. Women in Disney's Feature Animation* (Eastleigh: John Libbey, 2006), p. 126.

199 D. Quinlan, *Wicked Women of the Screen* (London: Batsford, 1987), p. 140.

200 'The Decay of Lying: An Observation', *Intentions*, in *The Complete Works of Oscar Wilde*, Vol. 4, ed. by I. Small (Oxford: Oxford University Press, 2007), p. 90.

201 Nissen, *Accustomed to Her Face*, p. 83-88.

the spectator to contemplate what Smith really looks like when she does not play one of her usual old crones. Reminding us a bit of her glorious Jocasta in Cocteau's *The Infernal Machine*,[202] her immensely beautiful Minerva looks like a tragic queen. At the same time, the actress has given to McGonagall a little touch of eccentricity which, at the most crucial moment in Hogwarts history (the *Piertotum Locomotor* spell, when the transfiguration teacher summons and animates the suits of armour), leads her to admit, with a mischievous smile: 'I've always wanted to use that spell!' These words may resound strangely, coming from the strict transfiguration teacher, but it reveals, *in ultimo*, a rich and multi-layered character.[203] It also definitely puts McGonagall alongside the stern but eccentric Mary Poppins and, more generally, all the good fairies in literature, from Cinderella's Godmother to Glinda the Good Witch. If there was a yellow brick road leading to Hogwarts, we all would be off to see its most wonderful wizard.

202 Directed by S. Callow, Lyric Hammersmith, 1986.

203 See T. Geier, '"Harry Potter" films: Home to great British actors', *Entertainment Weekly*, 15 July 2009 <http://ew.com/article/2009/07/15/harry-potter-films-great-british-actors-refuge/> [accessed 12 November 2016]. The journalist explained that the main reason why classically trained actors did so well in the *Harry Potter* movies was the noble British tradition of the panto. The grown-up stars of the films took 'a similar relish' playing their roles.

Spinster Act

It may seem a bit odd to compare a world-known blockbuster with a charming independent British movie. The fact is that Janet Widdington – the character portrayed by Maggie Smith in *Ladies in Lavender* (C. Dance, 2004) – represents a nuanced and multi-layered variation on the stern-but-with-a-heart-of-gold figure embodied by Mother Superior and Minerva McGonagall. Through this character, the actress even manages to subvert her own type, revealing the sensitivity that lies inside an apparently stiff and authoritarian woman. Filmed on location (notably St Ives, Helston and Cadgwith Cove, Cornwall) during the early autumn of 2003, *Ladies*

in Lavender was Charles Dance's first venture into directing. Having fortuitously discovered William J. Locke's eponymous short story (1916), the actor fell for this touching tale of an impossible love and wished to adapt it for the big screen. *Ladies in Lavender* tells the story of two middle-aged sisters living quietly together along the coast of Cornwall in the 1930s. They have reached an age and a peaceful equilibrium which allow the viewers to think that nothing will ever happen to them again. One morning, though, after a storm, the sisters rescue a young Polish man (Daniel Brühl) – in fact, a violin virtuoso called Andrea – who, having escaped a shipwreck, has been washed by the tide onto their beach. While they provide shelter and health care to this handsome stranger, Ursula (Judi Dench), the younger of the two, immediately feels desire growing in her heart and, experiencing love for the first time in her life, starts to behave accordingly. Having noticed the yellow flower that Ursula has put on Andrea's tray, Janet (Smith) clearly perceives her sister's infatuation for the very young man and, quite embarrassed, she tries at first to reason with her and to repress that misplaced feeling like a boarding-school matron would do. But when an attractive Russian woman, Olga (Natasha McElhone), interferes for the purpose of launching Andrea's career, Janet progressively feels empathy with Ursula and stands with her, doing her best to keep Olga at bay. Eventually, Andrea leaves to start his career in London and the two sisters resume their quiet life.

The critic Geoffrey Macnab was mostly receptive to the humorous side of the movie, seeing in Janet Widdington one of Smith's numerous variations-on-Bracknell, but also admitting that, despite a dowager-like haughtiness which showed up here and there, her comic timing was at its best.[204] According to him, a large part of the comical aspect of the film lies in the fact that its two leading characters are older, even 'considerably older', than they were in the short story which inspired it. On one side, it allows Dance to develop the comedic aspects of the story, the two sisters being old enough to be Andrea's grandmothers; on the other side, it also deprives the film of the 'intensity' it could have had.[205] In the movie, Janet and Ursula are not 'considerably' older than the original characters – according to Dance's screenplay, Ursula and Janet are nearly sixty,

204 'Ladies in Lavender', *Sight and Sound*, November 2004, p. 56.
205 *Ibid.*

certainly not, in any case, as old as some reviewers have pretended – and alleging such a thing also means to tactfully suggest that the two actresses were 'considerably' old, what was untrue. Besides, the critic seemed to imply that such a story, the love a woman suddenly feels for a man who is younger, becomes necessarily risible and grotesque when the woman is an ageing one. The older, the funnier. Such a vision could appear stereotyped these days. Ten years later, many movies targeted at older viewers have been released and love stories mixing senior and younger people are certainly not an object of ridicule. Making fun of Ursula and, in a lesser extent, of Janet, was certainly not the purpose of this production. On the contrary, Dance deals with his subject with tact and delicacy and the numerous comical elements only add to the picturesque atmosphere of the film. Everything here tends to demonstrate that it is never too late to fall in love. Ursula's story is pathetic, not because she is indeed older than the man she loves, but for the reason that there is no reciprocation. Andrea does not love Ursula; if he really did, he would forget her grey hair and her wrinkles, or ignore the scandal that an affair could raise in their small community. There is no love from his part, so there is no reason to fight against prejudice. Andrea is – quite conventionally – attracted to the young and pretty woman, Olga, but most of all, he is dedicated to his art. Actually, social conventions have the last word in that story. When writing the penultimate scene of the movie, Charles Dance had made a commendable attempt to justify Locke's enigmatic title, *Ladies in Lavender*.[206] In the original script, Janet and Ursula left a small bunch of lavender on a table before walking away from the Royal Albert Hall. Olga Danilov (who does not appear in this scene of the movie) was supposed to find it and put it in a vase. That short bit was eventually cut, but it echoed, in a certain way, the scene where Andrea gives a bunch of wild flowers to both the sisters. Janet very practically puts them in a vase, as if the young man's romantic gesture was to be immediately contained and disciplined.

Two sisters, but definitely not twin sisters. The diptych formed by the two leading characters could not be more contrasted, Janet and Ursula being

206 The critic from *The Times* (11 November 2004, p. 11) harmlessly joked about that title, as if it was Dance's unfortunate choice, admitting that, despite its odd title, which evoked the smell of mothballs, *Ladies in Lavender* was the most exquisite movie.

quite dissimilar. Sense against sensibility. Ursula, the younger of the two, is touching in her candour and spontaneity. At a mature age, she behaves like an impulsive young girl and the movie emphasises the childish aspects of her personality. On the beach, she runs to the water to paddle in it and splashes her older sister who quietly remains sitting on the sand. She reacts impetuously to every situation, getting quickly overexcited, speaking with a full mouth or sulking in a corner when disappointed. On the opposite side, Janet, the elder sister, embodies calm, authority and seriousness. She is the one who runs the house, makes decisions and takes on all the responsibilities. She incarnates the power in the microcosm that their little cottage is. Competent as a nurse, she drives the car, plays the piano and even speaks German when it is required. As much as Ursula incarnates the eternal child, Janet stands as the motherly, reasonable figure who restrains her sister's exuberance.

The motif of the opposite sisters is a common *topos* in literature and drama, and the Widdington ladies echo, among others, Deborah and Mathilda Jenkins in Elizabeth Gaskell's *Cranford*.[207] It has been exploited on the big screen as well, and *Ladies in Lavender* reminds us of other movies revolving around a pair of not-so-twin sisters. *Babette's Feast* (G. Axel, 1987) tells the story of a French cook, Babette, who escapes from Paris during the 1870 war and seeks refuge in Denmark, where she is given hospitality by two sisters. These two ageing women live together in a small cottage on the seaside, feeding the poor and cherishing the memory of their late father, a revered Protestant clergyman. More austere in their way of life than Janet and Ursula, the Danish sisters are nevertheless in a similar situation, sheltering a stranger in their home. No love story here – only implicit regrets, as we get to learn that both sisters rejected a devoted suitor in their youth – but a beautiful tale of friendship, generosity and thankfulness. The host, Babette, promises that she will never leave her benefactors and, having won the lottery, she spends all her money to thank them with a sumptuous dinner. If *Ladies in Lavender* and *Babette's Feast* both have the structure of a fairy tale,

207 In the BBC adaptation (2007), it was precisely Judi Dench who played the sweet, romantic Mathilda against a stern, authoritarian Eileen Atkins as Deborah. It is probably no coincidence if the stiffer of the two is played by an actress who, physically, belongs to the same category as Maggie Smith: tall and angular, Atkins herself excels in portraying imperious figures or pinched old bats.

with the irruption of a trigger component – the arrival of a stranger – in a well-settled routine, Andrea is far from having as much gratitude for his hostesses as Babette had. His career comes first, he leaves without a word to follow Olga, and when the two sisters travel to London to see him at the concert, the young musician abandons them in the theatre foyer to meet a certain Sir Thomas.[208] In *Ladies in Lavender*, the focus is clearly not on the notions of hospitality and thankfulness, but on the complexity of feelings.

From that point of view, another 1987 release is probably closer to Charles Dance's movie. Directed by Lindsay Anderson, *The Whales of August* is a small scale but exceptional production which reunited the star of silent film, Lilian Gish, and Bette Davis in her last role on the big screen. Gish and Davis play two elderly sisters, Sarah and Libby, who live on their own in a seaside cottage in Maine. With Libby (already blind and nearly disabled) getting more and more senile, Sarah contemplates their future with apprehension. Just like in *Ladies in Lavender*, the film sketches out a beautifully contrasted portrait of the two sisters; the sweet and docile Sarah (Gish) is bullied by her cantankerous, tyrannical sister Libby (Davis) whom she obeys like a dedicated servant. When Sarah is gently courted by an old Russian aristocrat, Mr Maranov (Vincent Price), Libby gets even grumpier, being jealous of her sister. Glued to their daily routine, the two women still behave like the girls they once were; Sarah has remained a quiet, romantic soul while Libby acts like a capricious, spoiled child. The critics who dared to write that Janet and Ursula looked like Andrea's grandmothers, certainly had never watched *The Whales of August*, the leading characters of which could easily be the Widdington sisters' old aunts. The passing of time is one of the major themes in *The Whales* and, indeed, it shows on screen. As Sarah, the veteran actress Lilian Gish looks like a well-preserved centenarian would look like these days and Bette Davis – who had been slightly disfigured by a stroke, in 1983, and was suffering from breast cancer when the movie was filmed – offers a heartbreaking vision; skeletal, her high cheeks emphasising her sunken eyes, her Libby looks like a frightening ghost. The two sisters argue and stand against each other, but in the end, both realise that the only true possession that time has left to them is their mutual love. They must make concessions and remain together. On that point, *The Whales* is very similar to C. Dance's film.

208 Ironically, this is no one else but Sir Thomas Beecham, the famous composer from whom the imaginary 'Beecham House' in *Quartet* (2012) has been named.

Although *Ladies in Lavender* was advertised as a vehicle for the two Dames sharing top billing, Smith remains slightly on the sidelines. Not that she has less screen time than Dench, but given her functional role in the story, she stands as a secondary character. Janet is only a witness of Ursula's passion for the young man, which is the main focus of the movie.[209] Suzie Mackenzie wrote that Smith brought a 'non-judgmental' sensibility to the part, so that we see her sister's distress through her eyes.[210] Maggie Smith may have a supporting role, but she makes the most of it. Janet Widdington could be considered quite a typical role for the actress, as an incarnation of reason and authority in the house, but this type is denatured here. The character embodies the perversion of the archetype of the 'perfect spinster', in the sense that the strong armour progressively cracks and reveals its weaknesses; as the story unfolds, it appears that Janet's actions and feelings are also driven by love. The character is not one-dimensional, and Janet Widdington proves to be a very emotive, fragile, loving person, something that is particularly suited to the actress, in the words of Charles Dance. The director explained that Maggie Smith showed a vulnerability that she was rarely able to reveal in movies. Most of the time, she portrays imperious women, sour and stiff, but beneath the façade, there is a real sensitivity that she brings out here.[211] However, unlike Ursula, her attachment is not of an erotic nature; she has rescued Andrea and expects to go on looking after him as she wants. Seeing Smith as a 1930s accomplished homemaker, cutting Andrea's hair or cooking a rather filling 'stargazey' pie for her guest is pure joy. Janet appears as a maternal figure whose tender love gradually turns into possessiveness and jealousy, firstly towards Ursula, then towards Olga Danilov. While she sees Olga as a troublemaker who intrudes in their lives and tries to take Andrea away from them, she also childishly squabbles with Ursula over the young man, although she has different interests. Ursula is deeply smitten with him, whereas Janet behaves like an overprotective, loving

209 See R. Moseley, 'A landscape of desire. Cornwall as romantic setting in *Love Story* and *Ladies in Lavender*', in *British Women's Cinema*, ed. by M. Bell and M. Williams (London-New York: Routledge, 2010), p. 87-91. According to Moseley, Dance's *Ladies in Lavender* explores the 'desiring subjectivity' of an old woman.

210 'You have to laugh', *The Guardian Weekend*, 20 November 2004, p. 41.

211 Quoted in S. Horwitz, 'Stirring the Depths', *Back Stage. The Performing Arts Weekly*, May 2005, 46.18, p. 38.

mother. That constant bickering funnily contrasts with the austere, stiff appearance of Janet and renews the usual Smith spinster type.

In fact, Olga stands as a second trigger component which definitively upsets the balance. From the start, she is the enemy, the functional 'opponent' to the protagonists and literally, as Ursula suggests, 'the wicked witch in a fairy story'. From then on, Janet becomes offensive and uses all her strengths to defend her sister against the meddling young woman who trespasses in their garden and nibbles at their cake without having been invited to do so. The rivalry with her younger sister soon has disappeared; she is no longer an 'opponent' to Ursula, but her most faithful 'helper', practically using lies and duplicity to ruin Olga's attempts to reach Andrea. But more than her fierce hatred for Olga, what is striking here is her fervent, absolute devotion to her younger sister. Witnessing Ursula's disarray and jealousy, Janet realises how much her sister feels for Andrea and, far from reprimanding her, she eventually comforts and supports the heartbroken woman, having herself lost her fiancé during the Great War. In her review, J. Mackenzie accurately described these successive stages (Janet being embarrassed at first, before feeling 'sympathy' and even true 'empathy' for Ursula); as the critic declared, only Maggie Smith could switch so aptly from irony to compassion. [212] Janet becomes so compassionate, that she feels – indirectly – her sister's desire, pain and frustration and finally shows her vulnerable side. When an angry Ursula accuses her of being insensitive, Smith's Janet gently replies: 'On the contrary.' Through Ursula's own passion, the stiff and reasonable Janet is contaminated with insane and irrepressible feelings. She is the one who organises the trip to London to see Andrea at the Royal Albert Hall. Quite unexpectedly for a spinster character played by Maggie Smith, sensibility has prevailed over sense.

***

Undeniably, Maggie Smith is often typecast. Not always, as some pretend, but quite frequently indeed. It can be asserted that the actress is typecast, most of the time, because of the lack of imagination of filmmakers who do not dare, unlike stage directors, to explore the infinite possibilities of

212 Mackenzie, 'You have to laugh', p. 41.

her talent. Maybe, from a more positive point of view, Smith is typecast because everyone in the industry knows she is simply better than anyone else in those parts. This advantage would play against her if she remained stuck with one unique role. Fortunately, this is far from being the case. With a career spanning almost six decades, the actress has never been busier than she was in the last five years and, despite the allegations of some, the parts she plays are quite different – not to say opposite –, giving her the opportunity to constantly reassert her incomparable versatility.

The roles which belong to her type are not necessarily comical parts. Most of the time, the women she plays are quite risible because of their bad faith or their caricatural behaviour, but the actress inevitably injects vulnerability or magnanimity in them. All her waspish dowagers have a softer side which makes them lovable. Moreover, Smith is typecast, not in one, but in two distinct categories: the haughty, grumpy aristocrat who embodies the British upper class, and the stern figure of authority, governess or schoolteacher, incarnation of discipline and common sense. Nevertheless, every time she is cast in one of these two types, the actress gives life to a character remotely different from the others – of the same type – she has previously played. For one type, there are many roles.

However, Smith's talent extends far beyond the narrow limits of typecasting. Her range is much wider, and it is precisely when she plays against type that we are able to contemplate a real genius at work.

2

TRANSFIGURATION MASTER

Metamorphosis and Characterisation

Protean Acting

Maggie Smith's type – which includes two subcategories, the grumpy snob and the tutelary figure of the housekeeper or the governess – only represents one part, one very small part of her range. With her piercing blue eyes, her aristocratic bearing and her tall stature, the actress ideally portrays all these posh or authoritarian characters, but to consider only this segment of her work is tantamount to omit the major part of her acting abilities. It would be quite unjust and simplistic to pretend, as some journalists do, that Smith always plays the same character, again and again. It would be even more pointless to compare every part she plays from Muriel Donnelly in *The Best Exotic Marigold Hotel* to Jean Horton in *Quartet* with the dowager countess in *Downton Abbey*, as if this overexposed role had become the yardstick by which every new performance has to be judged. Reading some articles, it looks as if she had never played anything else before and would never play anything really different from now. The last straw came with N. Hytner's *The Lady in the Van*. As inaccurate it may be, some critics were not discouraged from comparing Miss Shepherd to Violet Crawley. In a mitigated review, the critic Stuart Jeffries ironically wondered how Dame Maggie Smith was able to portray this woman who had fallen 'so low' and nevertheless play the part just like she plays her usual imperious lady roles.[213] Similarly, Matthew Bond, in *The Daily Mail*, pretended that Smith was channelling a 'down-and-out' dowager countess.[214] On the contrary, it is when the actress does not play her type that she gloriously reveals the incommensurable width of her range. Maggie Smith can play many roles which totally differ from the person she is by their psychological profile, their social status or their physical appearance. It is in the hiatus between what she does look like and what she is able to look like that lies her extraordinary aptitude for metamorphosis. Despite what those who know very little about her career (the awful thing is that a great number of tabloid journalists belong to that category) believe or pretend, Smith has never stopped diversifying her roles during the last twenty years. These two decades have given her the opportunity to tackle an infinite variety of parts and, every time, she has surprised the public, brilliantly demonstrating that she is a marvellous chameleon, able to wholly transform herself if the part requires it. It is the ultimate paradox for an actress who is – allegedly – pigeonholed in a type.

When describing the work of an actor who 'steps into the shoes' of

213 'Got any change? Why cinema struggles with homelessness', *The Guardian G2*, 5 November 2015, p. 10. Becoming more incisive, Jeffries pretended to be falsely amazed by the dame's versatility and ability to switch from a snobbish Violet Crawley to a repellent Miss Shepherd smelling of pee, only regretting that, whatever the part, Smith could never get rid of that 'sub-Lady Bracknell' imperiousness.

214 'With two Alan Bennetts and Maggie Smith channelling a down-and-out dowager countess, this touching true story of the woman who lived in a van on the writer's drive is a brilliantly British triumph', *The Daily Mail*, 14 November 2015 <http://www.dailymail.co.uk/home/event/article-3315458/The-Lady-Van-review-two-Alan-Bennetts-Maggie-Smith-channelling-dowager-countess-touching-true-story-woman-lived-van-writer-s-drive-brilliantly-British-triumph.html> [accessed 12 November 2016]. According to Bond, Miss Shepherd was nothing but a vagrant, unwashed, smelly dowager countess in rags, a less than elegant manner to suggest that Smith always gives the same turn.

a character, some theorists say he 'incarnates' that character. According to the Latin etymology, 'to incarnate' strictly means 'to get into the flesh', an equivalent of the usual French expression *entrer dans la peau du personnage* or the German verb *verkörpern*; in fact, it proves to be an overused word, quite inaccurate for defining characterisation. A theatre character, like any fictional figure, has no existence, no skin, no flesh. The actor is the only medium by which the character is given life. For the duration of the show, this is the actor who lends his flesh to the character. He lends him his body and his voice. Through the actor, the character gains a 'carnal' existence and immediately becomes tangibly present on the stage. Maggie Smith goes far beyond this first step. She does not content herself with lending her body and her face to the character. Her range is of such a width that, each time, she is able to adapt herself, in her appearance and her gesture, to the figure she has to portray. There is no proper word, in English, to denominate the fabrication of a character which is quite different from the performer who plays it.[215] Stanislavski's translators have pertinently chosen the expression 'building a character' which suggests the total creation of a fictional character by the actor. 'Characterisation' is a word that is often used to describe this process – that of giving life, through acting, to an 'unique and individual' figure[216] – and, although the term does not completely do justice to the idea of metamorphosis that the actor has to go through, it sounds the most appropriate.

In other European traditions, as well as in the United States, it is more usual to cast the actors according to their type. Most of the time, there is a physical adequacy between the part and the performer. French actors do not like much to be made-up and they reluctantly use wigs, that is why a casting director will preferably cast an actor who exactly looks the part. In contrast, in the UK, without generalising – all the more that the younger generation of actors favours movies and cinematic acting – characterisation is often part of the job. It is considered that an actor, as a chameleon, must be able to play almost anything. For the British actors, acting involves make-up, costumes and technical skills, and those are the tools that the performer uses to build the character. Laurence Olivier made a distinction between actors who 'start from the inside' and actors, like Alec Guinness,

215 The French call it *composition*.

216 See R. Boleslavsky, *Acting. The first six lessons* (New York: Routledge, 1933), p. 81.

who 'start from the periphery', professing that the actor who starts from the inside is more exposed to 'find himself' in the role he plays, than he has a chance to become someone else.[217] Unlike the method performers, actors of Smith's generation did not learn to recall feelings and sensations in order to put themselves in the character's emotional state. They know how *to make* it. They become the character only when they are on stage or when the camera rolls. They do not 'feel'. They simply 'act', but in so subtle a way that the audience never sees the huge amount of skill and effort that is required to obtain that result. While type refers to immutability, rigidity, even sclerosis – the actor being durably identified with a unique category of roles – characterisation requires a great deal of adaptability and resourcefulness from the performer. Whereas an actor playing his type only lends his body and his voice to the character he plays, an actor playing 'against type' has to build the fictional figure to which he gives life. To do so, he uses his innate means – voice, physical appearance, gesture – helped by technical skills and practical tools – such as make-up, wigs, costumes and props – which allow him to go through a total transformation. The protean actor who fully masters characterisation and transformation is able to play almost every role and to remain convincing.

According to Stanislavski, whose famous theory is too often reduced to the third part of its substance (overall, the part which corresponds to *An actor prepares*, that is the physical and psychological conditioning of the actor), characterisation is the prime requirement in acting. An actor should never be himself. For him, the advocates of the typecasting practice were the least talented actors, those whose range is not wide but rather 'one-sided' and who can play only one role. Stanislavski considered that a genuine, accomplished actor had to avoid typecasting and play all kinds of parts, what the theoretician called 'characterisation'. The actor had to be a character actor.[218] He also condemned these famous thespians who have such an overwhelming personality that they remain themselves in every part they play – without jeopardising their success and popularity, as the public gladly pays to see them playing themselves on stage or on screen.

---

217 Laurence Olivier talking to Kenneth Tynan, in *Great Acting*, ed. by H. Burton (London: BBC, 1967), p. 24.

218 *Stanislavski's Legacy. A Collection of Comments on a Variety of Aspects of an Actor's Art and Life*, ed. by E. R. Hapgood (London: Methuen Drama, 1981), p. 16-18.

The spectators do not see X, a character, they see a famous actor playing X. According to Stanislavski, an egocentric actor never stoops to transforming into the character. He is dressed as the character, but he nevertheless always remains himself: Stanislavski deplored that, in his time, there were actresses who were reluctant to transform themselves into an unbecoming character, preferring to adapt every role they played to their own personal appeal.[219] As the academic Raphaëlle Costa de Beauregard notices, the fact already existed in Shakespeare's time,[220] and later, at the end of the eighteenth century, critics compared the flamboyant acting of Sarah Siddons (1755-1831) with that – more restrained – of Ann Street Crawford (1733-1801). Unlike Crawford, Siddons never achieved total absorption in the part, she never effaced herself in the illusion of the scene. 'I have often thought Mrs Siddons a most wonderful actress; I have often forgotten Mrs Crawford *was an actress*,' the author of *Funereal Stanzas in homage to Ann Crawford* asserted in his preface.[221]

Characterisation should go without saying: every actor should be able to play any, or almost any role. In reality, very few actors are versatile enough to play an extreme variety of parts. Those who have the capacity to do so are regarded as phenomena, although they simply do their job. Jack Nicholson or the French actor Gérard Depardieu are past masters in the art of characterisation, although, precisely, they both have such an overpowering personality that it always overshadows the character they play. Robert De Niro, like Dustin Hoffman, and of course Daniel Day Lewis – the absolute chameleon actor – are more versatile, in the strict sense of the word. They are able to physically transform and become

219 *Building a character* (New York: Routledge, 1949), p. 22.

220 'The Staging of Dramatic Time in *As You Like It*', in *Shakespeare's As You Like It* (Paris: Ellipses, 1997), p. 108: 'They played several parts in a play until, after the 1580s, the fame of some of these actors made it quite impossible, their image being too well-known for any disguise to make them unrecognizable. On the other hand, their fame becoming a form of enticement for audiences to attend the plays, it must have encouraged a tendency to write plays for them [...] This must be seen as an innovation implying that they would be like cinema stars today, providing a double-layered entertainment, both as actors playing a part in the *diegesis* and as actors playing their own part in the performance.'

221 Anonym., *Funereal Stanzas, inscribed to the Reverend Memory of Mrs Ann Crawford, with a Comparative Dissertation between her Theatrical Merits and those of Mrs Siddons* (Dublin: Milliken, 1803), quoted in R. McDonald, *Look to the Lady. Sarah Siddons, Ellen Terry, and Judi Dench on the Shakespearean Stage* (Athens: University of Georgia Press, 2005), p. 28.

priests, businessmen or serial-killers, just like, a few decades ago, the French actor Michel Serrault and the Italian actor Marcello Mastroianni, who both excelled in tragedy as well as in farce. Yet, the fact remains that characterisation is more often associated with actors than it is with actresses. Great actresses who fully master characterisation are less common, probably because female performers are usually divided in distinct categories. The 'lead roles' – in other words the actresses who start with the gorgeous young debutantes – go on with the beautiful women and end playing the charming grandmothers. On the other side, the 'character actresses' exclusively get supporting roles despite their indisputable talent. Most of the time, these highly skilled actresses successfully specialise in playing unglamorous but juicy characters, like Margaret Rutherford in the past or, these days, Miriam Margolyes, Stephanie Cole or Linda Bassett. For her part, the marvellous Imelda Staunton has an immensely extended range and regularly plays leading roles, but she never plays the high-born aristocrats. Generally, actresses who belong to the first category are very conscious of their image and, preserving an enviable appearance as long as they can, they leave the less flattering parts – the servants, the desiccated spinsters or the wicked witches – to the second category. There usually is no interference whatsoever between these two categories of actresses. Rutherford was frustrated to be pigeonholed in farcical roles during her whole career and she dreamed of playing classical parts like her contemporaries Thorndike or Evans did. Her particular looks, which had earned her glory, were also an obstacle to her real aspirations. Far from being happy with that 'clown's face' which was worth a fortune, Margaret Rutherford was deeply affected by being a figure of fun, and she considered her looks an obstacle which prevented her from playing great female parts.[222] Therefore, aside from Meryl Streep[223] and few others, leading actresses are rarely versatile and adaptable performers, willing to be made-up in order to play characters who look ugly or considerably older. These roles, considered less gratifying, usually go to 'character actresses'

222 Johns, *Dames of the Theatre*, p. 125.

223 On Streep's malleability, see K. Fairclough-Isaacs, 'Mature Meryl and Hot Helen: Hollywood Gossip and the "Appropriately Ageing actress"', in *Ageing, Popular Culture and Contemporary Feminism*, ed. by I. Whelehan and J. Gwynne (Basingstoke: Palgrave Macmillan, 2014), p. 152.

who are more accustomed to transform themselves or whose physical appearance exempts them from using a heavy make-up.

Some people – and Maggie Smith herself – assume that she is a 'character actress.'[224] *Stricto sensu*, this old-fashioned expression refers, with often a negative connotation, to a performer specialising in small supporting parts. To end up as a character actress, in Hollywood's Golden Age, was the lot of many old glories of the stage who became pigeonholed in small supporting roles on screen, playing aunts, grandmothers, housekeepers maids or dowagers.[225] Generally, character actresses are not stars, they are not famous, only their face is familiar to the public. The only thing that Maggie Smith and that kind of character actress have in common is an extraordinary malleability. However, in Smith's case, this is not because of a plain and rather insignificant physical appearance, far from it, but thanks to her amazing chameleon skills. Unlike the typical character actress, she does not play a wide range of small parts – every time she is given a small part, it happens that she is actually typecast – and, most of all, she is a major star. Yet, it can be said that Smith is a 'character actress' in the sense that she is a giant of acting who amazingly masters, like very few others, the art of characterisation. Laurence Olivier himself claimed that he wished to be seen as a character actor, that is as a chameleon. He used to say that he was never more pleased than when he knew that he had tricked his audience, having been on stage for several minutes without being recognised. For him, acting was 'character acting' and necessarily involved props, transformation and characterisation.[226]

Maggie Smith masters the art of transformation at the highest level. Two of Smith's most successful roles on stage – Miss Shepherd in A. Bennett's *The Lady in the Van* and A in E. Albee's *Three Tall Women* – implied strong characterisation. Most of the time, the actress has to transform herself to give life to the characters she plays and her talent for metamorphosis is so staggering that it is quite difficult for the spectator

224 'Because I am, if anything, a character actress. I have been playing ninety-three for years now': not without irony, Maggie Smith said that to journalist Steve Kroft who clearly identified the actress with her 'old bag' type and was precisely interviewing her just as if she was a contemporary of Madge Kendal or Marie Tempest (*60 minutes*, CBS, 17 February 2013).

225 Nissen, *Actresses of A Certain Character*, p. 4-5.

226 *On Acting* (New York: Simon & Schuster, 1986), p. 90-91.

to persuade himself that she hides behind the character. Journalists and critics rarely point it out, but it is unthinkable that the same actress successively portrayed Grace Hawkins in *Keeping Mum* and Elizabeth in *The Lady from Dubuque*, or that the same woman who lends her features to the austere Mother Superior in *Sister Act* reveals (a bit of) her charms in *My House in Umbria*. This is not a famous thespian being dressed – like a paper doll – with the distinctive uniforms of an extensive gallery of characters, but the creation of many different figures of flesh and blood, each one having nothing in common with the others, apart from a (very distinctive) pair of blue eyes. Smith achieves the ultimate feat by not being recognisable from one part to another.

Trying to Blend In

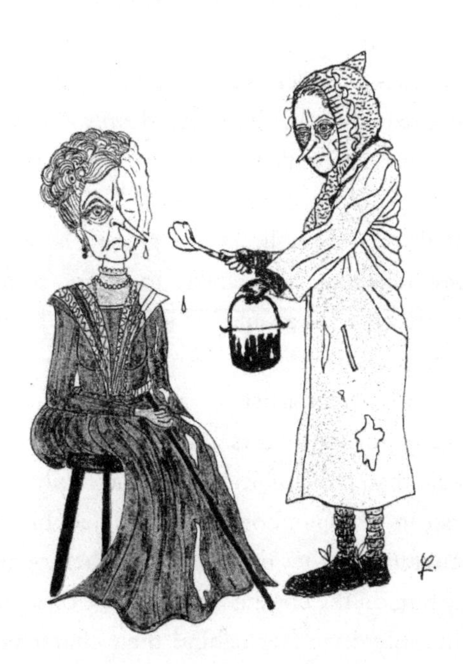

Not only does characterisation require a great deal of work from the actor, but it also implies some kind of neutrality and malleability. To be efficient on stage or on screen, an actor should not be 'performing' in everyday life. It seems obvious, even though it was not always the case in the past. According to Sacha Guitry (1885-1957), the famous French playwright and director, '*Il faut qu'un acteur ait l'air d'un acteur, même à la ville*', an actor must look like an actor, even off stage.[227] Actually, Guitry, who was an

227 D. Desanti, *Sacha Guitry, cinquante ans de spectacle* (Paris: Grasset, 1982), p. 48.

actor himself, behaved theatrically on and off stage and the audience expected him to do so. He resembled the characters he played or, more accurately, he created characters who resembled him. Sarah Bernhardt, who belonged to an earlier generation, embodied more than anyone else the larger-than-life figure of the diva-actress, always in performance.[228] Having seen Eleonora Duse and Sarah Bernhardt playing the same part, George Bernard Shaw gave preference to the Italian thespian rather than the French actress whom he found too theatrical: 'The dress, the title of the play, the order of the words may vary, but the woman is always the same. She does not enter into the leading character; she substitutes herself for it.'[229] In a book which focuses on the greatest Dames of the London stage, Eric Johns recounts that Sybil Thorndike herself blamed her illustrious predecessor Ellen Terry for the same reason. Thorndike deplored that the great thespian had played only one part in her career – that is herself – instead of tackling a variety of roles, admitting that maybe the audience would not have liked it.[230] Terry was a charismatic thespian who delighted the public by her grace; she was certainly not a protean performer. This flaw was peculiar to actors from the past, whose deeds and actions always took an aura of splendour. Even off stage, they were always in performance.

These days, the real great artists do not 'stage' their own lives. They do not put on a show for journalists. As a general rule, British actors are much more versatile than most of European and Hollywood stars and – at least for veteran actors like Gambon, McKellen, Jacobi, Atkins and others from the same generation – they do not project their own personality into the roles they play but, on the contrary, making use of a perfectly mastered technique, they humbly disappear behind their characters. Among some purists and theorists of the theatre, the French language – particularly precise in that area – establishes a distinction between the *acteur*, that is the hammy performer, and the *comédien*, that is the great, highly skilled actor. The French actor Louis Jouvet professed: 'The *acteur* can play only a few roles and he distorts the others according to his own personality. The

228 C. Joannis, *Sarah Bernhardt, Reine de l'Attitude et princesse des gestes* (Paris: Payot, 2000), p. 75: 'She needs to be extraordinary to be herself'.

229 'Duse versus Bernhardt', 15 June 1895, in *Dramatic Opinions*, I, p. 126-127.

230 Johns, *Dames of the Theatre*, p. 10.

comédien can play every role.'[231] Such a distinction could seem outdated or pointless nowadays but, in any case, it is still commonly accepted that the mediocre *histrion* makes a show of himself, whereas the true actor aims at invisibility. Most of the time, the more neutral and ordinary-looking the performer is in real life, the more extraordinary he can be when acting. The actor's face must be as insignificant as the neutral mask to allow him to play any role. Laurence Olivier considered that the physical neutrality of the actor was essential to the process of characterisation. He liked to see his face as a kind of 'blank canvas' that he was able to mould as he wished, confessing that it had always been a great joy for him to surprise the audience, and not be recognised.[232] Talking about faces he saw in public places, in the street or in the Tube, Olivier made a distinction between the 'modern man', who strictly belongs to the present time and would be unable to be placed in another period, and the 'period man', who could wear any costume and be placed convincingly in any period, just like paper dolls. Neutrality was one of Guinness's major assets, as the celebrated critic Kenneth Tynnan asserted. As Shaw used to say about Henry Irving, Tynnan considered that Alec Guinness had no face (what allowed him to go unnoticed when he entered a room) and called him a 'master of anonymity'.[233] Neutrality not only goes hand in hand with malleability and allows an actor to transform himself as much as he wants, but it also virtually creates a kind of retreat, a place of his own for the actor, where he can isolate himself from the public. As the biographer Mel Gussow explains, the immense Michael Gambon has no other purpose than going totally unnoticed in everyday life, professing that the less the audience knows about the actor, the better it is, otherwise it 'fucks up' his work. [234]

The fact is that some actors are too well-known to manage to completely disappear behind their character. However, the French movie

---

231 *Réflexions du comédien* (Paris: Éditions de la Nouvelle Revue Critique, 1938), p. 141.

232 *On Acting* (New York: Simon & Schuster, 1986), p. 30.

233 *Alec Guinness* (London: Barrie & Rockliff, 1961), p. 11-12. See also G. Macnab, *Searching for Stars. Stardom and Screen Acting in British Cinema* (London-New York: Cassell, 2000), p. 140; about Alec Guinness, the author evokes 'his inscrutable palimpsest of a face.'

234 *Gambon. A life in acting* (London: NHB, 2004), p. 35. See also p. 158, where he says that there is nothing worse than being an actor whose face is so famous that people recognise him in the street.

critic Christian Viviani suggests that the spectator does not necessarily seek to forget the actor who plays the role; to fully please and amaze the audience, the famous actor has to remain recognisable behind the character.[235] As the academic Stephen Booth notes, the true great stars never let the audience forget that they are actors playing a role; what is special about them is that they are always both themselves and the character they portray.[236] Indeed, the charisma and the popularity of the big stars condemn them to always play characters who resemble them or, conversely, to superimpose their own personality on the character they portray. This is exactly what Eugene Stelzig criticises in his study on the autobiographical genre, when defining the notion of 'stage presence' related to star performers. He claims that these very famous performers take on the identity of one character, although the spectators perfectly know that they do not see this character on the stage 'but rather Laurence Olivier or Maggie Smith'.[237]

It seems particularly inaccurate to use Smith as an example here. She is precisely not that kind of actor, even if some critics do see her celebrity as a handicap. In an excellent article published in *American Theatre* in 1995, Matt Wolf hailed the efficience of Maggie Smith's acting in Albee's *Three Tall Women*, also regretting that her personality sometimes engulfed the character. Wolf considered Smith's performance 'star acting' in the old sense of the word, as the actress, while honouring the part fully, still let her personality coexist with the character.[238] About her stage performance as Miss Shepherd, in *The Lady in the Van*, some reviewers reproached her to be too well-known to play the part. R. Butler claimed that the fact that the 'anonymous' Miss Shepherd was played by a very famous actress,

235 Viviani, *Le Magique et le Vrai*, p. 32.

236 'On the Aesthetics of Acting', in J. L. Halio and H. Richmond, *Shakespearean Illuminations. Essays in Honor of Marvin Rosenberg* (London: University of Delaware Press, 1998), p. 255-266. See also S. Kracauer, 'Remarks on the Actor', in *Theory of Film: The Redemption of Physical Reality* (Oxford: Oxford University Press, 1960), p. 99-100. Kracauer notes that the Hollywood star generally imposes a 'screen image' of himself, and this image determines and influences every performance he gives.

237 *Romantic Autobiography in England* (Farnham: Ashgate, 2009), p. 145-146. See also M. McNamara, 'Maggie Smith, the Magnificent', *The Los Angeles Times*, 3 January 2013, p. 1; according to the journalist, like any great actor, Smith is both totally immersed in character and instantly recognisable on the stage.

238 'The Pleasures of Bravura Acting in London', *American Theatre*, Vol. 12, Issue 2, February 1995, p. 67.

Maggie Smith, substantially skewed the reaction of the audience.[239] It is probably her glittering portrayal of Lettice Douffet, in Peter Shaffer's *Lettice and Lovage*, that gathered the most numerous criticisms of that nature. A critic even used a metaphor to describe Smith's overwhelming persona, saying that she is one of these actors who take on the part like they would a hat, and adapt it to suit their own personality and the taste of their fans.[240] Many reviewers compared Smith with Margaret Tyzack, her co-star in the play, in other words the mannered, overfamous star versus the chameleon actress. A critic from *The Observer* drew a parallel between them, saying that, whereas Tyzack was always the character she played on the stage, Smith, despite her talent, was always Dame Maggie Smith.[241] However, Tyzack herself denied these allegations, observing that, if some people were stars and not actors, she and Maggie were, above all, actresses.[242] In fact, even at her debut, Maggie Smith was labelled as a performer endowed with too much personality to be able to disappear behind a character. In 1965, the critic from *The Evening Post* was quite pessimistic about the young actress's characterisation abilities. Too much identifiable as Maggie Smith whatever part she was playing, she was not a 'self-effacing' performer like Alec Guinness, one of those 'who can sink themselves in a part without trace'.[243] Yet, Smith's whole career, especially in these last two decades, utterly proves him wrong.

In a book that John Gielgud wrote about some of the remarkable figures he had worked with, the great actor praised Edith Evans's malleability, remembering that, in his youth, he wished he could have a photograph of Evans. He never recognised her when she appeared on stage, as she always looked exactly like the part she was playing. [244] Maggie

239 'Driving Miss Crazy', *The Independent on Sunday Culture*, 12 December 1999, p. 4.

240 M. Hoyle, 'Lettice and Lovage', *The Financial Times*, 28 October 1987, p. 23. See also E. Pall, 'The Fine Art Of Disappearing Into a Role', *The New York Times*, 25 March 1990, p. 5; the critic considered that there was something about Smith that 'announces itself', as if it was impossible to see her in a play or a movie without recognising her.

241 A. Stephen, 'The very model of an actress's actress: Maggie Tyzack', *The Observer*, 10 June 1990, p. 46.

242 Pall, 'The Fine Art Of Disappearing Into a Role'.

243 D. Hatwell, 'Only in the theatre do I ever really come alive', *The Evening Post*, 24 March 1965, p. 34.

244 *Distinguished Company* (London: Heinemann, 1972), p. 112.

Smith also possesses the neutrality that full metamorphosis requires.[245] She does not dress in an extravagant or ostentatious manner, she behaves discreetly, always with both elegance and simplicity. A few years ago, she even affirmed that she could go unnoticed in public: 'I'm never recognised in the street.'[246] Many people come across her, in London or in Sussex, and few recognise her, as it is difficult to identify this elegant and unostentatious lady with the larger-than-life characters she usually plays. Only her eyes, when they are not concealed behind sunglasses, can betray her. Far from being a recluse in the Greta Garbo manner, she nevertheless flees boisterous parties and society events, and she is rarely photographed, except when she attends the odd premiere or awards ceremony. Of course, things have changed slightly with *Downton Abbey*, but it is certain that the actress does not seek publicity and does not aim to shine when she is not acting. In the late 1980s, the journalist Barbara Isenberg described an actress much more restrained in real life than she appeared on the stage or screen, an 'ordinary' woman ready to be metamorphosed once more by an 'extraordinary' role. [247] Just like Edith Evans or Peggy Ashcroft in the past, not only does Smith keep her private life away from the public, but she also rarely gives interviews. She loathes idle questions about acting or pointless comments on her current work. The actress's latest in-depth interviews were given in the late 1980s, when husband Beverley Cross (half-) opened the door of their home to journalists and photographers. But these interviews, rare and quite respectful of her privacy, were rather different from the glamorous reports from the late 1960s and early 1970s, when the Stephens, Robert and Maggie, gladly answered questions of journalists from *Life* or *Vogue* about their life and their common projects on stage and on screen. These days, the actress avoids the media as much as her popularity, ever increased by her TV success, permits it.

245 For M. Gussow, Gambon's face is a blank canvas waiting to be 'filled with expressiveness' and his body seems to change its shape when the role requires it. See Gussow, *Gambon. A life in acting*, p. 15.

246 A. McAfee, 'The Enigmatic Prime of Dame Maggie Smith', *The Evening Standard*, 3 September 1992, p. 24. See also M. Coveney, 'Our last great star', *The Daily Mail*, 4 November 1997, p. 9; Coveney wrote that, like Olivier, she could blend in with the crowd without being recognised. It has changed.

247 'The Many Reflections of Maggie Smith', *The Los Angeles Times*, 16 February 1988, p. 1. See also C. Fox, 'Grande dame of the old bags', *The Daily Telegraph*, 19 March 2007, p. 29.

That distant and restrained behaviour is nevertheless a key element in her work. Maggie Smith maintains a halo of mystery around herself, what irritates nosy fans and gossip hunters, but makes her portrayals even more convincing. The general public, who knows so well the Dowager Countess, has not a very clear idea of what Maggie Smith really looks like. In an article written in 1994, the journalist Mick Brown emphasised the sublime, elusive malleability of Maggie Smith's face, declaring that it was like 'a stage', an empty stage that was ready to be transformed and the exact shape of which no photographer could capture.[248] The public face of the actress never outdoes the face of Minerva McGonagall or Violet Crawley. Surprisingly, these characters look profoundly dissimilar, but it does not seem to disturb the spectators. For many people, these two images, alternatively or successively, coexist. Being underexposed, Maggie Smith lends her features even more easily to the various characters she has to portray, sporting effortlessly any kind of outfit. Although she regularly plays contemporary roles, period costumes suit her better than anybody else. Each time, she seems to have stepped out of an oil painting or a history book, and in his biography of the actress, Michael Coveney beautifully wrote that her delicate, malleable features lend themselves to every period of history.[249] On Smith, costumes do not look like costumes – even less like fancy dress, what is unfortunately the case for some young performers these days – and she always remains convincing. She could be a Roman matron (she has already played a Greek goddess), a medieval lady or a Georgian marchioness with the same authenticity. Undoubtedly, her physical appearance helps, as if her face and her frame had been built for that purpose, but she also possesses an innate talent for wearing with ease costumes of any style and any epoch. Her body seems to adapt itself to the outfit and she immediately adopts the ideal posture which exactly corresponds to the figure she portrays. Maggie Smith knows just how to swing a crinoline and nobody can sweep into a bow as gracefully as she does. Attending an 'In Conversation' event at the BFI Southbank in April 2017, the veteran thespian thanked the audience's standing-ovation by dropping an immaculate – and agile – curtsey that could have made many young aspiring actresses envious.

248 'Maggie, Moody and Magnificent', *The Telegraph Magazine*, 12 November 1994, p. 43.
249 *Maggie Smith. A Biography*, p. 151.

Smith's use of the costume is also part of her characterisation strategy. To become a dowager worthy of the name, the actress had to be transformed. Costume and make-up designers helped her to get rid of her physical vulnerability which would have seemed out of tune with the character. Susannah Buxton, the costume designer for Season 1, got her inspiration from Queen Mary to create the dowager countess's wardrobe, and made the actress carry a huge bustle draped in heavy fabrics.[250] Topped with oversized hats, her figure is certainly more imposing than elegant, but at least the goal is achieved. Under Violet's armour, Smith is – save the eyes – unrecognisable and conveys an indisputable authority. From then on, she has been physically identified with Violet Crawley to the point that, when *The Best Exotic Marigold Hotel* was released, in 2012, *Downton Abbey* fans were astounded when seeing Maggie Smith, their favourite dowager, wearing jeans and Converse to portray Muriel Donnelly. There was nothing to be amazed of. Reviewing W. Gaskill's *The Beaux' Stratagem* in 1970, the critic B. Nightingale described – so vividly and so rightly – her amazing talent for metamorphosis: 'A purr becomes a quiet growl becomes an ecstatic snap of the jaws: the cat turns chameleon turns crocodile [...] Who ever saw such biological bravura in a woman?'[251] Smith definitely is a protean creature, one of the most polymorphous actors ever.

250 W. Lee Adams, 'Downton Abbey's Costume Designer on How to Dress Like an Edwardian', *Time Magazine*, 19 February 2012 < http://entertainment.time.com/2012/02/19/downton-abbeys-costume-designer-on-how-to-dress-like-an-edwardian/?iid=sr-link1> [accessed 12 November 2016]. The purpose was to make the Dowager Countess – the dominant figure in the series – appear strong and powerful. Buxton made a distinction between costume and fashion; while fashion aims at making a person look thin and beautiful, costume emphasises the character and helps it develop.

251 'With a Human Face', *The New Statesman*, 1 January 1970, p. 560.

Mabel's Stratagem

Michael Redgrave celebrated 'the magic of verbal control, the understanding and manipulation of words' that characterised Edith Evans's acting.[252] More specifically, John Gielgud pointed out that the great thespian undeniably privileged her phrasing rather than her moves on the stage. Having directed Evans in several plays, from *The Importance* to Bagnold's *The Chalk Garden*, he compared her with these Murano glass figurines which slowly turn, but never move; she played with her

252 Redgrave, *The Actor's Ways and Means*, p. 30.

voice rather than her body.[253] When she played Lady Bracknell, Evans's performance was mostly verbal and it is as such that it was praised by the critics. Compared with Dame Edith's acting, Maggie Smith's appears essentially physical, based on facial expressions and eloquent gestures, what some critics have called a real 'body language'. The actress always makes a clever use of the props that are lent to her so that, in her hands, an innocuous umbrella turns into the most redoubtable javelin. In his rave notice on Smith's Bracknell, the critic C. Spencer drew a striking, hilarious picture of the fierce lady brandishing her umbrella 'like an offensive weapon' as if to stress her nasal razor-sharp inflections.[254] At the Aldwych, too, De Jongh, scrupulously checking all the key components of the Smith device – the pinched lips, the rolling eyes, the disdainful chin, also noticed that her parasol had become 'an instrument of command'.[255] If a parasol is an instrument of command, a walking stick inevitably becomes the most redoubtable bludgeon in the lady's delicate hands and Smith efficiently used it, in *Three Tall Women* first and, later, in *The Lady in the Van*.

In a recent article published in *The Guardian*, the novelist Tessa Hadley captured very well Maggie Smith's potential, asserting that the physical appearance and means of an actor – his face, his voice and his gesture – are endowments with which his talent has to 'negociate', and this gift is necessarily restrictive: he can transform himself only within the limits of his 'bodily repertoire'.[256] With a different face and a different body, Smith would not have been Smith and, precisely, Mother Nature generously gifted the actress who has at her disposal an array of particularly efficient tools. The most diabolic instrument of Maggie Smith's comical genius is incontestably her eyes. She has immense eyes of an infinite sadness which are simply magnificent when at rest, but become redoubtable or incredibly funny when she wants them to be so. To express fright, disgust, bewilderment or anger, her eyes widen to the point that they get round and protuberant like those of a night owl; Smith's eyes – huge, blue and

253 Quoted in A. Macaulay, 'The "perfect pitch" and classical versatility of Dame Edith Evans. Laughter beyond Bracknell', *The Times Literary Supplement*, 29 September 2006, p. 18-19. See also B. Forbes, *Ned's Girl. The authorized biography of Dame Edith Evans* (London: Elm Tree Books, 1977), p. 61.

254 Spencer, 'Dame Maggie's night of triumph'.

255 De Jongh, 'Dame Maggie handbags her way into history'.

256 'A walking, talking flame', *The Guardian*, 24 January 2015, p. 18.

incredibly expressive – are indubitably the most useful weapon in her performing arsenal. Her nose, which always remains unnoticed in her dramatic roles, suddenly looks longer and sharper when she plays comedy, and her chin, often held up, confers on her the elegant and irresistibly funny allure of a wading bird. Another of Smith's most evident tools is her mouth, which she is able to pucker or distort at will. Wrinkling her nose and pulling back her chin, the actress is able to enlarge, tighten or pinch her mouth, in order to look unrecognisable. This incomparable ability to pout and grimace gives an immediate cuteness to the most formidable figures she portrays; thanks to her hilarious faces, Constance Trentham and Betsey Trotwood become as funny and adorable as Muppets or cartoon characters.

However, despite all her talent for metamorphosis, Maggie Smith certainly cannot play any role. The range of characters she is able to portray is necessarily limited by her looks and her means. 'An actor can never altogether escape his form and his features. They are the medium of his art,' the journalist Edith J. R. Isaacs wrote in her essay on typecasting.[257] Beneath make-up and characterisation, some small part of the actor's appearance and personality always subsists, whether it is his voice, his eyes or his mannerisms:[258] on stage, Miss Shepherd – the Lady in the Van – had piercing, scary blue eyes with dark rings around them,[259] the same eyes Muriel Donnelly has in the first scenes of *The Best Exotic Marigold Hotel.* No matter how great his talent for transformation is, it is necessarily restricted by constraints of age, physical appearance and natural demeanour, although these limitations do not diminish the truth of the character. Nevertheless, it has to be admitted that, in Maggie Smith's case, these limits are extended very far. Of course, Smith will never play a teenager now, neither would she be convincing as a science fiction superhero (though that still has to be

257 Isaacs, 'Type-casting: The eighth deadly sin', p. 135. See also R. Speaight, *Acting: its Idea and Tradition* (London: Cassel, 1939), p. 29: 'Versatility is only admirable in so far it enables an actor to give a number of good performances [...]. An actor must recognise not only the truth of the character he plays, but the facts of his physical or temperamental limitations.'

258 Speaight, *Acting*, p. 25: 'The means of [...] interpretation are the personality and the physical habit of the player [...]. Acting is interpretation; it is not disguise.'

259 In the 2015 movie, Smith wears cinematic make-up which looks lighter and more natural, at least from the spectator's point of view.

proven), but she can portray characters of different ages or different social status, she can play women with a heart of gold as well as vile creatures, and she tackles with the same brilliance farce and tragedy. Just like Edith Evans, a master of versatility, Smith can become – as convincingly – a beggar or a servant, as well as a millionairess or a monarch. Her physical appearance and her pitch perfect technique allow her to play a very large number of roles. Moreover, even if her timbre of voice is so characteristic that her detractors make use of it to parody her, Maggie Smith is able to modulate it in any way she wishes, so that it fits the age, the social background or the nationality of the character; cockney accent for Muriel Donnelly, Scottish accent for McGonagall, South American accent for Caro Bennett in *The Divine Secrets of the Yaya Sisterhood* or quavering voice for Miss Shepherd and old Mrs Docherty in *Nanny McPhee and the Big Bang*. Maggie Smith's voice is completely malleable and, although her minor contribution to *Gnomeo and Juliet* (K. Ashbury, 2011) did not give her the opportunity to fully display her skills, she would do wonderfully well in dubbing animated movies. The actress manages to give unpredictable inflections to her voice, changing the meaning of a line by stressing the unexpected word in a sentence or, like she did in *The Importance of Being Earnest*, the unexpected sentence in a speech.

Her body language is equally expressive. Once called 'Lady of the Wrists' by the movie critic Pauline Kael, the actress is renowned not only for the acute precision of her timing – especially when she gives a subtle pause to cap a critical remark – but also for her fluttering fingers and wringing wrists. As a general rule, Maggie Smith confers on her character, when the script requires it, an inimitable and colourful demeanour, using repetitive gesticulations and mannerisms that inevitably annoy the naysayers. In a book dedicated to the great actors of the British stage, Brian Master undercuts Smith's virtuosity, reducing it to a merely caricatural mechanism. He regards her as a comic performer whose 'vocabulary' essentially lies in the extravagant use she makes of her bodily skills, especially that restless hand flapping which often makes her look like a signalman using flag 'semaphore'.[260] Over the course of the chapters, the author scrupulously castigates the voice, the technique and, generally speaking, the acting of an actress whom he obviously does not appreciate but nevertheless ranks among the 'great actors' he writes about. In reality, Maggie Smith has every

260 *Thunder in the Air. Great Actors in Great Roles* (London: Oberon, 2000), p. 128.

part of her body under control and she artfully makes use of the gift that the Good Lord has bestowed on her. T. Hadley's final point was that Smith's body proves to be 'intelligent' in itself.[261] In fact, the actress's body is as agile as her face is expressive. To cast her as a bed-ridden or wheelchair-bound character deprives the audience of half of her skills, even if she has proved several times that no wheelchair or Zimmer frame could prevent her from giving an outstanding and colourful performance.[262] It is a real shame that she has been playing mostly, for the last five years, ladies in need of a hip-replacement or old biddies leaning on a stick; Smith is built to move.[263] Every ounce of her body acts. She masters with an incredible agility all her joints and muscles, and alters at will the appearance of her figure or her face. In this respect, she has the same abilities as Alec Guinness who easily transformed himself without the help of make-up.[264] In 1993, the critic David Nathan commented on her performance as Bracknell, observing that, when she smiled at the curtain call, you were able to fully appraise the involvement of her 'facial muscles' in her characterisation.[265] Maggie Smith wrinkles her forehead or raises her eyebrows and instantly becomes unrecognisable. Just like a virtuoso, the actress makes use of her body as if it was an instrument. And that instrument is a Stradivarius.

To take but one example among a long list of characters, it could be interesting to observe the actress in action, in one of the rare parts of villain she has played until now, Mabel Pettigrew in Jack Clayton's *Memento Mori* (1992). Mrs Pettigrew is an obnoxious, evil but, paradoxically, good-looking woman. Precisely, it is through her body language that Smith

261 Hadley, 'A walking, talking flame'.

262 About her performance in *Three Tall Women*, Martin Spence wrote in *Midweek* (19 October 1995): '*Three Tall Women* (Wyndham's) shattered one of my dearest dreams. For years I have hoped to see Maggie Smith on a zimmer. There alone would her infamous hand gesture suffer inevitable restraint. But no.'

263 Approached by N. Hytner in 2002, Smith refused to play Winnie in Beckett's *Happy Days* as she was not enthusiastic at the idea of being buried to the neck during the play; see D. Rosenthal, *The National Theatre History* (London: Oberon, 2013), p. 701.

264 See S. Callow, *Being an Actor*, 2nd edn (London: Penguin, 1995), p. 184. As Callow explains, Laurence Olivier was an adept of make-up and prosthetics that he used to 'substitute' another face for his own. For his part, Alex Guinness successfully managed, 'by thought alone', and with the help of his facial muscles, to transform his face and become the character.

265 'The Importance of Being Earnest', *The Jewish Chronicle*, 12 March 1993, p. 17.

reveals the perversity of the attractive lady she portrays. Clayton wanted to adapt Muriel Spark's novel – a geriatric black comedy – since its publication (1959), but he had to wait for several decades before producers became interested in a story involving very old people.[266] Besides, when the movie eventually got funded, Spark rejected the screenplay which had been submitted to her and it had to be rewritten by Clayton's assistant, Jeanie Sims, who took account of the novelist's objections. Because of all these difficulties, the project was delayed but, at, least, it gave the director the chance to cast the actress he had always wanted to play the hateful Mrs Pettigrew. When the TV movie was released, he confessed that he would not have done it *without* Maggie Smith.[267] Muriel Spark would not have contradict; in April 1991, the novelist sent a letter to Clayton, confessing that she always found Maggie Smith 'magical'.[268] Still, the actress was much too young, then, to play seventy-three-year-old Mabel Pettigrew. The American critic Kay Gardella – who overall hailed Clayton's movie and Smith's performance – clumsily pretended that the actress was heavily made up to look the right age, and thus seemed to have stepped out of 'an English vaudeville house'.[269] Actually, Maggie Smith had not been made up to look older. On the contrary, as the action takes place in the years after WWII, her Mrs Pettigrew could easily be thought of as a quadragenarian or a young quinquagenarian of that time. Her hair immaculately swept high in an elegant French pleat, Smith wears tailored suits in the 1950s style which make her resemble a model for Dior's Nouvelle Vague. Beautiful, ambitious and calculating, the ominous Mrs Pettigrew is far too refined to stoop to attending upon old Charmian Colston (R. Asherson) who has just hired her as a housekeeper, and she tries as hard as she can to have the poor woman sent to a nursing home.

Like many of their acquaintances, the Colstons – Charmian and husband Godfrey (Michael Hordern) – receive anonymous phone calls of the scariest genre. The mysterious caller terrifies all these elderly Londoners by reminding them that their death is imminent and, above all, inexorable:

266 M. Church, 'The old school of funny turns', *The Observer*, 19 April 1992, p. 65.

267 L. Middlehurst, 'There's Nothing Like THIS Dame', *The Daily Mail*, 18 April 1992, p. 33.

268 Letter dated 2 April 1991, Clayton's archive, BFI collections.

269 K. Gardella, 'A "Masterpiece" to die for. "Memento Mori" is a most amusing PBS mystery', *The New York Daily News*, 22 October 1992 (page not known).

'Remember you must die'. Although a retired inspector (John Wood) conducts an investigation, the phone calls get more and more frequent and Mabel Pettigrew takes advantage of the troubled situation, blackmailing and threatening several members of the small community. As a fearsome legacy huntress, she associates with the impecunious son of her employers to extort some money from them, and even insinuates that she could poison Charmian if she wanted to. Mrs Pettigrew is a special role in Maggie Smith's career, insofar as this character is completely unsympathetic. The characters whom the actress usually plays are not hateful, they always reveal a softer side or an inner vulnerability that makes them touching or even lovable. Mabel Pettigrew does not go through a final redemption, she is simply defeated, confounded and fired. In *The Daily Express*, M. Paton praised her brilliant portrayal of a 'female Uriah Heep'.[270] Pettigrew is an evil woman, a poisonous flower and, like Violet Venable, she reminds us of many characters portrayed by Bette Davis.

To give life to Mrs Pettigrew, Smith does an amazing physical work. Her face could be compared to a palette of which she uses, like a painter, all the nuances, to alternatively express irony, disappointment, triumph, furor, hypocrisy and contrived naivety. A sweep of kohl underlines her very mobile eyes, round and penetrating like those of a bird of prey, and her red lipstick highlights a sardonic and toothy grin which strongly resembles the smile of Cinderella's wicked stepmother in the Disney movie. Quite accurately, the journalist from *The Washington Times* compared the actress's thin, pinched lips to 'snipping scissors'.[271] The critic Philip Strick, in *Sight and Sound,* also mentioned 'a scathing repertoire of sniffs, groans and glances.'[272] Mabel Pettigrew constantly winces, alternating triumphant smiles and disappointed pouts – she even becomes violent and ill-tempered when she hears that she will not inherit Lisa Brooke, her former employer – and most of Maggie Smith's performance lies in a physical tour de force. Lester Middlehurst wrote a rave notice for *The Daily Mail*, hailing an exceptional piece of work, where Smith, making the most of one infinitesimal vocal inflection or facial expression, gloriously

270 'Television Week-End View', *The Daily Express*, 18 April 1992, p. 33.

271 R. Dreher, 'Actors liven up "Memento Mori"', *The Washington Times*, 25 October 1992 (page not known).

272 *Sight and Sound,* June 1992, p. 56.

stole the whole show.[273] In his excellent monograph on Jack Clayton, Sinyard also pays tribute to the extraordinary skills the actress displays here, stressing the very special way Smith suggests deceitfulness with a slight cock of her head when she speaks, what distorts her inflection and give it a particular tone, imbued both with irony and duplicity.[274]

Moreover, it is essentially by a clever and well-mastered use of her body that Smith meticulously draws the character. It appears that the predatory housekeeper lurks behind every door in the house, spying her soon-to-be victims. Like a reptile, she creeps in everywhere and pops up at the most unexpected moment. In his review, B. Nightingale described Mrs Pettigrew as a deceitful, rapacious creature who ambushes the frail prey that Charmian Colston is. Affecting refined manners and false affability, Pettigrew surreptitiously lets show her true wicked nature.[275] As usual, critics seized the opportunity to compare Smith's character to different obnoxious or venomous animals. M. Coveney compared Mrs Pettigrew to a snake, whereas some others preferred to see her as a vulture. In *The Sunday Telegraph*, the journalist Sean Day-Lewis described the sinister 'hovering' of the 'vulture-housekeeper' that Mrs Pettigrew is: stalking and spying her soon-to-be preys, the rapacious Mabel eagerly awaits for the spoils that one of these old dears could leave her.[276] Furthermore, there were some reviewers who related the malevolent housekeeper to the fantastic bestiary. In *The Daily Telegraph*, R. Last, mixing the species, called Smith a 'would be siren' of seventy years whose brutal fierceness was that of a 'female basilisk'.[277] In the chapter he dedicates to *Memento Mori*, N. Sinyard analyses with great acuteness the scene where Mabel attempts to force old Charmian to have her medication dose for the second time. Maggie Smith uses her thin phalanges, articulated like the legs of a spider, to move the pills on the table as if they were pawns on a chessboard. Sinyard emphasises the fact that Clayton generates suspense focusing his camera on the outrageously red-varnished fingernails of Mabel Pettigrew who, at one moment, starts to perform a mysterious finger choreography around the pills, in the manner

273 Middlehurst, 'There's Nothing Like THIS Dame'.

274 Sinyard, *Jack Clayton*, p. 196.

275 'Triumph of the old-timers', *The Times*, 20 April 1992, p. 29.

276 S. Day-Lewis, Pick of the Day 'Memento Mori', *The Sunday Telegraph*, 19 April 1992, p. xxiv.

277 'Old Star shine brightest', *The Daily Telegraph*, 20 April 1992, p. 15.

of a 'spidery predator' ready to catch its quarry.[278] As dark and svelte as a giant *Tegenaria* (commonly, and quite properly, called 'house spider'), Mabel Pettigrew stalks her prey like a spider stalks the fly which foolishly ventures onto her trapping cobweb.

Mrs Pettigrew does not content herself in being fearsome and Machiavellian, though. She also hides a vulgar side which is quite rare among the characters whom the actress is accustomed to play. Mabel briskly knocks back the Colstons' whiskey, smokes like a chimney and, despite her respectable age, does her best to seduce the master of the house. Great amateur of stockings and garters, old Godfrey Colston is immediately corrupted by the dangerous charms of the new housekeeper – what gives Smith a good reason for revealing her perfect legs. Just after Lisa Brooke's funeral, when all the attendees gather in a tea shop, Mrs Pettigrew readjusts a recalcitrant suspender and meets old Godfrey's concupiscent eyes. She smiles, immediately realising that she will be able to take advantage of his weakness at any time.[279] Later, when she works as a lady companion at the Colstons', she goes down the stairs with a lascivious air – being well aware that Godfrey is gazing at her – and ostentatiously hitches up her skirt to adjust her stockings.[280] The spectator guesses, then, that she will use her charms and make the old man pay to contemplate her garters, just like the young Olive Mannering (Zoe Wanamaker) did previously. It is quite rare to see Smith portraying such a sensual, even provocative character. With some nail polish on their fingernails, the chaste hands which belong, in other films, to Betsey Trotwood or Janet Widdington become outrageously sexy when it comes to lighting a cigarette. Perfectly conscious of her sex-appeal, Mabel regularly checks her immaculate bun with one manicured hand, conspicuously sways her hips when walking and winks at the men she fancies, like Inspector Mortimer. Unquestionably, Mrs Pettigrew has a past as a seductress.

However, although she is terrifying, Mabel Pettigrew retains, thanks

278 Sinyard, *Jack Clayton*, p. 202.

279 This scene was inserted in the final script (shooting script by A. Kelley, J. Sims et J. Clayton), whereas it did not appear in the first version (P. Prince, March 1990). Thanks to Maggie Smith, it spices the movie with a delightful comical note.

280 In the initial script, the scene was located in Pettigrew's bedroom. Godfrey knocked at the door and entered. Sitting on a chair, the housekeeper raised the hem of her skirt – just like Olive used to do – to let the old man gaze at her thighs.

to Maggie Smith and her subtle, distanced approach – underpinned by insisting looks and high-pitched voice inflections – some aspects of a comical figure. Spark, who had been a great admirer of the actress since *The Prime of Miss Jean Brodie*, was particularly enthusiastic about her portrayal of Pettigrew. In a letter sent to Clayton after the release, she wrote that Smith was a perfect casting choice, making her Mabel Pettigrew a character simultaneously funny and scary.[281] Mrs Pettigrew certainly corresponds to one of the actress's most striking performances, all the more that she had to tackle with a kind of character she had never played until then, the evil woman. As glamorous as her Miss Pettigrew looks, she produces the same chilling impression as Anna Massey did in the unforgettable BBC series *Rebecca*.[282] Undoubtedly, Smith would have been the most outstanding Mrs Danvers, had she been cast in the part a few years ago.

281 Letter quoted in Middlehurst, 'There's Nothing Like THIS Dame'.

282 *Rebecca*, dir. S. Langton, BBC 1978.

Transfigured by Grace

Maggie Smith does not play only pinched aristocrats and commanding schoolmistresses, she also excels in playing against type. To play against type can be regarded as the unavoidable result of miscasting, when an actor plays disappointingly a part that he should never had played. With regard to Smith, to play against type is art brought to its utmost perfection. In the movie *Keeping Mum* (N. Johnson, 2005), the actress is the only one, among the cast, who illustrates the notion of full characterisation. She is the only one who has to go through a physical transformation to play her role. Despite being a master of disguise, Maggie Smith parsimoniously resorts to technical tools or artifices such as make-up, wigs and costumes. Aunt Augusta in *Travels in my Aunt* and Granny Wendy in *Hook* stand as two significant exceptions on a long list of old crones; those are the only parts which required that she wore a silicone mask to look older. For her other roles, even for the oldest characters she had to portray, she only wore a more or less pronounced make-up. Smith is an absolute performer. Not only does she fully become the character, lending this fictional figure her body and her voice, but she is more able than anybody else to transform her instrument. She skilfully uses her means and, if necessary, she also can outstrip them to totally morph into the character. Whatever the part, whatever the age or the physical appearance of the character, she will give a definitive performance. In 1984, interviewed by the filmmaker Mary Harron for *The Observer*, Smith complained about the fact she never had to play 'common people' on screen, admitting that she could count on one hand the parts she had played in 'modern dress', as she was never cast in an 'everyday' situation.[283] Bad luck. In *Keeping Mum*, the actress was cast in an everyday situation, but her character was everything but ordinary and, as Grace Hawkins, she was properly unrecognisable.

Keeping Mum is above all a comedy, carried by Rowan Atkinson in a role quite different from his celebrated Mr Bean. The story in itself is quite funny and unusual. Having served a forty-three year prison sentence for the murder of her adulterous husband, an elderly lady intentionally gets hired as a housekeeper in the home of her own daughter, Gloria (K. Scott-Thomas), who is married to the local vicar, Reverend Goodfellow (Atkinson). The energetic housekeeper – who pretends to be called Grace Hawkins although her real name is Rosie Jones – undertakes to solve all Gloria's conjugal and domestic issues, using murder when it is necessary. She gets confounded by her daughter at the time the situation is sorted out and, having accomplished her duty, the murderous Poppins leaves the now happy family as discreetly as she had come. Grace definitely is a mysterious character. She firstly appears as a voice-over – the voice of a woman who comes to rescue Petey, Gloria's little boy, who is regularly bullied by his fellow pupils – and the spectator does not get to see her. In her first proper

283 'Miss Smith and Betty the pig', *The Observer*, 18 November 1984, p. 25.

scene, she remains in the distance, as a silhouette, but no one could guess that the character is played by Maggie Smith. Dressed in a funny purple gored coat, Grace looks surprisingly short and stout. The lady is as round and beaming as Smith's characters are usually angular and sharp. When she meets, at last, the Goodfellows, we get to see more of her. Grace has a plump face, enlightened by the most cheerful smile. She is a sweet, adorable elderly lady who – apart from the eyes – does not look at all like Smith. In fact, 'elderly lady' is not exactly the word. Grace/Rosie was pregnant forty-three years earlier and she was at the most twenty-five by then. Accordingly, Grace must be in her late sixties and she is, by no means, what might be called an old lady nowadays. When she arrives at Reverend Goodfellow's home, she is immediately confronted with the nosy old neighbour, Mrs Parker (Liz Smith) and then, simultaneously, the spectator is reminded of another pairing of the two actresses. Smith and Smith – Liz and Maggie – played mother and daughter in Malcolm Mowbray's hilarious movie *A Private Function,* in 1984. It is quite a shock to see the two of them together again. While Liz Smith plays a similar character – the dotty old lady –, it is more striking to see what has become of the middle-class (but glamorous) Joyce Chilvers.

The actress has never looked so plain before. For the movie, Smith had to wear the wardrobe of a perfect lady parishioner, granny boots, carpet slippers, old-fashioned skirts and hand-knitted cardigans, that is the opposite extreme of the sumptuous outfits she usually wears on screen. In the way she dresses, Grace looks terribly outdated and common, and it is quite a treat to see Dame Maggie in the (sensible) shoes of a lower middle-class woman. The critic from *The Daily Express* joked that the most interesting aspect of the movie was to see 'the peerless Dame Maggie Smith in a tea cosy hat'.[284] Thanks to the costume designer, no detail had been overlooked. Thick woollen tights hid the actress's svelte ankles and made them look larger, while a grey wig, done into a grannyish perm, radically changed her appearance. Moreover, props and make-up apart, Smith stretches her astonishing ability to distort her jaw in order to enlarge the bottom of her face and lose these angular features which characterise her – a trick that she already used when playing, on stage, Miss Shepherd in *The Lady in the Van*. The result is breathtaking; Grace Hawkins stands

284 A. Hunter, 'Lazy comedy lacking laughs', *The Daily Express*, 2 December 2005, p. 44.

as a sweet, slightly plump granny, making the spectators forget that they are watching the actress who also plays the majestic Minerva McGonagall.

Maggie Smith adopts a very special posture when portraying the housekeeper – often turning her head one side and smiling – showing an apparent softness which seems too good to be true and hides a rather darker personality. We eventually discover that Grace is much more nervous and expeditive than we thought. In the football match scene, her odd behaviour suddenly suggests that the housekeeper has an interest in the Goodfellows' family issues. When she notices that Gloria and her American golf teacher, Lance (Patrick Swayze, in his last role), seem to be very close, she suddenly looks distraught, her large smile disappears and her face is invaded by sadness. This impression is confirmed when she accidentally answers Gloria's mobile phone and gets a call from the American guy. In a delightful quiproquo, Lance whispers to her that he intends 'to cover her body with coconut cream' and 'lick his way up slowly' to her most intimate parts. Grace's voice interrupts him sharply: 'That sounds lovely. When do we go?' The actress's facial expression is, of course, priceless, making this scene one of the funniest moments in the movie. Another scene, more moving, shows Grace preparing roast beef in the kitchen. Suddenly, the phone rings and her daughter Gloria leaves the room to answer the call of her American lover. Grace remains alone in the kitchen and her face starts to disintegrate. Her round face lengthens to transform into a thinner and more familiar one, that of Smith. She frowns, pinches her nose and becomes a figure of sorrow. It is a comedy, so we spectators know that we will laugh at the end, nevertheless Mrs Hawkins appears to be a more complex character than it seemed at the beginning. All these scenes aim at emphasising the housekeeper's surprising empathy with the Goodfellows' conjugal problems, preparing the revelation of Grace's real identity. Still, most of the comical efficiency of the film lies in the calm and the determination with which the woman kills off anyone – even the neighbour's little dog – who challenges her daughter's well-being. Grace Hawkins is a very clever and cunning woman (it can be assumed that she had to carefully investigate before finding Little Wallop, the charming hamlet where her daughter lives with her family) and she commits her murders in cold blood, never feeling any remorse afterwards. On the contrary, she remains quiet and relaxed, being proud of her crimes. In her own logic, she must do everything she can to remove any obstacle to Gloria's happiness, even if she has to commit murder for that. From that point of view, Grace is the most perfect mother.

That character represents a kind of interlude in Maggie Smith's career.[285] It was the very first time that she had to play a murderer and, on set, the crew jokingly nicknamed the actress 'Scary Poppins', seeing her character as a chilling version of P. J. Travers's heroine. The fact is that, just like Mrs Pettigrew (whose spectacles she has apparently borrowed from), Grace always makes sudden appearances and the other characters immanquably startle when she pops up. For that reason, the housekeeper represents not only a fairylike character, but also a disquieting figure which would have been a tailor-made role for an actress like Ruth Gordon. Grace is a well-organised, meticulous killer who protects her clothes from blood, wearing a plastic raincoat over her coat – just like Miss Shepherd protects her elaborate outfit from the yellow paint that she applies a bit too liberally. The motif of the murderous nanny is quite common these days on the big screen, at least in the thriller genre. But fifty years ago, *The Nanny* (S. Holt, 1965) already offered Bette Davis the role of a hair-rising housekeeper, a kind of negative of Mary Poppins. But, as suggested by V. Lawson in her biography of P. J. Travers, Davis's Nanny has come to kill, while Mary Poppins has come to work things out, to make 'order from disorder', and when it is all done, she can leave for her mysterious retreat.[286] *The Nanny* belongs, though, to another category, between horror and fantasy, in the vein of Polanski's *Rosemary's Baby* and Hitchcock's *Psycho*: Davis, terrifying, shivers up your spine, whereas Smith only prompts laughter.

Certainly closer to *Arsenic and Old Lace* or Ealing's classic *The Ladykillers*, *Keeping Mum* offers the actress one of her more original roles. Needless to say that there were, of course, a few critics who dared to assert that she was playing, once again, 'the same type'. When the film was released, the producer Julia Palau declared that the actress was cast against type because Grace was a murderer. In fact, the characterisation process mostly lies in the social downgrade. Grace Hawkins is a middle-class, impecunious woman; she is in professional reintegration after her long-term prison

285 S. Holden, 'Mary Poppins's Dotty Doppelgänger', *The New York Times*, 15 September 2006, p. 15. The critic rejoiced to see Maggie Smith playing on 'a lighter mode' than usual.

286 Lawson, *Mary Poppins*, p. 4.

sentence. Smith had never played a common middle-class woman and she had never played a sweet granny either. The actress playing upper-class characters most of the time, she never has to deal with prosaic matters and housework on screen. Here, we also get to see the housekeeper in action, what appears quite unusual; Grace masterfully irons clothes or ties a roast, activities that none of Smith's other characters could do without looking odd. It is quite hard to recognise the actress who played – five years earlier – the snobbish Countess Trentham, when seeing Grace Hawkins, in apron, opening the curtains to wake up her boss and hastily preparing an opulent breakfast for the whole Goodfellow family.[287] The picture looks like a TV advertisement for cereals and it is quite amazing to see how Smith merges well into that setting. She does look the part.

The film is only ten years old and it seems to have been slightly forgotten by the journalists who remain focused on her most recent TV role. In an apparently unostentatious comedy film, Maggie Smith gives one of her most mesmerising performances in terms of characterisation. Eyes apart – it would be quite difficult to hide these huge blue eyes – the actress is unrecognisable. Far, very far from Augusta Bracknell or Lady Gresham whom she would portray the following year in J. Jarrold's *Becoming Jane*, she adopts gestures and postures which are not her own and creates an original, compelling character. In other words, it is quite difficult to believe that Dame Maggie Smith herself stands behind that sweet old lady. For one hour and forty-five minutes, Grace Hawkins does exist and is a proper, real person who has nothing in common with the actress who plays her. Like Mother Superior in *Sister Act,* who seems to have escaped from a real convent, the viewers are tempted to believe that the production has hired a pensioner they met at the local supermarket. For once, Smith plays Mrs Patmore.

287 This is very sad that a hilarious scene that was in the script was eventually not filmed: it showed Grace trying to drive and crashing the car.

The Lady was a Tramp

Maggie Smith – the living incarnation of upper-class haughtiness – is not only able to portray servants and middle-class housewives, but she has no difficulty either to transform into the most repulsive bag lady. When Alan Bennett wrote his first account of Miss Shepherd's story in *The London Review of Books*, in 1989, he had absolutely no idea it would become a play. His only purpose was to put into words, in the form of an entertaining essay, his astonishing personal experience with a vagrant who incidentally got to spend many years in the driveway of his Camden house. As generous as naive, the famous playwright had invited Miss Mary

Shepherd (or more exactly, Sheppard, although it was not even her real name), an old lady with a disturbed mind, to park her derelict van in his drive for a few weeks and she eventually stayed for fifteen years. During these long years, Bennett had to cope with this obtrusive parasite, being alternatively amused, moved and exasperated by the old lady's behaviour. Although the playwright knew nothing about her background at that time – he would find out her real identity after her death and the publication of his autobiographical memoir – he got to discover bits and pieces of her story. Having studied the piano in Paris as a disciple of the virtuoso pianist Alfred Cortot, Margaret Fairchild (aka Miss Shepherd) gave up the music to become a nun, but failed twice as she was unable to accommodate herself to the life of the convent, and then escaped from a mental hospital where her brother had tried to have her kept. One day, a motorcyclist hit her van at a crossroads and died in the collision. Panic-stricken, the woman instinctively left the scene and evaded the police, making her way to destitution and homelessness. Of course, none of this appears in Alan Bennett's account which is essentially a pleasant chronicle on his daily encounters with his troublesome neighbour, but, a few years later, he decided to make a play of it, having, from the start, Maggie Smith in mind to portray the grumpy, filthy old lady.

Directed by Nicholas Hytner and produced by Robert Fox, the play opened in November 1999 at the Queen's Theatre. Having received rave reviews, it would run for nine months. It was undoubtedly a coup, as the production reunited one of the most celebrated British actresses, a highly successful writer and a prominent stage director. Bennett's original memoir was not easy to transpose on the stage and some critics blamed the playwright for having written what they considered a succession of sketches rather than a proper stage play. However, the chronology, which did not appear very clearly in the memoir, was more obvious here, and the audience witnessed the still vigorous, cantankerous woman of Act I slowly turning into the disabled – although no less cantankerous – old lady of Act II. The genuine originality of the play was the presence of two Bennetts on the stage, the inhabitant of Gloucester Crescent, 23 (the Good Samaritan who confronts the Lady) and the writer (slightly older, who stands as a caustic observer) discussing and arguing in front of the audience. The play gives rise to a reflection on human conscience, torn between guilt and generosity, and on the advantage that every writer takes from other people's lives. Since 1999, *The Lady in the Van* has had many revivals – all outside the West End – and its dramatic interest essentially lies in this interaction between the two Bennetts, whose reactions towards Miss Shepherd – successively embarrassment, disgust and sympathy – capture the attention of the audience. Nevertheless, to cast Maggie Smith as the titular lady was not insignificant. Played by her, the character gained an extraordinary aura. As expected, she appropriated Miss Shepherd forever, although it was indisputably a role against type for an actress more accustomed to play high-born ladies than tramps. The major consequence of such a casting was that it necessarily affected the balance between the protagonists. Less present – in terms of duration – on the stage, Miss Shepherd nevertheless caught the eye of the audience every time she emerged from her van, transforming the play into a one-star vehicle; with another actress playing the role, the balance is unavoidably different. Most of the critics extolled the exceptional quality of her portrayal, seizing on its realism. According to M. Billington, as the cantankerous Miss Shepherd, Maggie Smith gave her most 'disciplined' performance in many years, playing the part with admirable 'honesty',[288] while G. Brown commented on the technical perfection of her work. For Brown, Smith was no less than 'sublime' in the role of the repellent old eccentric. The critic praised her wondrous characterisation that gave life to a fearsome, ungrateful, but perfectly convincing 'creature of the wild'.[289]

Actually, Smith amazingly captured the wild manners of her character. The actress grasped not only the tics of the old lady,[290] but also the straight and pragmatic behaviour of someone who lives in the street. Miss Shepherd is always on the defensive, she is constantly quarrelsome, even towards those who give her a helping hand. As Billington underscored, she displays that ungrateful pride which belongs to people in dire need. She reluctantly accepts help, never expresses gratitude and even persuades

288 'Epitome of a hermit', *The Guardian*, 8 December 1999, p. 20.

289 'Maggie finds her perfect vehicle in the remade Van', *The Mail on Sunday*, 12 December 1999, p. 79.

290 De Jongh wrote that no other actor than Smith would be able to get a laugh with the appalling ordeals of old age ('The Van is merely a vehicle for Dame Maggie', *The Evening Standard*, 8 December 1999, p. 20).

her benefactors that she does them a favour when benefiting from their generosity. As noted by Billington, when presents are bestowed to her, this ruthless, unruly creature even 'bites' the hand which charitably feeds her.[291] She is an odious but nevertheless lovable character, as her lack of consideration and her bad faith rapidly get irresistible. Always convinced that she is right, with a frenetic diction which indicates a perturbed mind, Miss Shepherd delights us with her steadfast determination. Such an eccentric character offered Maggie Smith a chance to fully display her consummate abilities. Her deadpan comic timing did marvels with Bennett's funny dialogue and her larger-than-life impersonation was sublimated by Hytner's inventive staging, but, mostly, to portray Miss Shepherd represented a striking challenge. London theatregoers suddenly rushed to Shaftesbury Avenue to applaude, in the role of a 'urine-stinking old woman', an actress they had seen on television a few days earlier, playing a beautiful and majestic Queen Alexandra in J. Jarrold's *All The King's Men.*[292] This new part, which ran against the natural grain, allowed Smith to receive some of the ravest reviews of her career.

In *The Daily Mail*, M. Coveney's enthusiastic notice was illustrated by a full-length portrait of the lady in question, carrying a huge garbage bag. Smith had created a phantasmagorical, composite figure that some critics compared to different animals, from the saurian to the bird of prey. In his vibrant – and well deserved – panegyric, Coveney assumed that the chameleon actress obviously had fun playing a part that, for once, required a complete bodily transformation, and he developed on the feral quality of the formidable creature, seeing her as a hybrid (half-lizard, half-amphibian), fascinating and mostly daunting.[293] Her wagging tongue, that she flickered between her desiccated lips like a reptile would do, fascinated the reviewers who often compared her with a lizard, like Susannah Clapp (who pertinently mentioned her 'grandiloquent gestures' and 'lizard like' tongue springing out between her dried lips[294]) or Robert Butler (noting that Miss Shepherd constantly darts out her tongue, what makes her disgustingly resemble a frog trying to launch its sticky tongue

291 Billington, 'Epitome of a hermit'.

292 *All the King's Men* aired on television in November 1999.

293 'Maggie's got it in the bag', *The Daily Mail*, 10 December 1999, p. 56.

294 'Neighbourhood witch', *The Observer*, 12 December 1999, p. 7.

at flies[295]). Across the pond, the critic Paul Levy marvelled at Smith's fascinating performance, also mentioning the tip of her tongue which, 'lizard-like', darted out of Miss Shepherd's mouth.[296] As for N. De Jongh and B. Nightingale, they preferred the (more common) ornithological comparison. With that 'birdy-like' face, Smith was no more an exotic bird, but a wild-eyed raptor, as De Jongh wrote,[297] while Nightingale asserted that there was not another performer who could play Miss Shepherd better than Smith, whose aquiline profile and piercing eyes made the old lady in rags look like a battered, but frightening hawk.[298] Popping up out of her van like a predator springing out of its den, Smith was staggeringly realistic, to the point that she terrified Alan Bennett himself. Replacing the actor Nicholas Farrell on short notice for a matinee in November 1999, and thus playing his own role, the playwright had – just like Dr Frankenstein – to confront his 'creature' on the stage. In his own, hilarious style, the playwright recounts that his role necessitated that he stand next to the Lady and, years later, he remembers the scene vividly. Being that close to Maggie Smith in full costume, with her bulging eyes, her fierce expression and her formidable vigour, he felt insecure and he would have given anything to escape that crazy woman![299]

Paradoxically, as repellent and disgusting as she is, Smith's Shepherd remains amazingly grand and impressive. Against all odds, that tramp is also a lady. Repulsive and mentally unstable, Miss Shepherd is well-educated and talks with a certain refinement. In the manner of a queen in rags or a fallen empress, the old tramp rules over a Cour des Miracles – reduced to the size of Alan Bennett's front garden – populated by the toad, its friend the slug and the dozens of moths breeding in the plastic bags. As the critics noted, the actress perfectly rendered that narcissistic delirium that seemed to be Miss Shepherd's main pathology; the critic from *The Sunday Times* compared the lady to a proud sovereign who,

295 Butler, 'Driving Miss Crazy'.

296 'From Everyday Life to the London Stage', *The Wall Street Journal*, 17 December 1999, p. 15.

297 De Jongh, 'The Van is merely a vehicle for Dame Maggie'.

298 'Why the tramp was a lady', *The Times*, 9 December 1999, p. 50. A. Bennett himself talks about a 'pathetic scarecrow'. See *Writing Home*, 3rd ed. (London: Faber and Faber, 2006), p. 87.

299 A. Bennett, *Untold Stories* (London: Faber and Faber, 2005), p. 259.

having been banished from her realm, had lost nothing of her hauteur and innate authority.[300] Just like Prometheus, outrageousness – which is called hubris in the Greek tragedy, that is 'overestimation of one's own capabilities' – is probably her most prominent character trait. Despite her very particular way of life, the old lady feels equal to the high and mighty; she seriously considers getting elected Prime Minister and, thus, running the country from her van parked outside 10 Downing Street. Always imperious, categorical, never doubting of herself, she constantly asserts, the only nuance she brings to her assertions being that recurring, hilarious 'possibly' which punctuates, like a catchphrase, all her sentences.[301] But this 'possibly' aims more to raise doubt and insecurity in the mind of her interlocutor than to attenuate her statements. S. Morley compared her to Mrs Thatcher and, more generally, to all the great despots who see 'only right in (their) position'.[302] This natural authority is coupled with a certain sense of decorum. J. Peter emphasised Miss Shepherd's fascinating sense of 'pride, pomp and circumstance' which strongly contrasts with her battered appearance and her firm belief in her own superiority; she feels important, and thus concludes that she is.[303] In her daily life, the lady literally stages herself on her very own scene, getting in and out of her van like a Shakespearean actor got in and out of the tiring house. In fact, the character gravitates in a very particular sphere, from which any sane individual is excluded. Miss Shepherd lives in her own world, where politics and religion take a prominent place and her devotion tends towards fanaticism; her filthy, stinky den is the shrine where she daily implores the Virgin Mary. Quite appropriately, the play ends with an apotheosis in the literal sense of the term. It is not the chariot of the

300 J. Peter, 'Van of the moment', *The Sunday Times*, 12 December 1999, p. 16. See also De Jongh, 'The Van is merely a vehicle for Dame Maggie'. Paradoxically, Smith conferred an 'imperious grandeur' on this battered, smelly eccentric.

301 According to her personal logic, even her most insane assertions are common sense. The critic D. Nathan highlighted her unwavering 'independence of spirit' and sense of self, and, in a certain way, the coherence of her train of thought. *The Jewish Chronicle*, 10 December 1999 (see *Theatre Record*, 3-31 December 1999, p. 1633). She sees herself as someone perfectly normal, clean, elegant, and certainly not as an indigent woman.

302 'Bennett's Mad, Magnificent "Lady"', *The International Herald Tribune*, 15 December 1999 <http://www.nytimes.com/1999/12/15/style/bennetts-mad-magnificent-lady.html> [accessed 12 November 2016].

303 Peter, 'Van of the moment'.

Roman Emperor which is pulled up by a pair of eagles to the realm of the deities, but the old, derelict van which is hoisted to the House of God with the help of a pick-up truck crane.

Although she was a real person, Miss Shepherd acquired, through Smith's portrayal, a hieratic dimension. In *The Independent*, the critic P. Taylor waxed lyrical, comparing the battered old woman with a Rambo cap to some mythical heroine coming straight out of Priam's palace, a kind of dilapidated Hecub with a slight touch of eccentricity.[304] The actress conferred on the character a kind of ravaged grandeur which was quite disturbing. In his review, J. Gross rightfully pointed out that paradox: admitting that Miss Shepherd displays all the physical attributes of a grotesque figure, the critic nevertheless underscored the complexity of the character, whose dignity and regal composure strongly contrast with the sordid reality of her day-to-day life.[305] With her ambiguities and her poetical dimension, Miss Shepherd has much in common with another stage persona, the eponymous role in Jean Giraudoux's *The Madwoman of Chaillot* (1945). Just like the tramp imagined by the French playwright and immortalised by the great Marguerite Moreno,[306] Miss Shepherd remains, under her disgusting rags, as distinguished and proud as an aristocrat could be. Likewise, in her own way, she cares a lot about her appearance, sporting the most sophisticated outfits and headwear. A succession of rituals punctuates her life: her ritual prayers to the Virgin, the ritual maintenance of her multiple vehicles and the (more prosaic) ritual of the plastic bags, those that she kicks out of her van every day. The Madwoman's most famous monologue – where the old tramp describes her morning rituals, putting her false teeth in and generously applying antediluvian cosmetics on her face – slightly echoes Miss Shepherd's grandiloquent and pathetic arrangements:

---

304 'Lady and a tramp', *The Independent*, 9 December 1999, p. 11.

305 'It's clever and funny, but this van doesn't move', *The Sunday Telegraph*, 12 December 1999, p. 8.

306 Moreno (1871-1948) was one of the greatest French actresses in the first half of the twentieth century. In the second part of her career, she specialised in old crones and dowagers. The part was famously played, on screen, by Katharine Hepburn, in Bryan Forbes's *The Madwoman of Chaillot* (1969), and, on stage, by Angela Lansbury, in Jerry Herman's musical *Dear World* (1969).

> Of course, when you wake up, it is not always joyous. When you choose, in the Hindu box, your hair for the day, when you take your denture out of the only cup left after you have moved from Rue de la Bienfaisance, you may feel a little out of place in this lowly world. [...] Then, when you have washed your face with rosewater, and powdered it, not with this awful rice powder which does not nourish the skin, but with an old chunk of pure rice starch, when you have put on your jewels, all your brooches plus the little pins that the courtesans wear, and the Persian earrings with their teardrop pearls [...], then you are armed, you are strong, you are ready to start a new day (*The Madwoman of Chaillot*, Act I).[307]

The Madwoman of Chaillot uses her dilapidated parasol as a weapon, just like Miss Shepherd does with her walking stick,[308] and she indefatigably rereads, every morning, the same issue of her favourite newspaper:

> I read *Le Gaulois.* And I will not waste my time reading the news. I always read the same issue, that of October 7, 1896. It is by far the best one. It says all about the scandal of Countess Diane's lovers... There is a note on the fashionable corset à la Bressant and the last minute bulletin announces the death of Léonide Leblanc. She lived next door... Poor woman! Every morning, the news of her death gives me such a shock! I can't lend you my copy, though. It's in tatters (*The Madwoman of Chaillot*, Act I).

Maybe Miss Shepherd, who kept piles of rotting newspapers in her van, would have done and said quite the same.[309] In any case, it is as if the real person whom Bennett has turned into a literary character borrowed a lot from the fictional figure created by Giraudoux, that tramp who acts like a high-born duchess. Just like the Madwoman, Miss Shepherd behaves like an eccentric and sublime diva. Only Smith was able to convey to

307 J. Giraudoux, *La Folle de Chaillot* (Paris : Librairie Générale Française, 1991), p. 951-952.

308 On stage, Smith used Mrs Shepherd's real walking stick, carefully kept by A. Bennett; it still had some stains of yellow paint on it.

309 Oddly enough, it actually happens in another play by Alan Bennett; in *People*, Dorothy Stacpoole does read old newspapers.

the character that regal bearing which, despite all their talent, the other actresses who succeed her in the stage role generally fail to suggest.

While being a monstrous character – in the etymological sense of the word, that is 'extraordinary' – the redoubtable Lady gave Maggie Smith the best opportunity ever to fully display her acting skills. All the nuances, all the subtleties of the character are perceptible in her voice inflections. Most of the time, she vociferates, but suddenly stops and talks slowly to evoke her past or her traumas, breaking for one moment the heart of the spectator. C. Spencer noted that there were some moments in the play when Miss Shepherd seemed to get introspective, suddenly overwhelmed with 'anguish' and distress.[310] Miss Shepherd has the voice of a deluded, crazy woman when Bennett-the-character suggests that someone could collide with her van, shouting that no one is going to run into her. Spencer admitted he was captured by her performance, a prowess in terms of characterisation and technical precision; bundled in filthy rags and unrecognisable, Smith delivered her lines with the sharpest virtuosity.[311] Others, like B. Nightingale, lauded the accuracy of Smith's subtle approach, which made the character as hateful as pathetic. Without an ounce of sentimentality, she had skilfully developed the antithetical aspects of her character, fierce but vulnerable, making us pity a woman she had already made insufferable, callous and egotistic.[312] As John Russell Taylor explained in the glowing notice he wrote about the production, the actress makes use of her comical tools – those that some critics, in a reproving manner, call 'tricks' or 'mannerisms' – but she makes very clever use of them, with the sole purpose of serving the play. Playing Miss Shepherd, Smith may be considered as 'infuriating' and mannered as her character, but, precisely, he assumed that, aptly used,

310 'Bennett steers Smith to grumpy, grimy triumph', *The Daily Telegraph*, 8 December 1999, p. 3. See also De Jongh, 'The Van is merely a vehicle for Dame Maggie'; the critic noted that, at some point toward the end of the play, Maggie Smith's voice suddenly breaks as she recalls her past, the waste of her career as a virtuoso pianist and her aborted vocation as a nun, and the comical character turns into a tragic figure; Taylor, 'How an uninvited guest split Bennett's life in two'; P. Taylor described the heartbreaking moment where a soon-to-die Miss Shepherd, in her penultimate scene, recounts how easier it was for her to play the piano than pray; a priest warned her that music could deter her from God, and forbade her to play again, pretending that self-sacrifice would heighten her dividends in terms of spiritual growth. At this very moment, she realises that she has wasted her life.

311 Spencer, 'Bennett steers Smith to grumpy, grimy triumph'.

312 *Great Moments in the Theatre* (London: Oberon, 2012), p. 230.

these mannerisms greatly contributed to her outstanding characterisation.[313] Once again, her exceptional performance reduced her detractors to aporia. It is unquestionably very difficult to find the right words to criticise a work of genius. While blaming Smith's overpowering scene-stealing, N. De Jongh admitted its undeniable efficience, saying that, although the show was more a 'display' than a play, it allowed her to give a performance which lived up to her genius.[314]

The physical transformation was total. Made up with (false) dirt, wearing a greasy dishevelled wig and covered with layers of dubious coloured rags, Smith had taken the role with great zest and demonstrated an audacity that few actresses would have. Despite her status and her physical appearance, she did not hesitate to undergo a complete metamorphosis to become the dirty, smelly old tramp. The uniqueness of her performance lay in the fact that, whereas some actresses had reached old age before portraying such elderly figures, Maggie Smith was still young and beautiful when playing Shepherd on stage – as much as she was (less young but still) youthful and beautiful when reprising the role for the big screen, in 2014 – what increased the challenge. In *The Times Literary Supplement*, the journalist Robert Shore rejoiced in the fact that Alan Bennett's play allowed the audience the opportunity to see the extremely elegant Dame Maggie sashaying on the stage in the filthiest and most unflattering outfit.[315] Miss Shepherd perfectly exemplifies the absolute characterisation. This is just the kind of unglamorous part – a cantankerous, incontinent, repulsive old woman – that every consummate performer should dream of, and the actress had indeed great fun in playing it. In his diaries, Alan Bennett recounts how gladly Smith transformed herself into the lady, improving her elaborate make-up every night. Although she was continuously complaining about the difficulty she had to put on her heavy make-up (and the greater difficulty to remove it), the actress undoubtedly had fun being made up and transforming into Miss Shepherd, so that she even

313 'The Lady in the Van', *Plays International Magazine*, January 2000, p. 18. *Contra*, see A. Macaulay, 'Too many Alans spoil the broth', *The Financial Times*, 9 December 1999, p. 20. Macaulay was one of the rare reviewers who disliked the play and vigorously criticised Maggie Smith's portrayal, declaring that this consummate actress was, unfortunately, 'at her worst' here and gave a performance which was nothing but a compilation of all her famous acting tricks.

314 De Jongh, 'The Van is merely a vehicle for Dame Maggie'.

315 'Tough love to one side', *The Times Literary Supplement*, 24 December 1999, p. 17.

added leg ulcers as a personal touch.[316] Scrupulously following Alan Bennett's stage directions, the designer Mark Thompson and his assistants found Miss Shepherd's attire in different charity shops. These pieces of clothing did not look as worn as required, though, and they had to tear, damage and soil them with various ingredients, even using a cheese grater to wear out her coats.[317] The only problem the actress had to deal with was the costume changes; Miss Shepherd wore very complex panoplies, composed of sponges, dusters and different items that were impossible to adjust backstage, so the designer reduced her wardrobe to a minimum, one outfit with changing accessories. Nevertheless, poor Maggie had to contort herself, crouched in the van, to make changes to her costume and, long before the end of the run, the actress – whom Thompson described as tremendously 'athletic', rushing in or out the van and dealing with the props[318] – was covered with bruises. Miss Shepherd's outfit was probably not the most comfortable costume Smith had worn in her whole career, but she was pleased with this radical metamorphosis. As Thompson metaphorically suggested, she was glad to let the dirt wedge itself under her fingernails.[319] Not only had Maggie Smith gleefully agreed to look very dirty as Miss Shepherd, but she was actually dirtier than she seemed on the stage.[320] Bennett's play explicitly refers to faeces and constantly mentions the nauseating smell that emanates from the old lady. In fact, as some critics and spectators admitted, the audience had the impression that Miss Shepherd *smelt* on the stage. Thanks to the perfection of Smith's acting, the olfactory senses were stimulated by the visual ones.

Hunched, wearing huge worn shoes which made her look like a clown, the actress walked like a duck and it conferred a particular posture on her character.[321] In a notice for *Country Life*, M. Billington underlined

316 Bennett, *Untold Stories*, p. 265.

317 P. Majendie, 'It's a riches-to-rags role', *The Daily Telegraph*, 13 December 1999, p. 73. Each day, they used paint, soup or grease to add a finishing touch to her costumes.

318 *Ibid.*

319 R. Stringer, 'Dear Dame Maggie as you've never seen her before; Alan Bennett's famous bag lady comes to life…', *The Evening Standard*, 2 December 1999, p. 3.

320 N. Reynolds, 'Why a dirty look from Dame Maggie is worth £1million to the West End', *The Daily Telegraph*, 3 December 1999, p. 13.

321 See Billington, 'Epitome of a hermit'; M. Billington noticed Miss Shepherd's particular gait, and especially these 'splayed feet' which made her figure so recognisable; see also R. Gore- Langton, 'Tired old bag', *The Daily Express*, 10 December, 1999, p. 67; he evoked the delight to see Smith's 'splayed walk'.

that physical prowess. According to him, the part allowed Maggie Smith the opportunity to give the audience, not a mannered star turn, but the portrayal of a 'fully-inhabited' individual whom she defined, thanks to her prodigious body skills, by a very specific, accurate posture.[322] For his part, the critic J. Peter saw in Smith's performance a real masterclass of acting, applauding the strict accuracy and technical precision of this immaculate portrayal, which reflected, once again, the actress's acute sense of observation.[323] Maggie Smith's impersonation was indeed a mesmerising achievement, in terms of characterisation. However, her real tour de force lay in the fact that she managed to make her character look scary. Her Miss Shepherd was undoubtedly fiercer, much more frightening than the real person was. A close-up portrait, published in *The Daily Mail* in December 1999, shows an elderly lady with wild, bulging eyes;[324] never had the actress's magnificent blue eyes been so wisely exploited to make the audience feel fright and repulsion. While the real Mary Shepherd's gaze was lifeless, that of her character was sharp, even spine-chilling. R. Butler vividly described an angular face that, constantly tilted in Alan Bennett's direction, stared at him with large, deluded eyes.[325] Maybe Smith's Shepherd was not that resemblant – the pictures published by Bennett show a sad-eyed old woman whose face was sagging like that of a decomposing corpse – but she was much more expressive than the original. Expressivity leads to expressionism and actually, in her make-up, black was predominant. There were large dark circles around her sockets, contrasting quite strikingly with the whites of her eyes and her huge irises of an icy blue, two aquamarines which oddly glittered in this ravaged face. It was difficult to recognise the actress, because this face was definitely not hers.

In fact, far beyond the help that the make-up can supply to her, Maggie Smith knows how to grimace and transform her features. Mimicry and grimaces contribute more to her physical transformation than cosmetics. In *What's On*, the critic S. Marlowe hailed Maggie Smith's performance and also

322 'Theatre', *Country Life*, 16 December 1999, p. 66.

323 Peter, 'Van of the moment'.

324 'Dame Maggie, growing old disgracefully', *The Daily Mail*, 13 December 1999, p. 27.

325 Butler, 'Driving Miss Crazy'. In *Time Out*, 15 December 1999 (see *Theatre Record*, 3-31 December 1999, p. 1638), the critic J. Edwardes, observing that she had rarely looked that redoubtable in a stage role, imputed it to these large, bulging eyes constantly peering at an unfortunate Bennett.

described Miss Shepherd's face as 'a mass of tics and grimaces', as if the actress's muscles prevailed over stage make-up.[326] Usually thin ('angular' as people commonly say) and perfectly symmetrical, her face is nothing here but a distorted mask, with a squarish jaw and drooping mouth corners. In *The New York Times*, B. Nightingale marvelled at the actress's appearance, writing that her face had never been 'grimier', her nose 'beakier' and her eyes more 'bulbous'.[327] As explained by S. West, in the eighteenth century, comical performers were categorised according to their ability to use the muscles of their face: 'Parsons's theory of muscular motion served as a useful purpose in criticism of comic acting, as critics evaluated expression with reference to the muscular control of the actor.'[328] Closer to our time, Alec Guinness was renowned for his facial agility. As one of his biographers recounts, the great actor was gifted with the most extraordinary facial musculature, which allowed him to express a wide range of emotional feelings, and radically transform himself with a very 'small amount of movement'.[329] Just as well, Maggie Smith possesses this very rare gift which allows her to change her physiognomy by simply pulling back her chin. Immediately, her jaw seems to be larger and her neck sags, making the actress acquire a bit of this masculinity that some very old ladies have. This is the same process – which involves many of her facial muscles – that she used to become Grace Hawkins in *Keeping Mum* or *Downton Abbey*'s haughty dowager. However, as breathtaking as her physical metamorphosis can be, Smith never manages – probably because none of her roles has required it until now – to look ugly. Each of the characters she plays has, despite the toll of the years or the absence of any make-up, an indefinable grace to which the expressivity of her eyes greatly contributes. For the actress, this part essentially represented the height of characterisation.[330] Smith is not Miss Shepherd and, nevertheless, on stage, only Miss Shepherd was to be seen. Imperious, impressive and even beautiful under her armour of dirt, that tramp was, definitely, a lady.

326 15 December 1999 (see *Theatre Record*, 3-31 December 1999, p. 1641).

327 Nightingale, '"Lady in the Van" offers a Moral Behind the Laughter'.

328 West, *The Image of the Actor*, p. 129.

329 G. O'Connor, *Alec Guinness. Master of Disguise* (London-Sydney-Auckland: Hodder & Stoughton, 1994), p. 207.

330 Billington, 'Epitome of a hermit'. Billington, usually critical on Smith's excesses and mannerisms, found her portrayal quite convincing and considered this performance her best in many years.

A Violet Past Prime

Actresses from the past were inclined to lie about their real age. With the development of the media and the Internet, it is no longer possible for famous people to hide their date of birth. However, as surprising as it may seem, Maggie Smith's age remains a mystery for a large part of the audience. Not that she brilliantly succeeds in keeping it secret, out of vanity, as journalists never forget to mention it at every occasion. On the contrary, for years, Smith herself has been taking great pleasure pretending she was 'old', although her physical appearance and her energy denied such a statement. As early as 1985, when filming Merchant-Ivory's

A Room with a View in Florence, she wondered why she was still in demand and felt lucky to get film roles at her age.[331] In 2005, in an interview given to *The Times Magazine*, she even affirmed that, at her age, she had no chance to be offered roles anymore,[332] what sounds quite odd, considering the amount of work she has done since 2005 and how much in demand she still is. Being very insecure, Smith probably tries to reassure herself by telling a lie to get at the truth. Anyway, everything this rather self-deprecating actress says has always to be taken with a large pinch of salt; her humour is so dry and corrosive that it can easily unsettle those who come unprepared. Although she claims, not without humour, a venerable age that she has not reached yet, Maggie Smith conveys, offstage, quite a different image. Always stylish and discreetly elegant, with her thick, shiny hair impeccably cut, the actress sports jeans and jackets with the same gracious poise as she wears, on screen and on stage, the most elaborate period costumes. The difficulty is that she often plays, with an incomparable truthfulness, characters who are much older than she is and, although every tabloid regularly mentions her date of birth, a portion of the public has paradoxically lost track of her real age. This impression is probably even stronger on screen than it is on stage, because, as Christine Geraghty explains, there is no curtain call in cinemas, no moment at the end when the actor, out of character, takes a bow; in a movie, he remains identified with the character beyond the credits.[333] In 1985, the journalist Julia Bright already assumed that people probably thought that Maggie Smith had been a quinquagenarian for many years, and it was her punishment for portraying ageing spinsters.[334] Thirty years later, her reputation is, alas, well-established. For the general public, Smith is that famous actress who has specialised in playing old ladies, desiccated spinsters or ageing aristocrats, among whom the role of Minerva McGonagall looks like a

331 M. Billington, 'A Literary Film-Making Team Has a Go at E. M. Forster', *The New York Times*, 28 July 1985, p. 15.

332 A. Franks, 'Love's Labour's Lost', *The Times Magazine*, 26 November 2005, p. 27.

333 'Performing as a Lady and a Dame: Reflections on Acting and Genre', in *Contemporary Hollywood Stardom*, ed. by Th. Austin & M. Barker (London: Arnold, 2003), p. 106. In the recent London production of *Driving Miss Daisy* (Wyndham Theatre, 2012), the curtain fell on a weakened and a senile Miss Daisy sitting in her wheelchair, and a few seconds later, a youthful Vanessa Redgrave came back running to bow in front of the audience.

334 Bright, 'Delicious pin-head, all eyes and teeth'.

delightful break. A few years ago, an article in *Der Berliner Morgenpost* was entitled 'Maggie Smith: Für immer alt', implying that the virtuoso actress, 'forever old', was pigeonholed in the fourth age category.[335]

'Forever old' is quite excessive in fact. Thankfully, Maggie Smith does not play only very old lady roles; for the last twenty-five years, she has played several younger characters on screen and on stage. It must be noticed, though, that the characters she has recently portrayed are not so remote from her own age, but they belong either to the past – and thus their physical appearance corresponds to aesthetic criteria which are different from ours (Janet Widdington, Lady Gresham, etc) – or to a social status which justifies they look older than the actress who portrays them (Grace Hawkins, Miss Shepherd). Hence, almost every time she plays in a movie, Smith has to age to look the part. Such a casting could seem quite repetitive, but it must be quite enjoyable for a chameleon actress who looks at least ten years younger than her age in real life. Of course, it is not without risks, and the actress has to pay the price for it. By looking older every time she appears on screen while avoiding as much as possible any form of promotion, the actress encourages less informed people to imagine, in good faith, that she is and looks much older than her colleagues of the same generation. No one wonders if Judi Dench is going to retire in the upcoming months. No one marvels at Vanessa Redgrave or Julie Andrew's longevity. It is true that Smith has a long and glittering career behind her, but no way is she the doyenne of world cinema or Ernst Lubitsch's ex-muse. Time goes by quickly, of course, but she was only a quinquagenarian in the 1990s and she belongs to a very prolific generation – that of Olivier's legatees – which is still active and at the top of its game.

In her autobiography, published in 1996, Claire Bloom wrote that, in every actress's career, there is a moment when her real age delineates her professional 'identity', deterring producers to offer her new roles.[336] This applies more to the United States than the UK (where actresses over sixty-five are quite in demand), but it is irrelevant to describe Maggie Smith's very particular case. Some actresses play daughters, then mothers, but Smith

335 14 March 2012.

336 *Leaving a Doll's House* (Boston-New York-Toronto-London: Little, Brown and Co, 1996), p. 160.

played grandmothers immediatly, as she admits.[337] Unlike those thespians from the past who willingly remained stuck with young parts at the risk of looking ridiculous, Smith is one of the rare actresses who have prematurely aged through their roles. In a recent radio interview, being asked if she would be interested in playing senior women like Simone Signoret used to do or Charlotte Rampling recently did in *45 Years*, Isabelle Huppert chuckled and acerbically replied: 'Not yet! But later, I will see.' In terms of acting craft, such a reply seems disconcerting, as if this excellent actress had in fact a much narrower range than we could expect – especially from someone whom the interviewer had just described as 'the greatest French actress, the one who takes the most risks and who is the most versatile.'[338] For Huppert, to play an older woman at sixty-three is obviously pushing versatility too far, whereas Meryl Streep does not feel offended at being offered these roles. Perfect characterisation requires high skills that only the consummate actors possess and, like Streep, Smith's talent allows her to play any character at any age.

Still, the phenomenon is not that recent. Very few people remember that Maggie Smith was cast in old lady parts as early as her debut. A forgotten article from the US newspaper *The Sunday Mirror Magazine* already lauded the young actress's ability to transform herself, as she was portraying a one-hundred-year-old lady in the musical revue *New Faces* (1956) just created at the Shubert Theatre in Boston. This old lady role was the very first among many others which would follow years later and, at that time, the young Maggie was thrilled to do it:

> One of the loveliest faces [producer Leonard Sillman] has brought to these shores belongs to a young lady, a singing comedienne, just barely out of her teens, whose name, she swears, is really Maggie Smith [...] She has dark hair, and large blue eyes that look like two spoonfuls of the Mediterranean, and that clear, creamy, pink and white complexion that English girls like herself are supposed to have, but seldom do [...] "In one number," said Miss Smith, "I am an old woman of approximatively 102 years. In my other numbers

337 Bardin, 'Idole Chatter'.

338 'L'Interview d'Anne Sinclair', I. Huppert interviewed by the journalist Anne Sinclair, Europe 1, 19 March 2016.

I am much younger, however. In those, I am somewhere in the late 70's".[339]

The journalist raved about the contrast between the 'fresh loveliness' of the young performer and the more-than-respectable age of the roles which had been given to her. A blurry photograph shows a very young Smith dressed in a fur-necked suit – quite similar to the one that Constance Trentham wears in *Gosford Park*, with a Marcel wave wig which makes her resemble Bette Davis's Mrs Van Schuyler in *Death on the Nile*. For the spectators sitting in the first row, her centenarian was probably not completely convincing, but at least, without knowing it, Maggie Smith paved the way for a brilliant career as a character actress. Yet, in the definitive version of the show which opened in Broadway, at the Ethel Barrymore, two weeks later, these characters had disappeared from the programme, letting Smith shine, for some decades, in the full bloom of youth.

Quite soon, though, in 1972, an ageing George Cukor, offered her the opportunity to replace Katharine Hepburn at short notice. Cukor planned to adapt Graham Greene's *Travels with my Aunt* for the big screen and Hepburn, having contributed to the rewriting of the script, was not completely pleased with it. Rumours said that, following the commercial disaster that *The Madwoman of Chaillot* (B. Forbes, 1969) had been, the actress was not very keen on portraying another eccentric old lady. She simply refused the dates imposed by the studios and, consequently, was courteously dismissed. Having considered for one moment the possibility of casting Angela Lansbury,[340] Cukor, encouraged by Robert Fryer (the producer of *The Prime of Miss Jean Brodie*), chose the much too young Maggie Smith to play his Aunt.[341] At that time, Maggie Smith explained that Cukor and his producers were in trouble and, when Bobby Fryer offered

339 G. Prevor, 'Age Before Beauty. Maggie Smith has just turned twenty-one, But on Broadway She's a Centenarian', *The Sunday Mirror Magazine*, 8 July 1956, p. 2.

340 He changed his mind, because the actress was too strongly identified with Auntie Mame whom she had recently played on the stage, and he feared that his movie would be seen an onscreen rerun of *Mame*. Nevertheless, some critics established a parallel between the two characters.

341 R. E. Long, *George Cukor Interviews* (Jackson: University Press of Mississipi, 2001), p.79; Long writes that 'naturally', the British actress was asked to play Aunt Augusta and agreed. Naturally, as if it went without saying.

her the part, she could not say no. And it would have been unthinkable not to work with G. Cukor.[342] A few flashbacks were to be inserted in the film and its heroine would have to alternatively age and de-age on screen. Had he worked with Katharine Hepburn (who was sixty-three then), Cukor would have been compelled to use a younger actress to play those scenes. To cast Smith, in a very Brechtian way,[343] allowed him to easily resolve that difficulty; convincing or not, the British actress would be able to play Aunt Augusta along the whole story, from youth to old age. At a recent talk, the costume designer Anthony Powell – a long time friend of Smith – revealed that she was in fact quite reluctant to accept the role: 'Maggie Smith was blackmailed into doing it: she didn't want to, saying "I am thirty-seven years old, I have the rest of my life to be playing seventy-year-old ladies".'[344] Of course, some viewers might smile when seeing Maggie Smith alternatively as a (mature) teenager and a falsely wrinkled septuagenarian, but it was undoubtedly a great challenge and the actress, definitely resourceful, did quite brilliantly.

Sadly, the film was not received as well as expected, especially in the UK where it got rather mitigated reviews. Some critics complained that Smith, being much too young to play the role, overacted and heavily relied on her technical tricks to create a highly theatrical characterisation.[345] In *The Observer*, the critic George Melly reproached the superficiality of her performance; Melly saw Maggie Smith as a very intelligent (and mannered) actress, but he considered that, despite her efforts, her portrayal of this seventy-year-old 'champagne bibbing' eccentric was laborious and unconvincing. For Melly, the trouble was that, focusing mainly on Aunt Augusta's histrionics and eccentricities, Maggie Smith had sacrificed the 'irresistible charm' of Graham Greene's heroine.[346] Likewise, Roger Greenspun, from *The New*

342 Quoted in Q. Falk, *Travels in Greeneland* (London: Reynolds & Hearn Ltd, 2000), p. 116.

343 Brecht considered it a much more interesting experience to cast young actors in older parts. See M. Mumford, *Bertold Brecht* (Oxon-New York: Routledge, 2009), p. 71. See also B. Brecht, *Brecht on Theatre* (London: Methuen, 1964), p. 243; for him, it makes no sense to cast actors according to their age and physical appearance.

344 Conversation with A. Powell at the Cranbrook Film Society, 4 June 2008.

345 See E. Levy, *George Cukor, Master of Elegance* (New York: William Morrow and C°, 1994), p. 343.

346 'Troubles with my Aunt', *The Observer*, 18 February 1973, p. 34. See also T. Milne, 'Travels with my Aunt', *Monthly Film Bulletin*, January 1973, p. 60; the critic blamed Maggie Smith's 'comic-strip' assumption of old-age.

York Times, blamed her for turning the character into a caricature instead of inhabiting it. He admitted she was amazingly made up and had as much energy as five ordinary actresses, but it was 'the energy of caricature'.[347] Reviewers particularly criticised her heavy, exaggerated make-up which, according to them, made the character look surreal. In *Film Quarterly*, Stephen Farber declared that Smith was 'ghastly' made up as a septuagenarian; he disliked everything in it, from the overblushed cheeks to the ridiculous red wig, and he considered that this nasal, 'croaking' voice had turned Augusta into a frenzied mechanical puppet.[348] In *The Washington Post*, Tom Donnelly ruthlessly pretended that the actress looked like a woman who had been embalmed in pastry dough.[349] On the contrary, G. Cukor was very proud of her make-up, declaring in an interview that they gasped with admiration when seeing her make-up.[350] Every morning, Smith spent two hours at the make-up table, while a mixture made of latex rubber, spirit gum and cotton wool was artistically applied on her face. The skin was stretched as long as the make-up was getting dry, then relaxed to create impressive, deep wrinkles on her face. At the end of the shoot day, the thin layer of rubber was moisturised with castor oil, then carefully removed. Smith joked that she felt she was being 'peeled, like an old onion'.[351] It is surprising that her skin was able to tolerate, for several weeks, such a treatment without being irreversibly damaged. At any rate, no one can deny how brave it was for such a young actress to portray a quirky old crone, hiding her lovely face behind a 'hideous mask'.[352] It would be the same later on. The very beautiful Maggie would never hesitate – at fifty, at sixty and over – to age and transform her appearance for a role. But then, paradoxically, while the Academy had given her a Best Actress nod, the critics did not forgive her for her boldness.

In a more recent article, the critic Richard Lippe refuted these negative reviews, demonstrating that, on the contrary, the actress was

347 'George Cukor brings Graham Greene's "Travels with my Aunt" to the Screen', *The New York Times*, 18 December 1972, p. 56.

348 'Two Old Men's Movies', *Film Quarterly*, 26.4, 1973, p. 50.

349 'Dawdling, Creeping Unreality', *The Washington Post*, 28 December 1972, p. 1.

350 Interview by W. Hall, 1972 (see 'Travels with Cukor and Maggie Smith', in *George Cukor Interviews*, p. 79).

351 R. Reed, 'New Wrinkles for Maggie Smith', *The Washington Post*, 25 June 1972, p. 2.

352 *Ibid.*

able to humanise her characterisation and brightly switch from comedy to pathos. According to him, far from being a caricature, Smith's Aunt Augusta becomes, thanks to the actress's brilliant performance, a 'vibrant human being' as it appears in the more tender scenes.[353] Anyhow, her awesome, highly comical impersonation did not aim at realism. Helped by a flaming red wig, an insane wardrobe and the rail-thin figure of a (much too) meagre Maggie Smith, Aunt Augusta stirs and leaps with as much velocity as a Tex Avery character, jumping onto her bed as if it were a trampoline and extending her legs straight up like a gymnastics champion. In the end, Augusta Bertram's age is irrelevant; like an oniric figure or a cartoon character, this iconoclast lady who drags her nephew Henry into a frenzied road trip is ageless. Yet, as the French critic Jean-Loup Bourget noticed in *Positif*, the actress expertly suggests, beneath a supremely caricatural exterior, the profound vulnerability of her character: 'Maggie Smith's acting is quite remarkable, not – despite what critics have written – because of her caricatural side (her flaming red wig, her broken/heartbreaking voice, her birdlike nervous gestures), but mostly thanks to the real emotion that such a caricature conveys, making the hidden vulnerability of the character entirely convincing.'[354] Much deeper, more moving than it was considered at the time of the release, Smith's performance has been partially rehabilitated these days. Back in the 1970s, critics had probably omitted to notice that this character, who speaks with the same voice as Miss Shepherd and Mathilde Girard in *My Old Lady* – Maggie Smith has a special 'old lady' voice in her repertoire – was the result of an amazing work by a young actress. Not only is it remarkable, but it is also unique. Smith was probably the only actress in the world capable to play that impossible role and make Aunt Augusta lovable and touching.

More favoured by the cinephiles than by the general public these days, *Travels with my Aunt* did not have a very large impact on Smith's career or a hypothetic typecasting in the 1970s–1980s. She would go on playing young, then youthful women for a while. Still, she stooped to the spinster area with *A Room with a View* (1985) and more roles of the same kind would follow. It was not exactly a first go for the actress, as J. Guillermin's *Death on the Nile* had already offered her a spinster role,

353 See 'Travels with my Aunt: romanticism and aging', *CineAction*, 50, January 1999, p. 16.
354 'Le dernier carré', *Positif*, April 1973, p. 8.

although different; the very brusque Miss Bowers, a virago in the full sense of the word, has little in common with the shy, gawky character depicted by E. M. Forster. Nevertheless, thanks to Charlotte Bartlett and the huge success of Merchant and Ivory's movie at the box office, Smith's career was to undergo a significant transformation. From then on, many directors would have a new perception of the actress she was. At fifty, Maggie Smith was ranked among the mature actresses and thus she started to be pigeonholed in a category of parts. It seemed not surprising then, to see her playing the title role in Jack Clayton's *The Lonely Passion of Judith Hearne* (1987), adapted from Brian Moore's novel. However, Clayton, one of the greatest directors of the twentieth century, had certainly not cast Smith following such a prejudice, but simply because he considered her to be the most talented actress of her generation. She was not born to play a lonely spinster – as some people would pretend – but she could play one amazingly. However, although Maggie Smith played spinsters quite early in her career, she did not age as quickly on stage than she did on screen. One year before *A Room with a View*, she gave a definitive rendition of Millamant in Congreve's *The Way of the World*, directed by William Gaskill at Chichester Festival Theatre.[355] Eight years after having triumphed in Robin Phillips's celebrated production, in Stratford (Ontario), and even if she was not exactly the right age to play the part, Smith proved to be a magnificent Millamant and her performance is now cited as a reference in scientific publications and commented editions of Congreve.[356]

In actual fact, this is 1991 which would bring a major turn in Maggie Smith's career. She had not appeared on screen since *The Lonely Passion of Judith Hearne* when she was approached by no less than Steven Spielberg to play Wendy Darling in *Hook*, a film which can be seen as a sequel to Peter Pan's story. As everyone knows, the movie tells the story of a grown-up Peter returning to Neverland to rescue his children kidnapped by Captain Hook. Wendy is only a minor character who has very little screen time, but just like almost all the supporting roles played by Smith,

355 The successful show transferred later to the Theatre Royal Haymarket.

356 W. Congreve's *The Way of the World*, ed. by B. Gibbons (London: A & C Black, 1994), p. xxxix; it mentions that Smith's Millamant, a 'beribboned beauty' who lived up to the description that Mirabell makes of the character, won 'every possible laugh' thanks to her brilliant delivery.

she is one of the most striking figures in the movie. In his biography of Maggie Smith, M. Coveney recounts that Spielberg's original intention was to cast Peggy Ashcroft as Granny Wendy. Unfortunately, the great actress, weakened by several strokes and ailments, was not able to work any more (she would die in June 1991) and the director had to think of another British actress who could replace her. The tale, reported by Maggie Smith herself, says that her unexpected casting – considering Wendy's age – resulted from a joke made by the facetious Anthony Powell, the famous costume designer. The actress recounts that her friend was asked by Steven Spielberg, 'How old is Maggie Smith now?' and Powell imperturbably replied that she was ninety-two.[357] The story does not say how long it took for Steven Spielberg to discover the deception, but persuaded by Powell's enthusiastic praise of Smith, he eventually cast that uncommon nonagenarian. Although the role required from the actress interminable make-up sessions in order to make her look like a deeply wrinkled old lady, it also gave her the opportunity to gain lots of new admirers, ten years before the first opus of *Harry Potter*. With her usual brio, the actress convincingly portrays a woman who is supposed to be nearly forty years older than she was at that time. With the help of elaborate prosthetics, considerably more discreet and realistic than the make-up she wore in *Travels with my Aunt*,[358] her Granny Wendy is compelling. Smith having reached maturity, it was, of course, much easier to make her up than it had been in 1972, when she still had a very young face. Nevertheless, as convincing as her make-up was – and although the actress has not yet reached Wendy's age at the moment when these pages are written – it is more than likely that, thanks to the expressivity and the delicacy of her features, she will undoubtedly look younger, more beautiful and more hieratic in her (real) nineties than she looks in Spielberg's movie.

A whole generation discovered *Hook* in theatres around the world, realising years later that old Wendy was played by Maggie Smith. As if they had never heard about cinematic prosthetics, there will always be people who speculate about Smith's age, being puzzled by the fact that she does look younger now than she did in *Hook*, twenty-five years ago. Those who

357 J. Gordinier, 'Grand Dame', *Entertainment Weekly*, 15 March 2002, p. 34.

358 This wondrous make-up, made of pieces of foam latex, secured an Oscar nomination for its creator, the famous special make-up effects artist Greg Cannom.

have more carefully studied the film know that the actress also appears in a brief flashback, as a sixty-something Wendy. She is a beautiful, red-haired woman, whose voice suddenly cracks when she confesses to the young man who Peter Pan has become that she is too old to follow him: 'I can't come with you. I've forgotten how to fly. I'm old, Peter.' It is, without doubt, one of the most heartbreaking moments in the film – when we realise how ambiguous the love Wendy feels for Peter is – but it is too rarely put on Smith's credit. However, her most memorable scene remains the first one, when Peter Banning and his family arrive at Granny Wendy's London home. 'Hello, boy,' someone utters with a quavering voice, as if it intended to bring Peter back to his childhood.[359] When Peter looks up to the flight of stairs, we see a frail figure who stands against the half-darkness. Leaning on her cane, Wendy carefully climbs down the steps to welcome her guests. The scene cannot be watched in the same way these days, as, in the meantime, Maggie Smith has played many old lady roles. To see her with a white wig and a walking stick does not seem extraordinary. For the audience of 1991, Smith was unrecognisable and it is only when she reaches the bottom of the stairs, in full lighting, that the spectator is able to notice her sad but mischievous large blue eyes.

As Coveney points out, as soon as Maggie/Wendy appears on the screen, the movie switches to fantasy. Actually, in the real world (as opposed to Neverland), Granny Wendy is the only fairy figure. According to the American critic Brian D. Johnson, in *MacLean's*, Smith was the one who brought the magic of *Peter Pan* to life.[360] Just like any other good grandmother, Wendy tells stories – her own story, in fact – to her great granddaughter and, so tiny in her large bed, she strives to resurrect the memories of Peter, who has forgotten everything about his childhood and their common past: 'You know, when I was young, no other girl held your favour the way I did.' Granny Wendy incarnates nostalgia for the past; functionally, her mission is to bring Peter Banning back to the consciousness of his childhood and, at the same time, to send him flying to Neverland,

359 H. Sheehan, 'Spielberg II', *Film Comment*, 28.4, July 1992, p. 66.

360 'Return to Neverland. Steven Spielberg recasts the Peter Pan Syndrome', *Maclean's*, 104.50, December 1991, p. 64. See also K. Turan, '"Hook": In Search of Enchantment', *The Los Angeles Times*, 11 December 1991, p. 1; the journalist lauded Smith's glowing performance, emphasising the fact that the actress had the 'regal, overworldly air of the perfect fairy-tale enchantress'.

in search of his children whom Captain Hook has kidnapped. In some ways, Wendy Darling reminds us of another grannyish figure – as much moving in her time, but less known to the younger generation – the Ghost of Christmas Past in *Scrooge* (R. Neame, 1970). In this musical version of Dickens's *A Christmas Carol*, filmed by the director of *The Prime of Miss Jean Brodie*, the first of the three spirits who come to disturb Ebenezer Scrooge in his sleep is played by Edith Evans, dressed like an upper-class lady of the Georgian era.[361] Just like Granny Wendy, the ghost intends to awaken the hero's memory, bringing some scenes from his forgotten past to life. Still, although the two characters have in common the same aristocratic elegance, Wendy emanates a youthful freshness – 'Peter, do you like my dress?' she asks the indifferent businessman – and a kind of evanescent grace that the (paradoxically earthly) Ghost of Christmas does not have. Maggie Smith displays an ethereal creature whose flexible and willowy figure could belong to a Disney character. By her appearance, Granny Wendy can be thought of as Madame Adelaide Bonfamille, in *The Aristocats*, whereas Edith Evans's Ghost of Christmas Past resembles a portrait by Van Dyck, in a ruby red dress certainly inspired by St. Nicholas's cloak. It was one of Dame Edith's last roles and thus it added to her performance an even more moving dimension. In *Scrooge*, Evans appeared as a kind of nostalgic cameo which, in a certain way, suggested that she was herself a living testimony of bygone days, getting confused with the spirit to whom she lent her appearance.[362]

Wendy Darling would probably have had a similar resonance, had she been played by Peggy Ashcroft as her ultimate role. In the twilight of her career, Dame Peggy embodied a fragile strength as well as a youthful candour that both show in the character of Mrs Moore, in *A Passage to India* (D. Lean, 1984). From that point of view – although Spielberg was probably unaware of that –, Smith was the perfect choice to replace Ashcroft. Watching *Hook*, we get the impression that her Wendy could crack like an old porcelain doll, but she remains alive and brisk, driven by a kind of youthful energy which helps her to put into practice her favourite motto, 'No growing-up'. She is, and she will always be, Peter's Wendy. Casting a young and vigorous actress

361 See Forbes, *Dame Edith Evans*, p. 263-264.

362 G. Banu, *Les voyages du comédien* (Paris: Gallimard, 2012), p. 140-141. The elderly performer fully assimilates into the (elderly) character he plays. He reminds us of the past as much as the character.

in the part, Spielberg exempts us from this little twinge of sorrow that every spectator feels when seeing a very old actor performing on screen or on stage. Maggie Smith brilliantly manages to make the character wholly credible, while sparing us the painful sight of the old actor's frailty, much more heartbreaking than that of the character. The audience can fully enjoy her performance without the slight feeling of guilt or pity and, as paradoxical as it may seem, be profoundly moved by her Granny Wendy. How does Smith manage to make the spectator feel empathy and emotion through a performance which represents the pinnacle of characterisation? That is a mystery and it should remain so. It could be assumed that her portrayal of Granny Wendy was not without consequences on her movie career and the roles that would be given to her subsequently. From then on, she would regularly be offered very old lady roles, to such an extent that one part of the public has forgotten her real appearance. Alternatively queen mother, spinster or dowager, Maggie Smith de-ages very rarely and, when it happens, she often plays an authoritarian or cantankerous character. Quite aware of that situation, the actress herself jests about it, admitting that she has been stuck with the nonagenarian roles for years. At the *Quartet* press conference in 2012, a journalist asked her what she thought about playing much older ladies – it was obviously not the most relevant question, in the sense that Jean Horton, in *Quartet*, is precisely younger and more glamorous than the characters she usually plays! – and, as modest as usual, she replied she was just 'glad to get any role, even if they were all 90!'[363]

363 Press Conference for the release of *Quartet*, Empire Leicester Square, London, 15 October 2012.

Endgame

After Smith's memorable Wendy, another nonagenarian would follow. It would be a stage role, A in Edward Albee's *Three Tall Women*. Senile and incontinent, with her ghostly complexion and her haggard eyes, A remains until now one of Maggie Smith's most splendid performances, and maybe, on equal terms with Miss Shepherd, her greatest theatre role. To create A, the main character of his play, Albee found inspiration in his adoptive mother, Frances Cotter Albee, with whom he had always had difficult relations.[364] A – the three women in question being designated by the alphabet's first letters – is a wealthy New Yorker of very advanced years. Imperious, difficult, even tyrannical, this decrepit woman inflicts her mood swings and the pitiful sight of her ageing on two younger women, B (a middle-aged woman who is paid, as a lady companion, to look after her) and C (a young jurist who handles the elderly lady's legal and financial affairs). Act I is quite static – the main action consisting in A being led twice to the bathroom and put to bed at the end of the act – and essentially takes the form of a long monologue delivered by A, the narrative process getting constantly interrupted, not only by the remarks of the two other characters, but by aporia (due to the failures of the old lady's memory) and constant changes of subject provoked by the loss of her mental faculties. A tells stories of her past, pauses, loses her train of thought, gets angry, bursts into tears, then laughs like a young child and resumes her account of her life, before pausing again.[365] At the end of Act I, she suffers a stroke just before the fall of the curtain and the audience does not know if she will survive beyond the interval. Here, Edward Albee exposes the sordid decline of a woman afflicted by all the throes of old age. Bitter and intolerant, looking like a monster or a witch who is literally melting in front of the spectators, A crystallises all the prejudices about senility. Describing Smith's performance, the critic from *The Daily Telegraph* applauded the striking display of decrepitude she offered.[366] However, beyond that objective and cruel picture of old age, Albee simultaneously sketches out the striking portrait of a proud, brave, admirable woman who, still driven by her survival instinct, fights her last battle, just like these moribund animals the bodies of which are already half-devoured by insects and worms.[367] A is not dead yet. She is going to die and, precisely, Act II allows us to enter her subjectivity

364 See M. Gussow, *Edward Albee: A Singular Journey. A Biography* (New York: Simon & Schuster, 1999), p. 25-26.

365 Albee himself admitted that the actress playing A has to get a grip, from the outset, with that 'schizophrenic thing' and it is a major difficulty *(ibid.*, p. 358).

366 R. Gore-Langton, 'A tale almost too grisly to bear', *The Daily Telegraph*, 2 October 1995, p. 19.

367 E. Albee wrote in his introduction to the Plume Penguin edition (1994) that he really admired Frances Albee's pride and 'sense of self'. He recounted that, when she reached her nineties, she started to decline physically and mentally, and he was moved by her instinct of 'survivor' and her desperate struggle not to let go.

during the time of her agony.[368] The second act opens with a *coup de théâtre* as A's inert body is lying on a bed in the background and, at the moment when the audience supposes she has certainly died after her stroke, her double, a nonagenarian who is alive and well, makes a spectacular entrance. During Act II, the spectator eventually witnesses a proper interaction between the three characters who prove to represent the different ages of an unique individual. On the brink of death, A literally splits into three distinct women, the three women she has successively been during her life, and these three characters share their hopes, their experiences and their disillusions. The tripartition of the character opens up a diachronic and synchronic reflection on the meaning of life, the passing of time and, of course, on death. At this stage, A has acquired the distance she needs to be able to appreciate her whole existence and realise that the happiest moment in life lies in its end, 'when it's all done'.

Created in Vienna in June 1991, *Three Tall Women* was presented in Woodstock in July 1993, and then in New York in January 1994, with a cast which included two of Albee's favourite actresses, Myra Carter as A and Marian Seldes as B. After a successful run, the production was transferred to Broadway, at the Promenade Theater. The London revival took place during the Broadway season and the American producers, associated for the occasion with the British producer R. Fox, decided to open directly in the West End with a prestigious cast led by Maggie Smith as A and the marvellous Frances de la Tour as B. Directed by Anthony Page,[369] this lavish production benefited from a sumptuous scenery, refined in its smallest details, which had nothing in common with the austere set used for the creation in Vienna. After a triumphant first night at the Wyndham in November 1994, the production ran for five months to full houses. The success of the first run was such that the play was revived the following autumn with a partially renewed cast, Sara

368 See B. Murphy, 'Albee's threnodies', in *The Cambridge Companion to Edward Albee*, ed. by S. Bottoms (Cambridge: Cambridge University Press, 2005), p. 103-107. Also R. H. Solomon, *Albee in Performance* (Bloomington: Indiana University Press, 2010), p. 163: 'This act […] stages the near-death out-of-body experience that the bedridden A is going through.'

369 After the first stage director, Karel Reisz had resigned, for the reason that he struggled with Albee's play (and not because of Maggie Smith, as some journalists thoughtfully suggested). See B. Bamigboye's clarification, 'Reisz and a wronged Dame', *The Daily Mail*, 30 September 1994, p. 42.

Kestelman and Samantha Bond replacing respectively Frances de la Tour and Anastasia Hille. As M. Coveney asserted in an article he wrote a few years later, *Three Tall Women* is probably Smith's greatest success on the London stage and, with that play, she became the most bankable actress in the West End.[370] Reassured by the critical and commercial success of the production – although she had been scandalously ignored by the judges of the Olivier Awards[371] – Maggie Smith reprised her role with an unaccustomed serenity; a picture published in *The Evening Standard* in September 1995 showed a radiant Smith surrounded by her new co-stars, Bond and Kestelman.[372] Although Albee had always given preference to Myra Carter – whose portrayal was apparently closer to the character he had in mind – the playwright nevertheless admitted that Maggie Smith was dazzling as A. London critics unanimously praised the quality of her performance, enhanced by a first-class cast. In *The Mail on Sunday*, Louise Doughty declared that Smith was one of the greatest living actresses at the top of her game.[373] Act I is often described as A's solo turn, the two other characters interrupting only to punctuate and relaunch her discourse. In fact, A's kind of soliloquy is immensely long for the reason that the old lady never stops repeating herself. Myra Carter had great difficulty memorising it,[374] and Maggie Smith herself mentioned 'the horror of trying to learn it',[375] although – as she explained in a letter to Albee – she greatly enjoyed playing this text, where every word, every comma was accurate.[376] In Act II, the actress did even more justice to the role, with a sobriety that all the critics applauded. As impressive as

370 'Our last great star', *The Daily Mail*, 4 November 1997, p. 9.

371 See L. Jenkins, 'Actress is written out of drama accolades', *The Times*, 25 February 1995, p. 5. The critic quoted Robert Fox; the play's producer vehemently expressed his indignation after such an unjust snub. However, Smith was presented with the Evening Standard Theatre Award for Best Actress in November 1994.

372 M. Owen, 'Women having fun', *The Evening Standard*, 22 September 1995, p. 25.

373 'Widow's pique', *The Mail on Sunday Review*, 20 November 1994, p. 30.

374 Solomon, *Albee in Performance*, p. 188.

375 Owen, 'Women having fun'.

376 Letter quoted in Gussow, *Edward Albee*, p. 372. A few years later, stage director A. Page explained that, in *Three Tall Women*, Maggie's lines were very difficult to learn; having grasped the structure, the actress sometimes changed a few words, following her instinct like a 'jazz player'. See M. Shenton, 'Returning to one's roots', *Plays International*, October 1997, p. 12-13.

a queen of tragedy, standing as a tallish figure draped in a devoured velvet robe, Smith magnificently, precisely, delivered every line, making the audience alternatively laugh or feel sorry. Critics as well as academics mostly focused on that second act which provided the actress with the opportunity to give a subtle, well-measured performance. Many reviewers thought that Act II was more riveting than Act I, due to its original dramatic structure and the philosophical reflection it underlaid,[377] but it seems that most of them were judging Albee's play and its very special point of view, rather than Smith's performance. As pertinent as their arguments were, Act I can appear – in terms of acting technique and dramaturgy – even more compelling. The novelist Beryl Bainbridge declared that Smith's A was so aged, that she was 'no longer female', emphasising the ultimate paradox of the actress's magical performance: playing the role as a caricatural pantomime dame, Maggie Smith gave the most striking, chillingly convincing portrayal.[378] P. Taylor praised an immaculate, virtuoso rendition of senility, underlining the technical mastery of an actress who aptly used all her physical tools to give the most mesmerising rendition of old age and decrepitude: with her drooping eyelids, her angular, disdainful chin and her screeching, Maggie Smith's A was the embodiment of crumbliness.[379] To put it simply, Act I allowed Smith to shine and display her talent in full scale, offering to the audience – although she was still in her late fifties – a stunning impersonation of senility.

When the curtain rises, A is wriggling about in her cosy armchair, soothing with her palm the soft fabric of her dressing gown. The old, very old lady winces, pouts, shakes her head and indistinctly chuckles.

377 See Taylor, 'Three Tall Women', *The Independent*, 2 October 1995, p. 11; J. Kingston, 'Albee's revenge diluted', *The Times*, 30 September 1995, p. 19; J. Tinker, 'Dame Maggie walks tall', *Daily Mail*, 6 October 1995, p. 52; M. Billington, 'Caged by old age', *The Guardian*, 16 November 1994, p. 7; J. Gross, 'Three into one don't quite go', *The Sunday Telegraph*, 20 November 1994, p. 5. For an in-depth analysis of Act II, see N. De Jongh, 'Standing tall on this night of high passion', *The Evening Standard*, 29 September 1995, p. 7.

378 *Front Row: Evenings at the Theatre* (New York: Continuum International Publishing Group Ltd, 2005), p. 84.

379 'Mommie Dearest', *The Independent*, 17 November 1994, p. 30. On the superiority of Act I, see also J. Campbell, 'When Beckett comes to Broadway', *The Times Literary Supplement*, 25 November 1994, p. 17.

With just a few moves, the actress has established her character and the spectators immediately perceive that they are seeing a vulnerable, senile nonagenarian. It was a real tour de force by Smith, a high-flying performance which led her to make use of all the resources of her creative genius; for forty minutes, the spectators watched a masterclass of acting. The American critic Wendy Lesser eloquently commented that staggering metamorphosis which actually deprived the audience from seeing the actress. There was only the character on stage and Maggie Smith brilliantly made use of her physical tools to express frailty and decay: 'In place of the willowy, graceful, extravagantly flamboyant Smith, we are left with the woman Albee has given us: a deeply crotchety, severely hampered, gradually dying old woman.' The critic admitted that, even immobilised and disabled, the actress brought 'a magnetic force to the role'.[380] The technique Smith used to convey her physical decrepitude was amazingly convincing.[381] Her acting tools were elementary – essentially the abrupt changes of tone and the comical gestures – but they were used with a virtuosity that compelled admiration. The change of tone, quite frequent in her monologue, oscillates between anger – the anger over her own decay and her envious rage against her able-bodied entourage – and incredulity – that of the loss of her mental faculties. It was on these two states of mind, the anger and the loss of her faculties, that Smith had built her whole performance. Her voice goes through infinite modulations, from an almost inaudible murmur – the faint voice of an exhausted woman – to raucous shrieks of an unexpected strength. She never stops moaning, whining and, like those stubborn and infuriating elderly people who seem obsessed by an idea, repeating to herself again and again: 'Where's the pillow? Where's the pillow?' She hammers home her words, she repeats them but quickly forgets them as soon as her mind wanders, and then she pauses, suddenly lost. Albee's script imposes that convulsive pace on the performer's delivery. When talking, A constantly stops and changes her mind as she loses the thread of her thought. Sometimes cheerful, she also

380 'Three Tall Women by Edward Albee', *The Threepenny Review*, 62, 1995, p. 25.

381 See M. Esslin, 'Three Tall Women', *Plays International*, January 1995, p. 15: Maggie Smith manages to present senility 'without patronising or ridiculing it.' Also C. Hirschhorn, 'Chilling study of growing old without grace', *The Sunday Express*, 20 November 1994, p. 58.

can be ferocious, literally barking her recriminations and puffing out her chest like a rooster ready to fight. This impotent Lady Bracknell – the comparison was made by Sheridan Morley[382] – possesses that oblivious self-assurance and peremptory imperiousness that very old people often have and her bad faith is so evident that it is nearly disarming. The critic B. Nightingale, whose review was altogether more positive, emphasised the caricatural tone of Act I, where the leading character, as (magnificently) played by Smith, took the form of a grotesque, pitiful Pantaloon figure lapsing in her second childhood,[383] while N. De Jongh was more receptive to the pathetic accents of the play, evoking the poignancy that underlay Smith's performance: witnessing the struggle of that diminished but proud woman, the audience certainly could not remain unmoved.[384] Astonishingly, the actress managed to convulse the house, despite the pitiful and devastating view her character offered. The return from the bathroom – one of the rare moments when A leaves her armchair – could bring tears to the eyes; dramatically hunched, leaning on her walking stick and dragging her slender frame onto the stage, the old lady seemed to be on the verge of collapse. Instead of that, the audience burst out laughing as the frail creature started to bully her lady companion with a thunderous, nearly masculine voice. This scene was probably one of the funniest moments in the play, especially when the dying nonagenarian regained a sudden energy to grasp her cane and bang it on her armchair in order to expel the unfortunate C who was unduly sitting in it. It was another form of comic effect, a visual one, which prefigured a memorable scene from *David Copperfield*, when the redoubtable Betsey Trotwood, broom in hand, chases the temerarious donkeys walking on her patch of grass.

Old, feeble and stricken with a variety of ailments, A is nevertheless – when being played by Maggie Smith – hilarious, and even cute. The actress presented, more than in any other part, this birdlike facies which accentuated her comical appearance. Emphasised by a stylish bun, her pointy nose, her angular face, her bulging eyes as well as her frenetic gestures – those jerky moves of the chin – gave her an inimitable bearing and a pinched, obstinate expression which sufficed to make the spectators

382 Morley, 'Who's Afraid of Maggie Smith ?'.

383 'Smith's rage against the dying', *The Times*, 17 November 1994, p. 25.

384 'Standing tall on this night of high passion', *The Evening Standard*, 29 September 1995, p. 7.

laugh, even before she had spoken. Smith displayed an extraordinary physical technique, as Matt Wolf emphasised in a remarkable article published in *American Theatre.* Wolf described Smith's 'strong alert eyes' piercing through a fascinating make-up; for him, the actress was 'a physical wonder'.[385] Just as they did for her unique Lady Bracknell rendition, critics extended the zoological metaphor, especially J. Tinker in *The Daily Mail* (who humorously compared her to a little bird 'darting' its head to pick a worm, emphasising the frail old lady's unexpected 'birdlike' energy[386]) and C. Spencer, in the rather enthusiastic review he wrote for *The Daily Telegraph* (for his part, the critic decided to underline the character's forceful determination, comparing the redoubtable old lady to a decrepit, 'beady-eyed' bird of prey[387]). In *The Evening Standard*, N. De Jongh colourfully described Smith's performance; carrying the metaphor further, he evoked the 'croaking' voice and 'cackling' chuckles of what proved to be a composite bird. Half hawk, half chick, the fearsome animal played by Smith darts the paralysing stare of a basilisk.[388] Of course, it was through these hilarious faces that the actress put her proven scene-stealing strategy into action. While C is talking, A never stops reacting by pouts and grumbles. She is getting bored, obviously – she hilariously puffs out her cheeks, just like an impolite child would do – and the spectator, also bored by C's insipid speech, focuses on Smith. At another moment, she simply points her nose to peer at a cup on a pedestal table; the gesture is unsignificant, but her suspicious air is irresistible. Despite the talent of the rest of the cast, the actress steals the show, once again.[389]

Every time she treads the boards, every time she appears in a movie, Maggie Smith is systematically, irritatingly, scrutinised by the critics

385 'The Pleasures of Bravura Acting in London', *American Theatre*, 12.2, February 1995, p. 67.

386 'Enriched by Dame Maggie's old age tension', *The Daily Mail*, 16 November 1994, p. 3.

387 'Albee's drama torn from the heart', *The Daily Telegraph*, 16 November 1994, p. 3. See also M. Paton ('Tall story that's too tiresome', *The Daily Express*, 16 November 1994, p. 19) who noted that the actress, aging thirty years for the part, looked like an 'outraged owl'; S. Hemming ('Return of Three Tall Women', *The Financial Times*, 3 October 1995, p. 17) preferred to compare Maggie Smith, 'eyes blinking, mouth pursed', with 'a tortoise newly acquainted with the light'.

388 'Magnificent Maggie', *The Evening Standard*, 16 November 1994, p. 3.

389 Paton, 'Tall story'; the critic admitted that, performing again her 'megastar turn', Smith nevertheless gave a great display of her comedic skills.

who hunt for excess, as if they feared that this first-rate actress would dare to make the audience laugh too much.[390] *Three Tall Women* did not make an exception and, as expected, some reviewers blamed her for overacting. Even Mel Gussow, in his biography of Albee, finds it opportune to allude to her usual mannerisms and 'idiosyncratic' acting style, although he hailed the acuteness of her portrayal here, admitting that Maggie Smith completely merged into the character created by Albee.[391] In quite a harsh indictment of a play which had obviously bored him to death, J. Peter accused her of indulging in complacency; he blamed the fact that the performance was undermined by Smith's flamboyant dramatics, suspecting the actress of using her commanding star aura and her equally imperious inflections to make her audience laugh on cue.[392] Once again, as it had happened with *The Importance of Being Earnest*, there were critics who reproached her for acting funny in a comedy. They blamed her for making clever use of her means – her voice, her hands and her body – as if a great actor had to be blamed for being great and for doing his job better than anyone else. Fortunately, others, like Bill Hagerty from *Today*, lauded Smith's exceptional talent. For him, Maggie Smith's incomparable performance transformed a good play into an unforgettable, mesmerising masterpiece; with no offence to the rest of the cast, her overwhelming portrayal made an impressive 'one tall woman' act.[393] M. Wolf also underlined the greatness of Maggie Smith's performance, which exclusively aimed at serving Albee's play,[394] and R. Tanitch, for his part, dismissing the naysayers' criticisms, gave a definitive judgement on her portrayal: 'There will be those who will find the monologue […] over long. Dame Maggie, imperious, rouged, pale, frail, keeps her comic mannerisms on check (on the whole) and the performance, both witty and distressing, is a tour de force.'[395]

---

390 See, among others, C. Hirschhorn, 'Three Tall Women', *The Sunday Express*, 8 October 1995 (see *Theatre Record*, 24 September-7 October 1995, p. 1349). Hischorn joked that Smith, well aware that she was in a play and not a revue, gave a great performance.

391 Gussow, *Edward Albee*, p. 370.

392 'Monstrous Regiment', *The Sunday Times*, 20 November 1994, p. 24.

393 'Three Tall Women', *Today*, 6 October 1995 (see *Theatre Record*, 24 September-7 October 1995, p. 1349).

394 Wolf, 'The Pleasures of Bravura Acting', p. 67.

395 'Three Tall Women', *Plays and Players*, November-December 1994, p. 9.

Still, in some aspects, the lady looked a bit too spry for a weakened nonagenarian. N. De Jongh ironically remarked that the frail nonagenarian in floral gown, who was supposed to hold her last stand (the critic compared her to an 'old galleon' slowly sinking in deep waters), was fighting sometimes a bit 'too vigorously'.[396] Looking like a fragile porcelain doll with her delicate pallid complexion – a critic wrote that she was a crossbreeding between an albino rabbit and Dame Barbara Cartland – her senile lady could find her place in a Tim Burton movie.[397] In *What's On*, Roger Foss commented on the caricatural aspect of her appearance; according to him, with one arm crippled and the other one flapping to express helpless disapproval, the sour-eyed ancient lady resembled a kind of old 'dinosaur' ultimately recollecting memories of its antediluvian past. For Foss, it was too excessive, on the verge of 'parody'.[398] However, under the grotesque persona of that tyrannical old lady, Smith had created, paradoxically, a very human figure, as M. Billington acknowledged in his review. He lauded her acute portrayal of 'extreme old age', mentioning these inconsistencies of perception which denote senility: alternatively clear-sighted or confused, joyous or agressive, Smith delivered a 'consummate' performance.[399] P. Taylor considered that the actress had brilliantly built a truthful character, beyond caricature and excess,[400] and A. Macaulay, in *The Financial Times*, paid homage to a baffling performance, delivered by a master of characterisation. He marvelled at Maggie Smith's extraordinary assumption of senility, emphasising her scrupulous depiction of old-age despair, thanks to voice inflections and facial expressions that spectacularly confess the torments of helplessness and infirmity. The critic compared her performance to that of Myra

396 De Jongh, 'Magnificent Maggie'.

397 The critic David Baker said: 'Nearly dead, her arm pokes in the air like a robot claw.' See *Theatre*, November-December 1995, p. 27.

398 4 October 1995 (see *Theatre Record*, 24 September-7 October 1995, p. 1350).

399 Billington, 'Caged by old age'. See also K. Stratton's review in *Time Out*, 4 October 1995 (see *Theatre Record*, 24 September-7 October 1995, p. 1350).

400 Taylor, 'Three Tall Women'. Analysing Maggie Smith's performance, the critic P. Taylor underlined the mesmerising, meticulous accuracy of her portrayal of the very old lady, thanks to a clever use of her technical skills; with her incessant crying, her right arm constantly waving as if to compensate the stillness of the left one, her mischievous grins and her fits of anger, Smith's A becomes the most sublime, convincing incarnation of senile decay.

Carter, considering it 'more autocratic' and, despite acknowledging she employed some of her trademark comic devices, he asserted that, in Act II, she was a marvel of 'stillness' and restraint, giving one of her best performances of her career.[401]

In Act I, Smith's A is also the embodiment of old-age vulnerability,[402] what makes her more moving – more lovable, in a certain way – than she is in Act II, where she reappears as a vigorous, majestic old monarch. The delicate grace that emanates from the character makes her physical frailty more poignant; hunched in her armchair, with her arm in a sling, A remains very beautiful despite her age and her disabilities. Probably too beautiful to be completely convincing, she becomes even more pathetic.[403] The senile lady is nothing but a disintegrating body, ravaged by osteoporosis which irremediably shrinks her willowy figure; she desperately mourns her former enviable appearance, as if her height was still of importance now that death is imminent. Deprived of the use of her decalcified arm of which the doctor postpones the amputation, A progressively loses control of all her mental faculties and physical abilities. Every time her troubled mind becomes aware of that irremediable loss, the old woman bursts into tears. One of the most heartbreaking scenes shows her confronted to the sordid realities of physical dependence. Screaming and staggering, the old woman is accompanied to the bathroom by B, to satisfy an urgent need. A few minutes later, back in her armchair, she stops her own babbles, suddenly fearing that she is 'doing' in her panties. It was supposed to be a devastating moment but – with an undeniable cruelty – the audience was in stitches when seeing a resigned Frances de la Tour conscientiously feeling the cushion on which Maggie Smith was sitting. A's vulnerability is all the more heartbreaking that it is mixed with a profound antipathy. The old lady is irascible and full of rancour when contemplating her own deterioration; her failings are always compensated by her fits of rage and then, her vigour

401 'Three Tall Women', *The Financial Times*, 16 November 1994, p. 23.

402 M. Paton, 'Mesmerising Maggie defies the depression', *The Daily Express*, 30 September 1995, p. 27; the critic found her pitiable, but hilariously funny

403 With her Gothic make-up, A looked like a character in an Expressionist movie by Murnau or Fritz Lang, especially during the second run, in 1995. Actually, this irrealistic note served the metaphysical dimension of the play. By its pastel colours, the set also reflected like a mirror the magnificent Wyndham's Theatre, architectural tribute to femininity and to the woman who had inspired its decoration, the actress Mary Moore.

oddly contrasts with her frailty. With her despising, haughty, even racist behaviour, A is as hateful as pitiful. She has all the paranoiac obsessions that very old people have, the constant fear of being robbed and the perpetual conviction that everyone around her is a drunk – 'My sister drank!' becomes a catchphrase which punctuates her speech. Pity eventually wins over hatred and that monstrous character appears to be lovable, as Sarah Hemming wrote in *The Financial Times*: as paradoxical as it might seem, people feel empathy for her despicable, but pitious old woman facing decrepitude.[404] In a certain way, Maggie Smith's performance ruined Albee's initial project. 'We've got to really hate her,' he had warned Myra Carter before the first rehearsals in Vienna.[405] Unfortunately, Smith made us adore that insufferable, cantankerous, incontinent old lady the playwright wanted us to abhor.[406]

---

404 Hemming, 'Return of *Three Tall Women*'. See also A. Edemariam, 'Whistling in the dark', *The Guardian*, 10 January 2004, p. 23; the journalist recounted that Albee kept asking Page to make Smith look more unpleasant and, according to the stage director, it was a tricky task. Seeing a character losing control of their mind or bodily faculties, the audience necessarily feels empathy for them.

405 Solomon, *Albee in Performance*, p. 166.

406 Bainbridge, *Front Row*, p. 83. The novelist remembered that the audience at the Wyndham's adored the character played by Maggie Smith despite her fierceness and, as she jokingly remarked, some of them would have gladly exchanged their own mother for the distasteful old crone they saw on the stage.

The Craft of Ageing

Like Miss Shepherd in *The Lady in the Van*, A represents an exception among the theatre roles that Maggie Smith has played since the early 1990s. On stage, the actress has more often played her own age than nonagenarians. On screen, though, white wigs, canes and wheelchairs have become usual props for her. Curly bun for a majestic Duchess of York in R. Loncraine's *Richard III* or smart Marcel wave for the widowed battle-axe she plays in *Tea with Mussolini*, Smith wears with the same elegance all variants of white hair. However, despite her highly skilled characterisation technique, the chameleon actress sometimes experiences difficulties when confronting what can be called the historical perception of age. No one could deny that the perception we have of a character also depends on the historical period which that character belongs to. In *Ladies in Lavender*, the transposition on screen of a story originally set in the 1900s has generated a few incoherencies – which in no way diminish, though, the quality of this charming movie. 'Old ladies': this is what the Widdington sisters are called by the neighbourhood, as well as by the film critics. In the interviews that Charles Dance gave at the time of the release, he admitted he had chosen to make the two heroines a bit older than they were in Locke's short story – Janet was forty-eight and her sister, forty-five –, in order to cast the tandem of Dench-Smith. Dance explained that, as soon as he had read the story, he thought about the casting of the Widdington sisters; for him, Dench and Smith were the only candidates.[407] Was it really necessary to pretend that the sisters were older to have them portrayed by Dench and Smith, both sexagenarians then? The two actresses could easily rely on their talent and energy to play – without being ridiculous – women who were middle-aged in the 1900s – or, in the film's case, in the 1930s. A woman of forty-eight, in 1936, was not young, but on the contrary, she could already be regarded as an ageing woman. In fact, it looks as if, on second thoughts, Dance had not really made his characters older. Janet and Ursula, such as they appear on screen, do not resemble the 'old ladies' announced by some reviewers. The two women look certainly closer to their fifties than a venerable age that their physical vigour immediately denies. The Widdington sisters climb the stairs, run on the beach and even dare to venture on the rocks with an agility that could not belong to elderly ladies. Despite their grey wigs and that coloured foundation which gives them the tanned complexion of the natives of Cornwall's coastline,[408] Smith and Dench behave like two young girls.

407 C. Dance, 'Lavender Blues', *The Telegraph Magazine*, 16 October 2004, p. 54.

408 Paradoxically, Smith, who often plays nonagenarians on screen, had to wear an ageing make-up for portraying a character who is supposed to be younger than she actually is! During an interview, she nevertheless dared to pretend, with Judi Dench: 'Not a blade of make-up between us!' – an allegation which was not only wrong, but self-deprecatory (see Mackenzie, 'You have to laugh'). The make-up designer Fae Hammond used a warm brown colour to make Dench and Smith look like women who had spent their entire lives in Cornwall: 'Everyone who comes on to the make-up truck leaves a few shades darker and it all fits in well with the gorgeous overall colours of the film.'

There is necessarily a discrepancy when a performer of our time has to portray a character from the past. An actor in his sixties will have to transform himself – through the process of characterisation – to be convincing as a greybeard in Shakespeare or Molière. A sixty-year-old man has nothing in common, nowadays, with the very old person he would have been three centuries ago. The same problem occurred in the first season of *Downton Abbey*. The dowager countess was supposed to be seventy at the beginning of the story; in 1912, a woman of that age would have been regarded as full of years and, when browsing through old pictures showing upper-class ladies from this era, the viewer realises that the character could not have looked that youthful at seventy. Ironically, Smith, being older than the character, had nevertheless to 'age' to play her. Even more disturbing is the fact that, in Season 5, the dowager – suddenly involved in a romantic plot – seems to have rejuvenated in quite an inexplicable manner, although she is supposed to be eighty-two then. More beautiful than ever, Violet makes a rather parcimonious use of her cane and, now dressed by the very talented costume designer Anna Robbins, she sports much more flattering dresses which emphasise a figure that no old dowager of that time could have had. Who cares about verisimilitude, though, when an actress wears period costumes so well?

Not only do the characters from the past necessarily look older than our contemporaries of the same age, but in the case of the female performers, this evolution is even more noticeable. Today, it would seem quite inappropriate to offer a septuagenarian actress the parts that were played, at the same age, by Margaret Rutherford or Dame May Whitty. Apart from a handful of chameleon actresses, many would immediately throw the script away. In February 1926, the incomparable Ellen Terry attended the first night of a revival of *Much Ado about Nothing* at the New Theatre – today known as the Noel Coward Theatre. The audience was overwhelmed by the presence of the great actress who had been a remarkable Beatrice in the 1880s, and a few weeks later, the journalist of *The Washington Post* wrote a panegyric of the elderly thespian who was, then, just a bit older than Maggie Smith is now. He described her as a white-haired 'beautiful grandmotherly person', dressed in black and grey, who retained 'in her old age' the aura and dignity of her glorious years.[409]

409 'Ellen Terry wears her age with grace', *The Washington Post*, 21 March 1926, p. 9.

Such a description would fit none of our senior actresses nowadays. Smith, like her colleagues Dench, Atkins or Redgrave, looks years younger than her own age. To see Eileen Atkins portraying a decrepit, and then dying Queen Mary in the first series of *The Crown* (2016), is a pure delight when we consider how youthful and modern Dame Eileen looks in real life. Times have changed, of course, and now, actresses in their late seventies or early eighties – as beautiful and attractive as ever – have nothing in common with their dignified predecessors of the nineteenth or early twentieth century. In that time, roles got fewer and fewer for mature actresses, and, after a certain age, the loss of beauty, weight gain or poor health compelled them to retire, backing into anonymity and poverty. These days, when playing their own age, septuagenarians or young octogenarians portray youthful and sprightly women who are still sexually attractive. They still can be involved in a love story, just like Judi Dench in *The Best Exotic Marigold Hotel* (2012) or Anne Reid in the TV show *Last Tango in Halifax*.

When it comes to playing very old ladies, it gets more difficult to find and cast an actress who is the right age. Few, very few elderly actors and actresses are still active and insurance companies are always reluctant to get involved in such circumstances. When the actor or the actress is the right age to play the part, he or she does not have the stamina to endure several weeks of filming or to tread the boards every night. A in *Three Tall Women* is unquestionably much too long, too demanding a part to be played by a ninety-five-year-old actress.[410] Her talent excepted, this is certainly the other reason why Maggie Smith has been playing very old ladies for years. Most of the actresses of the previous generation were already dead or had retired for a long time and casting directors necessarily had to resort to actresses of her generation to play very old characters. Smith's amazing ability to transform herself – which allows her to play the most decrepit women – is combined with a phenomenal energy; it represents a considerable facility for the director and the production team. The producer Kevin Loader recently hailed the actress for the energy she displayed during the filming of *The Lady in the Van*. In her behind-the-

410 J. W. Fisher, 'Creating Another Identity', p. 75: 'The oldest character in Edward Albee's play, for example, awaits the nonagenarian who has the stamina to play not only her own age, but also the younger 72-year-old.'

scenes commentary, the actress and screenwriter Emma Thompson had also underscored Smith's fitness and agility on the set of *Nanny McPhee and the Big Bang* (2009), telling how the veteran actress, as fit as a teenage girl, acrobatically skipped up and down the precarious platforms.[411] Having brilliantly demonstrated how good she could be in those parts, the actress stands now as the ideal choice to play any nonagenarian or centenarian.

In 2013, when the American playwright Israel Horovitz decided to make his debut behind the camera, adapting his successful play *My Old Lady* for the big screen, he wanted to reunite an A-list cast for his first movie in order to ensure its success.[412] He sent his screenplay to Maggie Smith, asking her to play the titular character, Mathilde Girard. In an interview, the actress admitted that, while some people imagine that most actors are knee-deep in scripts, reality is much different; they have to do things as they turn up. When she read Horovitz's script, she found the story intriguing and was willing to play Mathilde, even if it was another nonagenarian part.[413] In the play, Mathilde was ninety-five, whereas she is only ninety-two in the film, but it does not change much; the actress was, once again, much younger than the role which was offered to her. Horovitz's movie eventually got mixed reviews, but critics unanimously praised the actors, Kevin Kline, Kristin Scott-Thomas and, of course, Smith who gives, as usual, an impeccable performance. As the director admitted, he wanted someone talented and very famous to play his 'old lady' and, understandably, he offered the part to Smith, an actress now specialising in that category of roles. Nothing out of the ordinary. What was less ordinary was that, for once, the actress had to do without any external help – wig, make-up or props – to play a part that is usually given to an older actress. In fact, Horovitz feared that the make-up would look artificial on her. Of course, it would be not only rude, but

411 E. Thompson, *Nanny McPhee and the Big Bang Film Diary* (London: Bloomsbury, 2010), p. 180.

412 I. Horovitz, *My Old Lady. Complete stage play and screenplay with an essay on adaptation* (New York: Three Rooms Press, 2016), p. 144.

413 K. Shattuck, 'Glad to Try "Something Terrifying". Israel Horovitz Directs the Film of His Play "My Old Lady"', *NYTimes.com*, 28 August 2014 <https://www.nytimes.com/2014/08/31/movies/israel-horovitz-directs-the-film-of-his-play-my-old-lady.html?_r=0> [accessed 12 November 2016].

mostly ridiculous to pretend that Maggie Smith could easily, naturally, be taken for a nonagenarian. It is not exactly the case, despite the actress's own allegations. In an interview for *The Telegraph*, she confessed – with her habitual causticity – to Elizabeth Grice that it was not necessary to make her up any more as she had eventually 'caught up' with herself! In parallel, the journalist commented that, on the contrary, the production team marvelled at her striking transformation into the very old Mathilde without the help of make-up or props and (according to her) they had every reason to do so, as the 'slight and chic' Maggie had nothing in common with a nonagenarian.[414] Actually, the transformation into old Mrs Girard does not work so well and, clearly, an adequat wig and a proper ageing make-up would not have been superfluous.[415] Her make-up is minimal – in any case, Smith wears just cinematic make-up, required by the lights, not aesthetical make-up – and, in accordance with the director's wishes, it looks quite natural indeed. The actress seems to be older than she is in real life, but she does not look like a nonagenarian at all. The age gap appears more clearly, though, on the stills from *The Second Best Exotic Marigold Hotel* (filmed a couple of months later, in the early weeks of 2014) or in the footage from The Evening Standard Theatre Awards ceremony where the actress was presented with a Lifetime Achievement Award, a few weeks after the production wrap of Horovitz's movie.

Despite this initial handicap, Smith bravely meets the challenge, using only her skills and technique to become Mathilde Girard. In an interview, Kevin Kline recounted how cast and crew were baffled to see her turning instantly into character. When she put on her old-lady attire, Smith transformed herself into 'this much slower woman'.[416] In fact, as soon as Mathilde appears on screen, the spectator can observe that this woman is definitely not Maggie Smith. Her figure and her attitude have changed. With a hunched back and her arms folded at her sides, she moves in a

414 E. Grice, 'Maggie Smith interview for My Old Lady: "If you have been around long enough you are an icon"', *The Telegraph*, 8 November 2014, p. 4.

415 As if Smith looked too old (?) to convincingly play the 'Old Lady', the publicists had the ridiculous idea to 'photoshop' her face on the film poster. The purpose was absurd and the result, disastrous.

416 R. Stein, 'Kevin Kline charms ladies old and young', *The San Francisco Chronicle*, 2 September 2014 <http://www.sfgate.com/entertainment/article/Kevin-Kline-charms-ladies-old-and-young-5717370.php> [accessed 12 November 2016].

very special manner. All her gestures are restricted. When sitting down in an armchair, she heavily slumps into it. She walks very slowly with her legs slightly apart as if she was perpetually trying to steady herself. The way she moves and her posture are, of course, key elements in her work of characterisation: 'Israel asked her if she could move into the next room a little faster. She said, "No. I'm an old lady and I can't move any faster". She had to remind him she was playing an old lady.'[417] To put it in a few words, Smith has changed her pace. She has this high-pitched, slightly hoarse voice she often uses when playing elderly women. She pants when breathing and speaks speedily, frantically, with the stubborn determination that very old people often have. Above all, the actress possesses this extraordinary ability to mobilise all the muscles of her face in order to transform it. Mathilde's face is tense, even contorted when she smiles. She puckers her lips to sip her wine and clinks her tongue, just like toothless old people do. All these details reflect a very scrupulous sense of observation. In one of the most striking scenes of the film, Mathilde – who is usually confined to the first floor – attempts to go upstairs to have a crucial talk with her daughter. Climbing each step needs enormous efforts and, desperately grabbing the banisters, Mathilde ascends the stairs with the greatest difficulty. Smith does not look ninety-two at that very moment. She seems to be more than one-hundred.

When he had imagined the character, Horovitz had been inspired by his own mother, an alert nonagenarian. When, years later, he chose to give the role to Maggie Smith, he probably thought that casting an actress too young for the part would make things easier in terms of verisimilitude. Not exactly, in fact. He wanted Smith to appear as a lively and alert very old lady, but of course, it was impossible for the actress to play the role in that manner. The only way she could 'act old' on screen was to make all her moves and gestures look slower, and to remain still, seated in her armchair, most of the time. In 1920, Sarah Bernhardt played the aged Biblical queen in Racine's *Athalie* and managed to create a powerful and formidable queen although she had one leg amputated. The critics acknowledged that the famous elderly thespian suggested movement while seated: 'Immobilised upon her palanquin, Athalie dominates the

417 *Ibid.*

stage as if she were standing [...] she leans upon the back of her chair, then sits erects again with so commanding an air that one forgets she is seated.'[418] This is the exact opposite which happens here with Maggie Smith as Mathilde; to remain seated is the only way for her to convey old age and hide the physical abilities of an actress too young for the role. If Smith had been too vigorous and alert when playing Mathilde Girard, her characterisation would have been deprived of any credibility. To cast an actor who is too young for the part forces him to transform himself, in order that the spectators could see what they expect to see. In fact, the actress had no other choice than playing the role according to our preconceptions of old age; she portrays the ninety-two-year-old lady whom the audience wants to see, that is the stereotypical image of a nonagenarian.[419] When watching a movie or seeing a play, the spectator needs codes of interpretation – just like, in ancient times, the Greek audiences were able to identify the characters in a comedy thanks to the distinctive mask each actor wore on the stage. Even if nonagenarians look much younger than their actual age these days, in fiction though, a nonagenarian still has to look old. But the real difficulty lies in the fact that a younger actress who plays a nonagenarian extremely well cannot be equivalent to an actress in her nineties who has remained fit and spry. The result is quite different. There is a slight mismatch between the actress's postures – always perfectly calculated, in Smith's case – and her physical appearance which sooner or later betrays her. The journalist from *The New York Times* described Mathilde as a vigorous, opinionated woman in her nineties showing few signs of decrepitude.[420] It was not accurate. In fact, Smith's Mathilde Girard looks more like a tired, faded woman in her seventies. Israel Horovitz was lucky enough to work with an actress

418 H. Bordeaux, *La Vie au Théâtre* (Paris: Plon, 1910-1921), V, p. 140-141, fully quoted in G. Taramow, *Sarah Bernhardt. The Art within the Legend* (Princeton: Princeton University Press, 1972), p. 97.

419 E. W. Markson, 'The Female Aging Body Through Film', in *Aging Bodies. Images and Everyday Experience*, ed. by C. A. Faircloth (Walnut Creek: Altamira Press, 2003), p. 99. The portrayal of the older female body in film is always biased; actresses adopt a look which is supposed to give information about the social status and the age of the character they are playing, but this stereotypical look may have nothing in common with the real-life appearance of the actress.

420 S. Holden, 'An Apartment in the Marais, With Complications and Family Secrets', *The New York Times*, 9 September 2014, p. 6.

whose professionalism and physical energy are both exceptional. It is all the more amazing to see Maggie Smith playing very old ladies that she is very fit in real life. As Horovitz pointed out, whereas many actors use a foam mattress when they have to fall onto the floor, Smith did several takes without using any protection. As he recounted: 'I thought, "I can't be the man who killed Maggie Smith." And I said, "I'm very impressed, that you could do that, Maggie," and she looked at me with this kind of sexy voice and said, "You'd be amazed at what I can still do."'[421]

In *My Old Lady*, Mathilde has a dull gaze but, at intervals, a mischievous twinkle suddenly appears in her eyes and the spectator wonders if it belongs to this enigmatic old woman who is teasing Mathias, or to Maggie Smith who considers with an ironic distance the character she is portraying. From time to time, when the tension loosens, the actress's beautiful face furtively shows beneath the surface and suddenly, she loses more than twenty years on the screen. At some rare moments, she straightens her back and immediately appears taller and more vigorous. When Mathilde wears her nightgown, Smith cannot delude the spectator; this is a granny nightgown, but the lady who is wearing it has the muscles and the frame of a younger woman. It is also here that her chameleon skills reach their limits. Despite all her talent, she is certainly too vigorous to be fully convincing and her morphology is not that of a decalcified centenarian. Nevertheless – and this is Maggie Smith's biggest achievement in that movie – her Mathilde is so compelling that the spectator feels almost uncomfortable after the screening. Critics praised her performance, indeed, but never mentioned her incredible prowess in terms of characterisation. As if they did not notice. This is perfect illusion, the ultimate goal that every actor should aim at. How does she do that? It is probably some magic, or something that is called genius and it goes far beyond technique and acting skills. In actual fact, very few actresses are able to transform themselves at sight so effortlessly. The French critic Henri Bataille once wrote about Réjane (1856–1920) – an actress as famous as Sarah Bernhardt in her time – that she had 'a rubber face': 'The concentric point is the nose. The

421 Press conference at the Cohen Media Group, September 2014. See L. Damon, 'Kevin Kline and Israel Horovitz discuss new film "My Old Lady"', *MediaMikes.com*, 10 September 2014 <http://www.mediamikes.com/2014/09/kevin-kline-and-israel-horovitz-discuss-new-film-my-old-lady/> [accessed 12 November 2016].

rest moves with agility around it, rises, lowers, tenses up or relaxes.' He emphasised her exceptional ability to age on demand, 'suddenly this facial mask – without moving, without fidgeting – alters, ages, visibly ages as if it was driven by a mysterious inner force... This woman is able to age instantly'.[422] In the review he wrote on *Three Tall Women* in 1994, P. Levy observed a similar phenomenon about Maggie Smith's performance. He recounted how her age altered several times during the play, going from a dying old woman to a more vigorous nonagenarian, and then discarding all the accumulated years for the curtain call.[423]

Oddly enough, it also happens that the character Maggie Smith has to play is made 'younger' for the needs of the production. For instance, Mrs Oldknow – a name which undoubtedly predisposes to wisdom – in J. Fellowes's *From Time to Time* (2009) is supposed to be the grandmother of young hero Tolly, although she was a centenarian in Lucy Boston's novel. In the *Chimneys of Green Knowe*, the second opus of Boston's *Green Knowe* series, Linnet Oldknow is a tiny, scrubbly, white-haired great-grandmother whose magical powers make her as fascinating as Granny Wendy in *Hook*. The movie shows a much more realistic grandmother, vigorous and tall, whose fashionable clothing – Maggie/Linnet sporting a very elegant side-buttoned coat – may seem a bit surprising considering the age she is. The young actor playing Tolly (Axel Etel) also looks a bit too old and too tall to play an eleven-year-old child,[424] thus the hero and his grandmother eventually make an odd couple. As the story is set in the early 1940s, Linnet could easily be taken for the fifty-something mother of the teenage boy. In a radically different context, the actress played Muriel Donnelly in John Madden's *The Best Exotic Marigold Hotel* (2012) and, like the other characters in the film, she has been made considerably younger in Ol Parker's screenplay. The novel which had inspired the movie, *These Foolish Things* by Deborah Moggach (2004), told the story of senescent – if not senile – old people 'outsourced' in India, in a former Bangalore hotel turned into a nursing home where they are supposed to spend their remaining years. Strangely, despite their ailments

---

422 H. Bataille, *Ecrits sur le Théâtre* (Paris: Editions Georges Crès et Cie, 1917), p. 94-95.

423 'Three Tall Women', *The Wall Street Journal*, 16 December 1994, p. 7.

424 The filming had been postponed to the end of 2008, because of Maggie Smith's health condition.

and disabilities, the characters created by Moggach were all septuagenarians, what could seem anachronistic these days. Septuagenarians often have their own parents still alive, and – unless they are ill or disabled – they certainly do not plan to settle in a retirement home themselves. Confined to a wheelchair because of a bad hip, Smith's Muriel is a vigorous and modern lower middle-class woman who seems to be in her late sixties. Cantankerous and racist to the point of caricature, she has very little in common with the character of the novel. Muriel Donnelly was initially a pitiful and decrepit old lady, weakened by her advanced years, whose only prospect was to spend the rest of her life in an exotic, cheap place where she would lose her points of reference. There was not much hope for her. On the contrary, in the movie, Muriel successfully goes through her hip surgery, regains her energy and, having found new goals to aim at, she starts a new life with new responsibilities. As the critic O. Glazebrook implied, the actors are all fabulous in their roles, but they definitely look too young to be convincing: the only resident who looks aged is Muriel Donnelly, and this is only because she is confined to a wheelchair.[425] Actually, in the movie, the nursing home run by Dr Kapoor has become a shabby hotel resort run by the young Sonny Kapoor, and the cast looks more like a group of senior tourists than a bunch of decaying old folks. Glazebrook noticed that, when Maggie/Muriel rises from her wheelchair, proving to be a youthful and energetic woman, she 'takes over' (and steals) the whole show.[426] Nevertheless, even in this small role, the metamorphosis which Maggie Smith goes through is spectacular. At the beginning, Muriel looks like an invalid, lying on a hospital bed, then sitting in a wheelchair. When she leaves the hospital, with a woolly beret on her head, she has a grumpy and wrinkled pale face that funnily reminds us of (the onstage version of) a clean Miss Shepherd wheeled back from the Day Centre. Progressively, Muriel acclimatises herself, changes her behaviour and becomes able to walk again. In the epilogue, she is quite a different person. Looking younger, more feminine and even pretty, Muriel is involved in the management of

---

425 'Golden Oldies', *The Spectator*, 25 February 2012, p. 56.

426 *Ibid.*

the Marigold Hotel.[427] In the sequel, released three years later, the change is even more radical, she has now turned into a real business woman, full of dynamism and wit. Only the ending could appear disappointing, as we suddenly learn, without any preliminary warning, that the character is going to die. However, in terms of acting, and despite her very limited screen time, the first opus indisputably gives Smith some meatier material, allowing us to witness the impressive evolution of her character.

In Dustin Hoffman's *Quartet* (2012), Maggie Smith portrays Jean Horton, an ex-diva whose financial issues force her to take refuge in a home for retired singers. Once again, the character she plays looks sensibly younger than the elderly character whom Ronald Harwood had created for the stage: 'She looks one-hundred,' one of the characters (of the play) comments, after seeing Jean on her arrival. It could be duly expected to see Maggie/Jean resembling A, her character in *Three Tall Women*, but there is nothing of that. Actually, in the film, Jean looks like the twin sister of Elizabeth – the Lady from Dubuque. Tall, blonde and sophisticated, she is an ageing, but beautiful woman who seems to be in her early seventies, but certainly not a very old lady. It is surprising to see the four leads in the film looking so young, much younger in any case than the actual residents of the Casa di Verdi in the documentary that had inspired Harwood.[428] Evading the delicate task to make the main actors look older, Hoffman decided to make the characters younger than they were in the play – Cedric Livingstone, played by Michael Gambon, was supposed to be ninety-one – and thus, despite Jean's bad hip and Cissy's mental disorders, they are still youthful and vigorous pensioners. In fact, as stressed by Dr Cogan (Sheridan Smith), Beecham House is not a 'nursing home', but a 'retirement home', for retired

427 Such a change seemed a bit sudden for some critics. See D. Cox, 'Why do films do such a bad job of portraying old people?', *The Guardian*, 28 February 2012 <https://www.theguardian.com/film/filmblog/2012/feb/28/films-bad-job-portraying-old-people> [accessed 12 November 2016]: 'A ratty old Hobnob addict can metamorphose into a finance whizz capable of rescuing an ailing business.' Also S. Falcus-K. Sako, 'Women, Travelling and Later Life', in *Ageing, Popular Culture and Contemporary Feminism*, p. 214: 'This change takes her from unpleasant bigot, who reluctantly travels to India to have an affordable hip operation, to efficient, hardworking woman, something symbolised by her movement out of the wheelchair. Her return to able-bodiedness is nevertheless problematic, both in its representation as almost miraculous and in its strong association with her usefulness.'

428 *Tosca's Kiss* (*Il Bascio di Tosca*), directed by D. Schmidt, 1984.

and disargented artists.[429] This was probably a clever way to justify the age of the four leaders, a bit too spry and alert to live in such a home, whereas numerous artists among the supporting cast were sensibly older.[430] This bias conveys a more optimistic tonality to the film, affirming, as the saying goes, 'it is never too late'. The four characters are too energetic, too valid to break our heart; they have not reached the end of their life, they still have a future. This slight change allows the introduction of a proper, convincing love story between Jean and her ex-husband. Far from being the ridiculous stock characters that they used to be in the past, these senior figures in movies are now involved in the same situations as young and middle-aged people are.

When Agnieszka Holland's *The Secret Garden* was released, in 1993, Maggie Smith was interviewed by the famous critic Barry Norman for his TV programme *Film 93*. When Norman asked her why she often played old ladies, Smith jokingly replied, 'Because I AM an old lady!'[431] More than twenty years later, it would still be a joke. The actress looks years younger than her age and, whatever she pretends, playing elderly women still requires some characterisation work from her. About Sybil Thorndike, the critics of her time said that the only way Sybil 'could convey old age' was by acting.[432] Thorndike had a particular longevity as a performer and she was able to keep, all her life, a vitality and freshness that made her appear graceful even in old age. Of course, it would be pointless to compare the Thorndike-Evans generation with the actresses of our time; at the same age, it is certain that Judi Dench, Eileen Atkins or Vanessa Redgrave will look younger than a 'youthful' Dame Sybil did. Still, the quote is relevant in the way it highlights one of the fundamental aspects of characterisation. The actor or the actress must be able to 'act old', just like he or she knows

429 A very recent article focuses on the fact that, in the movie, care and care workers are relegated to the background (see S. Chivers, 'The Show must Go On: Aging, Care, and Musical Performance in *Quartet*', *Modern Drama*, 59.2, Summer 2016, p. 213-230). However, from a realistic point of view, none of the four leading characters seems to need the kind of care provided in a nursing home, and when the author points out that Horton risks revealing the extent to which her age 'has affected her skill and appearance', it sounds as if she had watched another film: we do not hear Jean singing, but at least we can see her, and she has obviously no reason to worry about her appearance.

430 All were real musicians or singers, as D. Hoffman wanted them to be.

431 *Film 93*, BBC1, 4 October 1993.

432 Croall, *Sibyl Thorndike*, p. 510.

how to play love or hatred. In 2012, in Toronto, Smith gave a brilliant and witty acceptance speech for the Stratford Shakespeare Festival's Legacy Award which had just been presented to her, and she related an anecdote which had happened to her a few months earlier, on the set of *Downton Abbey*. In full dowager costume, struggling to get out of her armchair and leaving heavily on her cane, she had suddenly told her co-star Penelope Wilton: 'Why am I acting old? I don't need to!'[433] The audience laughed heartily, as the remark sounded quite irrelevant coming from such a spry lady. Undoubtedly, to portray an elderly lady, Smith still needs to 'act old', and fortunately, she does it better than anyone.

Maggie Smith is probably one of the rare actresses in the world who is able to portray characters on such a wide age scale. She can play any age, from maturity to very old age. In this regard, she outdoes her colleagues Judi Dench and Helen Mirren who usually play their own age,[434] and joins actresses such as Eileen Atkins or Vanessa Redgrave – who played a magnificent Miss Daisy in the London production of *Driving Miss Daisy* (Wyndham Theatre, 2011). Like Atkins and Redgrave, Smith has a very angular face which certainly helps her to age so easily. However, to cast her only in nonagenarian or centenarian parts would equate to deprive us of fifty per cent of her talent. Maggie Smith is always perfect when playing younger women, but oddly, journalists and critics do not seem to notice that she is precisely playing a younger role. She remains unclassifiable, incomparable in her malleability and her amazing capacity to effortlessly portray any character, outside of all temporal contingencies. As convincing when playing a senile woman as a very old performer could be, as attractive – when the part requires it, and it is, unfortunately, too rare – as many younger actresses, she can afford the luxury of alternating,

433 Maggie Smith resumed this anecdote more recently (radio-interview by D. Davies for NPR, 23 February 2016). What seems to be a funny behind-the-scene story – told by the self-deprecating Smith to reassert that she is a 'woman of many years' – is much more insightful than it appears. Whatever she says about her (supposedly 'very') old age, her instinct leads her to use her technical skills when it comes to playing an elderly character. For a full transcript of the interview, see NPR website, <http://www.npr.org/2016/02/23/467802382/maggie-smith-on-the-pressures-of-acting-you-want-so-much-to-get-it-right> [accessed 12 November 2016].

434 With regard to Judi Dench, *Chocolat* (L. Hallström, 2000), where she portrays an old lady who suffers from diabetes, represents a noticeable exception in her recent career.

at very short intervals, roles that no other actress could play at the same moment of her career. In fact, her range covers almost fifty years. She still can play quinquagenarians in eighteenth- or nineteenth-century period dramas as well as bed-ridden centenarians. Her means (physical appearance, gestures, voice) offer her innumerable possibilities and, at her age, Smith is able to portray – despite what she pretends – an immense variety of characters.

***

In his essay *On the Technique of Acting*, M. Chekhov wrote that the nature of the performer's body and physical means may impose limits to his acting, but he can always alter his body to a much greater extent than people generally think. A true, dedicated actor must have the desire and the ability to transform himself: this is the first requirement of his job.[435] In Maggie Smith's case, her physical appearance as well as her technique lend themselves to almost anything. Her range is extremely wide and she always makes the most of it, despite the fact that filmmakers tend to cast her in the same category of roles. The actress does a job of a prodigious acuity that makes her look different every time she appears on stage or on screen. She has absolutely no difficulty playing all stages of life, from an attractively spry maturity to senility and physical deterioration. She is also able to radically disfigure her enviable features, to the point that she comes very close to caricature or grotesque.

Smith's precise, mysterious technique is hers alone and it is not up to any of us to disclose it. Even if she wanted to disclose it herself, she probably could not. She undoubtedly has a gift, an innate sense of timing and dramatic effect that is impossible to grasp. In 1990, when she was playing Lettice Douffet in Broadway, a journalist rightly admitted that the 'magic' Maggie Smith performs on stage cannot be described in words.[436] That's it. To use Simon Callow's accurate metaphor, the 'Smith machine' has been programmed for phenomenal acting from the start. In 1986, the

435 *M. Chekhov's On the Technique of Acting*, ed. by M. Gordon (New York: HarperCollins, 1991), p. 99.

436 G. Anderson, 'A Celestial Smith in *Lettice and Lovage*', Pittsburgh Post-Gazette, 1 May 1990, p. 18.

multi-talented Callow directed Cocteau's *The Infernal Machine* at the Lyric Hammersmith and working with her – she played Jocasta – allowed him to subtly describe the genius of an actress he greatly admires. He compared her with an 'acting machine' and praised her ability to completely transform. Callow describes a slow, subtle process of metamorphosis which is initiated by the brain and results from an amazing capacity to adjust to the part she plays.[437] What is particularly overwhelming is the fact that the 'acting machine' appears to be more and more efficient as the years go by. Smith has nothing of a hammy thespian who plays every part the same way. She still is the amazing girl of the Oxford Playhouse, but she has certainly even bettered herself. She is simply better than she was at the Old Vic or in Stratford. She is undoubtedly at the height of her professional abilities.

437 Interview of S. Callow in R. Lewis, *Stage People* (London: Weidenfeld and Nicolson, 1989), p. 380.

3

THE LADY OF MANY PARTS

Maggie Smith or the Ultimate Versatility

Beyond Thalia and Melpomene

When the most recent part of Maggie Smith's career is considered, not synchronically, but diachronically – year after year since 1991 (*Hook*) – the diversity of the roles she has successively played seems amazing, all the more so because the actress is usually labelled as being typecast. The critic G. Macnab is one of the very few who ever dared to write that Maggie Smith has never been typecast and, being a master of high comedy, also excels in 'very dark roles'.[438] Actually, Smith *is* typecast. But the critic is right when emphasising the width of her range. Not only has the actress an exceptional ability to transform herself and turn into characters radically

438 'The Prime of her life', *The Independent*, 14 November 2015, p. 40. On her versatility, see B. Norman, 'Barry Norman on… the versatile actress Maggie Smith, a "grand dame" of stage and screen', *Radio Times*, 29 September-2 October 1992, p. 40.

different from her type (*The Lady in the Van*, *Keeping Mum*) or much older than she is (*Three Tall Women*, *My Old Lady*) but, whether she plays her type or 'against type', she portrays characters of an infinite variety.

Most of Smith's recent admirers – those who have discovered her through *Harry Potter* or *Downton Abbey* – have quite a partial view of her impressive career and, in any case, they have never seen her in a play. A few of them have heard about her award-winning performance in *The Prime of Miss Jean Brodie*, and the youngest ones know at least *Sister Act* and *The Secret Garden*. Fortunately, while only a small number of Maggie Smith's stage performances have been recorded (mostly her Shakespearean work, at Stratford's Festival, Ontario), all her onscreen portrayals are now immortalised for posterity on DVDs and Blu-ray discs, allowing her new fans to appreciate the magnitude of her career. Smith had played a great number of roles before being cast as Minerva McGonagall, and she has played many others since the end of the *Harry Potter* saga. The actress made her debut several decades prior to the first appearance of the dowager countess on television and she has survived her. Not only is she very popular, being an international star and one of the most revered British actresses, but she has also obtained professional recognition. Smith never stops garnering tributes to her glittering career on stage and on screen – she was made a Member of the Order of the Companions of Honour for services to drama in 2014, and she has recently been honoured with the Special Olivier Award (2010), the Stratford Shakespeare Festival's Legacy Award (2012), the Evening Standard's Icon Award (2013), the Critics' Circle Award for Distinguished Service to the Arts, and the Bodley Medal of Oxford's Bodleian Library (both in 2016). In addition, the actress collects nominations and awards for her most recent work; she won one Golden Globe, three Emmy Awards and four Screen Actors Guild Awards for her role in *Downton Abbey*, and her exceptional performance as *The Lady in the Van* earned her the Evening Standard Film Award for Best Actress in 2016, as well as nominations at the Golden Globe and the BAFTA Awards. These honours are not the reward of a past glory, though; hers is a prolific career, still developing fifty years after her debut and encompassing all genres: children's movies, popular comedies, period movies and modern drama (Bennett, Poliakoff, Albee).

At the same time, Maggie Smith's incredible new popularity does not lessen her prestige; whether she plays a cameo in a blockbuster or a leading part in an independent movie, she displays the same extraordinary acting skills. She alternates between leading and supporting roles. On screen, she has predominantly played small parts, secondary characters or cameos, and although her screen time is most often very short, the character she portrays inevitably becomes the most remarkable figure in the whole movie. In fact, Smith is a star cast in supporting roles rather than a supporting actress who has acceded to a stellar fame. Of course, no one can deny that leading roles get scarce for the actresses who are over fifty, and most of the parts for mature female performers are supporting ones, whereas older actors are still cast as title characters in movies. Nevertheless, the fact is unjust and absurd: many things still can happen to older women, they can love and be loved, they can suffer, they can be happy, they can commit a murder or get married. There is no limitation, in terms of plots. Until now, companies only sought scripts involving young heroes, relegating mature and elderly actors to the background, but, thankfully, they have realised that their productions should reflect our changing society. In the last few years, Smith also played several major parts, from Stephen Poliakoff's *Capturing Mary* to Nicholas Hytner's *The Lady in the Van.* Yet, as far as her career is concerned, the distinction between big and small roles is not relevant; even in the smallest part, she is frightfully good, carrying the scenes with her consummate timing. Without any doubt, the irresistible Maggie Smith is a redoubtable scene-stealer who always captures the audience's full attention. In 1969, a journalist from *The Guardian* joked that a special clause including 'Maggie Smith' should have been added to the famous proverb about never acting with children or animals on stage, as even when she was playing a supporting role in a movie, the actress managed to overshadow the leading actors themselves.[439] When Smith played in *Macbeth* at the Stratford Shakespeare Festival, the critic from *The New York Times* wrote that her Lady Macbeth, 'large and totally exposed', outshone the whole cast.[440] Among a cast as impressive as that of Altman's *Gosford Park*, Smith nevertheless manages to outdo the other actors; unquestionably, with a handful of short scenes, her Aunt Constance is the funniest and the most memorable

439 C. Stott, 'Actress on a banana skin', *The Guardian*, 5 June 1969, p. 11.

440 R. Eder, 'Stage: Vanya and Macbeth', *The New York Times*, 9 June 1978, p. 3.

character in the film. The actress inevitably overshadows her co-stars and her charismatic presence pervades the screen as soon as she appears, for no other reason than that she is the best. Writing on the formidable Marie Dressler's career, V. Sturtevant clearly redefines the notion of 'scene-stealing', asserting that, when a character actor draws more attention than the leading actor, he should not be called a 'stealer'. It is simply because he is better trained and more talented than him.[441] Of course, many actors are secretly jealous of Smith, although it is actually very challenging to play with such a consummate actress; she is so good, that she makes things easier for the other performers who have to keep up with her, enhancing the quality of acting. Nonetheless, it is quite impossible to upstage her and even the incomparable Judi Dench is endangered when co-starring with her colleague. Playing opposite Smith is nearly the same as accepting to go unnoticed.

Despite the fact that Maggie Smith is able to play any genre, she is mostly seen as a comedy actress; the critic Jack Kroll once stated that she seemed to be 'the Muse of Farce' herself.[442] The personality traits of the characters she portrays are often thought to be hers, and this is probably one of the reasons why she is so strongly identified with some roles. Just like she raised laughs with her nasal inflections and her wringing wrists forty years ago, she raises laughs with her one-liners and withering glances nowadays. Some blame her for doing 'her Maggie Smith turn', as if her acting abilities were restricted to that and the public did not expect anything else from her performances. During the run of *The Importance of Being Earnest*, Smith was accused of overdoing it to win the favour of the audience, even though she precisely had no possibility of departing from Wilde's text. To her credit, J. Gross honoured her impeccable rendition of Bracknell. According to him, Smith efficiently made use of body skills to give a masterful performance which, as flamboyant as it was, remained 'perfectly consistent' with Wilde's play.[443] Maggie Smith has an unfounded reputation which unfortunately precedes her. In an article written in 2002, the critic Sean Macaulay said that the actress's imperiousness and grandiose theatricality were better suited to stage than screen, referring to Smith's extraordinary mastery of her

441 Sturtevant, *A Great Big Girl*, p. 43.

442 'The Prime of Dame Maggie', *Newsweek*, 2 April 1990, p. 54.

443 'Lady Bracknell is some sour grand dame', *The Daily Telegraph*, 14 March 1993, p. xiii.

physical skills; from eyes to wrists, every muscle in her body acts and the theatrical flamboyance of her demeanour is enhanced by the nasal tone of a distinctive voice, fitted for command and grandeur.[444]

'Enlarge, enliven, enlighten!' was Lettice's famous motto in P. Shaffer's *Lettice and Lovage*. It seems that excess and extravagance have been banished from all forms of dramatic art these days, and even from comedy. For years, Maggie Smith has been accused of overacting. A long time ago, in the early 1970s, some critics tracked and castigated her mannerisms, blaming her for giving caricatural impersonations.[445] In 1975, an American reviewer hailed her performance as Amanda in Coward's *Private Lives* (Ahmanson Theatre, Los Angeles) but also heavily insisted on her much too flamboyant acting. He wrote that Smith's comic efficiency was too great to be matched by the more conventional levels of playing of her fellow actors, and her performance, despite being extraordinarily brilliant in its conception and execution, was almost 'too large to be contained by a stage'.[446] People often quote Walter Kerr, from *The New York Times*, who once said that the actress looked like a pair of scissors and was 'what is meant by alternating current'.[447] P. Kael would write vibrant lines on Smith's performance as Judith Hearne, but she was quite harsh about *Travels with my Aunt*, writing that Maggie Smith gave such a 'flustered', ridiculous performance, overloaded with excessive gesture and 'high-piping' screeches that, after a while, the viewer just wanted her to stop fidgeting and keep quiet.[448] Nevertheless, in four triumphal seasons at Stratford (Ontario), Smith brilliantly demonstrated that she was able to play tragic as well as comical figures, from N. Coward's Judith Bliss to Shakespeare's Cleopatra. Years have passed, and even if her reputation is firmly established, even if she is now seen as one of the greatest actresses in the world, there is always the odd critic who reproaches her for her too frenetic gestures or her

444 S. Macaulay, 'Play up, play up, and play the Dame', *The Times*, 31 January 2002, p. 14.

445 See, for instance, M. Knelman, *A Stratford Tempest* (Toronto: McClelland & Stewart, 1982), p. 37; for Knelman, she seemed to give a 'nightclub comic's' impression of herself. About her performance in *Snap* (Vaudeville Theatre, 1974), I. Wardle considered that, in comparison with the parts that Smith had previously played, it consisted in the most extraordinary display of mannerisms. See 'Laughs that do not deserve a clap', *The Times*, 14 March 1974, p. 15.

446 J. Aaron, 'Theatre in Review', *Educational Theatre Journal*, 27.1, 1975, p. 129-130.

447 W. Kerr, 'The New Young Lunts?', *The New York Times*, 22 February 1970, p. 1.

448 *Reeling* (Boston-Toronto: Little & Brown & Cie, 1976), p. 97.

exaggerated inflections. Some blame her elongated vowels, her nasal twang or her fluttering wrists, while some others dislike her pinched mouth and her haughty chin, even calling her a 'pantomime dame'. In 1984, the critic from *The Observer* did not like very much Smith playing Congreve, emphasising the most excessive, overwhelming aspects of her acting and delivery. He compared her geometrical posture to that of an Egyptian figure on a funeral stele, and blamed her exaggerated, mannered inflections which aimed at provoking laughs at any cost.[449] In contrast, proving the critics wrong, the director himself, William Gaskill, praised the actress's impeccable work and precise inflection: 'In the famous scene between Millamant and Mirabell, where they state their conditions for a good marriage, (Maggie Smith) would drop her voice on the word "lastly" [...]. On a line on which she could have easily got a laugh, she chose to say to the audience, "Take this bit seriously," and so gave the scene an unexpected depth.'[450]

In the late 1980s, the role of the extravagant Miss Douffet in *Lettice and Lovage* especially laid itself open to criticism. As Lettice, the actress displayed with a consummate virtuosity her comedic skills and, of course, some critics were too pleased, beyond compliments, to allude to her mannerisms. Among others, M. Billington highly praised her performance, but also eloquently described a body language he found a bit excessive; Billington humorously described Smith's notorious habit of extending her palms at a variable angle to her fluttering wrists, what gave her forearms the appearance of two wild winged creatures (two 'demented birds,' he said) desperately attempting to fly away.[451] Still, as most of them admitted, Smith – 'mistress of the histrionic gesture', according to a journalist[452] – brilliantly served Shaffer's play.[453] Twelve years later, in 1999, her sublime performance as Miss Shepherd in *The Lady in the Van* did not avoid criticism either. In *The*

449 M. Ratcliffe, 'Blurring the World's wit', *The Observer*, 18 November 1984, p. 27.

450 *Words into Action. Finding the Life of the Play* (London: Nick Hern Books, 2010), p. 144.

451 'Lord, Peter's whimsy', *The Guardian*, 29 October 1987, p. 22. The critic M. Hoyle evoked 'the clownish caperings' of Miss Tyzack's colleague ('Review of "Lettice and Lovage" at the Globe', *The Financial Times*, 28 October 1987, p. 23).

452 J. Beaufort, 'Maggie Smith's Brilliant Comic Inventions Brighten Broadway', *Special to The Christian Monitor*, 2 April 1990, p. 10. The critic G. Weales ('Maggie For the Fun of It', *The Nation*, 7 May 1990, p. 388) described her as 'so histrionic a storm'.

453 G. Rogoff, *Vanishing Acts. Theater since the Sixties* (New Haven: Yale University Press, 2000), p. 175; the author affirms that, even without Smith, Lettice remains a great role, but concedes that her 'animated-cartoon' wrists and high comedy tricks do not do the play any harm.

Financial Times, A. Macaulay declared that Smith's performance was a kind of caricatural patchwork, made of every 'acting trick' which belonged to the Maggie Smith's arsenal, from the nasal high-pitched inflections to the extravagant moves of the body, head-flickings and eye-rollings included.[454] You cannot please everyone, this is true, but most of these criticisms were unjust and paradoxical. If they were annoying and superfluous, these 'self parodic' mannerisms – as some journalists describe her acting[455] – would have wearied the public. There is nothing of the kind.[456] The spectators love Maggie Smith as she is and, on the contrary, they just ask for more. Far from disserving her, these excesses are an integral part of her technique and they efficiently reinforce her acting performance. In 2004, during the Australian revival of *Bed Among the Lentils*, the Australian journalist Susan Chenery wrote the most evocative paragraph on Smith's voice, a voice which is so fundamentally and excessively the authentic 'thespian voice' of the British stage, that it sounds like a conscious parody.[457] Basically, to dub Maggie Smith for foreign audiences is sacrilege. Sacha Guitry considered that, in the case of exceptional actors, dubbing was out of the question: 'The idea of dubbing a great actor is something barbarous [...] Never deprive yourself of a great actor's intonation, because his whole value lies in his intonation. To express his thoughts, the actor has at his disposal a certain amount of words which he has been entrusted with by the author, and also a physical expression which is his own. Each time there is a perfect concordance between these three elements, the goal is reached. But, two of these three elements are international: the intonation and the physical expression.'[458] Smith's distinctive voice and inflection are part of the mysterious alchemy

454 Macaulay, 'Too many Alans spoil the broth'.

455 'Best of the 20th century: stage actresses. Power and Performance', *The Guardian*, 22 September 1994, p. 15.

456 In view of her glorious career and her past and present successes, the despising notice which can be found under Maggie Smith's name in the *International Dictionary of Theatre* looks quite inane: '[Kenneth] Williams was a master of "high camp", known for his nasal delivery and his range of funny voices. His influence left its mark on her [...] The accusation that she too can be mannered and camp has dogged her career.' See *International Dictionary of Theatre-3. Actors, Directors and Designers*, ed. by D. Pickering (New York: St. James Press, 1996), p. 711.

457 'No ordinary Dame', *The Australian*, 13 March 2004, p. 16.

458 Foreword to *Les Perles de la Couronne* (The Pearls of the Crown), 1937, in S. Guitry. *Cinéma* (Paris: Omnibus, 2007), p. 561-562.

that her acting is. With that voice, with those mannerisms, she makes people laugh. She makes people laugh *more* than anyone else and this is probably what annoys some critics. Nearly thirty years ago, Christopher Edwards brilliantly underlined that paradox, admitting that, although she was undoubtedly a very mannered actress who excelled at a kind of 'rich comic exaggeration', he took a great pleasure in watching Smith's overacting, as no other actress could compete with her on that territory.[459] Years later, J. R. Taylor wrote similar comments on her dizzying performance in *The Lady in the Van*, stating that Maggie Smith, because of her mannerisms and acting tricks, was as 'infuriating' as the character she was playing, but her mastery of these mannerisms was incomparable and unsurpassed.[460]

Some critics have a much too intellectual approach of the performing arts. To act is to lend one's body, one's voice to a character one portrays in front of an audience who has paid to be entertained. If the show is advertised as a comedy, the spectators rightly expect to have fun. The first purpose of a play – in the way that Ancient Romans, and later Shakespeare and Molière, conceived it – is to please the spectators, whether they have to laugh or shed tears. More than anyone else, Maggie Smith has a particular talent for convulsing the audience with laughter. Her acting, her facial expressions and her timing are devastatingly efficient. She knows how to point out the right line, with the appropriate punctuation and the proper gesture or facial expression. Her pledge is fulfilled – the love that the public feels for her testifies it – and thus there is absolutely no reason to discuss and call into question the means and the tools she uses to reach that goal. Of course, her acting can be excessive, but why on earth should restraint and moderation – *aurea mediocritas*, as the Latins used to say – be regarded as the supreme values in a discipline (an art, in fact) the rules of which are constantly redefined? Excess and expressivity, when they are skilfully mastered, are much more proper to enthral the spectator than lazy tepidity, and caricature is one of the best ingredients of comedy. To provoke laughs, Smith manages to combine her mannerisms with a perfect ability to transform herself. Her technique is irreproachable and the result, devastatingly hilarious. The actress has turned her excesses into assets. That is all.

459 'A touch of spice', *The Spectator*, 31 October 1987, p. 51-52.

460 'John R. Taylor at the *Lady in the Van*, Queen's Theatre', *Plays International*, January 2000, p. 18.

Yet, to typecast Maggie Smith seems to be the most incoherent and paradoxical thing in the world; she is the most versatile actress ever. Those who pretend that her performances are 'phoned' from one role to another, or that she plays 'on automatic', are totally wrong.[461] They seem to pass over an entire part of her potential. The actress knows how to raise laughs, that is certain, but she also knows how to have the audience in tears. Commenting on her performance in *The Importance of Being Earnest*, M. Billington emphasised this dual proficiency. Although he did not fully approve of Smith's rendition of Bracknell, the critic paid tribute to her versatility and admitted that she was a kind of 'Jekyll-and-Hyde' actress, as good at conveying a devastating vulnerability as at provoking laughs.[462] Smith's ability to convey sadness and vulnerability is phenomenal, and very few performers master so brilliantly comedic and dramatic skills. In fact, there are some roles in which she merges completely (Mary Gilbert, Miss Shepherd, Jean Horton) and others (like Violet Crawley) that she plays with a certain distance, as if she made fun of the character. Nevertheless, her capability for restraint, when the part requires it, is too often neglected or omitted by the critics. What is probably confusing is that she can play comedy and tragedy with the same brio and some people apparently cannot admit or realise that the same actor can excel in both genres.[463]

461 See, for instance, N. Heller, 'Four's Company', *Vogue.com*, 11 January 2013 <http://www.vogue.com/article/fours-company-dustin-hoffmans-directorial-debut-quartet> [accessed November 2016]; the critic wrote that Smith was taking again the kind of imperious role she has been playing for hundreds of years. Also D. Thomson, 'Art and Age. The strange career of Maggie Smith', *The New Republic*, 24 August 2014, p. 49; Thomson asserts that Smith plays 'on automatic'. The latter is probably one of the most unjustly critical articles recently written about the actress: its argument in neither clear nor coherent.

462 'Theatre', *Country Life*, 18 March 1993, p. 73. See also S. Pile, 'Not playing the Dame', *Radio Times*, 23-29 March 2002, p. 38; the critic saw in her a 'mixture' of comedy and pathos. When the actress was appearing in Ronald Harwood's *Interpreters* at the Queen's Theatre (1985-1986), B. Nightingale praised her stunning versatility, writing that Harwood's play had given her the opportunity to remind the spectators of her stunning range; see 'In London, Two Actresses Shine', *The New York Times*, 1 December 1985, p. 3.

463 See Masters, *Thunder in the Air*, p. 30; Masters considers her a comedic actress, lacking 'the red corpuscle' when she tackles tragedy and pathos.

Drama Queen

Despite her regal bearing and her majestic elegance, Maggie Smith has – until now – rarely played royals. Judi Dench triumphantly appeared as Queen Victoria in John Madden's *Mrs Brown* (1997) and even got an Academy Award for her supporting role as Elizabeth I in *Shakespeare in Love* (1998), also directed by Madden, while her colleague Eileen Atkins is now seen as ideal casting for portraying Mary of Teck, having played the Queen Mother twice so far (*Bertie and Elizabeth*, 2002, and *The Crown*, 2016). With respect to Helen Mirren, she has undoubtedly cornered the marked with her fascinating impersonation of Elizabeth II, both on screen (*The Queen*,

2006) and on stage (*The Audience*, 2013).[464] Smith, however, is not so strongly identified with royalty for the reason that the rare queens whom she has ever played have been overshadowed by subsequent roles like Minerva McGonagall or the dowager countess. Nevertheless, to portray a dignified and sorrowful Duchess of York in R. Loncraine's *Richard III* (1995) has allowed her to brilliantly showcase her dramatic skills. Transposed in pre-war London, *Richard III* illustrates the fascinating story of an actor who enjoyed so much playing a part on stage that he spared no effort to have a movie made from it; Ian McKellen adapted Shakespeare's verse for the screen and asked Richard Loncraine to direct.[465] Of course, Maggie Smith – an actress for whom McKellen has as much affection as admiration – was to get a part in the production.

In this adaptation, Smith's very small role combines the character of the Duchess of York and that of fierce Queen Margaret in Shakespeare's play. Still, as usual, although the actress only appears in a few short scenes, she gives life to one of the most remarkable and moving figures in the story. Tall, willowy, with her white hair elegantly pulled up into a curly bun, the actress unquestionably embodies royalty.[466] If there had been a fundamental necessity to typecast Maggie Smith, she should have been typecast as queens. When she makes her entrance in the opening scene, arriving at the Palace for the Victory Ball with her granddaughter, she incontestably stands for the Queen Mother. In evening dress, the venerable Duchess of York is – according to Ian McKellen and Richard Loncraine's screenplay – 'tiara-to-toe, an Edwardian matriarch',[467] and this is as such that she appears in the family group photograph (which was used, later, as a movie still for the promotion). Impressively elegant with her sequined

---

464 Mirren played in turn Elizabeth I in a miniseries for HBO, in 2005. She also played a moving Queen Charlotte in Nicholas Hytner's *The Madness of King George* (1994), adapted from the eponymous play by Alan Bennett. Several actresses of the same generation – including V. Redgrave – have specialised in portraying queens on screen or on stage; see Richards, *The Rise*, p. 213-214.

465 Richard Eyre had directed McKellen as Richard III at the National Theatre in 1990 and later on tour, in Europe and in the US.

466 So that she resembled Queen Mary in 'scratchy 1930s newsreels'. See K. S. Rothwell, *A History of Shakespeare on Screen. A century of film and television*[2] (Cambridge: Cambridge University Press, 2004), p. 221.

467 I. McKellen, *William Shakespeare's* Richard III*: A Screenplay* (London-New York: Doubleday, 1996), p. 53.

black dress and her jewels parure, the elderly duchess presides with the utmost dignity over the ball, her vague smile hiding her inner torments. The next scene shows her attending her son Edward's deathbed, just after the death of her other son, Clarence, as the most dignified *mater dolorosa*: 'Alas! I am the mother of these griefs / On me pour all your tears'. It has to be noticed, here, that Smith plays the mother not only of Ian McKellen – who is more likely to be her husband or her brother on screen, as they belong to the same generation – but also of the late Nigel Hawthorne and John Wood, who were both sensibly older than her. I. McKellen was aware of that incongruity, but he considered that the character of the duchess should be played by an actress of high calibre. He could not have made a better choice. As he recounts, he had always wished to see Smith play his mother in the movie. Although she was much too young for the part, she was more able than anyone else to convey the 'emotional barrenness' of Richard's childhood.[468] Older, wiser, the duchess appears as an impressive and comforting figure.

Still, the matriarch is also the progenitor of a monster. Alluding to the tormented childhood of his younger son, she clearly voices her fears for the future: 'Now two mirrors of my husband's likeness / Are cracked in pieces, by malignant death. / And I, for comfort, have but one false glass, / That grieves me when I see my shame in him'. As Richard's bloody crimes follow one another, the Duchess feels overwhelmed by the cruelty of the man to whom she has unfortunately given birth and longs for her own death: 'Blood against blood, self against self. / Oh, let me die to look on death no more'. She will not die, though. She will leave England after having said her farewell to her wicked son, visiting him at his quarters. At the top of the stairs, the duchess confronts Richard to expose her griefs to him, as if this ultimate exchange announced his upcoming fall.[469] Actually, her speech turns into a curse, as she wishes him to die at war: 'Bloody you are: bloody

468 *Ibid.*, p. 144.

469 N. Vienne-Guerrin, 'Evil tongues in Richard III on screen', in *Shakespeare on Screen (Proceedings of the Conference organised at the Université de Rouen)*, ed. by S. Hatchuel and N. Vienne-Guerrin (Rouen: Presses de l'Université de Rouen, 2005), p. 254: 'Richard's mother's curse is heard in a sequence which first symbolically shows them as if coming from two sides of the world on the top of the stairs, thus suggesting that there is a gulf between mother and son and that Richard won't be long falling.'

will be your end. / Shame serves your life – and will your / death attend!'[470] Her farewell to the king precedes her departure to France. In furs with a matching toque which makes her resemble an old tsarina, the duchess leaves as majestically as she had first appeared in the opening scene, except that she looks much more vulnerable, having probably realised that she is helpless in front of Richard. To encapsulate Maggie Smith's contribution to the movie, the critic from *Cineaste* said that she was playing the duchess as a 'crusty grand dame' who spends most of the film quarrelling and bickering, blaming the infamous conduct of her wicked offspring and prophesying his doom,[471] but it did not do justice to her subtle and moving portrayal. More developed in the film than it had been on stage, the role of the duchess gives the actress the opportunity to portray a devastating, larger-than-life figure. This time, there was not an ounce of mannerism or comical irony in her characterisation. She makes a small supporting part a heartbreaking, outstanding performance. Like Sycorax, mother of Caliban, or Pasiphae, whose offspring was the Minotaur, she has given birth to an evil brood. She is not innocent herself, though. The duchess is depicted as the cruelest and most ferocious mother; having rejected her youngest child for his crooked body, she is partly responsible of his psychological troubles; feeling despised and hated by the person who had the greatest authority and influence on him, Richard has progressively become a monster.[472] In fact, Smith's duchess is quite similar to one of the most devastating figures in French

470 This scene was quite difficult to perform as Maggie Smith had to climb down the stairs in full costume and on high heels, but she found her way through it quite brilliantly, as McKellen recently recalled in his delightful monologue 'Women I've Filmed With' (Fine Arts Theater, Los Angeles, 19 November 2015).

471 G. Crowdus, 'Richard III', *Cineaste*, 22, 1996, p. 36.

472 J. N. Loehlin, '"Top of the World, Ma": *Richard III* and Cinematic Convention', in *Shakespeare, the Movie. Popularizing the plays on film, TV and video*, ed. by L. E. Boose and R. Burt (London-New York: Routledge, 1997), p. 74-75; in R. Loncraine's movie, Richard is obsessed with his mother, and his criminal behaviour is obviously linked to a childhood rejection. Each time the Duchess of York mentions his deformities of body or his criminal conduct, Richard is deeply hurt. His mother has rejected him for his deformities, and the rejection has shaped the evil man he is now. See also C. Chillington Rutter, 'Looking at Shakespeare's women on film', in *The Cambridge Companion to Shakespeare on Film*, ed. by R. Jackson (Cambridge: Cambridge University Press, 2006), p. 248; the author underscores the overpowering influence of the duchess on his son. When the matriarch delivers her farewell speech, 'To war take with you my most grievous curse', Richard finds no escape, being doomed for ever.

classical tragedy, Agrippina in Racine's *Britannicus*. She expresses the disgust and the terror of the mother who witnesses the progressive transformation of her already wicked progeny into a monstrous, murderous creature. Like Nero's mother, the duchess is appalled by the increasing cruelty of her son in his efforts to reign as an absolute tyrant, but she still outdoes him. She is the only person he fears and her curse will initiate his ruin. While Agrippina is a major character in Racine's play, the duchess has in fact few scenes and few lines, but thanks to the actress's extraordinary charisma, the character is elevated to the rank of a queen of tragedy.[473]

This is the same dignity, minus haughtiness and plus a touching humanity, that characterises the other royal figure that Maggie Smith has played on screen, Queen Alexandra in *All the King's Men* (1999). This excellent BBC production directed by Julian Jarrold, was adapted by the screenwriter Alma Cullen from a captivating account by Nigel McCrery which throws light on one of the most mysterious episodes of the First World War. In 1915, a company – formed of young workers on King George V's Royal Estate in Sandringham – joined the 5th battalion of the Norfolk regiment to fight against the Turkish soldiers at Galipoli, in the Dardanelles. On the decisive day of the battle, they walked towards the enemy but suddenly disappeared. Reportedly missing after the battle, they were believed to have been made prisoners by the Germans. Unfortunately, they never returned. A few years later, a mass grave was discovered and, obviously, the human remains belonged to the men from the 5th battalion. The truth was never publicly disclosed, though, and on the contrary, some people preferred to perpetuate the naive legend claiming that a cloud of mist had swallowed them up to heaven. What makes the story even more compelling and touching, is the fact that these unfortunate young volunteers had been trained by Captain Frank Beck – the estate's land agent of King George – who had insisted on accompanying his boys to the battlefield. Despite the refusal of her son who considered that Beck was too old to fight, Queen Alexandra publicly honoured his merits as an officer (offering him a pocket watch)

473 Nevertheless, the most delightful image of Smith's Duchess of York does not belong to the movie, but to the behind-the-scenes material. A priceless picture (inserted in the published version of the shooting script) shows the actress, in full costume, drinking with a straw from a can of Diet Coke.

and encouraged him to lead his soldiers to Galipoli. In quite an unexpected manner, the bonds which linked Queen Alexandra and Captain Beck were made of mutual respect and friendship. The Queen Mother admired the ageing officer immensely, and his devotion to the sovereign went beyond loyalty; he worshipped her like a goddess.

As Queen Alexandra, Maggie Smith has a charm, an aura and at the same time a down-to-earth gentleness which remind us of another royal figure, more often celebrated on the silver screen, Elizabeth of Austria. In some ways, her Alexandra resembles a mature Empress Sissi, memorably portrayed by the actress Romy Schneider in Luchino Visconti's *Ludwig* (1971). Kind, generous and incredibly graceful, Queen Alexandra is Captain Beck's heroine. When the Queen Mother passes ahead of the wedding feast of her maid, Peggy Batterbee – who is marrying one of the young soldiers – and asks Beck if he remembers her as a bride the day she married Prince Edward, he daringly replies: 'I'd never seen anyone so beautiful!' Never, although he is married himself. This subtle, unsaid affection explains why the Queen Mother becomes so concerned by the disappearance of the battalion, and especially by that of Captain Beck she had encouraged to follow his regiment. It is in fact one of Smith's shortest roles on screen, but nevertheless, played by her, what was a secondary part becomes a deeply moving and even pivotal figure in the story. Her appearances are rare and brief, but very efficient. The first scene emphasises the (almost) familiarity between the members of the Royal Family and their loyal servants. Queen Alexandra passes by the fields in her elegant automobile and kindly greets Captain Beck, complimenting him for having made 'fine soldiers' from the young workers of Sandringham's estate. Later when she sits at her dressing table, chatting quite informally with her young lady's maid about the upcoming departure of the Regiment, it seems to be her main preoccupation and this is Beck – invited to dine with the king – whom she chooses to lead her to the dining-room. Simple, generous, incredibly affable with her servants, the character played by Maggie Smith is far away from her stiff dowagers and haughty aristocrats. Just like she did when portraying the Duchess of York, the actress brilliantly embodies majesty and benevolence, a resplendent tiara crowning her red curls: 'The epitome of monarchical grandeur,' as the reviewer from *The Daily Mail* described her.[474] With regard to the age of the characters, Queen Alexandra undeniably looks too young to be the mother of the middle-aged George V and the mother-in-law of a robust Queen Mary. Born Princess of Denmark in 1844, Alexandra was seventy-one in 1915, thus slightly older than the actress who plays her on screen. Of course, Smith easily compensates the age gap with a dignified bearing and a slight limp in her walk[475] and, to pay tribute to the make-up and costume designers, she closely resembles Queen Alexandra as portrayed, in 1905, in Lukes Fildes's painting. As regal looking as she may be, the Queen Mother is nevertheless a model of restraint and the role gives absolutely no room for excess or mannerisms of any kind. The journalists who continuously pretend that the actress always plays the same part could not keep saying such allegations after seeing her as Queen Alexandra. In *The Guardian*, Mark Lawson stated that, even if Smith's recent performances had been 'a museum' of her typical acting tricks, she gave a convincing portrayal of Alexandra, although she was surprisingly conveying less imperiousness than usual.[476] Even more than in *Richard III*, her performance is all interiority and sobriety. With very few gestures, very few words, Maggie Smith subtly expresses the torments of her mind invaded by fear and guilt. She was the one who had convinced the king to allow Frank Beck to depart for the Dardanelles, and the regiment did not come back.

The second half of the TV drama intercuts scenes on the battlefield, images of dust and blood on the set of operation, with scenes in England, where anxiety progressively nurtures emotion and violence. However, in her mute sorrow, Queen Alexandra appears as the most luminous character in the story. Deeply worried by the events, she eventually understands that the men will never be back. The sequence when, at sunrise, she slowly walks in the corridor towards a large window represents probably one of the most pictorially beautiful scenes ever played by Smith. Her frail figure standing against the pale light of dawn, the ageing queen lifts the blind and the camera captures her profile as she gazes in the distance. She

474 P. Paterson, 'Peering through the mist', *The Daily Mail*, 15 November 1999, p. 57.

475 A serious illness had left Queen Alexandra with a stiff knee and a limp, but she nevertheless moved very gracefully. See G. Battiscombe, *Queen Alexandra* (Boston: Houghton Mifflin, 1969), p. 92: 'Society ladies were copying "the Alexandra limp".'

476 'Pride and Glory', *The Guardian*, 8 November 1999, p. 17.

sees the swans swimming quietly on Sandringham's lake, but her mind wanders elsewhere, far from Norfolk. Feeling guilty, she eventually leads inquiries to discover the truth and, when Reverend Pierrepoint Edwards, back from Galipoli, refuses to tell her the real story but gives her Beck's pocket watch, she faces her loss. The captain is dead, because of his courage, and also because of her foolish generosity. Without a tear, she contemplates his watch in her black gloved hand, but the actress makes that silent mourning the most devastating moment of the whole movie. Cleverly using her skills, Maggie Smith has an amazing ability to adapt her acting to the role she plays. She knows how to make the most of all her technical resources. She has huge means and uses them alternatively, at the risk of unsettling the critics who certainly prefer to put actors in distinct categories. For that reason, her genius often eludes conventional criticism. Journalists tend to diminish her talent in their reviews, always focusing on an infinitesimal part of it and rarely allowing the public to embrace it in its whole. Maybe the diamond has too much facets to be appreciated according to ordinary criteria. Smith is probably the funniest comedic actress ever, but she is also, concomitantly, the most devastating tragedian of our time.

Like a Dame

To be considered in a diachronic way, the actress's recent career has to be examined in the light of theatre and cinema history. In the matter of roles, Maggie Smith has inherited a long line of tradition. Of course, it may appear commonplace to compare her with her predecessors, as well as it is quite irritating to see some journalists desperately trying to find her a successor. 'The new Maggie Smith,' they say. There is no need for a new Maggie Smith. There is already one and she is magnificent. No one would say 'the new David Hockney' or 'the new Stephen Sondheim'. An artist is exceptional and unique. Yet, it must be admitted that, with regard to casting, the actress herself has followed the path of her predecessors, reprising some of the most famous roles of the literary tradition, on stage and on screen. Besides, Smith is certainly not a star of our time; she may wear jeans and use a mobile phone, she is nevertheless an old-fashioned actress. With her elegance, her excellent manners and her high professionalism, she has more in common with the greatest thespians from the past than with some young celebrities who are compared to her. She is simply one of the most revered actresses in the history of British theatre and cinema, although she probably differs, by her down-to-earthness, from her predecessors who expected the consideration due to their age and status. Maggie Smith's modesty is proportional to her talent, which is saying something. The actress is generally compared to Edith Evans, while, for her part, Judi Dench is often compared to Sybil Thorndike.[477] In any case, Evans and Thorndike were – in physical appearance and acting style – as different as Dench and Smith are different today, thus it is very tempting when comparing our dames to draw a parallel between them and the two most celebrated actresses of the mid-twentieth century.

Half a century apart, Evans and Smith occupy quite a similar place in the history of the London stage. Yet, while their careers, their roles and their technical skills can be juxtaposed, their one and only professional collaboration caused rather a short circuit than a fireworks display. In 1964, they co-starred in a National Theatre production of Noel Coward's *Hay Fever*, with Evans playing (a rather aged) Judith Bliss and Smith, a glamorous Myra Arundel.[478] It seems that, with her impetuosity, the young and talented Maggie slightly got on the nerves of the respectable Dame Edith, who was old enough to be her grandmother. M. Coveney recounts that, on matinee days, a thoughtful Maggie Smith made it a habit to play at top volume her favourite song of the moment – *Baby Love* by the Supremes – in order to prevent Edith Evans from taking a nap before the evening performance. Smith's ingenious tactic aimed at neutralising the fierceness

477 Dench even played Thorndike in *My week with Marilyn* (S. Curtis, 2011). See M. Coveney, 'A real drama queen', *The Independent Review*, 16 December 2004, p. 8. Here, Coveney is drawing a parallel between the two dames, whom he called 'the Edith Evans and Sybil Thorndike' of their generation, setting a waspish and private Maggie Smith against a generous and affable Judi Dench.

478 Coward himself directed that production. In fact, Evans and Smith had already appeared together in a TV production of the play (ITV, 1960), now lost. Maggie Smith played Jackie Coryton.

of her redoubtable enemy; deprived of her restorative sleep, the venerable thespian had less energy to remonstrate against the younger cast. From Dame Edith's point of view, the perspective was radically different. At her age and despite all her experience, she did not feel at ease, surrounded by these young actors who seemed derisive and hostile, especially 'the little Smith girl', as she bitterly called Britain's future leading actress.[479] With her advancing years and declining health, Edith Evans certainly found it difficult to be confronted with the insolent youth of the new generation and the play proved to be a personal failure for her. In her memories, Jean Batters – who was Evans's secretary – casts blame on Smith: 'At that time Maggie Smith was the darling of the Old Vic audience, but my opinion was that she over-acted as Myra Arundel, although the critics thought otherwise. Be that as it may, Edith found her difficult to play with.'[480] *Sic.* Did Dame Edith fear to be upstaged by her young co-star? It is highly possible. Conversely, in his autobiography, Laurence Olivier hailed the skills of his young company, with Maggie Smith at the head, regretting that Edith Evans had not been at her best, putting at risk the whole production. He related how E. Evans's performance strongly contrasted with the brilliance of his young actors; Evans had difficulty remembering her lines and, a far cry from her glorious former self, seemed lost in a part she was far too old to play.[481] The National Theatre company was made of young people whose talent was equalled only by their energy. At the moment when this extraordinary generation of actors was starting to emerge – the generation of Dench, Gambon, Stephens, Jacobi, McKellen, that is, chronologically speaking, Laurence Olivier and John Gielgud's legatees – the woman who had been, with Sybil Thorndike, the greatest actress of her time, was starting to decline, as her means and physical abilities were diminishing. The confrontation of these two generations was undoubtedly painful – a similar situation happened in 1917, when a young Edith Evans met an aged Ellen Terry[482] – and Smith's wicked Teppaz did not help to cement this relationship.

In a notice he wrote after Evans's death, the biographer John C. Trewin described her as very protective of her privacy off stage, while she was, on

479 Coveney, *Maggie Smith. A Biography*, p. 90.

480 *Edith Evans. A Personal Memoir* (London: Hart-Davis MacGibbon, 1977), p. 130.

481 *Confessions of an Actor* (London: Weidenfeld & Nicolson, 1994), p. 273-274.

482 See Forbes, *Dame Edith Evans*, p. 51.

stage, the most glittering performer.[483] Oddly enough, the same sentence could be used, in the present tense, to define Maggie Smith. The two actresses, who have both been ranked as national treasures, have followed quite a similar path in terms of career. Their respective backgrounds were completely different, though. Working as an apprentice at a milliner's shop and acting in an amateur company, Evans had not trained at drama school. She simply caught the eye of William Poel – a producer who was known, in the early years of the twentieth century, for his modernised approach of Shakespeare's plays – in an amateur production and eventually learned her craft on the job. As first-rate actresses, Evans and Smith both have played the leading parts of the English repertory, from Shakespeare to G. B. Shaw, Restoration comedy included. Fifty years apart, they have successively tackled lots of key roles: several major parts in Shakespeare,[484] Mrs Sullen in Fahrquar's *The Beaux' Stratagem*, Irina Arkadina in *The Seagull* and, more notably, Millamant in Congreve's *The Way of the World* – which was probably Evans's favourite part. In 1967, a (perspicuous) critic from *The Observer* was contemplating the future of the National Theatre's leading ladies, Joan Plowright, Geraldine McEwan and Maggie Smith, imagining Maggie Smith following in the steps of E. Evans with the great comic heroines, from Rosalind to Millamant to Lady Bracknell.[485] Indeed, Smith would play Rosalind in 1978 (Stratford Festival, Ontario), Millamant in 1976 (Stratford Festival) and 1984 (Chichester and Theatre Royal Haymarket) and, of course, Bracknell in 1993 (Aldwych). It is an ironic twist of fate that Smith even portrayed Epifania in *The Millionairess*,[486] a role that G. B. Shaw had written especially for Evans and that she did not want to play. All these parts belong to the classical repertory, as compulsory steps in the tradition

483 'Edith Evans's obituary', *The Times*, 15 October 1976, p. 19.

484 Among others, Viola, in *Twelfth Night*, Beatrice in *Much Ado About Nothing*, Mistress Ford in *The Merry Wives of Windsor*, Portia in *The Merchant of Venice*, and Rosalind in *As You Like It*.

485 R. Bryden, 'Our New Beatrice', *The Observer*, 26 March 1967, p. 21. See also W. Gaskill, *A Sense of Direction* (London: Faber and Faber, 1988), p. 57; talking about directing Farquhar's *The Recruiting Officer* at the National in 1963, W. Gaskill says that he had made a point of casting Smith as Silvia. From the moment when he saw her as Lady Plyant in *The Double Dealer*, he had perceived that, in the matter of Restoration comedy, she was the true heiress of Dame Edith Evans.

486 Not on stage, in fact, but in a TV adaptation of the play, filmed for the famous BBC 'Play of Month' (*Bernard Shaw's The Millionairess*, directed by W. Slater, 1972).

of the English stage, thus there is no great coincidence if both actresses played them in turn at some point in their career.

It would be more relevant, though, to examine which types both are identified with. In her maturity, apart from Lady Bracknell, Maggie Smith has – willingly or not – avoided Dame Edith's greatest successes, such as Mrs St Maugham in Enid Bagnold's *The Chalk Garden* or the Nurse in *Romeo and Juliet*. She nevertheless followed into Evans's steps in playing the classical type of the spinster, giving her rendition of Betsey Trotwood in Dickens's *David Copperfield*. Edith Evans was famous for being able to play any role. However, her consummate art of characterisation and her extraordinary ability to transform her appearance paradoxically did not prevent her from being pigeonholed in a category of roles. She was regularly cast in the same type. 'Versatility can be a danger. Familiarity breeds content', the drama critic J. C. Trewin wrote in his monograph on Evans.[487] Dame Edith's latest biographer, the director B. Forbes also underscored that fundamental incoherency, saying that paradoxically Evans's versatility did not allow her to avoid being typecast.[488] The same statement could be made, nowadays, about Smith.

Edith Evans and Maggie Smith have both, very early in their careers, specialised in authoritarian or cantankerous elderly – or very old – ladies. As early as 1914 (she was only twenty-six), Evans was given the role of Mrs Rhead in Arnold Bennett's *Milestones*, a woman in her sixties, and in 1926 (she was thirty-eight, then), she portrayed for the first time the nurse in *Romeo and Juliet*, [489] having played Queen Margaret in a production of *Richard III* the previous year. Evans and Smith have become – one in the 1940s, the other in the early 1990s – ideal casting for all these characters belonging to the old bag category. When they reached maturity, both actresses got typecast and followed very similar paths. From her sixties, Edith Evans started to play the kind of roles that Maggie Smith plays today. These characters can be divided into three categories:

- The upper-class ladies, the haughty aristocrats and the imposing figures who possess authority. Of course, everyone thinks of Lady Bracknell, the character with whom Evans remains most strongly identified and

487 Trewin, *Edith Evans*, p. 52.

488 Forbes, *Dame Edith Evans*, p. 131.

489 She would reprise the role later, in 1934 and 1961.

the role which Smith was unquestionable born to play. When people evoke Evans's Bracknell, the term 'dragonhood' reccurs quite often. In comparison, Maggie Smith has given a rather different reading of the role, but both have portrayed with the same panache the formidable Aunt Augusta. For her part, since her 1993 triumph, Smith has offered numerous variations on the same type, with characters such as Constance Trentham, in *Gosford Park*, Lady Hester in *Tea With Mussolini* and, of course, Violet Crawley in *Downton Abbey*.

- The very old women, senile and often disabled. Just like Smith today, Evans was renowned for her amazing versatility and her remarkable aptitude for metamorphosis. She was capable of portraying extremely old characters. Despite some rare forays into silent movies, Evans made her proper screen debut in 1948. Her first appearance on screen did not go unnoticed, as she was playing the very old Countess Ranevskaya in T. Dickinson's *The Queen of Spades*, a she-Faust who has sold her soul to the Devil. Thanks to a thick layer of caoutchouc and chemical products which gave her a wrinkled, leathery skin, the actress was supposed to look like an octogenarian – or, more exactly, like what an octogenarian was supposed to look like, in the late 1940s. Commenting on her performance, the critic from *The Sunday Chronicle* wrote: 'Dame Edith's countess is a figure of unforgettable senility, whose skull one glimpses beneath the skin. The skin itself is not so much wrinkled as smoked; and the words, croaked softly from an almost lipless mouth, carry a quality of frog's breath.' [490]
- The eccentric, extravagant ladies who more or less resemble Sheridan's grotesques. Within this category, Miss Western in *Tom Jones* (T. Richardson, 1963), one of Dame Edith's prominent roles on screen, or Josephine, the Madwoman of La Concorde, in *The Madwoman of Chaillot* (B. Forbes, 1968), could be mentioned. In the same vein, Maggie Smith has played characters such as Charlotte Bartlett in Ivory's *A Room with a View*, Lavinia Penniman in Agnieszka Holland's *Washington Square* and, on stage, Lettice Douffet in Shaffer's *Lettice and Lovage*.

However, although both have portrayed, at different times, the same characters, Maggie Smith disposes of a larger potential than Edith Evans.

490 Quoted in Forbes, *Dame Edith Evans*, p. 210.

As W. Gaskill once pointed out, Smith probably outdoes Evans thanks to her incredible ability to provoke laughs. In the matter of tragedy and dramatic roles, Smith has certainly nothing to envy Evans for, but unlike her predecessor, she is also a real comic genius. Gaskill analysed Maggie Smith's incomparable comic talent as a diptych: her wit and her 'clowning'. He admitted that very few actors have both, and Dame Edith Evans, whose roles Maggie Smith has often played, was no 'clown'.[491] Furthermore, as Smith has now reached an age at which Evans was in the autumn of her career, the range of parts she still can play remains much wider. It is obvious and normal that Maggie Smith looks much younger than Dame Edith did at the same age and, while the latter did not wear any ageing make-up to play the dowager queen in her last movie, *The Slipper and the Rose* (B. Forbes, 1975), the former still needs the help of a make-up designer to be convincing as a very old lady. Without being unattractive, Evans had an uncommon face and she was certainly more remarkable by her allure than by her beauty.[492] Over the years, her features thickened and even if her physical appearance was particularly adequate to portray dowagers and old crones, it would have prevented her from playing the younger, more attractive characters that are still accessible to Smith.

In any case, this parallel with the actress to whom she is usually compared provides us with a very convenient framework of analysis to examine, in terms of versatility, Maggie Smith's recent roles and, to begin with, those which belong to tradition – either the actress plays a character from the classical literature or an archetype of comedy. In fact, although the roles which correspond to her type are usually funny – her on-stage Lady Bracknell was as hilarious as her dowager countess is on television – the specifically comedic roles she has played are scarce and can be seen as traditional parts. Playing these roles, Smith comes after several generations of actresses but, far from betraying and corrupting these parts by the

491 'A rare source of wit', *The Observer*, 1 November 1992, p. 60. See also Wardle, 'All the angles'; Smith has two 'identities' as a performer, actor and clown.

492 When she met for the first time Edith Evans, in 1919, Sybil Thorndike was reputed to have said: 'I've just seen the most wonderful actress: she's almost plain, almost ugly, but she's absolutely marvellous'; quoted in Johns, *Dames of the Theatre*, p. 80. See also M. Billington, 'The greatest actress of her times', *The Guardian,* 15 October 1976, p. 17; he admits that she was not 'beautiful', but could convey beauty. As J. C. Trewin asserted, 'she could act beauty' (see Trewin, *Edith Evans*, p. 62).

excesses and mannerisms she is too often associated with, she has renewed them. Most of the time, she offers a new reading of the character and her performance eventually becomes the definitive one.

Journey with my Aunt

Just like Jane Austen's novels, Dickens's works have been adapted for the screen a great number of times, and *David Copperfield* makes no exception. Still, whereas the two latest adaptations have been released in a short interval of time (Simon Curtis's adaptation, for the BBC, in December 1999 and Peter Medak's, for TNT, just one year later), there has been none since then. It seems that Curtis's adaptation – better received by critics than Medak's with which it was, of course, systematically compared – has become the definitive one, just like the acclaimed BBC adaptation of *Pride and Prejudice*, in 1995. Curtis's version is probably less faithful to the novel than the previous ones, as the script deliberately focuses on a selection of scenes – such a plentiful novel being almost impossible to adapt for the screen because of the multiplicity of the subplots – but it eventually reinforces the readability of the story. In any case, the quality of this TV drama lies for a large part in Maggie Smith's unforgettable performance as Aunt Betsey.[493] At each period of time, there is a great actress to portray that character which is truly part of English heritage. 'The larger-than-life "Dickensian" character, sharply etched by behaviour, appearance and verbal tics, was the dream assignment of every character-actor,' the academic J. Marsh writes.[494] Every renowned actress, if she is the right age and has a physical appearance suitable for the part, is expected to play Aunt Betsey at some time. Appreciative of Adrian Hodge's script, the actress enjoyed playing this role, confessing that she was 'very, very fond' of Betsey Trotwood. She thought that Dickens (who performed his novels in public) always wrote good characters.[495] As the producer Kate Harwood asserted, Smith was the best cast possible for Betsey. When she accepted the role, it allowed the project to take off. The actress liked the script and was eager to play Betsey Trotwood, one of literature's most dramatic figures. According to Harwood, she is the definitive Betsey, an extraordinary mixture of sweetness and stiff eccentricity, which suits so well her marvellous comic timing.[496] Smith, more angular than Miss Trotwood herself, was obviously born to play her one day or another, as Miriam Margolyes – a good specialist of Dickens – explains: 'That's a particularly Dickensian thing, that Dickens characters have such defined shapes. It is quite wrong for me to be Betsey Trotwood when she is clearly an angular creature. That's why Maggie Smith is perfectly good casting.'[497] Abrupt woman with a heart of gold, Betsey Trotwood was a tailor-made role for the actress, prefiguring Minerva

493 N. Genzlinger, 'David Copperfield's Tough Boyhood and Yada Yada Yada', *The New York Times*, 15 April 2000, p. 566; the journalist mentions a Betsey Trotwood played 'with delightful perfection' by Maggie Smith.

494 'Dickens and film', in *The Cambridge Companion to Dickens*, ed. by J. O. Jordan (Cambridge: Cambridge University Press, 2001), p. 214.

495 See *Radio Times*, 18-31 December 1999, p. 8.

496 J. Herd, 'Dickens accessible for all', *The Australian*, 5 février 2000 (page not known).

497 Quoted in *Dickens on Screen*, ed. by J. Glavin (Cambridge: Cambridge University Press, 2003), p. 105. Author and performer of the excellent *Dickens Women*, M. Margolyes has great experience in Dickensian characters; see M. Margolyes-S. Fraser, *Dickens Women* (London: Hesperus, 2011). An American critic blamed this 'physiognomic' casting (E. Gibbs, 'Stocking fillers', *The Sunday Herald*, 19 December 1999, p. 53), complaining that every character is either an angel or a devil, according to his physical shape (the rounder the actor, the sweeter the character), and, when a plump Pauline Quirke makes an entrance, the spectators can guess that she is good-natured. It reflects, in fact, the categories of characters depicted by Dickens itself.

McGonagall she would play the following year alongside the same young actor, a certain Daniel Radcliffe. By her features, Betsey ranks among the figures of authority, these stern but fair women whom Smith portrays so marvellously. This time, though, she relies on the eccentricity of the Dickensian character to turn it into a comical figure.

Playing Betsey Trotwood, Smith was the latest in a long list of prestigious actresses, including Flora Robson[498] and Edith Evans. Oddly, Aunt Betsey is not, far from it, Dame Edith's most notable role. Despite an amazing cast – including Laurence Olivier, Michael Redgrave, Ralph Richardson, Cyril Cusack and Wendy Hiller – the 1969 adaptation (directed by Delbert Mann) looks a bit outdated these days and Evans's Betsey does not reach the greatness of the actress's most famous performances. It is one of her last roles on screen; she looks, from the start, far too old to play a middle-aged Betsey and her portrayal does not do justice to the extravagance of the character. George Cukor's *David Copperfield*, released in 1935 by MGM Studios, is generally considered the most faithful adaptation. The script scrupulously follows Dickens's chapters and one of Cukor's first concerns was to cast actors who looked like the characters or, more precisely, like Phiz's illustrations for the very first edition.[499] The American actress Edna May Oliver – who would become, a few years later, an amazing Catherine de Bourgh in Cukor's adaptation of *Pride and Prejudice* (1940) – did not look exactly like Betsey's drawing by Phiz, but her casting was an obvious choice. She would be a larger-than-life Aunt Betsey whose every gesture, every line was calculated to be in accordance with Dickens's text – especially in that particular way Betsey tucks up her skirt to put her feet on the fender. Famous for her mannerisms, her horsey profile and her energetic demeanour, Miss May Oliver had all the qualities required to play the part.[500]

Maggie Smith's performance goes beyond the traditional approach. The actress simply brings a new breadth to the character. She manages to transcend it, making Betsey's figure equally deeper and funnier. Patience Collier – in a 1974 version, directed by Joan Craft for the BBC – and Edith

498 In a BBC's series directed by J. Craft, January-April 1966, with no less than Ian McKellen as David Copperfield.

499 See *Film Adaptation*, ed. by J. Naremore (New Brunswick: Rutgers University, 2000), p. 127, n. 37.

500 Nissen, *Actresses of a certain Character*, p. 138: 'Oliver simply looked like something out of a storybook.'

Evans were peculiar but not funny. Maybe Smith's Aunt Betsey is not the most faithful to the novel, but she is the most delectable version of the character, to the point that she definitely outdoes the other actresses who have played the part. According to the journalist from *The Independent*, Smith is the 'ideal' Aunt Betsey. As he explained, when she appears on screen, Maggie/Betsey obviously stands as the successful result of a long process aiming to obtain the 'ideal' Betsey. She is stern, hilarious, comforting, tremendously eccentric, and totally unaware of it.[501] It must be noticed, though, that the darker side of Betsey's life – everything about her former husband and the furtive reappearances of that evil man – has been completely obliterated in Hodge's script. At some point, Betsey herself reveals that her husband has been killed by an elephant in India, although he was well alive in the other adaptations. In fact, in Curtis's version, Betsey Trotwood – a widow without the grief – has reintegrated, as a character, the spinster category. Freed from any conjugal authority, Aunt Betsey has the moral strength of a man and she is the one who protects the masculine figures who live in her house – David, of course, and the incredible Mr Dick. Being a spinster instead of a betrayed spouse, Betsey gains in *vis comica.*

According to Bergson, most of the comical effects result from 'something mechanical encrusted on the living'.[502] In fact, by her frenetic gesture, Maggie Smith conveys a mechanical aspect to her character. In the first episode, her Betsey looks like an articulated puppet, suggesting a rigidity which was in fact the main feature of the character imagined by Dickens: 'The setting sun was glowing on the strange lady, over the garden-fence, and she came walking up to the door with a fell rigidity of figure and composure of countenance that could have belonged to nobody else.'[503] With her repetitive movements and her exaggerated pouts, Smith's Betsey sometimes looks like a jumping jack or a cartoon character, outdoing, thanks to her vivacious, hilarious manners, all the other Betseys who have preceded her. Maggie Smith has transformed that colourful character – which was too conventionally portrayed after

501 R. Hanks, 'David Copperfield', *The Independent*, 27 December 1999, p. 12.

502 *Laughter. An Essay on the meaning of the comic,* transl. by C. Brereton & F. Rothwell (New York: MacMillan, 1912), p. 37.

503 C. Dickens, *David Copperfield,* Chapter 1 (Oxford: Oxford University Press, 1981), p. 3.

all these years – into a hilarious but very moving figure, a bit excessive as it suits a Dickens's character, but never hammy. Her Aunt Betsey is very funny, but neither caricatural, nor grotesque like Mrs Crupp, David's landlady (deliciously played by Dawn French, who got on very well with Maggie Smith during the filming) or Mrs Heep, who both correspond to Dickensian types. With Smith, Betsey loses a bit of the roughness that belonged to the character of the novel. She is elegant, refined and – unlike E. May Oliver's uproarious portrayal – she also reveals a softer, more vulnerable side which makes her instantly lovable. Betsey may be very stiff and brusque, she is not entirely the virago whom Dickens depicts in his novel and, at the risk of writing an oxymoron, it may be said that Maggie Smith's Betsey is often cute. Of course, the 1830s fashion and its wide-brimmed bonnets – deliciously curved like chanterelle mushrooms or sea snails – certainly help, but, thanks to the actress, some scenes of the film look like a naive painting.

The film opens on the profile of a woman standing against the darkness or, to be more precise, a pointy nose jutting out from under the brim of a black bonnet. At a slow, but determined pace, the woman walks towards the house where a very pregnant Mrs Copperfield lives with her maid, Peggotty. This first scene gives a rather chilling impression of Betsey Trotwood, who makes the same entrance as a maleficent fairy coming to cast a spell on a newborn.[504] The spectator does not know if he has to laugh or to wince when the grimacing face of the lady appears through the window, looking like a scarecrow or a Gorgon mask aimed at frightening the young children.[505] Dressed in black, wearing a feathered bonnet which accentuates her verticality, Maggie Smith, with her very mobile face, her neat features and her ever-moving chin, looks more birdlike than ever. This time, though, she resembles a sinister raven who has come to angrily peck in Mrs Copperfield peaceful nest. 'Miss Betsey Trotwood. You've heard of her… Now you see her!' she announces. However, as grumpy as she may seem, nothing has to be feared from this intriguing creature. As soon

504 H. Stone, 'Fairy Tales and Ogres: Dickens's Imagination and *David Copperfield*', *Criticism*, vol. 6, n° 4, 1964, p. 324: 'From outward view she appears to be a witch rather than a godmother. But her forbidding exterior and eccentric mannerisms are a fairy tale disguise.'

505 M. Hollington, *David Copperfield by Charles Dickens* (Paris: Didier, 1996), p. 59: 'Aunt Betsey pressing her face against the window pane (transforms) herself into a monster.'

as she gets rid of her coat and sits by the fire, waiting for the birth of her much-awaited great-niece, Miss Trotwood proves to be a very efficient comical figure. Unable to bear the screams of the parturient, she stuffs her ears with cotton balls and, at the height of her annoyance, she paces up and down the sitting room. Here, more than in any of her other films, Smith is considerably helped by her physical means. Her large blue eyes – so glamorous, in other contexts – become two mobile, bulging globes rolling in a bird facies distorted by horror and disgust. The actress has never looked so funny on screen. Unfortunately for her, the child is a boy, and to the great disappointment of the spectator (if he does not know the story), the strange lady leaves as quickly as she had come.

When the mysterious Aunt Betsey reappears, years later, it is in a much cosier setting than the austere Rookery.[506] The following episodes, in Dover first, then at Mr Wickfield's, in Canterbury, correspond to the second period in Betsey's 'progress'. She is ten years older than she was when she visited her niece Copperfield, but she has lost nothing of her energy. On the contrary. When the young David, exhausted after his long journey from London to the south coast, arrives at Betsey's home, his aunt, taken by surprise, falls over in the lavender bush she was lovingly pampering a few seconds earlier – proving, if necessary, that Smith was the perfect fit for playing a 'lady in lavender'! In fact, it is the only adaptation which shows Aunt Betsey flat on her bottom; one probable explanation is that the other actresses did not have, when they played Betsey, Smith's physical agility – Edith Evans cautiously sat on a bench, while Edna O'Brien fell very carefully – and, of course, it reinforces the comical efficiency of the scene. Oddly enough, a preliminary drawing by Phiz showed (under the legend 'I make myself known to my aunt') Aunt Betsey sitting flat down in the garden path, while the final etching shows her standing, haggard, with a rake and a watering can at her feet.[507] Maybe the illustrator had thought that the posture offended the dignity of the character – being unaware that, played by Maggie Smith, Aunt Betsey would *never* lose her dignity, whatever

506 Actually, none of the previous adaptations had offered such a beautiful home to Betsey T. By magic (and with the help of computer technology), the magnificent house of Houghton Hodge, Hampshire, was transferred to Dover's famous white cliffs.

507 H. Steig, *Dickens and Phiz* (Bloomington: Indiana University Press), 1978, p. 119 and fig. 77-78.

the situation. Always in motion, the actress has the quickness and the agility of a bird, displaying an uncommon stamina. Betsey Trotwood holds the reins of her cariole with an iron fist and shows the same amount of energy when it comes to chasing away the donkeys which recklessly venture on her patch of grass. From that point of view, the role represents a great physical challenge. In full costume, the actress runs amazingly fast and she waves a broom better than anyone else to knock out her unwanted guests. Such a part was perfect for Smith, as it gave her the opportunity to display her physical abilities. This bodily vigour is combined with verbal violence in the scene where she faces the Murdstones but, paradoxically, that very scene reveals at the same time all the inner tenderheartedness of Aunt Betsey, who gently caresses the cheek of David whilst he is asleep.

After a gap of several years – David's school years in Canterbury – the viewers meet Betsey Trotwood again; she has white hair but, nevertheless, she still looks as vigorous as before. While she walks the London streets with her nephew, she suddenly faints, having the feeling that a donkey is trespassing on her dear patch of grass. This is a very short scene, but it wonderfully showcases the actress's talent and facial expressivity. Suddenly, her blue eyes stare in horror, her face turns pale and, in total panic, the elderly woman suppresses a retching cough. To be fully appreciated, the scene must be watched on freeze frame mode, but, by its precision and verisimilitude, it stands as a masterclass in acting.[508] Two minutes later, the same Betsey radiantly smiles to Mr Spenlow who has just hired David as a clerk and, despite her white hair, she suddenly loses fifteen years and fleetingly appears as beautiful as the actress who plays her. Even more succinct, but quite emblematic, is the scene which corresponds to Betsey's arrival in London. Now ruined, after some misguided investments, she brings Mr Dick with her to seek refuge at David's place. Waiting for his return from the office, they sit with bag and baggage on the landing.[509] The picture on the screen could be compared to a painting, in the way it faithfully reflects one of Phiz's etchings – except that Betsey's caged birds

508 B. Garron, 'Air Time', *Hollywood Reporter*, 6 June 2000, p. 6; according to the critic, Smith's portrayal is so accurate that it makes her every scene 'a textbook study in acting.'

509 Dickens writes: 'My aunt sitting on a quantity of luggage, with her two birds before her, and her cat on her knee, like a female Robinson Crusoe' (*David Copperfield*, Chapter 34, p. 405).

are replaced by a couple of funny wooden budgies. 'I am ruined,' she says. Grasping a huge travel bag, with her wrinkled forehead, her raised eyebrows and her beaming smile, Smith, as cute as a little girl, is unrecognisable. The last (properly) funny scene is that of Uriah Heep's denunciation, when, more vigorous and energetic than ever, Aunt Betsey shakes a terrified Heep like a rag doll. However, at that point, the spectator has already noticed that the character's behaviour has gradually changed. Figure of incontestable authority in the very first scene, Betsey Trotwood progressively softens and eventually becomes a sweet old lady in the last few minutes of the TV drama. The most challenging aspect of this performance – in regards to Smith's versatility – lies in the fact that it represents a 'mise en abyme' of the metamorphosis process. The actress transforms into a character who goes through a transformation.[510] As her hair is whitening, Miss Trotwood gets more and more patient and serene, and, in the second part of the series, she is rather cute and lovable than properly funny. The critic from *The New York Daily News* perfectly captured that impression, asserting that her Aunt Betsey communicated so much kindness and spirit that the spectator wanted 'to kiss her on the screen'.[511]

Betsey Trotwood's first scenes belong to the pantomime genre. Aunt Betsey is presented as a female dragon, with brusque gesture and excessive attitudes which were already described, like stage directions in a script, in Dickens's novel. When she visits Mrs Copperfield, Betsey hustles and bullies the young woman, vividly complaining about her lack of maturity. Probably distressed by her ebullient guest, the young woman suddenly feels labour pains and her maid Peggotty has to fetch the doctor. The birth of a boy makes Betsey furious and she nearly knocks the poor doctor out. As early as this first scene, Aunt Betsey stands as an 'opponent'; she hates David who has the disadvantage of being a boy. When David reappears in Betsey's life, almost one decade later, his great-aunt has slightly evolved. Although she is terrified by the arrival of a boy at her home, she cannot

510 N. E. Schroeder-R. A. Schroeder, 'Betsey Trotwood and Jane Murdstone: Dickensian Doubles', *Studies in the Novel*, vol. 21.3, 1989, p. 268: 'Aunt Betsey develops from a Dickensian caricature to a psychologically convincing character [...] Part of what makes Aunt Betsey so endearing and so authentic is precisely the fact that she does change.'

511 Schultz, 'Splendid Copperfield', *The New York Daily News*, 16 April 2000 <http://www.nydailynews.com/archives/nydn-features/splendid-copperfield-fine-mchenry-article-1.859056> [accessed 12 November 2016].

resolve to leave him in the hands of the Murdstones and, with the help of Mr Dick, she will quickly learn to love him as her own child, David Trotwood Copperfield. From then on, whereas she remains a brusque and vigorous woman, her manners considerably soften and the dragon becomes, in the last scene, a sweet and loving grandmother as if – to make a comparison with Disney's characters – Maleficent has turned into Cinderella's fairy Godmother. 'She vanished like a discontented fairy': this is how Dickens describes Betsey's disappointment after David's birth.[512] The character, when played by Maggie Smith, actually performs the role of a fairy figure.[513] Having transformed into a 'helper', she becomes a counsellor and mostly a surrogate mother for David. She may not put up with donkeys on her green, but she spends a part of her fortune for David's education. Step by step, she will accompany him, like a guardian angel, at every stage of his young life. She protects him, but does not try to dissuade him to marry Dora Spenlow although it is obviously a mistake; *David Copperfield* can be regarded as a Bildungsroman and David must learn from experience to grow up and build his own personality. Betsey reveals herself to be a brave woman with a heart of gold. By her generosity and her tutelary benevolence, Betsey can be seen as a double of Minerva McGonagall, stern and fair at the same time. She is a stiff woman with a sweet heart, who wipes away a tear when leaving the little boy at Mr Wickfield's house in Canterbury. Slowly, her figure emerges through the story to take the final form of the affectionate old lady who, in the epilogue, holds in her arms (the long awaited) Baby Betsey.

In the two episodes of the series, Maggie Smith's performance as Aunt Betsey spans more than thirty years (if we consider David's age at the end of the story). The last appearance of an aged Aunt Betsey receiving in her arms her great-great niece did not exist in the previous adaptations. According to Dickens himself, she is at least eighty – which was a very respectable age in the first half of the nineteenth century –

512 *David Copperfield*, Chapter 1, p. 10.

513 It was inherent in the character created by Dickens. M. Slater, *Dickens and Women* (Redwood City: Stanford University Press, 1983), p. 275: '(Betsey) compels us to suspend our disbelief in the existence of real-life fairy godmothers'; see also Stone, 'Fairy Tales and Ogres', p. 829: 'Hundreds of details, from the grotesque portents which surround Miss Betsey's first appearance, to the magical sanity she infuses into Mr Dick's imbecility, add fairy-tale potency to David's succoring godmother.'

in that very last scene,[514] she is about sixty-five when she finds refuge in London after her bankruptcy and she is probably in her fifties when David arrives in Dover. This means that she is a quadragenarian, no more, in the first scene. Smith stands as the only Betsey Trotwood to have lived through the whole story, going through more than three decades, effortlessly jumping from one age to another and wearing, always convincingly, any hair colour. By comparison, Evans's Betsey, in 1969, kept the same appearance – that of an elderly woman – through the film, while Patience Collier, in the 1974 version, simply wore spectacles in the last scenes to suggest the passing of years. This double evolution, physical and moral, was made possible by the casting of Maggie Smith, as S. Curtis admitted: 'Other people could be the Aunt Betsey at the beginning or the Aunt Betsey at the end […] but Maggie is the only one who could be Aunt Betsey all the way through, showing how she develops.'[515] Only Smith was able to portray so convincingly the same character, from middle-age to old age, with a minimum of props and make-up. Only Smith was able to make the audience visualise Betsey Trotwood's evolution, from the farcical abruptness of the first scenes to the motherly tenderness of the last chapter. Successively harsh and soft, comical and vulnerable, the actress lets us witness the incredible and incessant metamorphosis of the character.

514 '(Aunt Betsey) in stronger spectacles, an old woman of fourscore years and more, but upright yet' (*David Copperfield,* Chapter 64, p. 714).

515 CBS press file, 2000. As the make-up designer Christina Noble pointed out, the passing of years was marked by the change of hair, the make-up itself being kept to a strict minimum.

The Dotty Chaperone

Although Henry James has rarely been held a master of comedy, it is in Agnieszka Holland's adaptation of *Washington Square* that Smith gives one of her most hilarious performances. Undeniably, the film was not as commercially successful as expected, but the critics were harsh on what they saw as a disappointing and superfluous enterprise, half a century after William Wyler's *The Heiress* which allowed Olivia de Havilland to pick up the Academy Award for Best Actress in 1949.[516] Still, Holland's film remains a very faithful adaptation of James's *Washington Square*, much closer to the novel than *The Heiress* was.[517] Because of the constant presence of an omniscient narrator, the text is all the more difficult to adapt for the screen, thus to transcribe in action and dialogue, not only the inner thoughts of the characters, but also the ironic judgment that the narrator passes on them, is certainly not an easy task. With regards to Maggie Smith's role, Aunt Lavinia, Holland has been able to give a new dimension to a character who was not particularly flattered in James's novel. Clumsily meddling in her niece's love affair, Lavinia Penniman only makes things worse and Henry James depicts a woman as stupid as she is secretive. In Holland's film, Lavinia reveals herself through several scenes – some are more developed than they were in the novel, while some others are new – which gradually draw the portrait of a cute and funny woman whom Smith's portrayal makes even cuter and funnier.[518] Ultimately, the actress gives life to a character whose presence illuminates a rather dark movie. An American critic wrote that Smith delivered the film's best lines 'with trilling, birdlike perfection'.[519]

As early as the first scene of the movie – after a prologue which crudely exposes the death of Mrs Sloper, as a consequence of Catherine's birth – Aunt Lavinia makes a theatrical entrance. A mature woman in full mourning emerges from her apartment to temper the enthusiasm of the young Catherine Sloper who is, as usual, overexcited by the return of her father

516 In this specific occurrence, any comparison was preposterous, as Wyler's film was based on the play by Augustus et Ruth Goetz (who adapted their own work for the screen) which was already loosely inspired by James's novel. Of course, the complex intertextual link which associates the novel with the play and its screen adaptation has unsurprisingly influenced the work of Agnieszka Holland and the screenwriter Carol Doyle, but it is nothing more than an influence. See K. Newell, '*Washington Square* "virus of suggestion": Sources Texts, Intertexts and Adaptations', *Literary Film Quarterly*, 34, 2006, p. 204-206.

517 S. Hunter, 'Henry James, Take Two', *The Washington Post Sunday Arts*, 12 October 1997, p. 1. Also C. Garbowski, 'The Modernity of Henry James and Agnieszka Holland's Washington Square', *American Studies*, XXII, 2005, p. 126.

518 D. Lodge, *Consciousness and the Novel. Connected Essays* (Harvard: Harvard University Press, 2002), p. 212: 'In the novel, she is mischievous, in the film merely comic or pathetic.'

519 A. Hornaday, 'Stuffy "Washington Square" fails to breathe much life into the Henry James classic', *The Baltimore Sun*, 17 October 1997 <http://articles.baltimoresun.com/1997-10-17/features/1997290052_1_washington-square-catherine-sloper-henry-james> [accessed 12 November 2016].

after his day of work. Dr Sloper (Albert Finney) reproaches his sister for her excesses, blaming her for providing his daughter with a frivolous education. That evening, Lavinia has secretly organised a small family gathering to celebrate her brother's birthday and, rather thoughtlessly, she intends to have Catherine sing a song. Unfortunately, the little girl panics and wets herself in front of the guests. This prosaic scene was largely criticised, not only because it did not exist in the novel,[520] but mostly because it sounded discordant with James's stilted universe. Nevertheless, it sheds light on Catherine's behaviour in the whole story, as well as on Lavinia's feelings for her niece. A close-up on the woman's beautiful, sad face reveals her disarray when she is confronted with the shyness and the discomfort of Catherine whom she seemingly truly loves. Lavinia stands as a protective, motherly figure for the little girl.[521] She is not exactly, here, the impecunious and opportunist aunt depicted by James in his novel and the spectator immediately feels compassion for her. In five minutes, Smith has established Lavinia as a lovable character. The actress now has plenty of time, one hour and forty minutes, to fully display all the resources of her comic genius.

Clearly, *Washington Square* cannot be seen as the most entertaining of James's novels – to the point that, when writing the screenplay for Wyler's film, Augustus and Ruth Goetz had shifted the central pivot of the plot onto Morris's betrayal and Catherine's final revenge – and Catherine Sloper (magnificently played by Jennifer Jason Leigh) stands as the most perfect anti-heroine. Yet, Holland has cleverly made use of the supporting character that Lavinia was, emphasising her comical side to beneficially counterbalance the cruel and painful aspects of the story.[522] A. and R. Goetz had deliberately made Lavinia a frivolous creature, more exasperating than funny; C. Doyle's screenplay has turned her into a winsome eccentric, joyous, funny and full of vitality. To cast Maggie Smith in the part had to be seen, of course,

520 In the novel, Aunt Penniman did not look after young Catherine. She settles in Dr Sloper's home quite lately, to become the young lady's chaperone.

521 K. M. Chandler, '"Her Ancient Faculty of Silence". Catherine Sloper's Ways of Being in James's Washington Square and Two Film Adaptations', in *Henry James goes to the movies*, ed. by S. M. Griffin (Lexington: University Press of Kentucky, 2002), p. 185; Chandler notes that Catherine has modelled herself after her extravagant aunt whose taste is deliciously grotesque.

522 See also J. A. Kassanoff, *Henry James' Daisy Miller and Washington Square* (New York: Barnes and Noble, 2004), p. 247; the author writes that Smith steals the show as Lavinia Penniman, and most of the film's humour lies in her performance.

as a supplementary asset, although it was a surprising choice, considering she usually plays stern or snobbish women. In reality, Agnieszka Holland simply wanted to work again with the actress whom she had directed in *The Secret Garden*, four years earlier.[523] In a recent thesis on James's cinematic adaptations, Jayson Baker pretends that Smith was 'miscast' as Lavinia Penniman: 'Penniman's willingness to betray her brother's trust seems to be an even more egregious violation given the frequency with which audiences have experienced Smith's snobbish and elite characterisations.'[524] In other words, according to the academic, as Maggie Smith often plays upper-class characters, she should stick to them because the audience is accustomed to see her as posh ladies. Such a conception would discourage any attempt of versatility. On the contrary, to portray Lavinia allows the actress to showcase once more her various and innumerable abilities in characterisation, far from her usual pinched aristocrats. Actually, what made the role challenging was the fact that Smith had to play a woman whom Henry James defined as 'an idiot', and Holland herself described Lavinia as 'not bad', but 'aggressively stupid'.[525] Despite all her talent, the actress physically shows too much intelligence and wit to convincingly embody ignorance and crass stupidity. In fact, Doyle's script takes some liberties with the novel, transforming Lavinia into a more complex, more captivating character. Mrs Penniman is no more a goose – the word is used by James himself – but a hypersensitive, romantic, exuberant woman who lives her romantic dreams through her niece's love story. While, at the beginning, she contents herself to meddle, trying to encourage Catherine and Morris's love affair, she gradually gets involved in the melodrama. She is funny because of her eccentricity and excesses, not because of her stupidity.

Visually speaking, Aunt Penniman is quite a noticeable character. In accordance with James's description, her outfits are overelaborate and Holland did not try to attenuate it and Doyle's screenplay describes Lavinia as a 'a big ambulatory Christmas tree'.[526] The peculiar thing about her is

523 G. Crnković, 'Interview with Agnieszka Holland', *Film Quaterly*, 52.2, Winter 1998-1999, p. 4.

524 *Imaginations: The Henry James literary and cinematic revival* (Providence: University of Rhode Island, 2012), p. 75.

525 R. Kempley, 'Agnieszka Holland: A War on Stupidity', *The Washington Post*, 12 October 1997, p. 7.

526 *Washington Square*, original script by C. Doyle, p. 107.

that, although she has been mourning for years, she manages to ally black colour with lots of lace, frills and ribbons. Widow of an austere clergyman, she nevertheless has a taste for overabundance in the matter of clothing.[527] In any case, Smith's Lavinia looks spruce and pretty, whereas James's Aunt Penniman was plain and old-fashioned. Her rustling dresses contrast with those of her much duller niece, and when she rushes down the stairs with her skirt tucked up, she brings to mind (a mature) Scarlett O'Hara running down the front path of Tara in *Gone with the Wind.* As expected, the crinoline suits Smith particularly well and even amplifies, thanks to its shape, her comical gestures. With her frilled taffeta skirt the width of which emphasises her slender waist,[528] Lavinia paradoxically looks as funny as elegant and raises laughs before having said one single word. The main reason lies probably in the blond ringlets which frame her angular, diaphanous face and whimsically wriggle like spiral springs at every move. Oddly, there is nothing properly ridiculous about her appearance, but everything in her is risible. Not only does Mrs Penniman have a passion for melodrama and romance, but she also behaves like an impulsive young girl whom only her persistent migraine can curb. In some way, she is much more youthful and impulsive than her niece is. For the role, Maggie Smith takes a North-American accent and speaks with a high-pitched tone which conveniently fits the manners of the babbling and always enthusiastic Lavinia. In the press file, the screenwriter pointed out that aspect: 'Aunt Penniman has a sense of fun and freedom. She has never let go of that drama and youth which so many others let go of very early.'[529] Here, Lavinia is much less haughty and more childish, 'girlish', than the character of the novel. At the engagement party of her other niece, she mixes with young people and even meddles in Catherine and Morris's first encounter. Feeling a lot easier than Catherine, she cheekily winks at the young man who politely compliments her. In *The Heiress*, Lavinia was an irritating, intrusive character – in the line of Molière's 'fâcheux' – who constantly interferes in

527 The costume designer Anna B. Sheppard commented: 'Aunt Lavinia's costumes are funny in a way. A widow of thirty years, she still wears black, but cannot keep from overdressing – even in black.' See *Washington Square* pressfile, p. 10.

528 Maggie Smith advised Jennifer Jason-Leigh – who had difficulties bearing the constricting garment – on how to wear a corset. See R. Lyman, 'James Follows Jane as Screen Writer of the Day', *The New York Times*, 7 September 1997, p. 66.

529 *Washington Square* pressfile, p. 7.

Catherine's matters of the heart; for the playwrights, it was the only way to visually transcribe the comments of the omniscient narrator. Holland goes even further and makes Lavinia an uproarious secondary character, a 'fluttery matchmaker', as the critic from *The Chicago Tribune* described her.[530] Inevitably, as wonderful as her prestigious co-stars – Leigh, Chaplin and Finney – are, the actress steals the show once again, in a very small part.[531] As soon as Lavinia has disappeared from the screen, the spectators long for her return and the critic Lisa Schwarzbaum humorously suggested that, maybe, the other actors wished Smith was a bit less mesmerising.[532]

Certainly, Smith does too much, but the character demands it. When Morris has dinner with the family and Dr Sloper takes him into the adjacent room to have a cigar and discuss about Catherine's future, Lavinia immediately peeps through the keyhole, like a nosy little girl. When Catherine accompanies Morris on the piano, Lavinia hilariously sings along, ruining their love song with her grotesque 'La la la'.[533] When she meets the young man in a shady bar to persuade him to secretly marry Catherine and put Dr Sloper in front of a *fait accompli*, she does not sound stupid like the character in the novel; she is mischievous, Machiavellian and even seductive. This scene corresponds to a crucial step in the character's evolution. Formerly an indiscreet go-between, Lavinia eventually (and unexpectedly) becomes a competitor for Catherine. She asks Morris for a lock of hair she is supposed to give to her niece, probably already intending to keep it for herself.[534] From then on, Lavinia's interest for Morris is made explicit. She

---

530 M. Wilmington, '*Washington Square*, a superb adaptation', *The Chicago Tribune*, 10 October 1997<http://articles.chicagotribune.com/1997-10-10/entertainment/9710100288_1_dr-sloper-morris-townsend-carol-doyle> [accessed 12 November 2016].

531 See, among others, J. Maslin, 'Clash of the Dazzling And the Meek, Again', *The New York Times*, 3 October 1997, p. 13. Also G. Murray, *Empire*, June 1998, p. 50: 'Smith, the stealer of all scenes'.

532 'Urbane renewal', *Entertainment Weekly*, 17 October 1997, p. 42.

533 It is a pity that Smith's voice has not been recorded on the soundtrack (original score by Jan A. Kaczmarek, Varese Editions). See Sadoff, *Victorian Vogue*, p. 174.

534 J. Bernard, 'It's fair and "Square". Victorian Heiress romance is par for the corset', *The New York Daily News*, 3 October 1997 <http://www.nydailynews.com/archives/nydn-features/fair-square-victorian-heiress-romance-par-corset-article-1.779194> [accessed 12 November 2016]. According to the critic, Maggie Smith could have expected an Oscar nomination 'for the funny, creepy way she demands a lock of hair from Morris' and then forgets to deliver it to her niece.

tries to divert the young man's interest for her own benefit. Some details are eminently suggestive: just like her parasol, the little handkerchief she uses to carefully wrap Morris's hair is deep red, as metaphorically ardent as the passion which inhabits her and, of course, in total discordance with her mourning attire.

The cutting of the tuft did not appear in the script and it judiciously announces, here, the following scene. Moments later, the viewers get to see Lavinia in the privacy of her bedroom. The place is cosy and full of trinkets like that of a romantic young girl. Mrs Penniman, with her hair in curlpapers – on Maggie Smith's head, the curlpapers alone are worth the trip –, takes a medallion from her drawers. She is wearing only her corset and her (red) petticoat, the colour of which can be regarded as eccentric and inappropriate for a widow in her mature years.[535] Lavinia lecherously looks at Morris's lock of hair, she sniffs and kisses it, before clutching the medallion to her heart. With no doubt, she does not meddle any more to serve Catherine's happiness; she clearly takes advantage of the situation. Thanks to Smith's subtle and hilarious performance, the scene is a piece of anthology and it is quite regrettable that so few critics noticed it, apart from the journalist from *The Washington Post* who did not hesitate to clearly assert that, basically, Lavinia wants 'a good hot shot of s-x' with the young man, even if she does not possess the words to express this idea.[536] When Catherine and her father embark on a trip to Europe, Lavinia finds another opportunity to get closer to Morris. In the novel, Lavinia promised her niece that she would dutifully entertain Morris's flame during her absence: 'I shall see him often, I shall feel like one of the vestals of old, tending the sacred flame.' However, it appears that the vestal is more forward than her sacred duty would allow her to be. In Dr Sloper's absence, she is the mistress of the house; in Catherine's absence, she behaves like Morris's

535 Red undergarments seem to be a leitmotiv through Holland's filmography, like Medlock's red dressing gown in *The Secret Garden*. The contrast was apparently deliberate, as the screenplay specifies (p. 59): 'She is in her underwear. And what underwear it is. Nothing we would ever have imagined to be under those black shifts. Satin and lace and courtesan type attire.'

536 S. Hunter, 'Washington Square: No Easy Pleasures', *The Washington Post*, 10 October 1997, p. 6. See also Matthews, 'Washington Square', *Sight and Sound*, June 1998, p. 60; the critic enjoyed the scene where Lavinia is shown 'fondling and sniffing' a lock of (masculine) hair.

most dedicated companion. Spectacularly dressed in salmon – the exact colour of the roses which now fill the Slopers' sitting room – with a galore of pastel lace and ribbons, the inconsolable widow is not mourning any more. 'It looks as if she's been in her niece's closet,' said the script.[537] Lavinia takes liberties with Morris, providing him with gestures of affection which reveal a great familiarity between them. A few months later, when she arrives at the port, radiant and all dressed in pale green, her enthusiasm betrays her. Catherine, who has become more lucid, realises that her aunt has interfered between them; the young woman's return sounds the death knell for Lavinia's romance. From then on, Mrs Penniman retreats to her proper place in the story and, in the last scenes of the movie, she is back in character; dressed in black again, she is relegated to the rank of 'relative'. Partly disinherited by her father, Catherine lives with her ageing aunt in the house which now represents her only possession. Despite a last (meddling) attempt by Lavinia, Catherine will remain single. Maggie Smith only makes a short appearance at the end of the film and, as disappointing as it can seem, it was necessary for the coherence of the whole story. The only comedic figure, played by a redoubtable scene-stealer, could not be too visible in the ending, without radically altering the tone of the film.

Yet, the part gives the actress a great opportunity to dazzle. Her legendary comic timing even increases the comical efficiency of the character. Every gesture, every facial expression is extremely precise and rightfully displayed. The scene where Morris informally visits the Slopers looks so spontaneous, that one could assume that it is improvised; Lavinia tries to improve the looks of her less-than-attractive niece, putting some ribbons in her hair and pinching her cheeks to bring colour to them, just before pushing her *manu militari* into the drawing room. All the action is scrupulously detailed and described in Doyle's script and Smith plays it like a music sheet, with an unsurpassed virtuosity; she never lets her technique show. Her timing and her energy have rarely been put so adequately to use for a screen role. She fidgets and wriggles like a cartoon character and, once again, this mechanical rhythm proves to be a powerful auxiliary of her acting. Lavinia Penniman evidently echoes some of Maggie Smith's previous roles, especially Charlotte Bartlett in *A Room with a View*. The two characters have a lot in common. Both women have a precarious social

537 See *Washington Square* script, p. 68.

status; as the chaperone of her younger cousin Lucy, Charlotte can travel around Europe thanks to the generosity of her rich cousins, while Lavinia lives at her brother's home. However, whereas Charlotte represents the ideal chaperone, prude, obsequious and excessively cautious,[538] Lavinia cuts a poor figure in comparison; although she is certainly more enthusiastic than the austere Charlotte, she is the least trustworthy chaperone ever, doing the exact contrary of what is expected from her. Far from preventing Catherine against ill-intentioned suitors, she hazardously encourages her to meet Morris and, being herself titillated by temptations which do not suit her age and her dignity, she tries to capture the attention of her niece's beau to the point that she causes resentment from the young lady.[539] Until the end, she will try to – unsuccessfully – interfere in Catherine's personal life. Still, Charlotte and Lavinia are both 'helpers', but this functional role is only a pretext. They are, above all, comical figures, who serve as a foil to the leading characters. 'Poor' Charlotte leaves the train at the wrong station, makes a fuss to be given some change to pay her taxi and eventually falls into her cousin's rose bush; being surprisingly lucid, she comments herself: 'What a nuisance I am!' Another similarity between Charlotte and Lavinia is the fact that, unlike Miriam Hopkins in *The Heiress*, Maggie Smith plays the character as a spinster. Her Lavinia has kept the freshness and the gawky spontaneity of a young girl. When she meets Morris in a brothel to provide him with advice, this great specialist in romantic intrigue and matters of the heart, suddenly gets scared when she realises that the occupants of the nearest box loudly copulate.[540] She vicariously lives Catherine's love affair, without the intention to go further. Although she used to be a married woman, she oddly seems to know very little about sentimental life and,

---

538 P. Kael, *Hooked. Film Writings 1985-1988* (New York: E. Dutton, 1989), p. 128; as P. Kael notes, Smith's Charlotte is nothing but the embodiment of prudery. She has always the pinched face of a spinster 'in eternal vigilance'. In *The Times*, the reviewer described Charlotte as the archetype of the desiccated spinster, an unfortunate creature constantly apologising and cautiously keeping away from matters of the heart. See D. Robinson, 'Masterpiece of enchanting fidelity', *The Times*, 11 April 1986, p. 15.

539 Whereas Charlotte Bartlett remains on the sideline. The – very sad – final scene of the film shows a lonely Charlotte, lying in her bed and reading the letter that her cousin Lucy has sent her from Florence.

540 Chandler, 'Her Ancient Faculty of Silence', p. 187; as Chandler explains, the juxtaposition of the two scenes suggests Aunt Lavinia's 'narrow conception of romance', which ignores any physical concerns.

like Emma Bovary, her experience of romance sounds more theoretical than practical. As a widow of a certain age, Lavinia embodies the type of what nineteenth-century French literature called the *oie blanche*, the young innocent girl who knows nothing about physical love but reads sentimental novels. Instead of portraying, like Hopkins did, an infuriating and mannered society woman, Smith plays a generic character, much heavier in comedic terms. One of the great achievements of Agnieszka Holland in this film is that she has turned the rebarbative character of Mrs Penniman into an archetypal figure; the spinster tantalised by desire is always a very efficient motif in comedy.[541]

That kind of character is indeed frequently involved in misunderstandings or impostures due to the fact that her vision of reality is always corrupted by her recklessness and her naivety. In English drama, this type is notoriously represented by two characters of the Restoration comedy, Lady Wishfort in Congreve's *The Way of the World* (1700) and Mrs Malaprop in Sheridan's *The Rivals* (1775). The ridiculous Malaprop – a 'weather-beaten old she dragon' – is convinced that she still is very attractive and thus liable to become a love interest, while the old Wishfort – despite being described as 'the antidote to desire' – uses prosthetics and thick make-up to hide the ravages of time. When the ridiculous spinster is involved, by accident, in a love intrigue, it necessarily raises laughs; on stage and, therefore, on screen, the elderly woman has nothing to do in the romantic sphere which is the preserve of young leading characters.[542] It is tolerated, though, that she interferes in young people's love affairs: the meddlesome spinster in *Tom Jones* (1749), immortalised on screen by Edith Evans, has only a very theoretical knowledge of the matters in

541 The figure of the ageing woman desperately trying to improve her appearance and attract men, has its origin in Roman Antiquity – with authors such as Martial, Juvenal and Ovid – and although the type itself does not exist in Latin drama, it appears for the first time in seventeenth-century French comedies, with the character of Bélise in *The Learned Ladies* by Molière (1672). Bélise is a frivolous and plain-looking spinster of a certain age who has confidence in her seductive power on men. When the young hero, Clitandre begs her to intercede with her niece Henriette whom he deeply loves, she mistakes his request for a declaration of love.

542 On that preconception, see E. A. Kaplan, 'Wicked Old Ladies from Europe', in *Bad. Infamy, Darkness, Evil and Slime on Screen*, ed. by M. Pomerance (New York: State University Press, 2004), p. 251.

which she pretends to be an expert.[543] All these characters have similarities with Lavinia in *Washington Square*. Although the respectable window of Reverend Penniman should direct her mind to spiritual aspirations and pious readings,[544] she does not think about anything but men and romance.[545] She obviously reads a lot of soppy novels, wears extravagant undies under her mourning dresses and meddles in her niece's love affair. Introducing the scene of the medallion, the patent concretisation of Lavinia's burning desire, Agnieszka Holland and Carol Doyle nearly shifted the movie into the comedic genre. There is only a slight distinction between Lavinia Penniman and Lady Wishfort. Wishfort looks ugly, and here probably lies the difference between comical figure and grotesque.

543 'She was, moreover, excellently well skilled in the doctrine of amour, and knew better than anybody who and who were together; a knowledge which she the more easily attained, as her pursuit of it was never diverted by any affairs of her own; for either she had no inclinations, or they had never been solicited.' See H. Fielding, *Tom Jones* (London: Penguin Books, 2005), p. 244.

544 Like the devout and utmost irritating Miss Drusilla Clack, in Wilkie Collins's *The Moonstone*, who is another hilarious example of the spinster type.

545 Sloper himself accuses her of fantasising about Morris 'She fantasises that the attention of all that abounding male energy in the front room is for her.' (*Washington Square*'s script, p. 80). See Maslin, 'Clash of the Dazzling'; as Maslin notices, the tremendously funny Aunt Lavinia is so fond of romantic melodrama that she takes pleasure in welcoming Morris, even if the 'gentleman caller' does not come to see her; S. Johnston, 'Washington Square' *Country Life*, 28 May 1998, p. 122; the author calls Lavinia a 'foolish old fusspot' with a great penchant for romance.

Into the Lean and Slippered Pantaloon

'All the world's a stage,' the melancholy Jaques famously declares in *As You Like It*, describing the seven ages that every man has to go through during his lifetime. Shakespeare's sixth age is the age of grotesque and ridicule, as the old man becomes the butt of others' mockery:

> The sixth age shifts
> Into the lean and slippered pantaloon,

With spectacles on nose and pouch on side,
His youthful hose, well saved, a world too wide
For his shrunk shank; and his big manly voice,
Turning again toward childish treble, pipes
And whistles in his sound (Act II, sc. 7).

Ridicule generally raises laughs. These laughs do not express connivance, though; the ridiculous individual is risible without being aware of it. Ridicule is usually believed to come from any deviation from the standards – the beauty, the sanity, the decency – or, in other words, from a difference which does not materialise a superiority but a deficiency. On the stage, the ridiculous character is unaware of his abnormality and he is all the more a source of fun because of his unwavering self-confidence. The more he sticks with his ignorance, the more his weak points get apparent, and the more his weak points get apparent, the less he is aware of them. Thus, the type has a huge comical efficiency on stage or on screen but, except if a young actor transforms to play the part, it often corresponds to a painful turning point in the career of an ageing actor who cannot play the young characters any more. Consequently, the grotesque character is the compulsory step for many actresses, after a certain age.[546] As everyone knows, the leading parts that older actors can play have no female counterparts and Maggie Smith herself has often complained about it in interviews. In 1992, she confessed to S. Morley that the difficulty for an actress of her age was that there was no transition, just one huge leap from Juliet into Lady Macbeth and then all the old crones.[547] Shakespearean theatre has not much to offer to mature actresses, except nurses and matronly figures (like the Nurse in *Romeo and Juliet* or Volumnia in *Coriolanus*),[548] and Restoration comedy keeps

546 I. Whelehan, 'Not to be looked at. Older women in recent British movies', in *British Women's Cinema*, ed. by M. Bell-M. Williams (London: Routledge, 2010), p. 171; as Whelehan suggests, in real life, the ageing movie star herself is often seen as a grotesque, the 'Dorian Gray' to her own eternal youthfulness on screen.

547 'Dial M for Maggie', *Radio Times*, 16-22 April 1992, p. 25.

548 Which were played by male performers on the Shakespearean stage. In France, although actresses had been allowed to tread the boards from the early years of the seventeenth century, old ladies parts in Molière's comedies used to be played by (elderly) actors. These days, some actresses and directors rebel against that unjust law, through gender-blind or all-female productions: in 2016, Glenda Jackson played King Lear at the Old Vic, while Harriet Walter appeared in an all-female Shakespeare trilogy at the Donmar.

them pigeonholed in a handful of characters, all risible and deprived of the attractiveness which usually characterises the female leading parts.

All the great British actresses have played the grotesques in the autumn of their career: Edith Evans, Flora Robson, as well as Sybil Thorndike and Gladys Cooper. In 1948, Evans eventually played Lady Wishfort and, as one of her biographers recounts, it was not easy.[549] Twenty-five years after her triumph as Millamant – probably her greatest success on stage, even if she is most remembered for her Bracknell nowadays – Dame Edith had to deliver the infamous line 'I look like an old peeled wall'. Of course, it was Wishfort who was speaking through Evans's mouth, but it is tough for an actress who has played the young female parts, then the leading ladies, to tackle the old crone roles. In 1953, it was Margaret Rutherford's turn to reprise Lady Wishfort at the Lyric Hammersmith, in a production staged by John Gielgud. In Rutherford's case, Lady Wishfort was only the latest in an impressive list of grotesques which corresponded, in fact, to her usual type. Rutherford would give her own rendition of Mrs Malaprop at seventy-five, in 1967. Yet, although the critics were in praise of her hilarious portrayal, they seemed to muddle up the character with the actress who played it. The celebrated critic Harold Hobson wrote: 'In her raddled, vain, manhunting, Lady Wishfort's most farcical and absurd rhetoric can be heard the echo of the authentic music of her vanished and betrayed romantic youth: there is something disturbingly sad, as well as uproariously funny, in this beauty become scarecrow.'[550] Make-up never suited Margaret Rutherford well and, from the production stills, with Lady Wishfort's cosmetics, she resembled a transvestite or, more exactly, the Auguste clown.[551] Of course, an actress does not play Wishfort or Malaprop at twenty-five and it must be painful, at some point in one's career, to enter this category of roles. The woman, object of sexual desire, is transformed into a pathetic buffoon. Things are changing, though, and mature actresses – who look younger than their predecessors – have fun portraying these characters, without having the disagreeable impression to be at the last turning point in their career. In

549 Batters, *Edith Evans*, p. 57.

550 Quoted by Keown, *Margaret Rutherford*, p. 56-57. With respect to Kenneth Tynan, after seeing the play, he described Miss Rutherford as 'a man-hungry pythoness' bustling about in her boudoir like a huge bumblebee. See K. Tynan, *A View of the English Stage, 1944-1965* (London: Methuen, 1975), p. 124.

551 Keown, *Margaret Rutherford*, p. 59-60.

1995, the late Geraldine McEwan played a dizzying, astonishingly sexy Wishfort at the National Theatre (where she had played Millamant in 1969), and Penelope Keith was a hilarious, but youthful Malaprop at the Theatre Royal Haymarket, in 2010.

As early as 1984, just at the time Maggie Smith was triumphantly playing Millamant in W. Gaskill's production of *The Way of The World*, she told N. De Jongh that, at her age, the grotesque parts (such as Mrs Malaprop and Wishfort) were 'looming'. [552] It would not be that surprising if Smith, in turn, lent her voice and her features to the key figures of the comical tradition. Nothing is less probable though. Not because the actress is currently unsure about returning to the stage, but mostly for the reason that Lady Wishfort seems to be too much classical a part to attract her.[553] Ridiculous and caricatural, Lady Wishfort comes close to the pantomime dame and, despite Maggie Smith's talent, it is difficult to imagine her in that kind of role. In 1988, she declared that Joan Plowright and her should do something about the fact that they were running out of parts. She said that actresses inevitably end up with the grotesques, for the reason that there are not many King Lears.[554] In March 2015, she declared to a journalist from *The Sunday Times* that she was reluctant to work again on stage, maybe because of the amount of energy it required, but mostly, she said jokingly, because she did not want to play an old crone feeding chickens in a Chekhovian play; Smith explained that, unfortunately, the older an actor gets, the grimier the parts become and, quoting the late Margaret Tyzack, she deplored the fact that, after a certain age, actresses are offered only dull or ridiculous characters that they did not enjoy playing.[555] Moreover, although Smith would never admit it, her physical appearance would make her a disservice. Even if she effortlessly ages when a role demands it, to make her look unattractive would require a lot more energy and talent from the make-up department. Her magnificent

552 'Millamant the magnificent', *The Guardian*, 2 November 1984, p. 19. The funny thing is that the journalist described her as a 'youthful, sexy fifty-one-year-old'. Not only was the actress younger than that then, but she had just had a full stock of theatre programmes redone because the notice stated that she was one year older than her real age.

553 Even if, as she recently declared at a Q&A event, she would have fun playing it (BFI and Radio Times Television Festival, BFI Southbank, 8 April 2017).

554 Isenberg, 'The Many Reflections of Maggie Smith'.

555 J. Utichi, 'Sorry, dear, but a dowager countess does not do selfies', *The Sunday Times*, 1 March 2015, p. 5.

blue eyes are too huge to leave room for ugliness or pitiful grotesque. The actress's face is naturally suited to express sadness and vulnerability which are not satisfactorily compatible with the farcical aspects of such figures: it is impossible to laugh at a character who inspire pity or affection. Back in 1984, when writing about Smith's performance as Mrs Chilvers in *A Private Function*, the filmmaker M. Harron celebrated 'a voice and a body made for elegant heroines'.[556] The major difficulty is that the actress has kept, at her age, a hieratic and spectacular beauty. On the stage, she still could play an older Millamant or a very mature Sullen – we got a glimpse of it in November 2013, at the National Theatre's 50th anniversary – certainly not Mrs Arcati or the nurse. Grotesque does not suit her queenly allure and vulnerable appearance.

Actually, Maggie Smith's occasional forays into that sphere are not her best performances. As always, she is convincing, but the comical impact is considerably reduced; the spectator does not laugh heartily. Instead, he is caught by an ambivalent feeling, a kind of unease, caused by the fact that the character, being more pitiful and lovable than downright ridiculous, calls for compassion rather than mockery. An example could be Mrs Docherty, in *Nanny McPhee and the Big Bang* (S. White, 2010). Old, wrinkled and white-haired, Agatha Docherty is slightly deranged and multiplies blunders. Of course, like most of the actress's onscreen roles, this is a supporting character whose only function is to make the (very young) audience laugh. With Docherty, though, Smith makes a glorious entrance in the gallery of grotesques. Not only does Mrs Docherty look like an elderly woman, but her mental state denotes an advanced senility. The comical disasters she regularly causes constitute her main characteristic. Functionally, she is not the one with whom the younger audience will identify: old, necessarily unattractive (as being old) and dotty, she is only a source of fun. Children laugh openly, but this is an incontestably cruel laugh. By an amusing coincidence, Maggie Smith encroaches here on a territory which belonged to her namesake, the late Liz Smith. Oddly, Mrs Docherty reminds us, in many aspects, of the characters L. Smith portrayed in the two movies the actresses have in common, *A Private Function* and *Keeping Mum*. Mrs Parker, Reverend Goodfellow's old neighbour in *Keeping Mum*, is a meddlesome figure whose habit is to always make an appearance at the worst moment.

556 Harron, 'Miss Smith and Betty the pig'.

Any of her intrusive interventions begins with the same sentence, 'About the Flower Arranging Committee…' a catchphrase that exasperates the other characters. Apart from this *idée fixe*, she is nosy and indiscreet like many idle old ladies. She feels persecuted and, at the same time, she is an easy prey for those who tell her lies. Even more resemblant to Mrs Docherty, Joyce Chilvers's mother in *A Private Function*, aka 'Mother Dear', gives evident signs of senility. Joyce never stops repeating 'She's seventy-four' to justify her mother's bewilderment and, to save face for the neighbours, she even dares to pretend that the old woman is the source of the terrible smell – caused by the pig's droppings – which had invaded her house. The only shopkeeper in the village, Mrs Docherty is not able to properly unwrap the merchandise she receives from her suppliers; she wades through the flour and fills the drawers of her little shop with treacle. During a picnic, the elderly lady even attempts to sit in a cowpat – 'a large mushy cow patty,' as a reviewer wrote. Someone thoughtfully prevents her from doing so, but nevertheless, she noisily (thanks to the talent of the sound technician) lowers herself in the very fresh cowpat. Any spectator under seven is supposed to burst out laughing and, of course, this film is targeted at very young audiences, but maybe there were other ways – more elegant than scatology – to use Maggie Smith's comedic skills. This is mostly a circus act, but as it often happens at the circus, the clown is more pitiful than risible. The last sequence – as Mrs Docherty has very little screen time in the two-hour long film – is thankfully quite different. In total contrast with the previous scenes, it is sweet, nostalgic and moving. Although Mrs Docherty appears to be senile and mentally disturbed during the whole movie, she seems to suddenly come to her senses in the very last minutes and proves to be the one who solves the enigma. She comforts the children who lament on Nanny McPhee's departure and also reveals her identity; she is Aggie, the baby who featured in the first movie, *Nanny McPhee* (2005). A radiant smile enlightens her face while she contemplates Nanny McPhee's magic harvest and a resplendent Maggie reappears – a bit discordantly – beneath Mrs Docherty's wrinkles and white curls. The film ends on that nostalgic note; the character was grotesque, the actress has made her touching. Pantaloon slippers definitely do not fit her.

Paradoxically, the most ridiculous character Maggie Smith has recently played is also one of the most glamorous. Yet, unlike Jean Horton in *Quartet*,

Emily Delahunty in *My House in Umbria* (R. Loncraine, 2003) represents a total characterisation. Freely adapted from William Trevor's novel by the screenwriter Hugh Whitemore, this TV drama provided the actress with the opportunity to portray a character quite unusual in regards to her regular casting. Considering the novel, Smith did not appear as an obvious choice to portray the plump quinquagenarian depicted by Trevor. Over-sophisticated, outrageously made-up and incorrigibly delusional, Emily Delahunty can be seen as a role 'against type' for Maggie Smith, far from her usual aristocrats, and very far from a brusque, sporty Muriel Donnelly or an austere Mother Superior. Anyhow, if the BFI movie theatre had been vast enough to accommodate Violet Crawley's innumerable fans for the screenings of *My House in Umbria* during the Maggie Smith Season in January 2015, there is no doubt that they would have hardly recognised the actress. Successful (as a writer of sentimental novels) and rich (she lives in a marvellous house in the Umbrian countryside), English expat Emily Delahunty – only one of her numerous pen names – has kept her looks intact, remaining a very attractive woman in her late fifties. Dressed in spectacular and very expensive clothes, she apparently has the most pleasant existence ever. One day in May, on her monthly trip to Milano where she is used to doing her costly shopping, a bomb explodes in the compartment she was sharing with several strangers. Some of her fellow travellers immediately die, while some others, like her, survive. Emily invites the three survivors from her carriage – an elderly general, a young German and Aimee, a little American girl who suffers from aphasia – to her sumptuous villa in order that they recover after the shock. As Emily's mind wanders to try to figure out who has placed the bomb and why, the four survivors forge a true friendship, living a quiet life, only disturbed by the arrival of Aimee's uncle, Mr Riversmith, claiming for his niece. Heartbroken at the thought of losing the little girl whom she has already made her surrogate daughter, Emily will try to woo Riversmith – a rather unpleasant academic specialising in carpenter ants – to reconsider and leave Aimee to her.

This is the main plot, a beautiful story of trauma, love and friendship, but this is not the most interesting aspect of the TV drama. What makes Emily Delahunty a complex, paradoxical character is the contrast between her outer appearance and her inner personality. Emily is the saddest person in the world. Sold for money by her parents (a couple of entertainers doing motorbike stunts who died shortly afterwards, in an accident), she was sexually abused in her teens by her adoptive father and, having run away from his home, after many wanderings, ended working as a prostitute in a shabby Moroccan café. The spectator does not get to know exactly how long Emily's troubled existence lasted, but she eventually bought a magnificent villa in Umbria, opened a kind of luxurious bed and breakfast and then, began to write bodice-ripping romance novels. She now has become a successful writer, some sort of second-rate Barbara Cartland, but it does not make her forget this painful past. Her only escape is her constant dreams, or more exactly the habit she has for inventing background stories for the people she meets, fictionalising and embellishing reality. Under her heavy make-up and her spectacular jewels, Emily is a wounded bird, a vulnerable creature. Many times deceived and exploited by men, she has remained alone in maturity and, just like Judith Hearne, she is a lonely soul, deprived of love. 'I was the only one not to have lost a loved one, having none to lose,' she says after the bomb attack. That explains why she is so generous and caring towards the other survivors, even showing maternal love to Aimee. The idea that the little girl will have to follow her uncle to Pennsylvania plunges her into despair. From the start, she puts all her efforts into being affable with Riversmith (Chris Cooper), but it only has the opposite effect. She quickly discovers he does not love his niece who suffers from post-traumatic shock and clearly represents a burden for him. Heartbroken, Emily feels helpless. Despite the kohl and the eyeshadow, rarely have Maggie Smith's blue eyes expressed such a deep sorrow, not since *The Lonely Passion of Judith Hearne* in any case.

In fact, Emily Delahunty has the same lonely addiction as Judith Hearne and carefully hides, not only her troubled past, but also her alcoholism. Being a heavy drinker, she behaves somewhat strangely and Mr Riversmith's hostility will increase her lack of confidence and her bewilderment, leading her to drink even more. Very soon, the character turns into an object of ridicule for Riversmith; he despises the fact that she writes cheap sentimental novels, knocks grappa at breakfast time and eventually attempts to seduce him. Deluded by false impressions, Emily humiliates herself in front of him, trying to catch his attention in the car during a day-trip to Sienna. Later, she suggests they have a drink and lures him to a very remote café where the man feels quite uncomfortable. She speaks too much, drinks too much and Riversmith, shocked by her behaviour, sees her as an old fool, lost in her dreams and her ridiculous fancies. All this blatantly appears on the screen, thanks to C. Cooper's perfectly balanced performance, but it takes Emily a long time to be aware of Riversmith's contempt. The most devastating moment comes later, when Aimee's uncle talks on the phone to his wife, telling her about Emily Delahunty. Driven by an unhealthy curiosity, or more probably by instinct, Emily secretly listens to the conversation and thus discovers that Riversmith considers her a dotty drunkard. The scene is short, but the pain and the disarray which take hold of her crystallise in Smith's eyes. Emily is deeply, irremediably hurt and the way the actress expresses those feelings represents a masterclass of acting in itself. Soberer and restrained, Emily's reaction is nevertheless as powerful as that of Judith Hearne when she realises that she was foolish to think that Madden wanted to marry her. Confronted to delusion, the truth is even more difficult to bear. Not only does Riversmith not find Emily attractive, but he makes fun of her behind her back. The ridiculous character usually does not know he is ridiculous. If he is aware of his ridicule, he becomes pathetic. In a last, tragic scene, Emily awakens Riversmith in the middle of the night to have a talk about Aimee's future. Already drunk, she brings with her two glasses and a bottle of grappa, hoping that alcohol will help to persuade him to leave the little girl in Italy. He is appalled and becomes even more so when Emily sits on his bed and inadvertently lets her dressing gown part, showing him her bare breast. Oddly enough, although the scene is certainly not erotic, it is even less grotesque. Riversmith is repelled by Emily's behaviour, but Emily is not physically repulsive; she is not an enamoured old crone like a modern Wishfort, but a smart, beautiful woman who is being ridiculed, because of her drunkenness, in front of a vile, insensitive man. The scene subtly lets the viewers wonder about Emily's real intentions and Riversmith's feelings: does he suppose, at that moment, that she intended to offer herself to him? It is difficult to say but, at least, Maggie Smith gratifies us with a devastating performance, all the more heartbreaking that the character is equally pitiful and touching. Emily's overflowing love and need for love totally annihilate the ridiculous aspects of the character. She may drink, she may write the silliest novels, she may have fanciful reveries, the spectator does not care. The critic from *Variety* commented that the character could easily have become caricature, but Smith's portrayal emphasises the pathos in the part.[557] Maybe another actress would have made Emily Delahunty a vulgar, grotesque woman; thanks to her vulnerability and elegance, the actress has transformed Emily into a poignant, lovable figure.

Unlike Trevor's novel,[558] Whitemore's screenplay ends on a high note. Riversmith flies back to the States, leaving Aimee to Emily who will be able to adopt her. Maternal love substitutes for conjugal love, making Emily happy. Having constantly, vainly tried to adapt the narrative pattern of her novels on reality, and thus distorting her vision of the world, she eventually decides to live her life to the fullest, 'seizing the day'. In the last scene, she has abandoned her heavy make-up and her sophisticated outfits for a simpler look, cotton dress and flat shoes. Ingeniously, the movie closes the loop, making Emily the heroine of a new story, the story she had started to write in the train, just before the bomb explosion: she had described an idyllic garden at twilight, full of blooming delphiniums and scented flowers, where a 'girl' in white dress was walking quietly, with a step 'as light as a morning cobweb'. With a light step, looking youthful in her white romantic dress, Maggie/Emily makes her way across a garden of Eden, starting a new life.

557 L. Loewenstein, 'My House in Umbria', *Variety*, 12 March 2003 <http://variety.com/2003/film/reviews/my-house-in-umbria-1200542866/> [accessed 12 November 2016].

558 In the novel, the old general dies, Riversmith brings his niece back to America and eventually puts her into a psychiatric institution.

The Poor Soul Sat Sighing

Unquestionably, Smith has no talent for grotesque. That does not mean she has never played risible, ridiculous characters, but these characters do not fulfil the requirements of a grotesque part. They do not raise cruel, despising laughs but, on the contrary, they make the spectator feel sorry for them.[559] One of the most disturbing, touching characters the actress

559 Even Charlotte Bartlett is moving and lovable. See R. Emmet-Long, *The Films of Merchant-Ivory* (New York: H. N. Abrams, 1997), p. 143; as Emmet-Long explains, Smith's Charlotte is a prim and apologetic spinster, but the character cannot be seen as a caricature. With her 'hollow eyes', she looks too vulnerable to be risible. She is comic at times, but undeniably touching.

has played on screen is Lila Fisher in *Love and Pain and the Whole Damn Thing* (A. Pakula, 1973), a secretive, clumsy, shy young woman who unexpectedly falls in love with Walter, an American boy significantly younger than she is, during a tour in Spain.[560] Lila never stops putting herself in awkward or ridiculous situations – she gets harassed by a weird Spaniard who emulates bird songs, she falls off her bed in the middle of the night or accidentally locks herself in the lavatories – and, whereas the viewers are tempted to laugh, her risible clumsiness is counterbalanced by her charm and vulnerability. Lila and Walter, both equally diffident and uncomfortable, gradually strengthen their relationship, even if the young woman obviously hides a much darker side. One night, she takes pills and drinks alcohol, in an attempt to shorten her own life. She does not die, but gets totally drunk, and the viewer realises that only Smith was able to convey this touching fragility to the pitiful wreck that Lila has suddenly become. This very scene, as devastating as beautifully acted, undeniably prefigures Judith Hearne's drunkenness in *The Lonely Passion of Judith Hearne*, in the way that the actress subtly manages to be alternatively ridiculous and moving. Despite their doubts and hesitations, Lila and Walter eventually become lovers and even then, just after their first romantic embrace, the young woman unexpectedly falls flat on her face, having her knickers twisted around her ankles. The situation is ridiculous but, strangely, we do not feel entitled to laugh heartily; there is something about that fragile woman that prevents laughs. In the very last part of the movie, Walter discovers that Lila is terminally ill and he proceeds to marry her although she is going to die soon. The tone of the story instantly changes, and what had started like a pleasant, light comedy turns into a devastating drama where Maggie Smith gives an incredibly moving performance.

Only ten years later, in the TV drama *Mrs Silly* (J. Cellan Jones, 1983), Smith plays a much more mature, but still unconfident character. Adapted from a short-story by William Trevor, *Mrs Silly* tells the misfortunes of a divorced, middle-aged woman, quite ordinary and normal tempered, but not rich, inventive or educated enough to make her beloved son, Michael, proud of her. Quite aware of her constant blunders and her propensity for

---

560 Quite surprisingly, Angela Lansbury – who certainly looked more mature, less vulnerable than Smith – had been approached to play the part. See J. Brown, *Alan J. Pakula. His Films and His Life* (New York: Back Stage, 2005), p. 116.

overtalking, she calls herself 'Mrs Silly', but her desperate attempts to please her son only worsen the situation. In the eyes of the young boy – enthralled by an upper-class way of life in his new school – his mother is an object of ridicule and he progressively drifts further away from her. Visiting the boy at school, Mrs Silly makes inappropriate comments and even dares to bore to death the headmaster with inept stories about her childhood. The last straw comes with Michael's confirmation day, attended by his father and stepmother, but also by his mother. During the reception which follows the ceremony at the school chapel, Mrs Silly – dressed with a gaudy blue coat and a red-feathered hat on her head – slips on the floor and falls flat in front of the numerous guests, making Michael definitively ashamed of her. When one of his schoolmates asks him who that ridiculous woman was, the boy tragically disowns the mother he loves so much, replying she is only 'some kind of aunt'. Shame has outstriped love and the last image shows the poor woman, alone, spending the evening in a cheap bed and breakfast next to the school. Once again, Maggie Smith's performance makes the audience hesitate between laughs and tears. The more ridiculous her Mrs Silly gets, the more touching and lovable she is.

As pitiful as Mrs Silly, but closer, by her fragility, to Lila Fisher, Judith Hearne is often seen as Smith's most outstanding performance on screen and J. Clayton's movie (1987), adapted from Brian Moore's excruciating novel, allows the viewers to witness the pathetic decline of a lonely, tortured and hopeless soul.[561] Having just moved into a seedy Dublin boarding house, Judith, a shy, mousy woman in middle age, is making a new start. She has spent the best years of her life looking after her aged aunt and now, lonely and penniless, she makes a living as a piano teacher. Unfortunately, she mistakes the attentions of her landlady's brother, James Madden (Bob Hoskins), who is just back from New York City. Overwhelmed by the exciting stories that Madden tells her – hiding the fact that he worked there as a hotel doorman –, Judith already imagines a new life as a married wife and, for his part, Madden firmly believes that she is a wealthy woman

561 A. Walker, 'The Lonely Passion of Judith Hearne', *The Evening Standard*, 5 January 1989, p. 28. The critic emphasised the many faces of Judith Hearne, praising Smith's incredible, unforgettable portrayal. Alternatively bold or apologetic, shy or candid, soaked with whisky or sober, Maggie Smith marvellously conveys all the anxieties and complexities of her character. With an amazing acuteness, the actress brings out the paradoxes of human suffering, making the film a magnificent 'aria of pain' and 'grace'.

whom he could lure into investing in his shady business. The story first takes the form of an improbable fairytale, before Judith comes to realising she had deluded herself. Losing her grip, she is taken captive by her old demons and sinks into alcoholism. Risible by her gawky manners when she does not know how to behave with Madden or when she exasperates the teen children of her friends, the O'Neills, Judith quickly turns into a pathetic figure; she loses not only all her piano pupils, but also her dignity. Totally drunk and even literally soaked with whiskey, she piteously sings in her room at midnight and, later, at the church, she shouts at the tabernacle and falls in front of it, dragging down the candlesticks and the vases from the altar. Unglamorous, pitiful, Judith's lonely downfall is painful to watch and no one else but Smith could have expressed vulnerability and despair conjointly with clumsiness and ridicule. The spectator certainly smiles, at times, but he cannot help but feel strong empathy with the character, shedding tears when witnessing Judith's gradual descent into hell. As Judith Hearne, Smith prevents us from any attempt to see her as a grotesque. The character is certainly ridiculous by many aspects, but no way is she risible; on the contrary, she makes the viewer feel uncomfortable. As P. Kael explained, the impression on screen is so vivid that we feel embarrassed and shameful for her. As the critic declared, playing Judith, Maggie Smith becomes the 'essence' of spinster. Shy, lonely, unloved, desperate and ridiculous, her Judith allows the spectators to experience the feeling of being a figure of fun.[562] The actress's physical fragility, combined here with her incomparable acting skills, forbids derision.

In fact, Maggie Smith has a unique air of vulnerability which makes the characters she portrays incredibly moving. Maybe it is a glimpse of sorrow in her large blue eyes, or the marmoreal complexion of her thin face. But Smith exudes sadness and frailty to the highest degree. It is difficult to imagine her portraying an ever smiling, beaming lady. The 'happiest', or 'coolest' character the actress has played in recent years is probably Caro Bennett, in *The Divine Secrets of the Yaya Sisterhood* (C. Khouri, 2002), adapted from Rebecca Wells's novel. It is certainly not the most memorable of her performances, but she undoubtedly gives a funny turn as Caro, a Southern belle in her sixties. Glamorous and sharp, Caro carries around an oxygen tank – having been a chain smoker, she suffers from emphysema – as well

562 *Hooked*, p. 411. Kael's review was first published in *The New Yorker* (28 December 1987).

as bottles of vodka. To see Maggie Smith in the movie is a joy in terms of characterisation; it is quite refreshing to see her swearing with a southern American accent, laughing loudly and guzzling Bloody Marys, whereas Caro is also one of the characters who, physically, most strongly resemble her. However, despite the fact that she plays a very funny woman, forceful and enthusiastic, and gets to delivers the sharpest lines of the script, the actress has to deal with too thin a material to give the performance which she would be capable of.

Quite different from Judith Hearne, the character Maggie Smith portrayed in *Capturing Mary*, twenty years later (2007), follows an opposite course, an ascending path from hell to redemption. The fears and demons associated with the past suddenly vanish, allowing the heroine to make a new start. Smith had already worked with the playwright Stephen Poliakoff in 1987, playing Halina in his *Coming in to Land* at the National. Captivated by the quite intriguing and original work that *Capturing Mary* was, she responded favourably when Poliakoff submitted the script to her, in 2006. As Smith recounted, the role was quite remote from those that she usually plays and she felt that Mary Gilbert, her character, was someone we could all relate to, because, if we had taken a different path, our lives would have been quite different.[563] The TV movie was part of a three-piece drama commissioned by the BBC, the other films being *Joe's Palace* (which starred Michael Gambon) and *A Real Summer* (already featuring Ruth Wilson, as a younger Mary). Smith certainly ignored, at that time, that it would lead her to give one of her finest performances on television. *Capturing Mary* is strange, unusual and in fact, not easy to comprehend. Yet, Maggie Smith's acting has never – and this is a word which must be used carefully – been so restrained and heartbreaking. The quality of her performance is beyond words, and her acting probably one step above her portrayal of Judith Hearne, which says it all.

Mary Gilbert is a woman of a certain age. She used to be a journalist, but a second-rate one, writing on gardening, antiques and other bland matters, although she had been destined for a much brighter future when she was young. Recently graduated from Oxford, Mary was then seen as

563 Maggie's interview quoted in *'Capturing Mary'* BBC Press Pack, 2007 <http://www.bbc.co.uk/pressoffice/pressreleases/stories/2007/10_october/02/mary.shtml> [accessed 12 November 2016].

one of the rising stars of London intellectual circles and, as such, was regularly invited to the glamorous – but very exclusive – parties that a certain Mr Graham gave in his luxurious town house. Although very daring in her judgments on the frozen, unchanging society of the late 1950s, Mary remained, in private, very naive and she felt a bit out of place among the most famous figures in politics or movies. At one of these lavish parties, she meets a mysterious man, Greville White, who lures her into following him to the wine cellar, where he tells her incredibly cruel and terrifying stories involving some famous people. Traumatised, the young woman tries to forget these things, but each time she meets Greville again, he attempts to have a hold over her. As she resists, he eventually manages to stand in her way, ruining her reputation and thus blocking her career. That is the story which is told to us through a great series of flashbacks of the 1950s and 1960s, almost all filmed in the hushed interiors of a magnificent house. Ruth Wilson was cast to play Mary in her twenties (although it did not seem an obvious choice; apart from their auburn hair, the two actresses do not really look alike in the film) but, despite the great amount of flashbacks, Smith remains constantly present through voice-over commentary, narrating these retrospective scenes with a hint of fear and bitterness. Rather sadistically, the director had asked the actress to learn the whole text by heart (instead of post-synchronising) in order to give more spontaneity to her delivery; older Mary was telling her story to Joe, and the flashbacks were added on her voice. As expected by Poliakoff, the result is picture perfect. The actress verbally narrates the story of her younger self, but what she shows when she is visually present on screen is the result of the bullying, the psychological rape which destroyed her career and her life. And that spectacle is mesmerising.

In the very first scene, Maggie/Mary rings the bell of a big house in a London residential area. The young caretaker, Joe, lets her in when she explains she would like to look inside this house where she spent time many years ago. As soon as the actress appears on screen, her face and mostly her eyes reflect dismay and vulnerability. Mary clearly is a woman who has lost confidence. Very conventionally dressed (although she is not yet an old lady), she exudes sadness and boredom. As he offers to show her around, she suddenly becomes nervous and refuses to see the rest of the house. She seems to be frightened, as if she was particularly anxious at the thought of visiting a house where – we will discover it gradually – she once experienced a psychological trauma. Revisiting the house amounts to revisiting her past. As young Joe has kindly served her a cup of tea, she accepts and lingers in the big hall, sippering her tea. Immersed in her thoughts, she suddenly knocks over the milk jug, with that touching awkwardness which belongs to all the vulnerable characters that Smith has played – Lila Fisher, Mrs Silly or Judith Hearne displayed the same clumsiness. When Mary agrees, at last, to let Joe guide her, room after room, through the vast and empty house, memories come flooding back and we finally learn her tragic story, that of a blighted fate. The viewer will never get to know, precisely, what Greville had told her, but it is, in the end, of no importance. Afterwards, Mary's career stagnated, she finally gave up journalism to become a writer and, then, still haunted by the memory of that dreadful encounter, she gave up writing and embarked on a chaotic way of life. She missed all the opportunities which came to her, until there were no more opportunities left.

Mary Gilbert in her seventies is the living result of Greville White's destructive exertion. Having remained single after a middling career, older Mary, disillusioned and anguished, is now deprived of all her confidence and has become an alcoholic. Severely addicted, she carefully keeps a flask in her handbag, while her pale and angular face seems to deny that she is a heavy drinker. Judith Hearne is probably the most striking role the actress has ever played (although Miss Shepherd is now challenging for the title), the one that would have deserved a third Oscar, in 1988. Mary Gilbert certainly is a less significant role in Smith's filmography and S. Poliakoff's movie has gone rather unnoticed since its broadcasting, in November 2007; yet, it must nevertheless be acknowledged that, in regard to acting, *Capturing Mary* showcases an even more amazing work. Or, more precisely, it reveals a higher degree of the actress's skills. Far from the excess and the mannerisms for which she is too often reproached, Maggie Smith gives quite a restrained, nuanced performance here. Mary is not a joyous alcoholic like an unmannered harridan or a drunken bag lady. She is an ageing woman, sad and lonely, who drowns her sorrows in alcohol. Like Judith Hearne, her physical vulnerability makes her penchant for alcohol all the more pathetic. No way does she look like a hard drinker. On the contrary, revealing herself gradually as the story unfolds, she carefully hides her addiction under a very respectable appearance, with tidy hair and plain, but elegant clothes which contrast with younger Mary's colourful dresses. It is only at the end of the movie that the viewer realises that, when older Mary arrived at the Graham house and rang the bell, she was coming straight from the park where she had abandoned herself to a violent fit of despair. In other words, in the first scene, the woman is already drunk and she will go on drinking afterwards, even before Joe's eyes. 'I was just keeping out of the winter cold,' she pretends. The actress suggests that from the start, but in a very subtle manner; standing in the hall, Mary did not stagger, but discreetly leans against a column.[564]

If it is a question of putting together an anthology of Smith's best scenes on screen, the moment when Mary Gilbert pathetically surrenders herself to depression in Kensington Gardens would be at the top of the list. During a walk in the park, Mary experiences a hallucination and sees Greville looking just like he looked in the 1950s. Devastated, she seeks comfort in alcohol and, getting totally drunk, she sobs loudly and stretches out on a bench just like an inebriate tramp. Her piteous and improper posture contrasts with her age and her neat attire. The pathos reaches its peak when a little girl stops short in front of the bench, looking at the drunk lady, and the child's mother promptly pulls her back from that dreadful exhibition. Here, Stephen Poliakoff favours us with two minutes of onscreen acting perfection.[565] This masterful scene looks natural – almost improvised – and its visual sobriety artfully conceals the acting process it implies. In praise of Smith's work, the critic from *The Times* commented that particular scene, which he described as an extraordinary performance by the actress;

564 R. Nelson, *Stephen Poliakoff: On Stage and On Screen* (London: Methuen Drama, 2011), p. 154. Nelson underlines Poliakoff's efficient strategy to make us acquainted with the character. Alternating flashbacks and present-day scenes, juxtaposing older Mary's voice and images of young Mary, the movie slowly discloses who Mary is (an alcoholic), versus who she could have been. The brilliance of Smith's performance lies in the fact that, retaining her dignity throughout, she subtly, gradually reveals her condition and the waste of her life. A few years ago, the actress Saskia Reeves praised Smith's physical acting in playing a drunk Judith Hearne, commenting on her facial and bodily expressions. The mouth, the eyes, even these angular fingers (which seem to belong to a woman who does not eat much), everything in Judith reveals her unhappiness, her loneliness and also her drinking problem. According to Reeves, Smith's extraordinary performance is based on that 'physicality'. See L. Francke, 'Equilibrium', *Sight and Sound*, September 1995, p. 19.

565 In his audio commentary, the director described Maggie Smith as 'a genius at work.' See *Capturing Mary*, Talkback Thames Productions/HBO Films for BBC, 2007.

huddled on her bench, plain, drunk and miserable, Maggie/Mary lets us witness her descent into hell, offering the most painful vision of human hopelessness.[566] The sight of this ageing woman who openly displays her distress and loses her dignity is the most devastating scene ever. It inevitably echoes several scenes from *The Lonely Passion of Judith Hearne*, especially the one where a dead-drunk Judith Hearne is singing loudly in her bedroom. Maggie Smith was certainly not born to play the jubilant grotesques but, on the counterpart, she is better than anyone at conveying an image of shame and misery. In fact, from Lila Fisher to Mary Gilbert, all these vulnerable and pitiful heroines represent just as many milestones on the actress's experimental pathway. The characters look alike, even if they are different in many aspects,[567] but the actress renews her performance every time, and, in doing so, constantly perfects her craft. Smith constantly learns from her successive performances to nurture new portrayals, she makes use of the work she has already done to give depth and relief to her upcoming roles. It is nothing but the normal – though rare – outcome of a dedicated and painstaking work. Every new character she plays corresponds to an evolved, more developed form of the one which has more or less inspired it. This is the case of Mary Gilbert. The character pertains to a type that the actress has already played in the past, but this new performance corresponds to a more advanced stage of research and elaboration. Regarding Smith, perfection proves to be perfectible.

566 D. Chater, 'Viewing Guide: Capturing Mary', *The Times*, 12 November 2007, p. 19.

567 For Mary Gilbert, finding the strength to revisit the house and telling her story to Joe, is way of letting the whole thing go. At the end, she looks serene: she is liberated from her demons.

Conversation Pieces

Coincidentally, several of Maggie Smith's roles belonging to the category of the vulnerable women share a common penchant for alcohol. The critic Charles Spencer once stated that Dame Maggie is the 'most extraordinary' drunk.[568] With no offence to the dame, the fact remains that it is the plain truth. Smith excels in playing these fallen, desperate creatures deprived of love who seek escapism in heavy drinking, and she gives life to the most touching and heartbreaking figures.[569] Most of these characters are victims –

568 C. Spencer, 'Dame Maggie's masterclass in comedy', *The Daily Telegraph*, 22 October 1997, p. 27.

569 S. Vineberg, 'Duet and Solos: The Pleasures of Alan Bennett', *The Threepenny Review*, 74, 1998, p. 26: '[Smith has] become the world champion at exposing the anguish of the lonely, the abandoned, the alcoholic, the sexually disenchanted.'

victims of others or victims of their own demons – whose hypersensitivity and vulnerability deprive them of any grotesque or laughable aspect. However, among all these poignant portrayals, Claire in E. Albee's *A Delicate Balance* and Susan, in A. Bennett's *Bed Among the Lentils* stand as exceptions. Despite the fact they are alcoholic and unfulfilled women, their main characteristic is that they escape, in turn, the sphere of the grotesques thanks to a particular ability to observe, judge and eloquently criticise, not only the way other people behave around them, but also their own failures. Gifted with words, intelligent and full of wit, they expertly master the art of using sarcasm and self-deprecation, making us laugh long before we laugh at them. It is needless to say that these roles of sharp, quick-minded women are tailor-made for an actress who is famously reputed for the same qualities. 'Wicked Wit of the West End', as her biographer humorously called her once,[570] Smith is unrivalled in terms of causticity and sharpness and has an incomparable talent for delivering deadpan one-liners. If her wit reinforces the social or moral superiority of the governesses and haughty dowagers whom she often plays, it sounds even more incisive when she plays characters whose stability is apparently challenged.

Firstly written as a TV series for the BBC, *Talking Heads* is undoubtedly one of Alan Bennett's most acclaimed pieces of work. Encouraged by the enthusiastic reception accorded to his first made-for-television monologue, *A Woman of No Importance* (1982), Bennett developed the concept, writing six dramatic monologues of which, oddly enough, *Bed Among the Lentils* was the only one he directed himself. The episode aired in May 1988, a few months before the UK release of *The Lonely Passion of Judith Hearne*; by a strange coincidence, the shooting of the BBC monologue had immediately followed that of J. Clayton's movie, allowing the actress to deliver two of her most extraordinary performances in a row. In *Bed Among the Lentils*, Smith plays Susan, the wife of a vicar who (partially, as the form of monologue implies breaks and innuendo) recounts the dull life which is hers.[571] Unsatisfied by her personal achievements – she had dreamt of becoming 'a wonderful woman' when she reached fifty, but she is obviously not –, and bored by

570 M. Coveney, 'The Profile: Dame Maggie Smith. Wicked Wit of the West End', *The Observer*, 16 June 1996, p. 5.

571 *Dull lives* being in fact the title that Bennett had considered first for his *Talking Heads*.

her sexless marital life,[572] Susan only finds comfort in sherry and wine. Irritated by the popularity of her husband, Geoffrey, with a 'fan club' of cackling, bigoted old parishioners whom she mimics and mocks, Susan refuses the protocol that is expected from a dignified vicar's wife and, secretly, disrespectfully rebels against God.[573] Having run up a debt with the local off-licence and dramatically knocked back the whole supply of communion wine during a flower arranging session, she now has to drive to Leeds to buy her sherry from Mr Ramesh, a young Indian grocer with whom she eventually sleeps (on a bed made with bags of lentils) having discovered for the first time the enjoyment of sex. Being inebriated on a regular basis, she has no choice but to comply with Ramesh's suggestion of attending Alcoholics Anonymous meetings. When she gets better, she discovers that Mr Ramesh has sold his shop to start a new life with his young wife elsewhere. Yet, she is now happy, pretending to be a 'new woman'. Nothing has changed, though, except that her vicar husband uses his wife's drinking problem to reinforce his own aura; her alcoholism was the cross he heroically had to bear, and he earns the esteem of the bishop for that. Now drinking fruit juice, her hair more stylishly done, Susan is still helplessly glued to the routine of her dreary life – having to attend both church and AA sessions – in the same way as Beckett's Winnie is buried in the ground of her desolate place.[574]

Maggie Smith's onscreen performance is a gem, forever saved on video. When it was eventually transferred to the stage – on the Minerva Studio stage in Chichester and at the Comedy Theatre[575] in London, in 1996, and then, in Australia and New Zealand, during spring 2004[576] – the

572 Like Joyce Chilvers, she is 'sexually starved,' P. Wolfe writes. See *Understanding Alan Bennett* (Columbia: University of California Press, 1999), p. 191.

573 By chance, Smith's Susan feels the same frustration as Scott Thomas's Gloria does, in the film *Keeping Mum*: Reverend Goodfellow is as neglectful as Geoffrey is, and Mrs Parker hilariously epitomises all the old spinsters who constantly fuss over Susan's husband.

574 J. O'Mealy, *Alan Bennett. A Critical Introduction* (New York-London: Routledge, 2001), p. 100. The author suggests that, metaphorically buried from the waist at the beginning, she eventually ends up buried 'up to her neck'.

575 Now the Harold Pinter Theatre, on Panton Street. Presented as a diptych (it coupled *Bed Among the Lentils* with *Soldiering On*, starring Margaret Tyzack), the play was directed by A. Bennett himself.

576 The production went on tour from March to May and, this time, Anthony Page was directing.

piece gained in depth thanks to the intimacy it created with the audience. Bennett acknowledged that he did not write *Bed Among The Lentils* with Smith in mind, but as he was writing it, he progressively saw her in the role and, thankfully, she immediately agreed to play Susan. While, on television, the camera focuses on her face, scrutinising every smallest expression, the staging of the monologue enlarged the perspective and gave the actress the opportunity to make use of her infinitely resourceful body language. A. Macaulay highlighted the greatness of her performance, particularly in the skilful way she used her physical tools and body language to express greyness and boredom. As the thin, 'lank-haired', dull-eyed Susan, Maggie Smith appears as the most perfect embodiment of social embarrassement.[577] Susan, as played by Smith, is a plain, mousy middle-class woman, miles away from the actress's usual grand dames. There is nothing unprepossessing in her face, but she cannot be called a beautiful woman. With no make-up, tastelessly dressed, she actually plays on appearances, proving to be a much more riveting dramatic persona than her insignificant exterior suggests. As the critic P. Taylor wrote about the stage performance, Smith managed to breathe 'marvellously mordant' life to the asexual, tiresome Susan.[578] Under unattractive looks, Susan proves to be the wittiest, bitchiest, funniest commentator on her own existence. As N. De Jongh suggested, her wit is a form of supreme resilience, that of those dull, unhappy people who feel the need to voice their resentment, even in that stoic, restrained, repressed manner. Commenting on Maggie Smith's stage performance, the critic praised her remarkable, masterful solo of 'raging calm' and sadness.[579] All understatements and implications, her delivery is sober, neutral, contrasting deeply with the irony and sarcasm it distils. Paradoxically, Susan is totally aware of her failure as a wife – she is the exact antithesis of what a perfect vicar's wife should be,

577 'Consummate Mistresses Of The Monologue', *The Financial Times*, 30 October 1996, p. 19.

578 'Theatre: *Talking Heads*', *The Independent*, 13 June 1996, p. 12.

579 'Singular triumph of the magical Dame Maggie', *The Evening Standard*, 11 June 1996, p. 6. See also A. Hunt, '*Talking Heads*: "Bed Among the Lentils" (A. Bennett)', in *British Television Drama in the 1980s*, ed. by G. W. Brandt (Cambridge: Cambridge University Press, 1993), p. 37: 'The cleverness of Maggie Smith's performance, and the knowingness she has brought to the character contradict the fatalism. The Mrs Vicar of Maggie Smith has demonstrated her survival skills [...] Resilience is implicit in Maggie Smith performance.'

having no talent for cooking (canned peaches topped with Carnation milk is apparently the best she can do) or entertaining guests, and feeling not the slightest concern for social conventions and appearances – and, at the same time, she is neither ridiculous nor grotesque. Admitting, with subtlety and self-deprecating humour, her dullness is a way to conjure it.

As Daphne Turner points out in her study on Alan Bennett, Susan's voice is constantly silenced; despite being 'subversive', her discourse is not a performative voice and Susan never can openly express her resentment. According to Turner, it is only when she talks with Mr Ramesh about her alcoholism that she can communicate.[580] Astonishingly, this remarkably eloquent speaker never manages to voice loudly, openly her thoughts. The monologue she delivers is the only way for her to express herself, gossiping about others or bitterly contemplating her disastrous everyday life. Seen through the prism of irony, the parish that Susan describes appears as colourful as insufferable, populated by a swarm of old bitches devoted to the sanctified figure of Geoffrey. In an in-depth article on *Bed Among the Lentils*, A. Hunt notices that one of the most effective elements in the monologue is the very casual language which Susan uses to talk about sacred matters: 'The language of gossip [...] brings God down to earth with a bump.'[581] Despised for not being the ideal vicar's wife, and also envied for being the wife of the vicar, Susan feels out of place alongside a husband who ignores and neglects her. Bitterly joking about the morosity of their sexual life, she reveals in fact the deep, painful frustration she endures; if she is supposed to 'offer her sex' to God as her vicar husband suggests to his parishioners, hers is not worth more than the ten pence she puts in the collection plate. Of course, Smith's precise, nuanced delivery emphasised each word, without any excess or affectation, and magnificently served Bennett's corrosive script. In *The Financial Times*, A. Macaulay pointed out the fact that her performance was unusually sober and restrained. Far from being mannered, Smith's gesture and delivery are incredibly 'economical'. Everything, in Susan's physiognomy, pertains to expressivity.[582]

The alcoholism topic is gradually inserted in her speech, but it comes as a confession only in the last sequence, when the problem is actually

580 *Alan Bennett: In a Manner of Speaking* (London: Faber and Faber, 1997), p. 57-58.

581 Hunt, 'Talking Heads', p. 25.

582 'Supremely Cast "Talking Heads"', *The Financial Times*, 12 June 1996, p. 21.

solved. Before that, only allusions clearly inform the audience of Susan's penchant for all kinds of spirits. She simply, casually refers to the fact that they have 'run out of sherry' at home, like others have run out of sugar or washing powder. Of course, every time it happens, her duty is to fetch a new bottle as soon as possible, even if the local grocer starts to look at her in an unfriendly manner because of the huge amount she owes him. Conscientiously, this accomplished housewife will drive to the next town to resupply with sherry. In parallel, the episode where she secretly drinks communion wine during a session of the flower arranging committee is narrated like an accident ('I slipped and rolled down the aisle'), even if she does not fool the other ladies. Verbally, in Susan's narration of the events, the appearances are safely kept, but every slight allusion, every silence and every facial or bodily expression of the actress reveals Susan's pathetic condition. Humorous and sarcastic in her witty speech, the woman is most certainly scorned and ridiculed behind her back. Subsequently, her encounter with Mr Ramesh, a twenty-six-year-old Indian grocer, leads to her (late) sexual awakening and raises awareness of her alcoholism; the young man urges her to join AA and she eventually recovers. Conversely – as paradoxes remain a constant in Susan's story – her recovery also corresponds to the end of her brief affair with the young Indian who leaves her to settle with his wife and start a new business. Giving up alcohol, Susan loses the only person who has had some consideration for her. It is evident that she will never experience sexual passion again. She will never get to know if sober is really *nicer*.[583] More carefully groomed than she was in the first scene, neat, poised and elegant, Smith's Susan is nevertheless unchanged. There is a fascinating subtext in the actress's performance; her improved appearance and quiet, ironic speech contrast strongly with the sad, immobile existence she is forever confined in.

The great artistry of Maggie Smith in portraying Susan is that she is at her most restrained. Her tone is neutral, her gesture minimal. She only suggests or alludes to the facts and the viewer has to construct his own interpretation

583 C. Spencer, 'Monologues with plenty of drama', *The Daily Telegraph*, 12 June 1996, p. 22. Spencer evoked the comical aspects of Smith's performance, from her amazing ability to deliver put downs with 'incomparable panache' to the joyful tone she uses to evoke sexual intercourse with Mr Ramesh, and its most touching moment, when her voice breaks to mention the end of their affair.

of the events she narrates.[584] It is in the huge contrast between what the actress says, simply, casually and often wittily, and what she makes visible on the stage that the devastating efficiency of her performance lies. A bit like Miss Schofield (Patricia Routledge) in *A Woman of No Importance*, who goes on talking cheerfully about her social influence at work although it is clear that she is dying on a hospital bed, Susan offers an image of physical frailty which contradicts her verbal easiness. As the critic Clare Bailey noted in *The Times*, it takes some time before the audience becomes aware that Susan is actually drunk; staggering her way to her chair, the woman obviously has a blurred perception of the reality.[585] The Susan who lives her life seems, through Smith's acting, much more vulnerable than the Susan who comments on it. Bennett is definitely very adept at dual characters, but, playing the role on the stage, the actress added a third dimension to the part, giving as Susan one of her most complex and subtle performance, as M. Wolf suggested in his rave review. The critic emphasised the fact that, although Maggie Smith was renowned for her tricks and mannerisms, she never once succumbed to those famous vocal flourishes which are usually part of her acting technique (making a disservice to the character), giving her most wonderful performance ever.[586] J. Tinker's enthusiastic notice, in *The Daily Mail*, echoed that amazement; the critic declared that Smith's portrayal of Susan was, without any doubt, one of the most outstanding stage performances she had given in her career, adding that no other actress could successfully achieve that combination of self-irony and vulnerability.[587] Restrained, sober, incredibly funny and

584 K. McKechnie, *Alan Bennett* (Manchester: Manchester University Press, 2007), p. 171. As noted by the author, there is a deep, complex subtext to the play, which is left to the audience's imagination.

585 'Storytelling with finesse', *The Times*, 28 October 1996, p. 20.

586 'Review: "Talking Heads"', *Variety*, 3 November 1996 <http://variety.com/1996/legit/reviews/talking-heads-3-1200447876/> [accessed 12 November 2016].

587 'Smith is ahead of the rest', *The Daily Mail*, 14 June 1996, p. 53. See also M. Coveney, 'A sure finger on the pulse', *The Observer*, 16 June 1996; the critic asserted that the spectator is both enthralled by Maggie Smith's genius and, watching her performance, carried away with 'joy and grief'; J. Peter, 'Talking Heads', *The Sunday Times*, 16 June 1996, p. 15; Peter compared Susan's hopeless misery with that of a poor bird caught in a trap which cannot stretch its broken wings, commenting on her dull, forlorn face that sometimes lights up when she evokes Mr Ramesh; B. Nightingale, 'A Pair Of The Best', *The Times*, 12 June 1996, p. 39; the critic emphasised Smith's ability to move the audience from laughter to tears and to suggest, through subtle nuances in her delivery, Susan's awareness of her own failure.

devastatingly heartbreaking, Smith's performance is regarded as one of her most elaborated, artistically chiselled masterpieces.

The following year, willing to tackle a new role, the actress discussed with Anthony Page – one of her favourite stage directors – to decide which play she could choose for her West End comeback. Albee's *A Delicate Balance*, a play both realistic and absurd which won the Pulitzer Prize in 1966, was her choice. 'We talked of several options. Ibsen's *Ghosts*, Beckett's *Happy Days*. But this is the one she wanted to do,' A. Page said in an interview.[588] Produced by Robert Fox, the play opened at the Theatre Royal Haymarket in October 1997, after a short pre-London tour. Although she was the one who had initiated the project, Smith was not, this time, centre-stage and the leading characters were played by Eileen Atkins and John Standing. Agnes (Atkins) and Tobias (Standing) form a late middle-aged American couple, living in a large, comfortable suburban house. After forty years, their marriage has turned into a sexless and morn companionship and they are both inhabited by a sense of waste and regret. Agnes's sister, Claire (Smith), lives on the premises, imposing on them the sight of her perpetual drunkenness. As extrovert as Agnes is restrained, Claire firmly refuses to be described as an 'alcoholic'; she has no addiction, drinking is for her a deliberate choice. To Tobias who asks her why she refuses to return to the meetings of the AA, she explains that those are alcoholics, whereas she is just a drunk. Her drinking is wilful, a deliberate evasion from reality that the academic Allan Pero recently described as an imperious necessity; she must be drunk to legitimate her presence in the household and to deny her alcoholism would forbid her to stay (and observe) any longer.[589] Claire analyses and comments on the others' behaviour, but she is unable to resolve her own problems and prefers to stay on the sidelines. Presenting herself as the only lucid person in contrast with her 'unconcerned or uncaring' relatives, her sister Agnes proves to be the one who maintains the balance in the family's life. Their thirty-six-year-old daughter, Julia, has divorced for the fourth time and, seeking refuge in their home, discovers that her childhood bedroom is now occupied by Harry and Edna who have just arrived and plan to stay

588 J. Christopher, 'Actors. Turn your backs', *The Observer*, 19 October 1997, p. 72.

589 'The Crux of Melancholy: Edward Albee's A Delicate Balance', *Modern Drama*, 49.2, 2006, p. 176.

for an undetermined period. These intruders are in fact Tobias and Agnes's long-time friends who also seek refuge in the house, having escaped from their own home as they were paralysed by an indescribable fear, all the more frightening that nothing justified it. As the house is now full of guests, this unexpected invasion will underline the breakdown of family and friendship, in a home which cannot sustain its own limited, precarious stability.

In terms of presence on stage, Claire is in fact a very slight role for Maggie Smith: her character makes rare, short appearances in Acts I and II, and she is nearly absent in Act III. In his review, R. Butler declared that if Albee had known that Smith would play the role thirty years later, he would have 'moved' her centre stage![590] Still, it goes without saying that, as usual, the actress skilfully steals the show despite the excellence of the rest of the cast. Soberer, all the more that her role was probably the most challenging one, Eileen Atkins's performance was unanimously hailed, while, of course, some critics disliked what seemed a bit mannered or excessive in Smith's part. M. Billington entitled his review 'Pantomime Dame', blaming her for stealing the show when playing a supporting part. For him, not only was the actress a bit too famous to blend in with an impeccable cast, but, due to her excessively comic genius, she undermined what was, an Albee script, a figure of conscious waste and self-destruction. Conspiring with the audience, fluttering her wrists, Smith seemed to give a solo turn as Claire. Billington considered her performance 'revue-sketch stuff', declaring that it was only when she was in repose, listening to Harry and Edna's (frightening, though absurd) account, that she brought out the depth and complexity of her character.[591] R. Butler also pointed out her unavoidable scene-stealing in a secondary role, humorously explaining that, as soon as she made an entrance, the play suddenly slid off the secondary road and onto the motorway. He explained that the name of Smith was the antithesis of 'ensemble acting' as it is quite difficult not to disappear when playing opposite her.[592] A. Page's comments dismissed any reproach of that kind, emphasising the actress's extraordinary genius and trying to define the essence of her rigorous working process; all her efforts aim

590 'The grand dame tips the Balance', *The Independent on Sunday Section 2*, 26 October 1997, p. 7.

591 *The Guardian*, 23 October 1997, p. 10.

592 Butler, 'The grand dame tips the Balance'.

at, not only capturing the truth of the scene she plays, but, also, skilfully revealing its comical subtext, giving the most convincing rendition of the part.[593] Actually, to the greatest delight of the audience, Smith perfectly performed the function that has been assigned to her character. In his very enthusiastic review, the critic C. Spencer admitted that, although Smith is accustomed to steal the show (even when playing a supporting role), Anthony Page's meticulous direction had forbidden her to do so and, on the contrary, allowed her to surreptitiously reveal, through a sober and nuanced performance, Claire's vulnerability.[594] In fact, Claire represents an external eye on the action. Most of the time, the character stands as a jester who entertains the company with her joyful, self-deprecating comments or crucifies the other characters with her acerbic putdowns, as P. Taylor asserted in his rave notice, comparing Smith's sleek, bulgy-eyed Claire with an inebriated but glamorous fool just 'kept upright' by booze, who spends her time wittily mocking what happens around her before having her glass refilled one more time.[595] Through this stage role of a troublemaker, Smith experienced, to a certain extent, the artful mastering of the one-liner. With her provocative banter, she softens the atmosphere of the house. In his review, N. De Jongh lauded her remarkable comic performance, in a part that was a refreshing departure from her usual casting. Her hilarious Claire, stretched out on the sofa, contented herself with sneering and scoffing at the whole family while sipping her vodka, what was an uncommon, though magisterial performance by Maggie Smith. De Jongh nevertheless acknowledged that the actress had erased the most painful, pathetic aspects of the character, especially 'the sense of danger' of Elaine Stritch's sorrowful alcoholic on Broadway.[596]

Far from being a pitiful woman whose wrecking would be painful to watch for the spectator, Claire is even more sympathetic thanks to her penchant for alcohol. As suggested by B. Nightingale in his review for *The Times*, with her sarcastic comments and her corrosive self-deprecating humour, that eccentric, enticing drunkard almost makes the audience forget her addiction.[597] Full of

593 M. Wolf, 'Three's a crowd pleaser', *The Times*, 15 October 1997, p. 41.

594 Spencer, 'Dame Maggie's masterclass'.

595 'Sisters of mercy?', *The Independent Eye*, 23 October 1997, p. 1.

596 'Dame Maggie's comic turn as Claire gets the balance right', *The Evening Standard*, 22 October 1997, p. 16.

597 'Family that preys together', *The Times*, 23 October 1997, p. 18.

wit, but also slender, flawlessly groomed and, ultimately, quite attractive, Smith's Claire looks certainly too neat and too well-preserved to be fully convincing as a drunkard, especially as the drunkard she is supposed to be, according to her sister Agnes – who evokes 'the vomit and the tears' (Act I). It serves, in any case, the idea of a probable flirtation between her and her brother-in-law, suggested by Albee's stage directions. As Claire herself bitterly implies, Tobias and Harry both had sex once with her. Light and agile, she contorts herself on the sofa to have her glass filled as often as she can, miles away from the conventional image of the swollen, red-faced old drunk slumped in an armchair. In his review, the critic R. Butler highlighted the sexiness and effortless elegance of that uncommon drunk, who nimbly stretched across the sofa 'in search of a refill', before sinking her pointy nose deep into the brandy glass with the most disdainful nonchalance.[598] Not only does Claire sneer wittily, but she also mocks her own weaknesses. In Act III, literally 'playing the drunk', she puts some vodka in her breakfast orange juice and staggers slightly to her feet. But despite her constant drunkenness, she witnesses and analyses quite wisely the situation she observes around her, her fierce blue eyes peeking through the blonde fringe of an immaculate bob. In fact, as a drunk, Claire has that clear-sighted wisdom that belongs to Touchstone, the fool in Shakespeare's *As you like it*. She is the only person who faces the truth and sees the absence of love in the family. In some ways, the character can be seen as a seer, a clear-sighted observer who predicts what is going to happen and, on the verge of metatheatricality, Agnes herself points it out.[599]

Claire has few scenes in the play, but each of her appearances raises all the laughs, as Robert Hewison observed. Far from blaming Smith's American accent (as some reviewers usually do), he praised her legendary timing and her ability to have the house in stitches as soon as she enters the stage; she makes the cleverest use of her props, yodelling with an accordion or waving an empty glass to have it refilled.[600] This insightful fool behaves as badly as she wants to, and, as if she aimed to provoke her sister, she stretches on the sofa, balancing a glass full of brandy on her forehead. In

598 Butler, 'The grand dame tips the Balance'.

599 See D. Murray, 'An overdone delicacy', *The Financial Times*, 23 October 1997, p. 15; the critic compared Smith with the joyous 'boozer' that Elizabeth Spriggs had been in 1969, insisting on her clear-sighted, 'fey' quality. She sees everything.

600 'Struck by fear', *The Sunday Times*, 26 October 1997, p. 15.

the following scene, she takes pleasure in recounting her latest shopping experience, when she tried to buy a topless bathing suit from an 'eighteen-nineties schoolteacher type' shopkeeper, and just for hearing Smith acting out the scene and saying 'I'm in the market for a topless swimsuit', the theatre ticket was worth its price. In another scene, when the tension is at its height, Claire enters with an accordion, plays it and yodels while the other characters have an important discussion. That strange – and irritating – behaviour can be interpreted as a kind of escape for a woman who refuses any commitment in the family's life; to make some noise is a way to cover, to annihilate an embarrassing discussion. Anyway, it was very difficult for the audience of the Theatre Royal Haymarket not to laugh heartily when seeing the dame in action, 'yodelling' with the utmost self-confidence.[601] What is certain is that the character has nothing pitiful or ridiculous about her. On the contrary, she is a witty and deliciously comical figure, unquestionably seductive. Unlike Billington, some other critics considered that Maggie Smith's acting was exceptionally restrained in this play.[602] The actress did not offer a one-layered, monochrome performance. Beyond the humour and the hilarious wisecracks, she let the despair and the awareness of a wasted life appear. Seeing Maggie/Claire, Martin Esslin noticed hints of regret and sadness behind her playful jibes.[603] In any case, this role gave the actress the rare opportunity to raise laughs with an alcoholic character, on the opposite side of her usual casting; all the other alcoholics she had played were pathetic, deeply moving figures.[604] Seductive, mischievous and exquisitely witty, her Claire was absolutely

601 M. Owen, 'Peeling back the years', *The Evening Standard*, 10 October 1997, p. 30. Maggie Smith had great fun appearing with that small accordion on stage. She only regretted that she could not make as much noise as she wanted with it, as the other actors had to keep speaking while Claire was yodelling.

602 S. Brownrigg, 'A plague of fear', *The Times Literary Supplement*, 31 October 1997, p. 24. The critic was surprised to see Maggie Smith giving such a sober reading of the part, maybe regretting that, a far cry from *Who's Afraid of Virginia Woolf?* main character, her quiet Claire cut a less formidable figure than we could have expected in a play by Edward Albee.

603 'Martin Esslin at A Delicate Balance', *Plays International*, November 1997, p. 21.

604 Maggie Smith herself acknowledged that playing Claire was refreshing; see Owen, 'Peeling back the years'. It was a kind of relief for Maggie Smith to be freed from her usual wigs, corsets and ageing make-up, and to tread the boards in skinny trousers. She admitted that the part was much less demanding, physically, than that of the very old A, in *Three Tall Women*.

lovable, leaving some spectators – like T. Paddock – frustrated not to be able to see more of Smith, as addictive as the vodka her character never stops knocking back. The critic deplored that her time on stage was far from being as 'plentiful' as the spirits which regularly refilled her glass, regretting to have to leave the theatre without getting 'one more shot' of the 'undiluted Dame'.[605]

Unlike Susan and Claire, Madeleine Palmer, the character whom Maggie Smith played in David Hare's *The Breath of Life* (2002), is not an alcoholic. She enjoys, at the dawn of old age, a semi-reclusive retirement, having been abandoned by her longtime lover, Martin, a radical lawyer who has now started a new life in America with a young woman. Far from being downbeat by this socially uncomfortable situation, Madeleine, a former museum curator and Islamic specialist, has found a new anchorage on the Isle of Wight, where she lives a bohemian life which ideally suits the independent, strong-minded woman she is. Her quiet routine is suddenly disturbed one day, when she is visited by the novelist Frances Beale (Judi Dench), Martin's ex-wife, and the confrontation of the two women, both abandoned by the same man, leads to a compelling – and often intricate – reflection on memory, burying of the past and resilient serenity. As the unconventional Madeleine, Smith gave an amazingly virtuoso performance, playing for once her own age after a succession of old lady parts on the screen, and proving once again she was highly capable of restraint in acting. In the very first scene, she managed to suggest annoyance without saying a word, letting for a couple of minutes her body and her face express her profound irritation. Joyful and serene when she enters the stage with her books, she suddenly loses her quiet confidence when Frances rings at the door. In his review, M. Wolf noted that Maggie Smith's first minutes on the stage, before Dench's entrance, represented 'a master class all of their own'.[606] Seductive, clever and tremendously sharp, Madeleine handles irony with the utmost dexterity. Billington considered that Smith was giving an immaculate rendition of

605 '*A Delicate Balance* at the Theatre Royal Haymarket', *WhatsOnStage.com*, October 1997 <http://archive.is/bVJBo> [accessed 12 November 2016].

606 'Two Great Dames in Search of a Play', *London Theatre News*, December 2002-January 2003, p. 2.

Madeleine's 'waspish' irony,[607] while P. Levy, in *The Wall Street Journal*, underscored the obvious similarity of wit between the character and the actress who portrayed her, writing that Madeleine's dialogue was 'pure Maggie Smith', deliciously funny with a subtle touch of camp.[608]

The encounter between the two seasoned veterans, Dench and Smith, at the Haymarket, had been announced like the theatrical event of the decade – just like Norman C. Hunter's *Waters of the Moon* had reunited, on the same stage, Evans and Thorndike in 1953[609] – and the run was sold out weeks ahead of the opening night. Still, both parts were not equal. Maggie Smith's role, more engaging – as she was the mistress versus the deceived wife – and funnier, was judged better than that of Judi Dench, who nevertheless delivered an impeccable performance. In M. Coveney's view, despite the fact that both actresses had top billing, the play was undoubtedly Smith's. As Coveney pointed out, Maggie's Madeleine was the one who 'set the pace', one step ahead of Judi's Frances, and who was able to assert her superiority over her, as mistress of her husband.[610] For his part, C. Spencer praised Smith's masterful nuanced portrayal, hailing her tremendous performance and stressing one particularly moving scene where Madeleine recounts how she met Martin again, after many years; then, suddenly, with a crack in her voice, a tearful Smith brings out an unexpected vulnerability.[611] Brilliant and sharper than ever, the actress nevertheless subtly infuses her performance with grief and regret, as M. Wolf suggested; the character played by Smith is a woman who once wanted everything and who has eventually 'settled for next to nothing'.[612] The confrontation with her lover's ex-wife leads Madeleine to self-awareness. Talking to Frances and revisiting her past, she

607 'The Breath of Life', *The Guardian*, 16 October 2002, p. 25.

608 'There's Nothing Like 2 Dames on a London stage', *The Wall Street Journal*, 18 October 2002, p. 8.

609 Forbes, *Dame Edith Evans*, 221. When promoting the play, the journalists pointed out the fact that it was the first time, in the history of the English stage, that two Dames appeared together. See also C. Duff, *The Lost Summer. The Heyday of the West End Theatre* (London: Nick Hern Books, 1995), p. 113-118.

610 'Why Maggie takes our breath away', *The Daily Mail*, 18 October 2002, p. 25.

611 'A breath-taking night with Hare and two great dames', *The Daily Telegraph*, 16 October 2002, p. 5.

612 '"The Breath of Life" Opens in London', *Variety*, 17 October 2002 <http://variety.com/2002/legit/reviews/the-breath-of-life-2-1200545401/> [accessed 12 November 2016].

realises her own failures and withdrawals. S. Clapp beautifully suggested that Maggie Smith managed to age within full view of the spectators. Comparing that to a 'slow fading' of the lights, barely perceptible, the critic noted that, gradually, Smith was becoming less vivid, almost pallid in Act II.[613] However, Madeleine resolutely remains modern and nonconformist. As the critic Peter Roberts jokingly noticed, it would have been quite improbable, in her time, to hear Edith Evans delivering a line such as 'I love orgies'.[614] Neither would we have got to see the venerable Sybil Thorndike crawling barefoot around the place, picking leftovers of an Indian take-away. Glowingly radiant and simultaneously vulnerable, gloriously witty and discreetly regretful, Madeleine is probably not Smith's most memorable or riveting performance on the stage in comparison with Lettice Douffet or A, but the role pinpointed, at least, the actress's almost forgotten ability to portray seductive, emotional, 'love-able' women of her age.[615]

---

613 'Ladies who lounge', *The Observer*, 20 October 2002, p. 11.

614 'Peter Roberts at *The Breath of Life*', *Plays International*, November-December 2002, p. 18.

615 N. De Jongh, 'Truly there is nothing like these Dames', *The Evening Standard*, 16 October 2002, p. 14. The critic emphasised that aspect, declaring that it had been years (Smith had played Millamant, in *The Way of the World*, eighteen years earlier) since the actress had played her own age, after a succession of old dowager parts. According to De Jongh, David Hare's new play allowed her the rare opportunity to give a sober, but magnificent performance, devoid of any mannerism, in the part of this wry, disenchanted retired museum curator in her sixties. At one point, Maggie/Madeleine revealed the truth about her affair with Martin in a heartbreaking, emotional confession, and it was probably her most stunning scene.

Looking the Part. Or not

Most of the time, people praise actresses who have dexterously turned a disgraceful face to professional advantage and made us forget, thanks to their talent, the absence of any attractiveness. In the case of Maggie Smith, it is the exact contrary. The young Margaret Smith who made her debut on the Oxford stage in the mid-1950s was regarded by one of her admirers – a young playwright named Beverley Cross – as an extremely beautiful young girl. When she was about to appear in his second play, *Strip The Willow* (1960), he clearly described the actress (rather than the character) in the stage directions: 'She is about twenty-five and very beautiful. As elegant and sophisticated as a top international model. A great sense of fun. A marvellous girl.' As time goes by, her features got sharper and the young woman acquired a more sophisticated elegance. At thirty, the actress who was now 'Maggie' Smith had the diaphanous face and the regal bearing of a queen of tragedy and she rapidly became a star of the British stage. The truth is that her physical appearance had little in common with that of the actresses who, in Europe or in the United States, hit the front pages of magazines. Tall, willowy, with a fair complexion and delicate features emphasising a pair of huge blue eyes, Smith had nothing of the luscious, sexy and provocative creatures showcased by the cinema of the 1960s. However, in England, she stood as the most prominent stage actress of her generation. Smith's incontestable grace was transcended on the stage and conveyed an extra dimension to her flamboyant acting. On screen, though, the actress rarely got the opportunity to make the most of her flattering looks. When she appeared in a movie, the young actress did not play the seductress or the passionate lover. The role which got her an Academy Award for Best Actress in 1969, Miss Jean Brodie, was that of an iconoclast, narcissistic and dangerously possessive schoolteacher. Brodie is an intriguing, megalomaniac and secretly vulnerable spinster, certainly not a *femme fatale*. Despite her undeniable beauty, the actress looked too angular and too thin to incarnate sensuality, and her appearance was not consistent with the expectations of the movie directors in the early 1970s. Oddly enough, the only film which did justice to Maggie Smith's physical attractiveness was a hilarious comedy, *Murder by Death* (R. Moore, 1976) where she made with the excellent David Niven a smashing couple of detectives, Dora and Nick Charleston. Dressed in a splendid low-necked evening gown, her magnificent red hair beautifully bobbed, Smith definitely proved she was able to play a very sexy and sophisticated woman. Not sooner than five years later, another movie, *Clash of the Titans* (D. Davis, 1981), made use of her flattering looks. 'You, Thetis, lovely goddess of the sea', these are the words – written by B. Cross himself, who penned the screenplay – with which Zeus (Laurence Olivier) addresses Peleus's mythical spouse. Yet, with her slender frame draped in an immaculate *peplos* and her curled bun, Maggie/Thetis resembles more a chaste vestal about to perform ritual libations than the turbulent goddess she is supposed to play and, in any case, she looks like the antithesis of the sensual Aphrodite, portrayed by Ursula Andress. Obviously, Smith's physical attractiveness, despite being incontestable, was never regarded as one of her major assets.

Many actresses are reputed for having had a 'second career'. The former sex-symbol, who had fallen into disgrace at forty, gloriously returns to the studios at sixty-five or seventy to play the grandmothers or the shameless old ladies. To make another comparison with Evans, it can be noticed that there was, globally, two essential phases in Dame Edith's movie career: her first appearances in silent movies and her comeback, in the 1960s, as elderly ladies. Bette Davis's career followed a similar course and, a few years before the death of the actress, her work enjoyed a revival in interest.[616] Seriously ill and devastatingly weakened by her ailments, Davis died too early, but if God had given her life, she would certainly have delivered outstanding performances until a very old age. Cinema does not like mature women – even if this age limitation, having been slightly shifted, applies more to sexagenarians than quadragenarians these days – but, on the counterpart, it clearly needs elderly actresses, even if it has only very small, ungratifying parts to give them. Surprisingly, unlike some actresses who, having been very beautiful in their youth, are relegated to less flattering roles when they reach maturity,[617] Maggie Smith has had quite a different career path. Actually, she started playing old ladies long before her age and paradoxically, years later, her physical appearance still allows her to play younger, attractive women when filmmakers are daring enough to cast her against her dowager type. 'Of course, there are laughter lines,' as Emily Delahunty concedes in *My House in Umbria*, but the actress's face impresses by the fineness of her features and the expressivity of her eyes. In an article for *The New York Times*, in 1979, Flora Lewis described a tall, svelte young woman, with shining red hair, freckles and very pale skin, wide blue eyes, sharp bones and very long fingers

616 S. Chivers, *The Silvering Screen. Old Age and Disability in Cinema* (Toronto: University of Toronto Press, 2011), p. 39; Chivers notes that her film career revived only when she played in a horror movie.

617 It was the case with Dame Gladys Cooper, a radiant beauty in her youth, who kept playing a succession of old ladies on stage and on screen from the moment she reached fifty.

constantly flickering.[618] The portrait drawn by the American critic seems, hair colour apart, nearly timeless.

Maggie Smith is very beautiful. She was beautiful at her debut, she was in her forties, she still is now, in the 2010s. A few years ago, as she entered a new decade, *The Guardian* chose to celebrate her birthday by having her posing for a photo session on the rooftops of London; in a cardigan, without any blade of make-up, Smith was resplendent.[619] Nonetheless, being very unconfident about her looks, the actress replied once to the journalist J. Rees (who complimented her on her 'bony, bonny' face) that she hated her appearance and was never comfortable when acting for the screen; she explained that the actor can create an illusion on stage, while he cannot avoid the camera.[620] It must be admitted, though, that, when we watch *Quartet* and several of her recent films, her self-deprecating comments seem rather irrelevant.[621] Smith is naturally – at a time when so many stars go under the knife – spectacularly beautiful, thanks to a perfectly structured face emphasised by high cheekbones, a diaphanous complexion and a pair of huge aquamarine eyes. Therefore, she has absolutely no merit not to have resorted to plastic surgery. Some journalists seem puzzled by the fact she has been brave enough to keep her natural face, unlike many other actresses of her generation or even younger. Actually, Maggie Smith simply does not need it to remain beautiful at her age – and this is the fact that journalists should marvel at. Moreover, if she had facial surgery, it would neutralise her expressivity, one of her most efficient acting tools.

Usually, pantomime dames and comedic actresses are definitely not beauties. Ugliness is often seen as a deviation from the norm and it represents a valuable asset when it comes to provoking laughs. An ugly woman makes us laugh – even if, subsequently, we feel empathy with her – and a comic

618 'Maggie Smith Finds the She on Stage is Easier to Know than One at Home', *The New York Times*, 12 September 1979, p. 26.

619 Pictures in Mackenzie, 'You have to laugh'.

620 Rees, 'The grand dame returns'.

621 See, for instance, J. Miller, 'Maggie Smith is already anticipating the Dowager Countess's Death on *Downton Abbey*', *Vanity Fair*, 7 March 2013 <http://www.vanityfair.com/hollywood/2013/03/maggie-smith-downton-abbey-dowager-countess>[accessed November 2016]. Having often played nonagenarians, Smith nevertheless concedes that it must be very difficult to do for the actresses who have always been beautiful (implying that she does not belong to that category).

performer is generally more successful at having the audience in stitches if he is physically disadvantaged; the atypical looks of the famous actress Marie Dressler were her main force. Unlike Margaret Rutherford, whom her physical appearance had her cornered in the grotesque type, Smith does not have the plain or unprepossessing appearance that normally secures a brilliant career in comedy. Even if the years have put their mark on her face, they have not altered her beauty. An aged actress, disfigured by the passing of time is a painful, pathetic vision. In the preface of Marguerite Moreno's autobiography, the French literary critic Robert Kemp wrote heartbreaking comments on what he called 'Moreno's metamorphosis':

> The hieratic muse, whose pre-Raphaelite grace [...] stood out in her portrait by Levy-Dhurner, had become one of these old women painted by Goya. Time had not been kind to her. While some other actresses refuse to acknowledge their age, she makes the most of what the advancing years have done to her [...] Marguerite Moreno did not hide from the public the ravages of time. She made use of them, she amplified them. She profaned her face and her body. She had become the caricature of herself. [622]

Maggie Smith has nothing in common with these mature or elderly actresses who are cast in a certain type – battle-axes, redoubtable mother-in-laws or curmudgeons of any sort – because they simply look the part. She has not an off-putting appearance. Her face does not possess the asperities of Edith Evans's and her figure cannot be mistaken for that of the imposing Rutherford. As A. Nissen points out, there was, at least in the 1940s, a typical dowager's appearance: 'They came in all sizes but tended towards "large", as if significance must be accorded to their pronouncements at least partly because of their *avoir du poids*. Certainly, they gave a whole meaning to the term "throwing your weight around".'[623] Specialising in old bags and risible spinsters, Smith unexpectedly does not have the right looks to play these roles. On the contrary, her enviable physical appearance could

622 M. Moreno, *Souvenirs de ma vie* (Paris: Editions de Flore, 1948), p. XXVI-XXVIII.

623 *Mothers, Mammies and Old Maids*, 65. See also S. Harper, 'From *wholesome girls* to difficult d*owagers*. Actresses in 1930s British Cinema', in *British Cinema, Past and Present*, ed. by J. Ashby and A. Higson (London: Routledge, 2000), p. 147.

be seen as a handicap. But the actress has more than one trick up her sleeve and she expertly knows how to turn that major inconvenience into the most efficient comical tool. In one of the best articles ever written about Smith, Irving Wardle alluded to her striking performance as Myra Arundel in *Hay Fever*, a role which already revealed the chameleon abilities of the young actress. Her celebrated mouth, able to switch from a genteel smile to the venomous grin 'of a stoat at bay' was already there and this beautiful young lady would have turned into the most repellent creature if the play had required it.[624] Maggie Smith still is 'that beautiful girl' and, at the pinnacle of high comedy, she wonderfully masters the art of transforming herself if the part requires it. Her capacity for metamorphosis is visually breathtaking and has an unrivalled comical impact on stage and on screen. When it comes to make the audience laugh, her audacity has no limits. The slightest pout, precise and judiciously calculated, transforms her physiognomy. It is quite astonishing to see that such a beautiful woman is able to become so hilariously expressive. Far from deserving her, her beauty contributes to her versatility. The physical transformation also works in reverse order, and Maggie Smith manages, if the role demands it, to sublimate her own beauty. This is an amazing phenomenon that M. Coveney subtly describes in his biography of the actress: Smith is able to radiate an absolute attractiveness, even more perfect than hers is, whenever she needs to. If *The First Wives' Club* (H. Wilson, 1996) does not represent the highlight of her filmography, the film allows the spectators to appreciate the hiatus between the parts which are usually offered to Smith and her real potential. Dressed to the nines and perched on stilettos, Gunilla Garson Goldberg looks like the queen of New York's jet-set and the viewer could have difficulty recognising, under the furs and the pearls, the actress who played the plain Susan, in Bennett's *Bed Among the Lentils*. Of course, every appearance of the glamorous Gunilla provokes laughs as the character is highly caricatural, however, it may be wondered why directors have made so little use of Maggie Smith's stunning looks.

624 Wardle, 'All the angles'.

Mother Dear

In 2006, maybe somewhat tired of the large array of old bags she had played on the big screen, Maggie Smith decided to escape her usual typecasting for her highly expected return to the West End. Having just got rid of Grace Hawkins's comfortable boots, she hastily borrowed the high heels of Edward Albee's Lady from Dubuque to tread the boards again after a five-year absence. The spectator who had watched *Keeping Mum* at the end of 2005 and booked a seat to see the same actress at the Theatre Royal Haymarket eighteen months later had good reasons to feel disconcerted. In Albee's play, Smith appeared more stunning than ever, having probably never looked that glamorous in a part since *Murder by Death*, in 1976. Seeing her in that role allowed the audience to dispel some of the preconceptions that M. Coveney referred to in a vibrant notice on his WhatsOnStage blog, enjoining any spectator who identified Smith with the wrinkled old crones she played in movies to rush to the Haymarket 'to drink deep at the true Maggie fount'.[625] When comparing the Lady from Dubuque with Dora Charleston, her character in *Murder by Death*, it appears that time has definitely been kind to the actress. Thirty years later, Smith sported with the same allure a similar bobbed hairstyle and, although her face has gained wrinkles, her Lady looked like a very attractive woman at the height of her beauty.

The plot of *The Lady from Dubuque* is not easy to follow. On the East coast of the United States, in the 1980s, three young couples play 'Twenty Questions' at the end of a merry evening. Jo, their hostess, has terminal cancer and the unbearable pain leads her to abruptly express her grudges against her friends and her absent mother, an overweight, pink-haired recluse who lives in New Jersey. The atmosphere getting irksome, the party has to end earlier than expected. Now alone with her husband, Sam, Jo asks him to take her upstairs. The stage remains empty for a few seconds and the audience can reasonably believe that Act I has ended, but then, a mature, very elegant lady makes an entrance, followed by Oscar, her black companion.[626] The curtain falls and, after the interval, Act II begins at the moment when Sam discovers these two intruders comfortably seated in his living room. Although she does not correspond to the description that has been given of her in Act I, the mysterious lady persists in pretending she is Jo's mother, coming from Dubuque to assist her daughter in her last moments. Act II focuses on a reflection – sometimes not accessible to the average spectator – on identity; none of the characters who successively re-enter the stage admits the identity that the Lady from Dubuque claims to be hers. Only Jo, climbing down the stairs, falls into the arms of her so-called mother. Who exactly is the lady? The play ends with ellipsis points as Jo is

625 Entitled 'There's nothing like a Dame', this post was written on May 2007, but it was unfortunately removed from *WhatsOnStage*'s new website, a few years later.

626 And not her chauffeur, as M. Coveney – probably confusing for one moment Elizabeth with Miss Daisy – asserts in his book (*Maggie Smith. A Biography*, p. 267).

carried back to her room where she dies peacefully. Created in Broadway in 1980 and panned by New York critics, *The Lady from Dubuque* had to close shortly after its opening night. To plan a London revival, twenty-seven years later, represented a major challenge and it was predictable that such a puzzling work – it is often considered an experimental play – would not appeal to the largest audience; the play certainly was more suited for the audiences of the National Theatre or the Donmar. However, although the production cannot be seen, in terms of box office, as a commercial success, the critics – and even the less favourable ones – unanimously hailed Maggie Smith and the subtlety of her acting.[627] N. De Jongh thought that the actress's extraordinary performance gave the play an 'emotional' focal point, as, for once, Smith was setting aside her famous acting tricks and mannerisms to create an intriguing character; portraying the enigmatic Lady, she was using a register of more 'serious' emotion, similar to what she had conveyed in *Three Tall Women*.[628] Tim Walker's review was just as complimentary, saying that Maggie Smith was giving a masterclass in stage acting; portraying the mysterious Lady from Dubuque, alternatively funny and moving, Smith dominated every scene.[629] In *The Independent*, Taylor commented on Maggie Smith's tremendous portrayal of Elizabeth, praising her subtle, witty delivery of lines combining comical irony ('Pink hair? On purpose?') with metaphysical overtones,[630] while G. Brown compared Smith's performance to a sparkling, multifaceted 'diamond' whose innumerable qualities are impossible to define.[631] From that point

627 See T. Zinman, *Edward Albee* (Ann Arbor: University of Michigan, 2008), p. 99-100.

628 'Dame Maggie's heavenly allure as angel of death', *The Evening Standard*, 21 March 2007, p. 25. The critic Benedict David was in awe of Smith's 'sphinx-like' interpretation; see 'The Lady from Dubuque', *Variety*, 21 March 2007 <http://variety.com/2007/legit/reviews/the-lady-from-dubuque-1200509537/> [accessed 12 November 2016]. One of the less positive reviews, that of C. Spencer, implicitly referred to the somewhat abstruse message of Albee's play, foreshadowing the unenthusiastic response of the West End audiences. The critic deplored the fact that Maggie Smith obviously distanced herself from her character. Although Spencer admitted that Smith, all wit and glamour, was giving an immaculate performance, he thought that the 'ironic detachment' with which she delivered her lines seemed to reflect her own doubts about the play. See 'Maggie draws the short straw this time', *The Daily Telegraph*, 21 March 2007, p. 33.

629 'An angel's kiss of life', *The Sunday Telegraph 'Seven'*, 25 March 2007, p. 24.

630 'Dame Maggie magnificent as ministering angel', *The Independent*, 21 March 2007, p. 13.

631 'Mystery of Maggie, the Angel', *The Mail on Sunday*, 25 March 2007, p. 75.

of view, the common enterprise of Maggie Smith, Anthony Page and Robert Fox was a great success.[632] Undoubtedly, the play gave the actress the opportunity to brutally break with her most recent portrayals on screen – the 'old crones' evoked by Coveney, Constance Trentham in *Gosford Park* and Janet in *Ladies in Lavender*, as well as, in a different genre, Grace Hawkins in *Keeping Mum* – and to develop through characterisation some aspects she had not tackled in her previous roles. According to Albee's stage directions, she played 'a stylish, elegant, handsome woman', 'splendid' in her late fifties or early sixties, but mostly, she embodied the dual figure of the mother and the seductress. Elizabeth is a protective, caring mother, a kind of angel or tutelary spirit who has come to provide her dying child with a final comfort. In *The Sunday Times*, Christopher Hart hailed Maggie Smith's magnificent performance, emphasising the unexpected gentleness of the Lady from Dubuque who, from the start, stands as a magnanimous figure.[633] Smith was perfectly convincing in a part which is usually not hers, even if several of the characters she has previously portrayed could be identified with the motherly figure. Lady Hester raising her grandson (*Tea with Mussolini*), Betsey Trotwood adopting her great-nephew (*David Copperfield*), Emily Delahunty looking after Aimee (*My House in Umbria*) or even Minerva McGonagall defending Harry Potter against Voldemort and his allies, all are surrogate mothers.

Tall and vigorous whereas her dying daughter appears frail and sickly, the lady who comes from Dubuque is a reassuring, comforting mother. Sophisticated and impeccably groomed, she also represents the paradigm of the mother, the ideal *belle dame* that every little girl wishes to become one day. In the Seattle production, a few months earlier, the American actress Myra Carter offered quite a different rendition of the character; she was a frail, withered elderly woman whose concubinage with the spry Oscar appeared quite improbable. Unsurprisingly, Maggie Smith gave a top-class performance, making the most of her perfectly mastered timing which always does marvels in Albee's plays. Elegantly dressed in a classy two-

632 A. Page wanted to direct *The Lady from Dubuque* as soon as he saw the play, in 1980. Years later, he submitted the project to Maggie Smith who was looking for a stage role she could play, after Hare's *The Breath of Life*. The play was a difficult one, but she decided to do it.

633 'That's the way to treat a lady', *The Sunday Times Culture*, 25 March 2007, p. 18.

piece outfit by Jean Muir, she literally dazzled on the stage. Oddly – in comparison with the roles the actress is usually identified with – it was through physical beauty that she transcended the character. Willingly or not, Smith's Elizabeth closely resembled Frances Cotter Albee, Edward Albee's adoptive mother. Blonde, tall and extremely smart, the lady from Dubuque remains, in maturity, a stunning woman.[634] The biographer Mel Gussow has inserted some pictures of Albee's stepmother in his book, and it is obvious that, with her bobbed hairstyle and her blonde colour, Maggie Smith looked a lot like the sophisticated Mrs Albee. M. Wolf considered that Smith was 'resplendent', looking far away from our image of a 'Dubuque matron'.[635] Smith had played a caricatural avatar of Frances Albee in *Three Tall Women*, but she eventually portrayed her in *The Lady from Dubuque*. None of the other actresses who had played the character before had been that close to Albee's vision of the Mother. This glamorous – but mysterious and impalpable – woman embodies the perfect maternal figure through the shape of a comforting Angel of Death, as a counterpoint to the imperfect maternal figure Frances represented in real life (Albee had very difficult relations with his adoptive mother). Who is the lady from Dubuque? No one knows and, after all, it does not matter. What she represents is more crucial than her actual identity. Elizabeth is not a proper character. She fills a function.[636] As G. Brown asserted, Elizabeth is the 'embodiment' of motherhood, a functional figure that intervenes when one character needs this substitute figure to deal with some painful events like the death of a loved one.[637] In Albee's drama, the maternal figure is associated with physical beauty and sophistication – in the most frivolous sense of the word, hairstyle, make-up and jewels – and the actress materialised remarkably that glamorous image. While illness irremediably estranges Jo from her husband, depriving

634 Maggie Smith was quite satisfied with her appearance (as Elizabeth, of course, otherwise she would never acknowledge her own beauty) and she even thought that she looked a bit like the always elegant Angela Lansbury.

635 '*Rose Tattoo* and *Lady from Dubuque*: lesser-known American classics make a study in contrast', *The International Herald Tribune*, 23 April 2007 <http://www.nytimes.com/2007/04/23/arts/23iht-lon25.1.5404962.html> [accessed 12 November 2016].

636 G. McCarthy, *Edward Albee* (London: Macmillan, 1987), p. 148; for McCarthy, Elizabeth clearly is a 'substitute speaker', invented by the playwright to fulfil a function. One character needs a mother, Albee creates her.

637 Brown, 'Mystery of Maggie, the Angel'.

her of all her sensuality and substance, her alleged mother is all charm and femininity. Making the soberest navy outfit sexy, Maggie/Elizabeth crossed and uncrossed a pair of splendid legs that *Downton Abbey*'s viewers had few opportunities to admire in the TV show. It is a questioning of the traditional scheme according to which a daughter is always more attractive than her ageing mother and physical attractiveness only belongs to youth. It is also a provocative statement by Albee (at least for the United States in the 1980s), who puts on stage a scandalous and unexpected common-law couple reuniting a mature white woman and a black man, slightly younger.

In fact, Elizabeth represents the Woman in the whole acceptance of the term. While the three other female characters, all in their thirties, go through conjugal issues, the Lady from Dubuque seems to be perfectly fulfilled in her personal life. The couple made by Oscar and Elizabeth could be seen as shocking in the eyes of traditionalist and reactionary people, but it never appears ridiculous or unconvincing. An older looking Lady would make their relationship grotesque and highly doubtful, adding a new interrogation to a play which probably includes too many unsolved questions: do they really make a couple, as they pretend to? Here there is no doubt and the two characters display a real chemistry which shows, not only in their verbal exchanges, but also in their acutely synchronised gestures. At one moment, Smith's acting involved impressive footwork which did not appear in the stage directions. Instead of presenting her palm to Oscar so that he could slap it with his own hand, she lifted her leg up and presented him with her foot that he quickly slapped, raising bursts of laughs in the audience. The gesture, which made use of the actress's proven agility, would have looked acrobatic and risible with Myra Carter's elderly Elizabeth or Irene Worth's compassed Lady. Full of energy, carnal, the character portrayed by Maggie Smith represented the ideal, blossoming woman that Jo, young and already dying, would never be. Although she appears mainly in Act II, Elizabeth nevertheless remains the title role and Smith captured the attention of the audience as soon as she put one foot on the stage, at the very end of Act I.[638] Not exactly when she made her entrance, in front of the audience,

638 T. Meacham, 'The Centrifugation of Iconic Actors and Characters: Daniel Radcliffe/Alan Strang and Maggie Smith/The Lady from Dubuque', *Western European Stages*, 19.2, Spring 2007, p. 31; the author remarked that Maggie Smith's entrance announced the real start of the show, and the actress 'effortlessly' overshadowed all the other actors.

but earlier, when her steps resounded backstage, on the wooden floor. Significantly older than the rest of the cast, the actress effortlessly dazzled, outshining all the other female performers on stage. In *The Spectator,* the critic Lloyd Evans described the Lady as the 'most watchable' thing that was offered to the spectator's eyes, admitting that, despite her age, Maggie Smith's charm was intact, as magical as ever.[639] Waxing lyrical, the critic Paul Callan defined Smith as the shining, dazzling, sparkling 'monarch' of the stage, emphasising the incomparable stage presence of one of the country's greatest actresses (and, as hyperbolic as these adjectives may seem, they were in fact quite accurate to describe her magisterial performance).[640] Not only did Smith deliver a wonderful masterclass of acting, but she also gave life to the radiant quinquagenarian described by Edward Albee. A bit older than B and much younger than A in *Three Tall Women*, the Lady from Dubuque incarnates the serene and poised woman in full bloom.

639 'A Touch of Magic', *The Spectator*, 31 March 2007, p. 52. See also S. Hemming, 'The Lady from Dubuque', *The Financial Times*, 23 March 2007, p. 11; the critic thought that Smith, with the subtle irony and quiet authority which were hers, brought a lighter, more enticing tone to the play.

640 'Dazzling Maggie's star turn', *The Daily Express*, 23 March 2007, p. 53. According to J. Edwardes, Maggie Smith brought 'a grace and restraint' to the part; 'The Lady from Dubuque', *Time Out*, 28 March 2007 (see *Theatre Record*, 12-25 March 2007, p. 332).

Lithe Spirit

It is highly dubious that many fans of *Harry Potter* or *Downton Abbey* have ever heard of *Curtain Call* (1998). However, in this much lesser known movie, Maggie Smith gives a devastating performance as a glamorous and touching character. Directed by Peter Yates (*The Dresser*), *Curtain Call* is certainly not the film the celebrated director is remembered for and its banal title – it changed three times during production – does not disclose much of the plot. This romantic comedy tells the story of a young book publisher, Stevenson Lowe (James Spader), who encounters difficulties at work – his new boss introducing questionable commercial policies in the publishing company – as well as in his private life – he is reluctant to make a commitment with his girlfriend (Polly Walker), although she would like to get married. Lowe buys a huge furnished old house before discovering it is haunted by a couple of ghosts, Lily Marlowe (Maggie Smith) and Max Gale (Michael Caine). Quite bothered by these unexpected guests, the young man finds at the same time comfort in them. The two ghosts, who were famous Broadway actors in the 1930s, become friends with Stevenson and provide him with advice to resolve his conjugal problems. It soon appears that the pair of love advisers does not make such a harmonious couple, never stopping bickering and exchanging scathing remarks. Nevertheless, as the film progresses, the two complicated romances – the one of the living young people and the one of the ghosts – develop and get resolved in parallel. Stevenson resigns from his job, creates his own publishing company and proposes, at last, to his girlfriend, while the elderly actors get reconciled. All's well that ends well, and the very first book published by Lowe Publishers is nothing but a superb album in tribute to Max and Lily's career.

Regarded as an average, mushy 'romcom', *Curtain Call* proves to be an exquisite movie with an outdated charm which, had it not been produced fifty years later, would have been quite suited to the 1950s. It went unnoticed, though, and it could have been much worse as it went through a lot of difficulties which challenged its theatrical release.[641] Actually, this commercial fiasco hides tremendous performances by Maggie Smith and Michael Caine, successfully teaming for the second time on screen. Arguing all the time, their characters nevertheless make the most assorted duo, just like the unforgettable Barries did in *California Suite*, twenty years earlier.

641 The making of the movie was announced in May 1996, with actor Jason Robards Jr as Max Gale and the beautiful Anne Bancroft as Lily Marlowe, but it got postponed, and these two characters were recast. With Michael Caine and Maggie Smith replacing Robards and Bancroft, the film was eventually shot on location, New York City and Washington D.C., during the winter of 1997 (in the very same Brooklyn house where the TV drama *Lily in Love* – starring Maggie Smith as Lily, and Christopher Plummer as her actor husband – had been filmed in 1983). Despite an A-list cast and an award-winning director, no distributor was willing to get involved after post-production, and the rolls stayed for more than one year in a cupboard. Then, Encore Media Group bought it for its Starz TV network and it eventually aired on US television in December 1998 and got a limited release, later, under the title *It All Came true.*

Caine joked about that, saying that they were shooting 'Geriatric Suite'.[642] That was funny, but quite unfair, their characters being equally attractive as Sidney and Diana Barrie were, if not more; Lily Marlowe and Max Gale have a supreme distinction and an old-fashioned charm which make them instantly lovable. Besides, Caine and Smith are certainly no less handsome in their mature years and, on the contrary, in *Curtain Call*, they form quite a convincing couple, more glamorous in fact than the younger one. The chemistry between the two actors is obvious. Both visibly had fun playing these two old glories of the stage and they slightly overact for the greatest pleasure of the spectator. Mischievous and also quite oversensitive, Max and Lily belong, as ghosts, to the fairy character category. Lily is jealous of her husband with whom she constantly squabbles and both stand as comical figures of troublemakers, developing the well-known theme of the poltergeists who suddenly erupt into living people's existence. One delightful scene shows Max/Caine spying from the stairs on the young couple dancing and lovingly kissing, as if he was envious of them. Suddenly, Lily appears and strongly advises him to stop at once, but she cannot help but linger herself to spy in turn on the two lovers.

It is probably fortuitous, but the evanescent Lily in her fluffy negligee of grey feathered velvet echoes Elvira's ghostly figure in Coward's *Blithe Spirit*, just like she was portrayed on screen by Kay Hammond in David Lean's movie (1945). Maggie Smith wears with an incomparable ease the extravagant outfits of her character and, by contrast with the other female figures in the movie, Lily Marlowe's refined elegance looks deliciously outdated. More than ever, it seems obvious that the Marcel wave is definitely one of the hairstyles which suit Smith's angular profile the best, as if the 1930s waves had been designed especially for her. For the movie, the actress had to wear a Hollywood star's wardrobe, all in black and pearl grey, ornated with sequins, fur and ostrich feathers, her only coloured outfit being the incredible Cleopatra disguise she wears at the New Year's Party; this is certainly the kitschest attire viewers have ever got to see Maggie Smith in, but she sports it like nobody else. Although the actress no longer has, thank goodness, the frightfully rail-thin figure she showed when filming *Travels with my Aunt* in 1972, she still possesses that flexibility that characterised her Aunt Augusta and Lily's muslin dress floats around her supple, slight

642 Owen, 'Peeling back the years'.

body. The grey outfits – an elegant two-piece tweed suit with a fur collar and a ravishing side-buttoned coat which emphasises her slender figure – amusingly remind us of Epifania Fitzfassenden in George Bernard Shaw's *The Millionairess* (BBC, 1972). The opening scene of the TV drama, where a very sophisticated Epifania, all dressed in grey with silver fox fur, gets out of her limousine and makes a theatrical entrance at her solicitor's, is undoubtedly one of the more typical samples of Maggie Smith's wonderful timing. More than twenty-five years after having played Epifania, the actress, as sparkling as ever, could rival her younger self. Lily is a sharp woman, as vivacious and quick-witted as a musical heroine, undulating in her kitsch wardrobe or, as chic as feisty, negligently playing with her glamorous accessories.

One day, Stevenson Lowe fortuitously walks up the stairs to the attic of his house and discovers the proper home of his guests. The attic has been decorated in the manner of a Broadway dressing room, filled with old costumes, crystal pendant chandeliers and theatre memorabilia – noticeably old posters from the time of Gale & Marlowe's glory (an attentive viewer would recognise pictures from *Travels with my Aunt* and Robin Phillips's production of *The Way of the World* at Stratford, Ontario). In this baroque setting, halfway between Ali Baba's cavern and Sarah Bernhardt's apartment, Caine and Smith seem particularly at ease, although their characters, egocentric and hammy beyond measure, never stop bickering under Lowe's bewildered eyes. Lily reproaches Max for his innumerable affairs, while he accuses her of being a harridan. They quarrel like naughty children, but also compete with humour, wit and elegance. Yet, what could be taken for a witty and playful jousting quickly proves to be a conjugal crisis. The old couple pretend to solve Stevenson's conjugal problems, but they are apparently unable to solve their own. As Lily later confesses to Stevenson, they still feel the resentment of their last years together, when they had irremediably kept their distance from each other. As usual with Maggie Smith, the vulnerable side of her character promptly outdoes the comical aspects of Lily's behaviour. The fact that Max Gale and Lily Marlowe are ghosts also adds a nostalgic tone to the film, the two characters being haunted – if one may say so – by regret, bitterness and awareness that, for them, things will never happen again. With her ethereal fragility, the actress appears as the most charming, touching ghostly figure ever, although her Lily looks certainly less gothic and spectral than Minerva McGonagall in the last episode of *Harry Potter*. Max jokingly calls her 'the Queen of Pulchritude' and, seeing Smith's exquisite Lily, the spectator cannot think that he uses this word in an exclusively ironic meaning.

The most striking part of Maggie Smith's performance corresponds to the last two scenes. After the foolish moment when Max and Stevenson have come back home totally drunk and Lily has violently slapped Max who immediately fell asleep, she explains to Stevenson how they met, at the New Year's Eve Ball in 1927. She now misses the Max Gale whom she fell in love with and also regrets that they spent the last years of their lives in reciprocal indifference: 'Now, it's too late. It's just too late.' This is a devastating moment and Smith is simply magnificent. However, the very last scene turns out to be a happy ending. Working to save Stevenson's relationship, Max and Lily return to the New Year's party as ghosts and unexpectedly fall in love again. At the end of the ball and the beginning of the New Year, their passion rises from its ashes. Dancing together, they revive their first date and mutually declare their love for each other. 'Lily, you are a hell of a girl. And I love you,' he shyly says. 'I love you too,' she replies. 'Till death do us part,' Max had ironically whispered earlier in the movie. Death cannot part ghosts, though, and their love is more vivid after death than it had ever been. Max and Lily dance the last waltz in an empty ballroom and progressively vanish from sight, although they will be around for ever. Together. As eternal lovers, like Tristan and Isolde. Subtly filmed by Yates, this scene is incredibly moving and aesthetically gorgeous, arguably representing the most romantic moment in Smith's whole filmography. For once, the actress does not play a lonely woman, but she is an element of a marital couple and the object of a man's desire. Maggie Smith is absolutely compelling as a woman in love, not only thanks to her attractiveness, but also for her ability to express the vulnerability and the sincerity of the character so well. There is nothing funny or odd about it. Smith can play a ridiculous old spinster if she wants to, but she also can play the moving and grand heroines, poles apart from the grotesque characters that are too often given to actresses of a certain age. *Curtain Call* also illustrates the fact that some of her roles echo others, sometimes at quite a large interval of time. This minor production foreshadowed a much more publicised film, the plot of which was built around a similar pattern: a couple of ageing (but well alive) artists who reconcile and fall in love again after having been separated for decades. Fifteen years after Peter Yates's movie, Smith, still as attractive as ever, would be involved, again, in a love story. A hell of a girl, definitely.

The Prime of Miss Jean Horton

As early as 2007, enthralled by Ronald Harwood's successful play *Quartet*,[643] Tom Courtenay encouraged the playwright to make a movie from it. He would play Reginald Paget, and his old friend Albert Finney, the lustful baryton Wilfred Bond. Enthusiastic about working again with such gifted actors – who both had co-starred in P. Yates's adaptation of *The Dresser*, in 1984 – Harwood suggested the name of his friend Maggie Smith for

643 The play opened in September 1999 at the Albery Theatre (now the Noel Coward Theatre), with Alec McCowen (Reggie), Donald Sinden (Wilf), Stephanie Cole (Cissy) and Angela Thorne (Jean).

the role of Jean Horton, a temperamental and haughty diva. However, like *Curtain Call*, which it surreptitiously echoes, *Quartet* walked an uneasy path and the pre-production went through many vicissitudes. The whole project might have fallen into oblivion,[644] but the producer Finola Dwyer eventually submitted the script to Dustin Hoffman who had expressed the wish to direct a movie. Moved to tears by Harwood's screenplay, Hoffman immediately agreed to do it and, of course, his name greatly helped the producers to raise funding. Having nothing in common with a Hollywood product, *Quartet* proves to be a sweet and moving piece of work which is certainly much more than the 'feel-good movie' that some critics considered it. It is mostly a vibrant tribute to performers in their golden years, expressing the view that talent does not fade with age.[645] Filmed in October 2011, in the enchanting scenery of Hedsor House (Taplow, Buckinghamshire), *Quartet* is coloured by autumnal nuances which metaphorically convey the proper background to the story.

Harwood's script – which evidently reminds us of Noel Coward's *Waiting in The Wings* (1960)[646] – tells the story of three elderly singers (Reggie, Wilf and Cissy) living in a retirement home for musicians. As the home faces financial issues, a gala involving the residents is being organised to raise money, but the arrival of Jean, Reggie's ex-wife, will upset the calm atmosphere of the institution. Humiliated by her new status and embarrassed to be confronted with her former husband, Jean behaves quite haughtily, refusing to take part and to sing the quartet of *Rigoletto* which the four singers were famous for. However, she will eventually find a new meaning in her life and fall in love again with Reggie. The movie differs from the play by one noticeable detail: Reggie, Wilf, Cissy and Jean are still able to sing, well enough at least to perform in public, while the characters of the play could not sing anymore and had to

644 The enterprise obtained the support of BBC Films and Headline Movies with the help of Mark Shivas (executive producer of *Memento Mori*), but was jeopardised a few months later, after Shivas's premature death. In the meantime, Richard Loncraine (who had been approached for directing the film) got involved in another project. See C. Gant, 'Singing for the Cinema', *Sight and Sound*, January 2013, p. 16-17.

645 The same idea has been exploited, more recently, by Sorrentino, in *Youth* (2015): the main character is an old conductor (Michael Caine) who, despite being retired and reluctant to be back on the stage, eventually agrees to conduct again.

646 "The Wings" being in fact, like Beecham House, a home for retired actresses.

use subterfuge to fool the audience. So, what was originally a cynical farce involving four old dears who were more or less decrepit – in fact, four types corresponding to the major opera tessitura, baritone, tenor, soprano and mezzo – turns into a more poignant drama, and the characters gain considerably in depth and humanity. Billy Connolly plays Wilf, originally a redoubtable Pan on the loose, who appears as a joyous prankster rather than a libidinous old fart. Pauline Collins brings her sweetness and her touching sensibility to Cissy, saucier and less lovable in the play than she is here, in the film. Tom Courtenay rejuvenates and humanises Reggie, who was a grumpy and introverted old man in the play. With regards to Michael Gambon, he brilliantly develops a character who was mentioned, but actually never appeared on the stage. Gambon makes Cedric a delirious and jubilant figure who strangely looks like the effeminate cousin of Albus Dumbledore – whose wardrobe he has obviously borrowed.

It comes as no surprise that, once more, Maggie Smith steals the whole show. The first fifteen minutes of the film consists of an introductory scene which prepares for Jean's arrival, that is Smith's much expected entrance. As soon as she sets foot in Beecham House, the spectator is riveted by her. The role emphatically demonstrates that the actress is perfectly able to escape the narrow limits of typecasting to give life to a character who is the complete opposite of the parts that are usually given to her. Maggie Smith admirably knows how to make the audience feel pity and empathy with her and, although she excels in playing prudish spinsters, she is perfectly convincing as a woman in love. Of course, while praising her performance, some journalists did not miss the great opportunity to make a comparison with the unavoidable Dowager Countess. In *The Mail on Sunday*, Matthew Bond wrote that Smith conveyed a bit of Violet Crawley's imperiousness to the character (when saying 'I never took less than twelve curtain calls'), admitting that she combined it with a touching fragility.[647] The reviewer of *The Evening Standard*, though enthusiastic, declared that it was *Downton Abbey* relocated in a care home.[648] In one scene, though, having had enough of being

647 M. Bond, 'Dustin's brilliantly British pitch-perfect', *The Mail on Sunday 2*, 6 January 2013, p. 12.

648 D. Malcolm, 'Hoffman's on song for his feature debut', *The Evening Standard*, 4 January 2013, p. 34.

pressured by her fellow residents to perform at the gala, Jean angrily drops the F-word at breakfast and there were critics who marvelled at Dame Maggie using such an expression on screen. Things should change slowly now the TV show has come to an end, but some people feel the necessity to compare every part she plays with that of the Dowager, indicating either blind incomprehension or a malicious intent to reduce the merits of an actress who is maybe a bit too talented to be unanimously hailed. The subtlety of her acting was totally missed by the critic from *The Irish Times*, who described a 'phoned' and linear performance, Smith's Jean spending half the film examining her fellow residents as if they were 'maggots burrowing their way through her morning muffin'.[649] Recurrent comparisons and assimilations to their most famous part is unfortunately the common fate of popular TV stars, but in the case of such a protean actress, it sounds unjustified and vacuous. On the contrary, Jean stands as an exception in her recent filmography, as underlined by Brian Kellow in *Opera News*; he declared that it was one of her 'freshest' characterisations since a long while.[650] Of course, the character is an imperious and whimsical diva – there was nothing surprising about this in a play about operatic performers – but Smith portrays Jean exactly as the role was written in Harwood's script. Tailored to fit the actors who had been cast in the parts, the adaptation for the screen actually gives a more human dimension to Jean Horton. In the play, she was a caricatural figure, with all the excesses of the stereotypical diva; grumpy and stubborn, on the verge of tears every time someone says something unpleasant or upsetting to her, Jean was in fact quite an antipathetic character. She appeared as a man-eater – the number of her husbands has dropped from five to two in the movie – extravagant and neglectful just like the cicada in the fable. In the film, the character allows Maggie Smith the opportunity to display a great variety of emotions, from fear to sorrow. In *The Telegraph*, Jenny McCartney emphasised the complexity of the character played by Maggie Smith; Jean is imperious, ironic and even cruel, but she also reveals, at times, her vulnerability.'[651] Jean Horton is a captivating character who constantly oscillates between dry humour and dramatic intensity. Her

649 D. Clarke, 'Quartet', *Irish Times*, 4 January 2013, p. 12.

650 'On the Beat', *Opera News*, 77.7, January 2013, p. 8.

651 'Quartet review', *The Telegraph*, 11 January 2013, p. 17.

caustic wittiness and her violence hide in fact a real sensibility, what makes the role of 'a snug glove of a fit', as the journalist of *The New York Observer* noted.[652] Horton – as Ronald Harwood had immediately realised – was a perfectly fitting role for the actress.

Although the character's back-story is less explicitly revealed in the film than it was in the play, the spectator perceives easily – through Smith's nuanced performance – her anxieties. More than the stage character, Jean makes the viewer feel sorry for her and her disarray strongly reminds us, at times, of Judith Hearne's. Fortuitously, the main action begins with her arrival and, just like the heroine of Clayton's movie, the former diva arrives in a car, peering through the window. While Judith was smiling, rejoicing at the thought of starting a new life in Dublin, Jean, bitter and scared, feels like she is getting buried alive. Her devastated face which appears through the window of her sumptuous flat on Fitzroy Square, then through that of the car, sharply contrasts with the *joie de vivre* which prevails at Beecham House. The image of the framed window reappears several times in the movie and is always associated with Jean, in the manner of a visual filter which isolates her, the vulnerable caged bird, from the external world. From the start, the character is related to sorrow and bitterness. With her navy outfits – smart but a bit out-of-date – and her frail appearance, Jean embodies the nostalgia of the past or, more precisely, the regret. Humiliated, she has to settle in a home only because she has nowhere else to go, being unable to support herself. The humiliation is double though; she also knows that she will be confronted with her ex-husband, Reggie, who left her the very day they had married, after she confessed an infidelity to him. Throughout the entire movie, Jean is overcome with shame, quite aware of her own downfall; Reggie split up with the successful young diva she was once, but financial circumstances have eventually made an old person of her. Philip French, in *The Observer*, considered that Jean Horton was one of Maggie Smith's finest performances, allowing the actress to bring her vulnerability to a 'grande dame' who becomes aware of the impending loss of her gifts

652 R. Reed, 'Hoffman's Directorial Debut is a Delicate Narrative Laced Together with Ego and Mortality', *The New York Observer*, 8 January 2013 <http://observer.com/2013/01/quartet-hoffmans-directorial-debut-is-a-delicate-narrative-laced-together-with-ego-and-mortality/> [accessed 12 November 2016].

and privileges.[653] While being used to playing strong and authoritarian ladies who never abase themselves, Smith portrays quite a different character here. Jean always has to swallow her pride. Like *Capturing Mary*, Jean's story tells a reversal of fortune, but whereas Mary Gilbert has lost her glamour, *Quartet*'s heroine still looks like a queen. This is probably the most challenging aspect of the character. There is a gap, a huge gap between Jean's physical appearance and her inner feelings, and it makes her even more pathetic.

In the play, Jean explains, through a monologue, the reasons why she refuses to perform with her friends at the gala in honour of Verdi's birthday. She lost her voice many years earlier and she cannot sing any more. 'My gift has deserted me,' she says. The scene is heartbreaking and the situation, hopeless; thus, the four old singers will eventually use playback to mimic the quartet of *Rigoletto*. In the movie, the situation is rather different. Being a perfectionist, Jean simply stopped singing because she could not bear the pressure of the critics any more, as her vocal abilities were inevitably going to diminish with time. She has lost her confidence, but not her voice. A very moving scene shows her alone in her room, hiding to listen to her old recordings and remembering, with a heavy heart, her past glory. Jean is perpetually mourning for her younger self. In fact, the character in the movie greatly resembles the actress who plays her – this is not fortuitous, D. Hoffman wanted it to be so – and Jean's reluctance to sing echoes, of course, Smith's own doubts about returning to the stage. In an article written in 1997, ahead of *A Delicate Balance*'s opening, the critic S. Morley quoted Smith's own words from a previous interview, saying that the problem about success is that it is always harder, every performance being a 'potential catastrophe', and these words oddly echo Jean Horton's.[654] Jean's corrosive humour is very close to that of the actress (the put-downs on Sir Beecham and laxative, as well as the stairlift episode are among the lines that Harwood has added to his script with Maggie Smith in mind), but it has, of course, deeper and bitterer tones. That vindicative behaviour can

653 'Quartet. Review', *The Observer*, 6 January 2013, p. 24.

654 'Drama queen of ice and fire', *The Scotsman*, 11 September 1997, p. 16. See also R. Higson, 'Theatre's gentle queen', *The Australian*, 6 March 2004, p. 11; Smith thinks that it is getting harder and harder to perform, admitting that she had some kind of 'blind confidence' at her debut, but, after many years, she realises how difficult it is.

be seen as a reaction of self-preservation in her despair. When wounded, the most inoffensive bird can be aggressive. Nevertheless, although she is fallen, the queen remains a bitch. A succession of emotionally strong scenes reveals the harshness of her temperament – she makes a scandal at breakfast, shouting rudely at her friends, and fiercely hits the poor Cissy who was presenting flowers to her to beg her pardon – but the character begins to change in the last third of the film. Cissy's fainting (of which she is partly responsible) makes her feel remorse, while her discussion with her old flame Frank White awakens her. She is still alive, so she must seize the day. Cissy herself manages to persuade her: if she does not take part in the gala, her greatest rival Ann Langley will sing the finale. This is an unbearable thought for Jean who decides to take part. She immediately regains her pride and her enthusiasm, triumphantly entering the dining-room arm in arm with Reggie. The spectators cannot fail to notice, then, that the two former singers make the most attractive, well-matched couple. From that point of view, the movie shows evident similarities with Federico Fellini's penultimate piece of work, *Ginger e Fred* (1986), which also displayed a couple of old performers. In this movie, sexagenarians Amelia (Giulietta Masina) and Pippo (Marcello Mastroianni), formerly successful tap dancers who have retired forty years earlier, agree to reunite for a last show on television. The difference lies in the fact that, unlike Jean and Reggie, Amelia and Pippo, aka Ginger and Fred, stand as an anachronistic couple, the relics of a forgotten past. On stage, Mastroianni whispers to Masina: 'We are ghosts, we come from the shadows and there we return.'[655] In comparison with them, Jean and Reggie do not appear as ridiculous, old-fashioned artists whose last performance seems risky and pitiful. On the contrary, the story implies that they are still able to perform and, as lovers, they still have a future.[656]

The complicated story of Jean and Reggie eventually prevails over the main plot – the preparation of the gala in honour of Verdi. Under Hoffman's impetus, Harwood's farce has become a touching love story. Reconciled at last, Jean and Reggie decide to marry again. While this happy

655 'Siamo dei fantasmi che vengono dal buio e nel buio se ne vanno.'

656 Mastroianni's character falls on stage during his laborious tap dance performance and, after this ultimate and fugitive encounter, the two aged dancers separate for good, in a gloomy Stazione Termini.

ending was merely sketched out in R. Harwood's play, the movie provides their romance with a real denouement which is as sweet as it is believable considering the age of the characters. In the play, Jean's presence is a constant humiliation for Reggie who failed to consummate their marriage and such a positive outcome was not possible; Reggie's 'problem' being not yet solved – even if Wilf suggests that he try pills of a certain kind – there is no question of the couple marrying again. Writing the screenplay, Harwood has removed the risible aspects of Reginald's character and, on set, Hoffman followed the same path. Reggie is certainly upset by the arrival of his ex-wife who once betrayed him and ruined their happiness – he never married again, disappointed by a *donna* a bit too *mobile* – but he has no reason, here, to be embarrassed and ashamed of himself; unlike the stage character, he is not sexually impotent. In the end, the film may lose in comical efficiency – some juicy lines have disappeared – but it certainly gains in intensity and emotion. Jean has to obtain Reggie's forgiveness to be able to live in peace at Beecham House and, in actual fact, she will get much more than a pardon.

Despite the weight of the past, Jean and Reggie's reconciliation is predictable from their first confrontation. Their discussion, in the chapel, is a devastating scene. Reggie, profoundly hurt, fights against himself to repel a woman he still loves as fondly as the first day he saw her. Jean, guilty and heartbroken, abandons her pride to beg for his forgiveness and bursts into tears. As a perfect gentleman, Reggie lends her his handkerchief and that insignificant gesture is in fact the true catalyst for the renewed romance. Smelling a fragrance of Cologne that she used to know so well, Jean suddenly realises that she has never stopped loving Reggie. The next scene shows them having a walk on the estate, exchanging languorous looks on a bench and listening to a serenade. Quite humorously, their final engagement is foreshadowed by the bucolic romp of Angelique and the young gardener. 'We weren't doing anything!' the boy protests. 'Neither were we,' Jean mischievously replies, probably with some naughty intentions in mind. In the same way, the invitation to dinner – the purpose of which was to persuade Jean to sing the quartet from *Rigoletto* – would be a date if Cissy and Wilf were not present. Jean amorously gazes at Reggie who does not really know how to react. The last scene, the gala, corresponds to the denouement of the love story. At Dustin Hoffman's request, the costume designer replaced the Renaissance costumes that should have been used for the finale with evening outfits. The dressing scene was a very funny moment in the play, but it went against the romantic ending that the director wanted for his film. Thanks to Wilf's meddling, the two lovebirds admit they still love each other and Reggie, a few seconds before entering the stage, proposes to a delighted Jean, who accepts – in typical Maggie Smith mode – his proposal: 'Were you serious?' Many have blamed Hoffman for having cut in the editing room the finale which showed the quartet singing,[657] but he replaced it with a subtler shot of a delicate eroticism. A visually beautiful close-up on Jean and Reggie's entwined fingers suffices to metaphorically suggest an intimacy which has nothing indecent or grotesque about it. Reggie is a handsome and still vigorous man, and Jean has little in common with the decrepit diva in the play who struggled to walk and staggered on the stage when singing. She is an ageing – but not aged – woman of breathtaking beauty. For the first time after a long interval (*My House in Umbria* was released in 2003), it was refreshing to see Maggie Smith playing a woman who is younger, very attractive and even sexually desirable. It is quite a rarity for her to portray characters who are romantically involved. According to the production notes, the actress was very pleased with that role: 'It's very rarely that you get an even faintly romantic story for elderly people, and we are all creaking around but it was great to do.'[658] Maybe no one would be bold enough to submit to her such a script, but – the same could be said about Judi Dench – Maggie Smith could still be convincing and touching in a love story. Her range easily extends to that. On stage, Dench has recently played quite a dashing Titania and Vanessa Redgrave a more controversial Beatrice; Smith would still be able, if she wanted to, to play one of Shakespeare's greatest heroines. Of course, such a suggestion sounds merely odd to anyone who has only the Dowager in mind, but her performance as Jean Horton allows us to imagine the actress as a resplendent shakespearean lover in an age-blind production, not to say a mature Millamant. She has played the role in her late forties, she

657 It is a shame, but it is also quite understandable. Despite their talent and an intensive training before the shooting with a vocal coach (see J. Utichi, 'Old hands still on song', *The Sunday Times Culture*, 23 December 2012, p. 15), the four leading actors are not opera singers.

658 *Quartet* pressfile, p. 10.

could play it now. Jean Horton's character is the brightest proof that Smith still can play a woman in love or a love interest, what would have been inconceivable for an actress of the same age thirty years ago.

From that point of view, Hoffman and his director of photography, John De Borman, seem to have – aesthetically speaking – fallen in love with the actress they were filming, every shot emphasising her mature beauty.[659] Rarely had Smith been so magnificently photographed on screen. She was certainly glad to portray, for once, a gorgeous lady, if only to remind the general public she was definitely not a centenarian lingering in nonagenarian roles. Too often pigeonholed in old crone parts, she appears, when escaping her type, outstandingly gorgeous and charming. The lovely scene when Jean is checking the mirror produces an effect that is quite the opposite of the one expected. It can be assumed that the character was supposed to lament, when contemplating her reflection in the mirror, in the way Ronsard's heroines mourn their lost beauty; in fact, the ageing woman is still stunning and probably aware of it. Unlike Muriel Donnelly, Smith's character in *The Best Exotic Marigold Hotel*, who sometimes looks like a tomboy, Jean Horton radiates an exquisite femininity and she is by far, across all generations, the prettiest girl at Beecham House. When she makes an appearance, at breakfast time and starts shouting at her friends, the harridan has the marmoreal complexion of a Madonna. The most stunning shot of Jean Horton is undeniably that of the final music rehearsal, in the chapel. Jean sits in silence, while the string quartet plays *Rigoletto*'s 'Bella figlia dell'amore'. In her mind, the vocal part is superimposed on the music and the camera lingers on the actress's sad and magnificent face. No one else than Smith would have been able to express the vulnerability and the contradictions – the pain and the anger – of Jean Horton. Even if the character makes the viewers laugh thanks to her diva demeanour, emotion wins and we feel sorry each time she bursts into tears. Therefore, Jean represents a kind of synthesis of Maggie Smith's acting abilities. This is a leading role, which

659 P. Travers, 'Quartet', *Rolling Stone*, 31 January 2013, p. 69; the critic hailed Dame Maggie's magnificent performance in the role of an imperious and witty diva. But mostly, he praised the talent of the cinematographer J. De Borman which magnificently highlights the actress's 'timeless beauty'. In the audio-commentary, Hoffman describes the actress as 'a stunning woman', one of those few who 'get more spectacular looking the older they get.'

appears to be the exact opposite of her usual type and implies comical aspects and emotional depth. Jean Horton is as beautiful and attractive as Elizabeth, the Lady from Dubuque, was. She is as haughty and acerbic as *Gosford Park*'s dowager, Constance Trentham, was. She is as desperate and vulnerable as Mary Gilbert was, in Poliakoff's *Capturing Mary*. The ending corresponds to the apotheosis of Jean's renaissance. Radiant and now more imperial than imperious, Miss Horton is the uncontested star of the gala and she makes the most spectacular entrance. Watching the movie, we may wonder if the spectators gathered in Beecham House's Great Hall give an ovation to the soprano Jean Horton, or to the actress who plays her. It is both intriguing and devastatingly moving. Dustin Hoffman was certainly aware of that ambiguity which served his intention. *Quartet* can undoubtedly be seen as a poignant tribute to Smith's beauty and talent. Harwood's play was all about a quartet. Hoffman's movie turns to be – with no offence to the rest of the cast – the most devastating aria.

Conclusion

At some point, this book has to be brought to an end. With N. Hytner's *The Lady in The Van*, Maggie Smith is at the peak of her career. Or, it is to be hoped, at a *temporary* peak. For decades, she has undoubtedly been ranked among the greatest actresses in the world and her professional merits are acknowledged by all. However, as surprising as it may seem, Smith still improves her craft over time. Her career has followed an uninterrupted crescendo since the early 1990s, and it has even taken another turn in the 2000s. Not to mention the worldwide success of *Harry Potter* and *Downton Abbey*, with her breathtaking performances in *Gosford Park*, *My House in Umbria*, *Ladies in Lavender* or *Quartet*, she has reached the pinnacle of her talent. She has never been that moving. She has never displayed such amazing skills. She is an unclassifiable, incomparable actress who belongs to the most glorious British acting tradition, but, at the same time, has gone far beyond the limits reached by her predecessors. She renews the classical literary roles and often gives a definitive rendition of them, but she also sets herself apart by her very particular career path. At her age, unlike the actresses of the previous generations, she cannot be cast as a grotesque character. Her sense of wit, her physical appearance and, most of all, her vulnerable side do not permit it. When she is ridiculous, she is essentially pathetic and, therefore, deeply moving. She breaks our hearts instead of provoking laughs. She is arguably one of the actresses of our time who are the most able to express vulnerability and despair.

In one of his numerous essays, the theatre theorist Edward Gordon Craig compared the gradual development of an actor's talent with the concentric rings which appear when a tree trunk has been sawn. Its cross section shows thirty, forty or sixty annual rings, each ring corresponding to the growth of the tree in one year. For Craig, the older an actor gets, the greater his talent become, just like the tree rings increase in number.[660] Such an image reflects quite accurately Smith's painstaking dedication to her art. Some critics or journalists reproach her for always playing the same role and giving the same performance. It is untrue and unjustified, but it cannot be denied that there are affinities and resonances between several of her parts. *Death on the Nile* (1979) and *A Room with a View* (1985) announced her future spinster roles, and *Travels with my Aunt* (1973), eighteen years before Spielberg's *Hook*, foreshadowed a long and successful career of very old lady on the big screen. But, above all, many of the parts that the actress has recently played represent new incarnations of characters whom she portrayed years ago – not bland and sterile lookalikes, but elaborate, developed and artistically chiselled figures. Every new performance gets nourished, not by the personal experience of the woman she is, but rather by her previous work, when she played similar parts. Like several actors of her generation, Maggie Smith is currently at the height of her acting abilities. In an interview, she once said that it was a pity that parts got fewer when actresses were older, because those were much more skilled than they were in their youth; it is most unfortunate that the parts become scarce one day, because it happens, precisely, at a time when the actor gets into grips with the whole process of acting or, at least, has a full mastery of his skills. And then, although he is at the top of his game, there are not many parts left.[661] As the American director Robert Lewis – the founder of the Actors Studio – taught, when you are an artist, it unfailingly takes you a whole lifetime to perfect whatever you are trying to achieve, and you always die too young. [662] Blessed with immense talent, boundless energy, Smith never stops surpassing herself and bettering her skills. Recently interviewed about working with her in *The Lady in the Van*, Alex Jennings simply acknowledged: 'I think she's the greatest we've got really. I think the range of the works that Maggie can do and has done and can still do and

660 E. Gordon Craig, *Le Théâtre en marche* (Paris: Gallimard, 1964), p. 242. This book is an augmented edition of *The Theatre Advancing* (1919), translated in French.

661 Isenberg, 'The Many Reflections of Maggie Smith'. See also D. Lister, 'Theatre's trap for a Dame in her prime', *The Independent*, 6 March 1993, p. 3.

662 *Method – or Madness?* (London-Melbourne-Toronto: Heinemann, 1960), p. 54.

will do is extraordinary. She can sing, she hasn't done enough singing in her career, she should've done more musicals in my book. I mean, you know, a fantastic, fantastic body of work.'[663]

Throughout the years, Maggie Smith has become a master in the art of giving self-deprecating interviews. Nothing but pessimistic prospects and depressing considerations about her work and her (in)ability to do it, all things that – thankfully – her actual zeal denies. To extend the floral metaphor already used by M. Coveney in his updated biography of the actress when he evokes – more or less tactfully – the 'last phase, or late flowering of "Maggiepanthus Smithsoniensis"'[664], Maggie Smith could be accurately identified with a rose. The petals have harmoniously opened one by one over time and it has taken decades for the promising rosebud to become a perfect rose. Everything was there since the beginning, but the passing of the years has allowed it to grow, then to magnificently blossom. The Smith rose is now in full bloom, and her age is completely irrelevant. 'Perfect flower is nearly old,' as Israel Horovitz smartly wrote in *My Old lady*. In December 2014, a couple of weeks ahead of her birthday, the actress attended the Sun Military Awards ceremony in London. Stylishly dressed in a multicoloured jacket and black trousers which emphasised her elegant figure, she looked stunning. The late Dame Edith Evans would have certainly been irritated seeing 'the little Smith girl' looking so youthful and pretty at an age when she herself looked like a dignified old lady. In fact, Maggie Smith's attractive, very malleable appearance allows her to play a vast range of parts. She can play as convincingly the most decrepit centenarian as well as a glamorous sixty-something woman in love. She is remarkably, naturally beautiful, but her aristocratic beauty – that time does not seem to wither – allows her any transformation, as if it had been created to equitably serve Thalia and Melpomene. With the bearing of a queen and the comic genius of a clown, Smith still can play almost anything, even if some filmmakers, lacking imagination, prefer to cast her as a stock character. The immensity of her talent should not be assessed by reference to her ability to play Janet Widdington or the

---

663 Alex Jennings interviewed about *The Lady in the Van* for Sony Pictures Classic, see <http://www.ramascreen.com/interview-alex-jennings-talks-to-me-about-maggie-smith-and-the-lady-in-the-van/> [accessed 12 November 2016].

664 *Maggie Smith. A Biography*, p. 273.

Lady from Dubuque, but rather with regard to the fact that she is able to portray the two of them. By comparing a picture of Jean Horton with one of Miss Shepherd, it goes without saying that there is a considerable gap between them, with enough room for the actress's huge talent. She is not a former beauty reconverted into old crones. She can be *both*, alternatively. This kind of versatility is theoretically impossible. In practice, with Miss Smith, that is the fact. She has reached the utmost, absolute versatility. She can play characters which are not compatible.

Of course, this study might be blamed for its lack of objectivity, but objectivity has certainly never been, at any time, the guiding principle of these reflections. The arid, rigorous, precise objectivity highly required in scientific studies seems out of place in artistic matters that only enthusiasm, instinct and passion can nurture. It is a boundless admiration for Smith's work and masterful technique that has initiated and inspired this book. May the author be forgiven for having been, throughout these pages, admiring. In *Quartet*, D. Hoffman gave the actress a beautiful quote from Rainer M. Rilke's *Letters to a young poet* to read aloud: 'Works of art are of an infinite loneliness and nothing can reach them so little as can criticism. Only love can grasp them and keep hold of them and be just to them.'[665] Maggie Smith has already won innumerable awards. These days, it is certain that she has nothing left to prove. She works for the enjoyment she gets, as a performer, from portraying new characters and also for the pleasure she gives to the audience. At this point, it is not about judging or criticising her performances, the quality of which is, not only professionally, but unanimously, hailed. Let's grasp and keep hold of her work with the thankful, loving admiration it deserves.

Exactly nine years after *The Lady from Dubuque*'s closing night, Maggie Smith trod the boards again at the Theatre Royal Haymarket, her favourite venue in the West End, for a special charity gala.[666] Her appearance was short, but long enough to allow her to have the house in stitches. Having made a much applauded entrance, she performed an ample, intriguing but graceful gesture in Lettice Douffet mode and started to declaim a Shakespearean speech at the utmost speed, with that characteristic high-pitched, girlish

665 *Letters to a young poet*, 23 April 1903.

666 *A Right Royal Knees Up*, organised by the Royal Theatrical Fund in honour of Her Majesty the Queen's 90th birthday, Theatre Royal Haymarket, 5 June 2016.

voice she obviously still possesses – but rarely uses these days, when playing Mathilde Girard and other nonagenarians. Unfortunately, the grandiloquent thespian was quickly, too quickly, hooked from the wings and pulled off the stage by a redoubtable hooded Grim Reaper (who was revealed to be Derek Jacobi), despite her fierce resistance and the vehement protests of the audience. Twice she reappeared, for another short sketch where she took revenge on Jacobi and also for the finale, all the cast dancing and joyously singing along. Majestic and impressively beautiful, but still devastatingly funny, the actress was magnificent and divine. Waiting backstage at the Haymarket may have struck a chord with her and, whether intentionally or not, the actress brilliantly demonstrated not only that the 'acting machine' – as Simon Callow called it – is in perfect working order,[667] but also that she still is the West End's most glittering star. But better was still to come. A few months later, taking part in the *Peter Shaffer Memorial Gala* at the National Theatre,[668] Maggie Smith performed a large excerpt from the opening act of *Lettice and Lovage*, recreating one of her most famous stage roles, the role that the playwright had written as a tribute to her comedic skills. Callow himself, standing a few steps behind, was looking at Smith in full action, waving and extending her arms, wringing her wrists and marvellously delivering the funniest lines ever written by Shaffer – the epic scene when Lettice enthusiastically describes the perilous stairs of Fustian House. She had the script at hand, but barely looked at it, knowing by heart a part that she played for so long and still plays so well. A quarter of a century after the Broadway production, the actress proved that she was highly deserving of Shaffer's gift and her sparkling rendition of Lettice Douffet, forever unsurpassable.

Smith is currently at the top of her game. Be sure she can go higher.

---

667 Just before she returned to the London stage to play *The Lady from Dubuque*, in March 2007, director A. Page affirmed that Smith's instincts were 'just as sharp, if not sharper, than they ever were.' (C. Fox, 'Grande Dame of the old bags', *The Daily Telegraph*, 19 March 2007, p. 29).

668 *Peter Schaffer Memorial Gala*, National Theatre, 30 March 2017.

Epilogue – Up there with God. An Apotheosis, possibly

In December 1999, while *The Lady in the Van* was having a successful run at the Queen's,[669] Alan Bennett wrote in his diary that there were lines he had forgotten to include, especially a striking tableau, depicting Miss Shepherd standing next to her van on the barren hills of the South Downs, and fiercely gazing across the Channel like 'a figure from a Shell poster' of old times. [670] This poetic vision needed more than fifteen years to materialise but, eventually,

669 A. Bennett and N. Hytner had to present the play in the West End because of Smith's 'aversion' to the Southbank building (Rosenthal, *The National Theatre History*, p. 722). The play would run successfully until June 2000, Smith having never missed a show.

670 Bennett, *Untold Stories*, p. 260.

in 2015, the film version of Miss Shepherd's adventures came to our screens, renewing once again the fruitful collaboration of Hytner and Bennett. And, of course, Maggie Smith was to be at the wheel. As early as 2000, just after the closing of the play in the West End, a movie had already been envisaged, as the critic Matt Wolf reported in *The Times*. At that time, it seemed unthinkable that another actress could play the part on screen; according to Hytner, no one could play it better than Smith.[671] Precisely. In fact, when R. Fox had attempted to extend the triumphal run of the play, he realised that Smith simply cannot be replaced in that role.[672] Not surprisingly, now that the movie has been made, it asserts itself as one of the very best performances that the actress has ever given. According to *Variety*, Miss Shepherd was one of the most tailor-made leading roles of her career and the movie could be viewed as 'The Maggie Smith Show',[673] while the critic from *The Telegraph* celebrated an exceptional achievement, comparing the role to a miraculous gift bestowed upon Smith and acknowledging that, in return, she rewarded the audience with 'the Maggiest of Maggie Smith performances' she had given of late.[674] In

---

671 'Hollywood diary', *The Times*, 13 July 2000, p. 21. A. Bennett started to write a first draft the following year (see M. Wolf, 'Van in working order', *Variety*, 2 April 2001, p. 33), at the same time as R. Fox was planning to bring the West End play to Broadway, with the author himself as Bennett-the-writer. Unfortunately, the project never came to fruition and, in 2002, instead of reprising *The Lady in the Van* in New York, Maggie Smith starred in Hare's *The Breath of Life* at the Haymarket.

672 N. Reynolds, 'Cinema may be the next stop for Bennett's *The Lady in the Van*', *The Daily Telegraph*, 27 May 2000, p. 22; Fox considered replacing Smith (who had already agreed to extend her six-month run to nine), but he realised that the task was impossible, as it appeared that the actress was 'irreplaceable'.

673 G. Lodge, 'Toronto Film Review: "The Lady in the Van"', *Variety*, 12 September 2015 <http://variety.com/2015/film/reviews/toronto-film-review-the-lady-in-the-van-1201581616/> [accessed 12 November 2016].

674 T. Robey, 'Maggie's smelly perfection', *The Telegraph*, 14 September 2015, p. 27. See also B. Grant, 'The Lady in The Van. The Dame gives this lady in van-tastic portrayal', *The Jewish Chronicle*, 13 November 2015, p. 45; in this enthusiastic notice, Grant explained that the film was, undoubtedly, Smith's triumph. It proved, if necessary, the incomparable, extraordinary genius of an actress who, after such a performance, would deserve, as the critic suggested, to be made a 'double Dame'. However, as N. Hytner explained, Smith was very careful not to overplay the part on screen. See J. Llewellyn Smith, 'The truth about directing Maggie Smith', *The Telegraph*, 12 November 2015, p. 37; in the interview, Hytner recounted that Smith had made a point, before they started filming, of asking that he hold her back from being 'too demonstrative' on screen. Having played the part on stage for so long, she was worrying about giving a too theatrical rendition of it.

fact, it is simply the kind of performance that can be expected when someone gives a sublime actress a part which is worthy of her prodigious talent. The movie format allowed an opening of the space and made it possible to insert several outbreaks on the seaside. Writing his screenplay in collaboration with Hytner, Bennett eventually got Miss Shepherd to drive across Sussex and to contemplate the sea from Broadstairs beach. Whether she looks like a figure from a Shell poster or not – the lady voraciously eats fish and chips out of greasy newspaper –, it does not really matter, but at least, finally, Alan Bennett's vision has come true.

Almost everything that was in the play has been maintained and even focused on in the movie. The viewers get to visualise facts or events that were just mentioned and, apart from a few exceptions, all the funniest scenes are there. The dirt and its corollary, the smell, the two most prominent characteristics of the titular lady, are omnipresent but come by small touches, so that the movie never falls into sordidness or scatology.[675] Still, Miss Shepherd's odoriferous trademark, impalpable but persistent, pervades the whole story, to the point that even the church minister has to provide against the smelliest of his parishioners. 'There is air-freshener behind the Virgin,' he helpfully informs anyone who enters the confessional after her. Miss Shepherd has as much bad faith as she had in the play. When Alan Bennett offers her the chance to park in his driveway, she opens large innocent eyes and feigns surprise. She haughtily declines to use the public toilet facilities as 'they smell' and spurns with high contempt the sweets and treats that the generous residents of the Crescent give her. No, Mary Shepherd has no gratitude for anyone and she never says a thank you. She even looks half incredulous, half offended at the kind neighbour who has just offered her a helping hand to open a jar of marmalade. Despite the squalor surrounding her, the tramp lady affects the same contemptuous air as Constance Trentham does every time her chambermaid helps her to open her Thermos bottle. Her delusions of grandeur have no limits, and the movie adaptation illustrates, quite spectacularly, Miss Shepherd's incredible pride and patrician hauteur. Towards the end of the film, an ambulance comes

675 To complete the Shepherd's 'panoply', the typical sanitary towels are hanging there, but the viewer will see them only if he looks for them. Even the most disgusting details are subtly displayed.

to take the old woman to the Day Centre and this rather prosaic scene unexpectedly presents a first kind of ascension (before the proper, final one which crowns a life of Catholic religiousness). The ambulance hoist pulls up the wheelchair where a regal Shepherd – beaming and proudly holding her two canes which look like sceptres or Hand of Justice sticks in her dirty fists – reminds us a bit of Queen Victoria on Sir George Hayter's painting. In his diary, A. Bennett admits that, in her own way, the lady had some kind of distinction when she left for the Day Centre, and her grimy face expressed that 'resigned satisfaction' Maggie Smith has so well captured in the film.[676] The playwright eventually made that clear in the script, Miss Shepherd asking if they could do it again, as she would like 'another go'! American critics probably expected a linear biopic, following the usual outline of any screenplay. Bennett's work, put into images by Hytner, is much deeper and more original than that. The final Ascension – replacing, thanks to cinematic special effects, the ascension of the van at the end of the play – is nothing but a clever, hilarious staging, in Monty Python mode, of Titian's *Assumption of the Virgin* which decorates the hall of the convent. Traumatised by the crash in which she was involved many years earlier, the lady is nevertheless a thrill seeker. We get to see, on a full scale, Bennett pushing the wheelchair up the Crescent and Miss Shepherd rolling down, her carpet-slippered feet raised up, with the most jubilant smile. Maybe less spectacular, but as much comical, the painting of the van is another moment of exception, the lady enthusiastically splashing the van with a mix of yellow paint – 'crushed-mimosa', as Bennett describes it – and Madeira cake crumbs. In all of these scenes, whatever the frame, whatever the setting, everything shows and happens on Maggie Smith's face. Unlike the stage, the camera permits close-ups which emphasise the actress's brilliant acting. She cleverly makes use of every muscle of her face and her huge, expressive eyes say more than any sentence would do.[677]

Every inclination to have compassion for the indigent old lady is thankfully tempered by her irascibility and confident authority. The story

676 Bennett, *Writing Home*, p. 115.

677 M. Wolf, '*The Lady in the Van*. Maggie Smith reprises a celebrated stage role, this time for keeps', *The Arts Desk*, 13 November 2015 <http://www.theartsdesk.com/film/lady-van> [accessed 12 November 2016]

never gets sentimental and when the audience begins to feel sorry for her, she delivers one of her cheeky, brutal one-liners. In *The Independent*, G. Macnab aptly highlighted the depth and range of emotions displayed by Smith, who conveys, not only a sense of guilt and anguish, but a 'Mother Courage-like' perseverance. The character she plays may be highly dislikeable, but the spectators cannot help admiring her and, paradoxically, seeing this repellent creature as a 'tragic heroine'.[678] As N. Hytner commented, Smith is able to do a lot with very few words or very limited gestures and, in fact, it is in the smallest details that her portraying is the most touching.[679] When Miss Shepherd drives her newly yellow-painted Reliant to Broadstairs, what is supposed to be a succession of very funny scenes turns to be as emotional as comical. She walks on the beach, eats fish and chips, enters an ice cream parlour to buy herself a copious sundae – which Lady Hester, in *Tea with Mussolini*, would certainly not approve of! – and finally rides a roundabout, rubbing shoulders with a couple of young kids who do not seem impressed at all. That last scene is priceless and the old tramp, triumphantly sitting side-saddle on a yellow duckie (that she has probably chosen because of its colour), does look as proud as Mary Poppins on the Merry-Go-Round. But behind these funny images, the situation is heartbreaking; Miss Shepherd simply wants to have the same kind of fun that normal people have. Although she has cut herself off from society, she eventually wants, at times, to be part of it. That is probably why she does not hesitate to enter the parish hall to have tea among the other pensioners and, unexpectedly, listen to the music. No way would the real Miss Shepherd have looked that cute and lovable,[680] but it joyously enlightens the story.

A major difference between the play and the film adaptation is that the latter is angled for giving prominence to Miss Shepherd's backstory, emphasising the fact that her life had been thrown off track by the

---

678 'A brilliant portrayal of a truly odd couple', *The Independent*, 13 November 2015, p. 44.

679 'I know nobody who is able to do more with a brief moment's silence, with a line. When she's given material like Alan Bennett gives her, you see the art of acting at its very height. She's rightly a legend, but she's a legend because she can do so much with so little. She is the most extraordinary actor.' (N. Hytner interviewed at the LFF Gala Premiere, Odeon Leicester Square, 13 October 2015).

680 The costumes help a lot here. Difficult to keep a poker face when we see Maggie Smith wearing that funny knitted hood, or those huge sunglasses with a scarf which makes her oddly resemble Mrs Thatcher whom she simultaneously watches on television.

crash she was involved in. Already known as a difficult and somewhat mentally disturbed person, she would be forever obsessed with her guilt. In the film, that event – it corresponds to the prologue which precedes the opening credits – is presented as the turning point in her life. A devout Catholic, Miss Shepherd turns into a disturbingly tormented soul, forever overwhelmed with guilt which shows in her very expressive way of praying. She prostrates herself frenetically, while loudly imploring God for mercy. This aspect was already present in the play, but here, the fact does not appear like a strange ritual, celebrated by a batty old woman, but like the paroxystic expression of her guilt and fear.[681] Unlike the play, the movie develops an aetiology of Miss Shepherd's uncommon behaviour which puts the spectator in a position to measure her social and physical decline – how a smart, accomplished young lady turns into a tramp – as well as to imagine what her life could have been if that traumatic event had not happened. In a radio interview, Smith confessed that she had often wondered, when preparing the role, if Miss Shepherd had sometimes thought about her backstory – the great gift she had and her wasted life – when she was alone in her van,[682] explaining why her performance is devastatingly imbued with this sadness. This idea of a tragic fate underpins the character study and transforms a very funny play into a hilarious, entertaining, but essentially poignant movie.[683]

It has been tempting, at different times in this book, to compare Maggie Smith's career path with that of Edith Evans, in order to stress, not the similarities, but mostly the differences between the two great thespians. Once again, it is of interest to draw a parallel between *The Lady in the Van* and a remarkable – although long-forgotten – movie

681 P. Bradshaw, 'Maggie Smith as the muse in the driveway', *The Guardian G2*, 13 November 2015, p. 19. In a very positive review, Bradshaw lauded a 'terrifically good' performance by Maggie Smith, particularly emphasising the excruciating sense of guilt that the actress brings out in her portrayal.

682 Radio-interview by D. Davies for NPR, 23 February 2016.

683 S. Papamichael, '*The Lady in the Van*: "Maggie Smith is wicked fun to watch"', *Radio Times*, 12 November 2015 < http://www.radiotimes.com/news/2015-11-12/the-lady-in-the-van-maggie-smith-is-wicked-fun-to-watch> [accessed 12 November 2016]. The journalist praised Smith's incomparable comic timing and a hilarious performance which never tips into caricature, though underlining the pathetic tone of the story. Through a moving portrayal, the actress perfectly brings out the traumas of a vulnerable, disturbed mind.

which starred Dame Edith in a similar role. Adapted from a novel by Robert Nicolson and directed by Bryan Forbes, *The Whisperers* (1967) tells the painful story of Margaret Ross (Evans), an impoverished elderly lady who lives in a desolate area in the North of England.[684] Having been abandoned by her husband many years earlier, she barely subsists on a meagre allowance that she receives through National Assistance and regularly goes to the reading room of the local library to keep her feet warm. Mrs Ross's lonely existence is suddenly disrupted after she finds a parcel of stolen money that her son has hidden in her apartment. Instead of returning to a decent living, she gets kidnapped and robbed by a stranger, catches pneumonia and loses her mind, before being reunited with her unscrupulous husband, who, soon after, abandons her for the second time; at the end, the poor woman resumes her reclusive routine. The two stories have in fact much in common. Like Miss Shepherd, Mrs Ross is a disturbed mind, an old woman who suffers from hallucinations – she imagines that her neighbours are continually spying on her through her wireless radio or whispering to her through the kitchen pipes – and delusions of grandeur – she adds the acronym DBE to her signature, having persuaded herself that she is the daughter of a rich bishop. Her hygiene is not that better than Mary Shepherd's; she wears dirty worn clothes and her flat, cluttered with garbage and old newspapers, is not much cleaner than the derelict van parked in Bennett's driveway. As Margaret Ross, Edith Evans gives the most powerful and restrained performance ever. Her impersonation is so compelling – especially in the way she eats a slice of bread – that, at times, it becomes unbearable to witness Mrs Ross's misfortune.[685] While Smith's Shepherd is an irascible and determined harridan who argues with everyone she meets, Mrs Ross lives as a recluse, in total loneliness, and she hardly speaks, only muttering to herself. While Shepherd is a bundle of nerves, jumping in and out her van or shouting loudly at (musical) people, Ross has the slowness and the frailty of old age. This

684 Originally set in Glasgow, the movie was shot in the suburbs of Manchester, at a time when whole areas of the city were being destroyed by bulldozers to make room for concrete high-rise buildings.

685 As B. Forbes said in an interview, explaining what Edith Evans's supposed method was: 'Her method is that she is simply a great actress.' See Forbes, *Dame Edith Evans*, p. 257.

is arguably one of Evans's best portrayals and she gave a masterclass in characterisation, amply deserving all the awards she got for it.[686]

When Dame Edith portrayed Mrs Ross, she was both a dignified elderly lady and one of the two most revered British actresses of the time, along with Sybil Thorndike.[687] Her main transformation for the part was to become, on screen, an indigent and uneducated woman.[688] Likewise, for Maggie Smith, who has now accumulated on her person all the honours which Evans had been previously gratified with, and who is well-established as one of the finest and most famous actresses in the world, becoming Miss Shepherd is also a changing of social class. From that point of view, *The Lady in the Van* allows Smith to elegantly thumb her nose at those who constantly accuse her of being typecast; Shepherd is the most perfect antithesis of Violet Crawley. But here, Smith's characterisation works on two levels. She transforms herself twice, going through social *and* physical change. Not only has she to become a repulsive vagrant woman, but she also has to age for the role. These days, Maggie Smith is even older than Miss Shepherd was at the end of her life, but as Hytner said, Miss Shepherd was no 'spring chicken'; he also admitted that Smith was perfectly convincing in 1999 but, fifteen years later, she had more to bring to the part – in terms of age but also, certainly, in terms of technical experience.[689] Nevertheless, the actress still has to 'age' when she plays Mary Shepherd at sixty. Time has passed since the stage production, but Smith does not resemble Miss Shepherd more these days and, fifteen years later, her characterisation

686 Not only was Evans nominated for the Academy Award for Best actress, but she received the Silver Bear for Best Actress Award at the 1967 Berlin Film Festival, the BAFTA Award, the National Board of Review Award, the New York Film Critics Circle Award, and the Golden Globe Award, all for Best Actress. Maggie Smith, for her part, was overlooked by the Academy in 2016, just like she unjustly had been in 1988 (*The Lonely Passion of Judith Hearne*). *The Lady in the Van* was probably too British a film to completely satisfy the US voters, but Smith's performance was an incomparable, mesmerising work of characterisation which would have certainly been honoured in other times.

687 Coincidentally, Sybil Thorndike's last stage role was that of an old vagrant revisiting her past, in J. Graham's *There Was An Old Woman* (Leatherhead, Thorndike Theatre, 1969).

688 Forbes, *Dame Edith Evans*, p. 257: 'She wore no make-up other than a little powder, she was dressed in the old clothes and was the Mrs Ross of my imagination come to life.'

689 N. Curtis, 'Nicholas Hytner interview: "My luckiest break is that I am Alan Bennett's director of choice. I respond strongly to the way he writes"', *The Evening Standard*, 5 November 2015, p. 42.

was still a challenge. Not only do people sleeping rough or living in the street age quickly, but also, thirty or even twenty years ago, a woman of the age Maggie Smith is today would have looked much older. Receiving her Evening Standard Film Award for Best actress in February 2016, she vehemently claimed that 'there wasn't a blade of prosthetics', a deadpan joke which had the audience in stitches. The make-up department had certainly not used the kind of prosthetics the actress wore for *Travels with my Aunt* or *Hook*, but the combination of false dirt, make-up and highly-skilled facial expressiveness could easily compensate. In the movie, Miss Shepherd's ageing process covers not only the fifteen years she stayed in Alan's garden, but much more in fact.

The very first sequence of the movie takes the form of a flashback, which is followed by a cut to Gloucester Crescent 23, sixteen years later. According to the screenplay, the opening scene – in fact the tragic accident that would be the turning point in her life and lead her to marginality – takes place in 1960. Miss Shepherd died at seventy-eight, in 1989; she was nearly sixty when Alan Bennett had the luck (or the misfortune) to cross her path for the very first time, in 1969. So, when she appears for the first time on the screen, Mary Shepherd is only in her late forties. This is not a problem for our chameleon actress who is, as everyone knows, slightly older. With brown hair carefully tied in a neat bun, Maggie Smith wears a strict grey flannel skirt suit, an immaculate corsage and a cute matching toque. Mary Shepherd has nothing of a glamorous lady, but with her blue eyes, her pale complexion and her delicate features, she has the same kind of fragile beauty that Judith Hearne had in J. Clayton's movie. Besides, if her mousy appearance reminds us of Miss Hearne's, middle-aged Shepherd also resembles, thanks to her austere elegance and her dated outfit, to a less sophisticated Mabel Pettigrew. Yet, while Muriel Spark's venomous character certainly would have had enough sanity and self-composure to keep calm and hide from the police, Mary Shepherd, overcome with guilt, is caught in a downward spiral. We just catch a glimpse of a forty-nine-year-old Shepherd when she disappears to give place to the sexagenarian, the lady with a van whom Bennett met one day in the late 1960s, near Albany Street. More than fifteen years have passed (we are now in 1976), and time has not been kind to her. Prematurely aged because of her particular way of life since the accident and dressed in filthy rags, Miss Shepherd is unrecognisable. Only her grey van allows the spectator to identify her. Long greasy grey hair has replaced her immaculate bun, and nothing of her former elegance remains in her shapeless figure wrapped in layers of dirty clothes. Maggie Smith excels in portraying the physical decline of a woman that life's events have permanently damaged. However, although the most sedentary of the vagrants stayed fifteen years in Alan Bennett's vicinity, the ageing process is difficult to perceive on screen for the reason that the lady already looks quite old at sixty – except that she gets dirtier and dirtier as time goes by. Very subtly, though, Miss Shepherd ages; quite nervous and quick at the beginning, she gradually become slower, even if the canes and the wheelchair she proudly uses are more an element of decorum – to manipulate people and make them pity her – than a medical equipment that is needed. Usually renowned for her majestic bearing, Smith adopts the character's typical, curved posture in the wheelchair – the comparison with real pictures is breathtaking – and, through her portrayal, the actress truly resurrects Miss Shepherd. Her face does not properly wrinkle, but gradually sags as if it was made of modelling clay or rubber. Just as she did on the stage, the actress masters once more, and without any great help of make-up, the art of transforming her face by distorting it. The very angular Maggie Smith manages brilliantly to transform her sharp and delicate features into this flabby batrachian mask.[690] Still, Miss Shepherd was a more caricatural, stylised character on the stage than she is in the movie. Not only was Smith's stage make-up heavier (her cinematic make-up looks more natural), but the character was, rather than a human being, a fascinating creature who – like the living organisms which, according to the 'spontaneous generation' theory developed by Aristotle, arose spontaneously in decaying flesh, rotten garbage or mud – seemed to arise from a pile of dirty rags, just in front of the audience. In his stage directions for his play, Alan Bennett mentions, stage left, a bundle of dirty rags from which, progressively, the lady emerges before getting on her

690 See C. Shoard, 'Dialogue and dame shine on Bennett's driveway', *The Guardian*, 14 September 2015, p. 15. The critic wrote a glowing review, celebrating Smith's exceptional ability to simultaneously provoke tears and laughs in the same performance. She also compared Miss Shepherd's 'gummy' face to that of a fierce 'tortoise', full of anger and determination.

feet.[691] That stylised character gets humanised in the film, becoming much more lovable and anchored in reality.

Yet, the character keeps its typical shapeless, androgynous appearance – which protects her like an armour – throughout the whole movie, except in the very last minutes. When she ultimately arrives at the Day Centre to be given a bath, clean clothes and good food, the van's creature becomes a woman again. An old woman, a frail and white-haired woman, but a woman. The editing itself is contrasting and shocking. In the first scene, we see Miss Shepherd in her wheelchair entering a bathroom; the sight is heartbreaking, almost embarrassing. The viewer comfortably seated in front of the screen, realises that it is a predominantly *true* story. Her face and her clothes are maculated with dirt, her long unwashed hair looks like greasy dreadlocks and her legs are enfolded in layers of very filthy socks.[692] What is amazing is that one sense arouses another here. Through imagination, the sight immediately suggests the stench. Just like she did on the stage, Smith literally *smells* on screen,[693] but this time, we are not supposed to laugh. She certainly stinks, but she breaks our hearts. Taking no notice, the young nurse begins to undress the old woman. Quite charitably, the camera spares us of what follows, but promptly cuts to a more astonishing scene. A slender elderly woman, wearing a bathrobe, walks slowly in the corridor, helped by the same nurse. This is a clean Miss Shepherd and it takes you a few seconds to recognise her, as her hair wrapped in a towel (a favourite headgear for Maggie Smith in movies) reminds us more of Jean Brodie, Diana Barrie or Emily Delahunty than of the pitiful creature we saw in the previous scene. This contrast between the condition of the old woman, whose death is imminent, and her figure, slight and feminine, is as intriguing as it is touching. In his diaries, Bennett wrote that indeed, when Mary

691 *The Lady in the Van*, Act One (London: Faber and Faber, 2000), p. 5.

692 Thinking of the dedication with which an actor like Daniel Day-Lewis prepares for each of his roles, and reading the detailed account that Alan Bennett wrote on Miss Shepherd's personal hygiene, Maggie Smith's relatives, colleagues and close friends should feel very fortunate that she is definitely not a Method actress.

693 J. Solomons, 'Maggie Smith puts in a spirited and fragrant performance as a cantankerous vagrant', *The Lady*, 27 November 2015 <http://www.jasonsolomons.com/the-lady-in-the-van-movie-review/> [accessed 12 November 2016]. In a very funny way, Solomons affirmed that, through Smith's extraordinary performance and immaculate rendition of the role, Miss Shepherd's celebrated 'odoriferous concerto' literally reached, in the cinema, the spectator's nostrils.

Shepherd had come back – washed and dressed in clean clothes – from the Day Centre, the 'fragile beauty' of the old lady had surprised him.[694] It was certainly much easier to suggest that on screen than it was on the stage, and Hytner makes the most of it, beautifully. In the following scene, the nurse gently combs and plaits her long white hair. 'You are MOT,' she kindly says to the elderly woman. For the first time, Miss Shepherd appears vulnerable, touching and feminine. To check her reflection in the mirror, she stretches her neck like a turtle, a cute little turtle now deprived of her protective shell of filth and rags.[695] It is almost disturbing to see her looking so different from her usual – dirty – self, but what is fascinating here is to visualise the *mise en abyme* of the actress's impersonation. Maggie Smith manages to transform herself twice; having become that repulsive and asexual creature that Miss Shepherd is, she eventually turns into a frail, vulnerable and rather beautiful old lady – who nevertheless looks miles away from the elegant and youthful actress who plays the part. Her performance is, physically speaking, a tour de force.

In terms of drama, this is also, arguably, one of the most devastating scenes Smith has ever played. Helping herself with her pair of canes to the lounge of the Day Centre, Miss Shepherd notices a piano and laboriously walks towards it. Slowly, reluctantly, she opens the lid and attempts to play a few notes, hesitates, then starts to play, forcefully, a romantic piece of music. The camera does a close-up on Miss Shepherd's fingers running swiftly over the key notes, which alternates with beautiful shots of her sad, emaciated face.[696] The footage is quite long – too long for some critics who judged it unnecessary – and this poignant, heartbreaking

694 See also, about the 1999 play, Billington, 'Epitome of a hermit'. The critic evoked that beautiful, heartbreaking scene, Maggie Smith's face suggesting the old woman's fragile beauty.

695 It was exactly Nicholas Hytner's own vision of the scene. In a Q&A for US journalists, he explained that Maggie Smith 'shows the turtle pulled out of her shell. She looks happy to see herself cleaned up, but it feels as if she's naked'.

696 See S. Vineberg, 'Tour de Force: Maggie Smith in The Lady in the Van', *Critics at Large*, 28 December 2015 <http://www.criticsatlarge.ca/2015/12/tour-de-force-maggie-smith-in-lady-in.html> [accessed 12 November 2016]. Vineberg brilliantly highlighted the greatness of that scene, when the viewers see Miss Shepherd's hesitation before touching the keys, her 'unsureness' about her ability to play a few notes and then, her 'uncertainty' in her reaction to her own success at playing; Smith's face and expression amazingly display all that.

scene is enough to turn the film comedy into a drama, to the point that it draws tears from viewers. Suddenly, the funny, eccentric, cantankerous Miss Shepherd becomes a character as moving as Judith Hearne or Mary Gilbert were, and then the viewers realise that it is maybe Maggie Smith's greatest ever performance. Ultimately, Mary Shepherd sees that she has wasted her gift and also her life, except that, unlike Hearne or Gilbert, she cannot have any hope for a better future. Clean and freshly confessed, she has got herself ready to meet the Almighty and, of course, the sorrow which fills Smith's blue eyes suffices to express the regret of her whole existence.[697] The intercutting with the following shot, which shows the old woman lying, nearly asleep, in her van, beautifully emphasises the feeling of regret. She realises that it is too late, stops playing the piano and returns home.[698] The piano sequence belongs to those that Alan Bennett himself attributes to his own imagination – he calls them 'departures from the facts' – just like, in the play, he featured Miss Shepherd speaking about the past, although she never actually did. It is quite probably what he would have wished to have happened.[699] Sadly, Miss Shepherd never got to play the piano again (obviously, Camden Day Centre was not Beecham House), but this imaginary scene is supposed to be real in the film.[700] In a soft semi-darkness, the character reveals itself as the most striking figure the actress has ever inhabited on screen and on stage. This white-haired elderly lady (she was only seventy-eight then, but her looks correspond to

697 'Knowing what he now does about Miss Shepherd which he did not know when she was alive, the Miss Shepherd of *The Lady in the Van* is infused with a real sense of regret and of what might have been that Bennett does not claim to have noticed during her lifetime.' (*The Lady in the Van* press file, Sony Classics, p. 8).

698 In his foreword to the *Complete Edition*, N. Hytner praises her ability to stretch her portrayal to suggest that she is playing what actually happened and, at the same time, what Bennett would have wanted to happen. See A. Bennett, *The Lady in the Van. The Complete Edition* (London: Faber and Faber, 2015), p. 6-7. See also T. Gray, 'Directors and Their Troops: Nicholas Hytner on His "Lady in the Van" Artisans', *Variety*, 4 December 2015 <http://variety.com/2015/artisans/news/lady-in-the-van-director-nicholas-hytner-artisans-1201652313/> [accessed 12 November 2016].

699 In the introduction to the play, Bennett writes that he would have liked her concert career to have outlasted the war or to have resumed afterwards (Bennett, *The Lady in the Van*, p. xvi).

700 Although some viewers might see it as an oneiric scene, imagined by Miss Shepherd while she was already asleep in her van. The very subtle intercutting leaves it open to interpretation.

a woman in her mid-nineties by now), dressed in clean clothes, does not even resemble Mary Shepherd. Played by Smith, she has an ethereal grace, a delicate frailty, everything that the lady has definitely not in the rest of the movie.[701] If she was homeless and destitute, no doubt that Maggie Smith would look like the most miserable homeless and destitute person ever, and benevolent people would probably fight for offering her assistance. More than the stage, the cinema and its close-ups bring us closer to Miss Shepherd's vulnerability. It does not enlarge the story, it gives it depth. Emotionally, 'Maggie has stripped herself naked,' Hytner declares in the audio commentary of the film. Only a movie could allow the audience to see, behind Shepherd's filthy armour, the little turtle without her shell.[702] Only Smith, supreme chameleon, was able to make these two antithetic facets of the same character cohabit in one film.

As much as the actress is remarkably able to transform herself into a very frail elderly woman, the role is paradoxically one of the most demanding old lady parts ever. Far from being slow or physically disabled, the ageless Miss Shepherd remains strong and perpetually on the move.[703] She runs to cross the street, she hurries to Alan Bennett's bathroom, she goes after the children playing music and, mostly, she never stops getting in and out of her derelict van. That is the reason why it is an old lady role which could not be played by a very old actress. The performer must be fit enough to climb in the van easily and then pop out of it like a Jack-in-the-box. Not only does Maggie Smith look much younger than her real age, but she also has – despite what she jokingly pretends – huge resources of energy when it comes to playing a part. Everyone on set, from Hytner to Bennett, praised her professionalism and dedication to the role. At the press conference which preceded the premiere, Bennett insisted on the physicality

---

701 Miss Shepherd had certainly not that frailty in reality. Although she became frailer with age and illness, the real Miss Shepherd was robust, very tall ('nearly six foot') and built like a man.

702 This image is particularly revealing. When she has shown, reluctantly, her wrist to allow the doctor to take her pulse, she promptly closes the window. At that moment, the van window looks strangely like the operculum of a whelk or a winkle. She withdraws herself in her van just like a frightened mollusc withdraws itself in its shell. See also S. Holden, 'Homesteading in the Driveway', *The New York Times*, 4 December 2015, p. 11. The critic compares the character to an animal which takes refuge in its den.

703 That can explain, maybe, her great physical resilience despite her way of life.

of the performance, especially in the devotion scenes; having to prostrate herself at the church, in the middle of a crossroads or, worse, inside the van, the actress gave of herself unsparingly and did as many takes as it was needed.[704] For Smith herself, the greatest inconvenience was getting bruised every time she had to climb into the van and having to spend hours in a very constricted and uncomfortable place. It was worse on the stage, because she used the van for her change of costume, but, as she jokes, 'It was a long time ago. I could handle it.' According to N. Hytner, she still handles it brilliantly. In an interview, the producer Kevin Loader also underlined the fact that the shooting began early and finished very late every day, and it took place, during eight weeks, in a very cold and wet Camden. Despite all the difficulties, the enjoyment that the actress takes in playing Miss Shepherd once again, clearly shines out from the screen. Loader thought that the actress's dedication was motivated by the high challenge that this characterisation represented.[705] As much as Hytner and Bennett would not have made the movie without her, Smith really wanted to play Shepherd on screen and thus her commitment was total. In his book, *Balancing Acts*, N. Hytner reveals that the actress even went to the Bodleian Library in Oxford to have a look at Miss Shepherd's papers.[706] After such a long and brilliant career, Smith works as if she still had everything to prove. Her costume and make-up reflect the same concern for accuracy. Her outfits were very professionally 'broken down' and worn out by Angels Costumiers, and her make-up, designed by Naomi Donne, took more than one hour: 'A lot is about putting mud under her fingernails and into her hands, making it look

704 Bennett, *The Lady in The Van. The Complete Edition*, p. 36. Here, A. Bennett explains how the pious Miss Shepherd prostrated herself at church when receiving the host, and how the priest had to bend down to put it in her mouth. When filming that scene, Smith had to prostrate herself too, as many times as required by the takes, 'without complaint or assistance'. On Smith's amazing dedication, see also J. Gerard, 'Q&A: Nicholas Hytner and Alan Bennet On Dame Maggie Smith's 15-Year Squatter', *Deadline*, 8 December 2015 <http://deadline.com/2015/12/nicholas-hytner-alan-bennett-maggie-smith-lady-in-the-van-1201659769/> [accessed 12 November 2016].

705 S. Feinstein, 'Downton Dowager is happy on tramp's pay', *The Sunday Times*, 26 October 2014, p. 4.

706 Hytner, *Balancing Acts*, p. 151. Alan Bennett donated his literary archive to the library in 2008.

like someone living in a rather unconventional place.'[707] As one critic wrote, Hytner managed to film, thanks to Smith's breathtaking incarnation, the 'definitive version of the events' narrated by Bennett.[708] The fact that the movie was shot in the very street and the very house where the events had actually occurred helped a lot, of course, but what was ever more striking is that Bennett confessed in interviews that Mary Shepherd's image had faded from his memory. Now, he can only see her with Maggie Smith's face, what certainly is, in spite of appearances, the greatest compliment ever for an actress who is as gorgeous as proteiform.[709] She has definitively made the role her own.

An indeed, as if perfection still could be improved, her portrayal is even more accomplished than it was on the stage. Maggie Smith, reprising the role for the third time, gives an absolute performance, now preserved for posterity.[710] She transforms herself, ages and even de-ages, has the viewer in stitches and reduces him to tears, and elaborates a multi-layered figure, endearing and insufferable, vulnerable and imperious. If the actress's career was a fireworks display, that piece would be the grand finale, the crowning of a glistening record. But we must hope that it is not. Smith is still full of energy and greedy to put her teeth in new parts. After a magisterial Miss Shepherd, a grumpy dowager and several nonagenarians, it would be fun to see her returning, for a change, to some younger and more glamorous characters, and putting at use again, like a polymorphous fairy, her magic.

707 Feinstein, 'Downton Dowager is happy on tramp's pay'. Fortunately, Smith was daily made up for the role. For the movie *Vagabond* (1985), directed by Agnès Varda, the French actress Sandrine Bonnaire had to wear dirty clothes and did not wash her hair for two months.

708 D. Sexton, 'Maggie Smith is glorious', *The Evening Standard*, 15 September 2015, p. 39.

709 'It's almost not a performance. She just became Miss Shepherd, the person I knew.' (A. Bennett interviewed by S. Wright, 'Steve Wright in the afternoon', BBC Radio 2, 11 November 2015).

710 She also starred in a radio adaptation of the play (along with Adrian Scarborough, Marcia Warren and Alan Bennett as himself) recorded for BBC Radio Four in 2009.

Select Bibliography

ACTING AND TYPES

Banu G., *Les voyages du comédien* (Paris: Gallimard, 2012)

Boleslavsky R., *Acting. The first six lessons* (New York: Routledge, 1933)

Booth E., 'On the Aesthetics of Acting', in J. L. Halio and H. Richmond, *Shakespearean Illuminations. Essays in Honor of Marvin Rosenberg* (London: University of Delaware Press, 1998), p. 255-266

Burge J. C., *Lines of Business. Casting Practice and Policy in the American Theatre, 1752-1899* (New York-Berne-Frankfurt am Main: Peter Lang, 1986)

Burton H. (ed.), *Great Acting* (London: BBC, 1967)

Callow S., *Being an Actor* (London: Penguin, 1995)

Capra S., *Theater Voices* (Laham-Toronto-Oxford: Scarecrow Press, 2004)

Davis A. M., *Good Girls and Wicked Witches. Women in Disney's Feature Animation* (Eastleigh: John Libbey, 2006)

Fisher J. W., 'Creating Another Identity: Aging Actresses in the Eighteenth Century', *Journal of Aging and Identity*, 4.2, 1999, p. 57-78

Gaskill W., *A Sense of Direction* (London: Faber and Faber, 1988)

Gaskill W., *Words into Action. Finding the Life of the Play* (London: Nick Hern Books, 2010)

Geraghty C., 'Performing as a Lady and a Dame: Reflections on Acting and Genre', in *Contemporary Hollywood Stardom*, ed. by Th. Austin and M. Barker (London: Arnold, 2003), p. 105-117

Gordon M. (ed.), *M. Chekhov's On the Technique of Acting* (New York: Harper Collins, 1991)

Hapgood E. R. (ed), *Stanislavski's Legacy. A Collection of Comments on a Variety of Aspects of an Actor's Art and Life* (London: Methuen Drama, 1981)

Harper S., 'From Wholesome Girls to Difficult Dowagers. Actresses in 1930's British Cinema', in *British Cinema, Past and Present*, ed. by J. Ashby and A. Higson (London: Routledge, 2000), p. 137-165

Isaacs E. J. R., 'Type-Casting: The Eighth Deadly Sin', *Theatre Arts Monthly*, Vol. XVII, 2, February 1933, p. 131-137

Jouvet L., *Réflexions du comédien* (Paris, Éditions de la Nouvelle Revue Critique, 1938)

Kaplan E. A., 'Wicked Old Ladies from Europe', in *Bad. Infamy, Darkness, Evil and Slime on Screen*, ed. by M. Pomerance (New York: State University Press, 2004), p. 239-253

Kracauer S., *Theory of Film: The Redemption of Physical Reality* (Oxford: Oxford University Press, 1960)

Lewis R., *Method – or Madness?* (London-Melbourne-Toronto: Heinemann, 1960)

Mudford P., *Making Theatre. From Text to Performance* (London-New Brunswick: The Athlone Press, 2000)

Nissen A., *Accustomed to Her Face: Thirty-five Character Actresses of Golden Age Hollywood* (Jefferson, North Carolina & London: McFarland and Cie, 2016)

Nissen A., *Actresses of A Certain Character* (Jefferson, North Carolina & London: McFarland and Cie, 2006)

Nissen A., *Mothers, Mammies and Old Maids. Twenty-Five Character Actresses of Golden Age Hollywood* (Jefferson, North Carolina & London: McFarland and Cie, 2012)

Olivier L.' *On Acting* (New York: Simon & Schuster, 1986)

Quinlan D., *Wicked Women of the Screen* (London: Batsford, 1987)

Quinn M. L., 'Celebrity and the Semiotics of Acting', *New Theatre Quarterly*, 6, 22 May 1990, p. 154-161

Richards S., *The Rise of the English Actress* (London: MacMillan, 1993)

Speaight R., *Acting: its Idea and Tradition* (London: Cassel, 1939)

Stanislavski C., *Building a character* (NewYork: Routledge, 1949)

Stanislavski C., *My Life in Art* (London: Eyre Methuen, 1980)

Stokes J., *The French Actress and her English Audience* (Cambridge: Cambridge University Press, 2005)

Tincknell E., 'Dowagers, Debs, Nuns and Babies: The Politics of Nostalgia and the Older Woman in the Sunday Night Television Serial', in *Aging Femininities. Troubling Representations*, ed. by J. Dolan and E. Tincknell (Newcastle: Cambridge Scholars, 2012), p. 53-65

West S., *The Image of the Actor. Verbal and visual representation in the age of Garrick and Kemble* (New-York: St. Martin's Press, 1991)

Wojcik P. R., 'Typecasting', *Criticism*, Spring 2003, 45.2, p. 223-249

ACTORS

Batters J., *Edith Evans. A Personal Memoir* (London: Hart-Davis MacGibbon, 1977)

Bloom C., *Leaving a Doll's House* (Boston-New York-Toronto-London: Little, Brown and Co, 1996)

Coveney M., *Maggie Smith. A Bright Particular Star* (London: Gollancz, 1992); updated edition: *Maggie Smith. A Biography* (London: Weidenfeld & Nicolson, 2015)

Croall J., *Sibyl Thorndike. A Star of Life* (London: Haus Publishing, 2008)

Desanti D., *Sacha Guitry, cinquante ans de spectacle* (Paris: Grasset, 1982)

Fairclough-Isaacs K., 'Mature Meryl and Hot Helen: Hollywood Gossip and the "Appropriately Ageing actress"', in *Ageing, Popular Culture and Contemporary Feminism*, ed. by I. Whelehan and J. Gwynne (Basingstoke: Palgrave Macmillan, 2014), p. 140-154

Findlater R., *The Player Queens* (London: Weidenfeld & Nicolson, 1976)

Forbes B., *Ned's Girl. The authorized biography of Dame Edith Evans* (London: Elm Tree Books, 1977)

Fothergill B., *Mrs Jordan. Portrait of an Actress* (London: Faber and Faber, 1965)

Gielgud J., *Distinguished Company* (London: Heinemann, 1972)

Gielgud J., *Early Stages* (San Francisco: Mercury House, 1987)

Gussow M., *Gambon. A life in acting* (London: NHB, 2004)

Hadley B., *Leading Ladies* (London: Robson, 1992)

Joannis C., *Sarah Bernhardt, Reine de l'Attitude et princesse des gestes* (Paris: Payot, 2000)

Johns E., *Dames of the Theatre* (London: W. H. Allen, 1974)

Karbo K., *How to Hepburn: Lessons on Living from Kate the Great* (New York: Bloomsbury, 2007)

Keown E., *Margaret Rutherford. An illustrated study of her work with a list of her appearances on stage and screen* (London: Rockliff, 1956)

Lewis R., *Stage People* (London: Weidenfeld and Nicolson, 1989)

Martin-Fugier A., *Comédiennes. De Mademoiselle Mars à Sarah Bernhardt* (Paris: Seuil, 2001)

McDonald R., *Look to the Lady. Sarah Siddons, Ellen Terry, and Judi Dench on the Shakespearean Stage* (Athens: University of Georgia Press, 2005)

Moreno M., *Souvenirs de ma vie* (Paris: Editions de Flore, 1948)

Morley S., *Gladys Cooper. A Biography* (London: Heinemann, 1979)

Morley S., *Sybil Thorndike. A Life in the Theatre* (London: Weidenfeld & Nicolson, 1977)

Morley S., *The Great Stage Stars* (London: Angus & Robertson, 1986)

O'Connor G., *Alec Guinness. Master of Disguise* (London-Sydney-Auckland: Hodder & Stoughton, 1994)

Olivier L., *Confessions of an Actor* (London: Weidenfeld & Nicolson, 1994)

Redgrave M., *The Actor's Ways and Means* (London: Heinemann, 1979)

Simmons D. L., *Margaret Rutherford. A Blithe Spirit* (London: Sphere Books, 1985)

Steen M., *A Pride of Terrys* (London: Longmans, 1962)

Sturtevant V., *A Great Big Girl like Me. The Films of Marie Dressler* (Urbana-Chicago: University of Illinois, 2009)

Taramow G., *Sarah Bernhardt. The Art within the Legend* (Princeton: Princeton University Press, 1972)

Trewin J. C., *Edith Evans* (London: Rockliff, 1954)

Tynnan K., *Alec Guinness* (London: Barrie & Rockliff, 1961)

Vanbrugh I., *To Tell my Story* (London: Hutchinson & Co, 1948)

HISTORY OF THE STAGE AND DRAMA

Bainbridge B., *Front Row: Evenings at the Theatre* (New York: Continuum International Publishing Group Ltd, 2005)

Bataille H., *Ecrits sur le Théâtre* (Paris: Editions Georges Crès et Cie, 1917)

Bennett A., *Untold Stories* (London: Faber and Faber, 2005)

Bennett A., *Writing Home*, 3rd edn (London: Faber and Faber, 2006)

Coveney M., *The Aisle is Full of Noises. A vivisection of the live theatre* (London: Nick Hern, 1994)

Dircks P. T., *Edward Albee. A Literary Companion* (Jefferson N. C.: MacFarland, 2010)

Duff C., *The Lost Summer. The Heyday of the West End Theatre* (London: Nick Hern Books, 1995)

Donohue J., 'Reception and Performance History of *The Importance of Being Earnest*', in *Oscar Wilde in Context*, ed. by K. Powell and P. Raby (Cambridge: Cambridge University Press, 2013)

Eyre R., *National Service. Diary of a decade at the National Theatre* (London: Bloomsbury, 2003)

Eyre R., *Utopia and other places. Memoir of a young director* (London: Bloomsbury, 1993)

Gordon Craig E., *Le Théâtre en marche* (Paris: Gallimard, 1964)

Grissom J., *Follies of God. Tennessee Williams and the Women of the Fog* (New York: Knopf, 2015)

Gussow M., *Edward Albee: A Singular Journey. A Biography* (New York: Simon & Schuster, 1999)

Hytner N., *Balancing Acts* (London: Jonathan Cape, 2017)

Jackson R., 'The Importance of Being Earnest', in *The Cambridge Companion to Oscar Wilde*, ed. by P. Raby (Cambridge: Cambridge University Press, 1997), p. 161-178

Kaplan J., 'Wilde on the stage', in *The Cambridge Companion to Oscar Wilde*, p. 249-275

Knelman M., *A Stratford Tempest* (Toronto: McClelland & Stewart, 1982)

Masters B., *Thunder in the Air. Great Actors in Great Roles* (London: Oberon, 2000)

McCarthy G., *Edward Albee* (London: Macmillan, 1987)

Nightingale B., *Great Moments in the Theatre* (London: Oberon, 2012)

O'Connor J., *Dramatizing Dementia. Madness in the Plays of Tennessee Williams* (Bowling Green: Popular Press, 1997)

O'Mealy J., *Alan Bennett. A Critical Introduction* (New York-London: Routledge, 2001)

Rogoff G., *Vanishing Acts. Theater since the Sixties* (New Haven: Yale University Press, 2000)

Rosenthal D., *The National Theatre History* (London: Oberon, 2013)

Solomon R. H., *Albee in Performance* (Bloomington: Indiana University Press, 2010)

Stokes J., *Oscar Wilde: myths, miracles and imitations* (Cambridge: Cambridge, University Press, 1996)

Stokes J., 'Wilde Interpretations', *Modern Drama*, 37.1, 1994, p. 156-174

Tanitch R., *Oscar Wilde on Stage and Screen* (London: Methuen, 1999)

Thompson J. J., *Tennessee Williams' Plays. Memory, Myth, and Symbol* (New York: Peter Lang, 2002)

Turner D., *Alan Bennett: In a Manner of Speaking* (London: Faber and Faber, 1997)

Tynnan K., *A View of the English Stage, 1944-1965* (London: Methuen, 1975)

Vineberg S., 'Duet and Solos: The Pleasures of Alan Bennett', *The Threepenny Review*, 74, 1998, p. 24-26

Wolfe P., *Understanding Alan Bennett* (Columbia: University of California Press, 1999)

Zinman T., *Edward Albee* (Ann Arbor: University of Michigan, 2008)

MOVIES AND ADAPTATIONS

Ashby J.-Higson A. (ed.), *British Cinema, Past and Present* (London: Routledge, 2000)

Baker J., *Imaginations: The Henry James literary and cinematic revival* (Providence: University of Rhode Island, 2012)

Brown J., *Alan J. Pakula. His Films and His Life* (New York: Back Stage, 2005)

Chandler K. M., '"Her Ancient Faculty of Silence". Catherine Sloper's Ways of Being in James's Washington Square and Two Film Adaptations', in *Henry James goes to the movies*, ed. by S. M. Griffin (Lexington: University Press of Kentucky, 2002), p. 170-190

Chillington Rutter C., 'Looking at Shakespeare's women on film', in *The Cambridge Companion to Shakespeare on Film*, ed. by R. Jackson (Cambridge: Cambridge University Press, 2000), p. 241-260

Chivers S., *The Silvering Screen. Old Age and Disability in Cinema* (Toronto: University of Toronto Press, 2011)

Crnković G. P., 'Interview with Agnieszka Holland', *Film Quaterly*, 52.2, Winter 1998-1999, p. 2-9

Crowdus G., 'Richard III', *Cineaste*, 22, 1996, p. 34-37

Dickens on Screen, ed. by J. Glavin (Cambridge: Cambridge University Press, 2003)

Dyer R., *Stars* (Londres: BFI, 1979)

Falcus S.-Sako K., 'Women, Travelling and Later Life', in *Ageing, Popular Culture and Contemporary Feminism*, p. 203-218

Falk Q., *Travels in Greeneland* (London: Reynolds & Hearn Ltd, 2000)

Film Adaptation, ed. by J. Naremore (New Brunswick: Rutgers University, 2000)

Gillispie J., 'American Film Adaptations of "The Secret Garden": Reflections of Sociological and Historical Changes', *The Lion and the Unicorn*, June 1996, 20.1, p. 144-145

Horovitz I., *My Old Lady. Complete stage play and screenplay with an essay on adaptation* (New York: Three Rooms Press, 2016)

Hunt A., '*Talking Heads*: "Bed Among the Lentils" (A. Bennett)', in *British Television Drama in the 1980s*, ed. by G. W. Brandt (Cambridge: Cambridge University Press, 1993), p. 19-39

Kael P., *Hooked. Film Writings 1985-1988* (New York: Dutton, 1989)

Kael P., *Reeling* (Boston-Toronto: Little & Brown & Cie, 1976)

Kempley R., 'Agnieszka Holland: A War on Stupidity', *The Washington Post*, 12 October 1997

Lawson V., *Mary Poppins, She Wrote* (New York: Simon & Schuster, 2013)

Levy E., *George Cukor, Master of Elegance* (New York: William Morrow and C°, 1994)

Loehlin J. N., '"Top of the World, Ma": *Richard III* and Cinematic Convention', in *Shakespeare, the Movie. Popularizing the plays on film, TV and video*, ed. by L. E. Boose and R. Burt (London-New York: Routledge, 1997), p. 68-80

Long R. E., *George Cukor Interviews* (Jackson: University Press of Mississipi, 2001)

Long R. E., *The Films of Merchant-Ivory* (New York: H. N. Abrams, 1997)

Macnab G., *Searching for Stars. Stardom and Screen Acting in British Cinema* (London-New York: Cassell, 2000)

Marchalonis S., '*Filming the Nineteenth Century*: "The Secret Garden" and "Little Women"', *American Transcendentalist Quarterly*, 10, 4, 1996, p. 273-292

Markson E. W., 'The Female Aging Body Through Film', in *Aging Bodies. Images and Everyday Experience*, ed. by C. A. Faircloth (Walnut Creek: Altamira Press, 2003), p. 77-102

Marsh J., 'Dickens and film', in *The Cambridge Companion to Dickens*, ed. by J. O. Jordan (Cambridge: Cambridge University Press, 2001), p. 204-223

Matson R. W., 'An Autobiographical Allegory: Franco Zeffirelli's Tea with Mussolini', in *Repicturing the Second World War. Representations in Film and Television*, ed. by M. Paris (New York: Palgrave Macmillan, 2007), p. 39-54

McCabe B., *Harry Potter: Page to Screen* (New York: Harper, 2011)

McKellen I., *William Shakespeare's* Richard III*: A Screenplay* (London-New York: Doubleday, 1996)

Modern British Drama on Screen, ed by R. B Palmer and W. R. Bray (Cambridge: Cambridge University Press, 2013)

Moseley R., 'A landscape of desire. Cornwall as romantic setting in *Love Story* and *Ladies in Lavender*', in *British Women's Cinema*, ed. by M. Bell and M. Williams (London-New York: Routledge, 2010), p. 77-93

Naremore J., *Acting in the Cinema* (Berkeley: University of California Press, 1988)

Nelson R., *Stephen Poliakoff: On Stage and On Screen* (London: Methuen Drama, 2011)

Newell K., '*Washington Square* "virus of suggestion": Sources Texts, Intertexts and Adaptations', *Literary Film Quarterly*, 34, 2006, p. 204-211

Pidduck J., *Contemporary Costume Film* (London: BFI, 2004)

Rothwell K. S., *A History of Shakespeare on Screen. A century of film and television* (Cambridge: Cambridge University Press, 2004)

Sadoff D. F., *Victorian Vogue. British Novels on Screen* (Minneapolis-London: University of Minnesota, 2010)

Sinyard N., *Jack Clayton* (Manchester: Manchester University Press, 2000)

Stokes S. S., 'Painting the Garden: Noel Streatfeild, the Garden as Restorative, and Pre-1950 Dramatizations of *The Secret Garden*', in

In the Garden. Essays in Honor of Frances Hodgson Burnett, ed. by A. S. Carpenter (Lanham: Scarecrow Press, 2006), p. 169-187

Thompson E., *Nanny McPhee and the Big Bang Film Diary* (London: Bloomsbury, 2010)

Vienne-Guerrin N., 'Evil tongues in Richard III on screen' in *Shakespeare on Screen (Proceedings of the Conference organized at the Université de Rouen)*, ed. by S. Hatchuel and N. Vienne-Guerrin (Rouen: Presses de l'Université de Rouen, 2005), p. 245-262

Viviani C., *Le magique et le vrai* (Aix-en-Provence: Rouge Profond, 2015)

Whelehan I., 'Not to be looked at. Older women in recent British movies', in *British Women's Cinema*, ed. by M. Bell and M. Williams (London: Routledge, 2010), p. 170-183

Zeffirelli F., *Franco Zeffirelli. The Autobiography* (London: Arena Books, 1987)

ARTICLES ON MAGGIE SMITH

'In her Prime: actress Maggie Smith', interview by Charles Osgood, CBS Sunday Morning, 20 January 2002

Bardin B., 'Idole Chatter: Maggie Smith', *Premiere Magazine*, April 2002, p. 92

Brown M., 'Maggie, Moody and Magnificent', *The Telegraph Magazine*, 12 November 1994, p. 43

Calkin J., 'Portrait of a Lady', *The Telegraph Magazine*, 7 November 2015, p. 32-33, 35, 37 and 39

Coveney M, 'A rare source of wit', *The Observer*, 1 November 1992, p. 60

- 'A real drama queen', *The Independent*, 16 December 2004, p. 8-9
- 'High anxiety through a veil of tears and laughter: Interview Maggie Smith', *The Observer*, 26 May 1991, p. 51
- 'I'm very scared of being back on stage', *The Evening Standard*, 2 March 2007, p. 34
- 'The Prime of Dame Maggie Smith', *The Observer*, 6 September 1992, p. 41
- 'The Prime of Dame Maggie Smith', *National Film Theatre Programme*, September-October 1992, p. 2-7

De Bertodano H., 'The shyest star you've ever met', *The Sunday Telegraph*, 19 February 2002, p. 3

Fox C., 'Grande dame of the old-bags', *The Daily Telegraph*, 19 March 2007, p. 29

Franks A., 'Love's Labour's Lost', *The Times Magazine*, 26 November 2005, p. 24-25, 27 and 29

Gardner L, 'Smith and moans', *The Guardian*, 15 October 1997, p. 14-15

Grice E., 'Maggie Smith interview for My Old Lady: "If you have been around long enough you are an icon" ', *The Telegraph*, 8 November 2014, p. 4

Herbert I., 'Maggie Smith', *The Stage*, 4 November 2010, p. 21

Hiscock J., 'A Great Dame', *The Evening Standard*, 4 July 2003, p. 27

Isenberg B., 'The Many Reflections of Maggie Smith', *The Los Angeles Times*, 16 February 1988, p. 1

Koenig R., 'Maggie Smith: The greatest Dame of all', *The Independent*, 9 March 2007, p. 2-4

Kroll J., 'The Prime of Dame Maggie', *Newsweek*, 2 April 1990, p. 54-56

Levin B., 'She's nothing like a dame', *The Times*, 30 December 1994, p. 16

Liptay F., 'Maggie Smith. Zivilisierter Ungehorsam', in *Film-Konzepte 1: Komödiantinnen*, ed. by T. Koebner and F. Liptay, 1, 2006, p. 154-160

Mackenzie S., 'You have to laugh', *The Guardian*, 20 November 2004, p. 36-39

McAfee A., 'The enigmatic prime of Dame Maggie Smith', *The Evening Standard*, 3 September 1992, p. 24

Miller T., 'Spell Binding', *The Telegraph Magazine*, 10 November 2001, p. 44-45, 47 and 49

Morley S., 'Drama queen of ice and fire', *The Scotman*, 11 September 1997, p. 16

- 'Profile: Maggie Smith', *European Travel and Life*, May 1990, p. 57-59
- 'There's nothing like a dame!', *Theatregoer Magazine*, September 2002, p. 18-20

Middlehurst L., 'There's Nothing Like THIS Dame', *The Daily Mail*, 18 April 1992, p. 33

Olliver V., 'The Prime of Ms Smith', *The Times*, 7 February 1986, p. 11

Rees J., 'The grand dame returns', *The Sunday Times*, 12 September 2010, p. 3-5

Vineberg S., 'Maggie Smith', *Salon.com*, 6 June 2000 <http://www.salon.com/2000/06/06/smith_12/> [accessed 12 November 2016]

Wardle I., 'All the angles: Farce or tragedy, stage or screen – no role seems beyond Maggie Smith', *The Independent*, 28 February 1993, p. 50
Wolf M., 'There is nothing like this Dame', *The New York Times*, 18 March 1990, p. 37, 51-53 and 55

Selective Index